10/13

modernism

modernism

Michael Levenson

Yale UNIVERSITY PRESS

new haven and london

Published with assistance from the foundation established in memory of Henry
Weldon Barnes of the Class of 1882, Yale College.

Yale University Press books may be purchased in quantity for educational, business,
or promotional use. For information, please e-mail sales.press@yale.edu (U.S. office)
or sales@yaleup.co.uk (U.K. office).

Set in Minion and Nobel type by Integrated Publishing Solutions, Grand Rapids,
Michigan.
Printed in the United States of America by Sheridan Books, Ann Arbor, Michigan.

Library of Congress Cataloging-in-Publication Data

Levenson, Michael H. (Michael Harry), 1951–
    Modernism / Michael Levenson.
      p. cm.
    Includes bibliographical references and index.
    ISBN 978-0-300-11173-6 (alk. paper)
1. Modernism (Literature)   I. Title.
    PN56.M54L48 2011
    700'.4112—dc22

                          2011014179

A catalogue record for this book is available from the British Library.

This paper meets the requirements of ANSI/NISO Z39.48-1992 (Permanence of
Paper).

10 9 8 7 6 5 4 3 2 1

To my mother, Rose, and for my father, Howard

CONTENTS

ILLUSTRATIONS FOLLOW PAGES 54 AND 218

introduction:
the spectacle of modernism

Modernism may have disappeared as a living cultural force, but it maintains its provocation for all who try to understand it. To live within our own modernity is to be anxious about our place in time, the future of culture, and the fate of the changes that the modernists sought to achieve.

This book offers a new account of Modernism. Thanks to the work of many scholars over the past two decades, it is now possible to offer a broader and more synthetic history than would have been possible in an earlier generation. In this respect, the present book is as much a tribute to the achievements of my contemporaries as it is the product of my own researches.

Any history, especially a history of Modernism, must begin with the myth of origins. Was there a first modernist? Even to pose the question is to hear the sound of folly. We look back to Edgar Allan Poe and further back to Lord Byron and then back again to Laurence Sterne. François Villon can be a precursor, as can Catullus or Petronius. Any distinguishing mark of Modernism, any sign or signature, such as discontinuity, collage, literary self-consciousness, irony, the use of myth, can be traced back to the furthest temporal horizon. To try to identify an elusive beginning or to propose clinching definitions is to play a game with changing rules. Yet even without boundaries and definitions, much needs to be said.

In European and American culture of the past two centuries a sense of rupture and novelty pervaded the collective consciousness. The reasons are familiar: revolutions in France and in America; the age of steam industry; railways; urbanization; class conflict; religious doubt; the spread of empire; the struggle between the sexes. These different dimensions of change followed varying historical pathways but converged and accumulated until

1

the discourse of novelty became inescapable. An act of testimony often appeared in nineteenth-century life: an elderly individual would summon the memory of an entirely different world in childhood. The evocation of the landscape before the railways was one common figure. But the telling event came within the curve of a single life; the vivid contrasts between green and gray, slowness and speed, national unity and class conflict, occurred inside one living memory.

Modernity remains haunted both by a search for novelty and by the recollection of precursors. This double sense creates an abiding instability, a sense of modernity as inescapable but undecidable. Perhaps we are not modern, or not yet modern, even as we feel that we have crossed a threshold in history. Such undecidability is both a condition of our scholarship and the episode itself. As Susan Stanford Friedman has observed, "Modernity is not solely a fixed set of characteristics that might have appeared in a given space and time, such as the European Enlightenment or the twentieth-century avant-garde in the arts. Nor is modernity exclusively the principle of rupture."[1] Throughout the past two hundred years, we hear a breathless chanting of the word "new" and then the uncertain recall of precedents. We may take it as the fate of modernity that its origins must remain in question and that we can never be sure that it *is* a modernity. Even as we talk incessantly about living through "new times," the origins of the newness are contested.

In an early essay, "Richard Wagner in Bayreuth (1876)," later published in *Untimely Meditations,* Friedrich Nietzsche unveiled a scene of revolutionary transformation. The theater of Wagner, the mythic musical grandeur of his opera—this, says Nietzsche, was something "altogether new," appearing with "no warning signs, no transitional events."[2] It pierced the complacency of modern life. It shattered the feeble art and literature that had impersonated a living culture; it united "what was separate, feeble and active" (209). Through his long appreciation Nietzsche exults in the thought that the sleep of culture is coming to an end, that we might escape the complacency of modernity and revive the power of artistic vision. Moreover, what appears within the music will not be contained there: "everything in our modern world is so dependent on everything else that to remove a single nail is to make the whole building tremble and collapse" (209). Because Wagner's art has achieved the "highest and purest effect" that theater can reach, it will inevitably bring "innovations everywhere, in morality and politics, in education and society" (210). In his most emphatic tones, Nietzsche anticipates the rupture. "For many things the time has come to die out; this new art is a prophet which sees the end approaching for other things than the arts" (199). This rapturous embrace completes an exemplary modernist scene: a revolutionary philosopher recognizes his vision incarnated in revolutionary art. Nietzsche welcomes the creative destruction that will become a rhythm in modernist ambition. Set against a society organized around comfort and respectability, appetite and nostalgia, a true art will violently recover something ancient that has been forgotten, even as it creates something new that has never been anticipated. It will necessarily be out of harmony with its own time. All who attend the Bayreuth Festival, proclaims Nietzsche, "will be felt to be untimely men: their home is not in this age but elsewhere" (198). Even when he turns against Wagner, bitterly regretting the betrayal of vision, Nietzsche remains the partisan of "untimely men" and of radical renewal in the arts that will overturn the bases of culture.

Another performance shook the complacent at nearly the same moment. Henrik Ibsen's *A Doll's House,* which appeared in 1879, created a notorious sensation in its final sequence. The decision of Nora Helmer to cross the threshold, leaving husband and children behind, was a reverberant act. The shock recurred two years later when *Ghosts* portrayed the mental dissolution of Oswald Alving, the too-young inheritor of his father's syphilis. Ibsen was writing in a key sharply different from Wagner's: his plays of the 1870s turn from mythic universality to the precision of the "problem play." Between Wagnerian allegory and the Ibsenite "topic" stretches a vast distance, but both authors shared a contempt for the timid bourgeoisie. Between the strivings of Wagnerian love and the attack of the syphilis bacterium lies the wide terrain of modernist provocation.

But Ibsen and Wagner share something else. Their work confirmed the spectacle of modernity, the advent of successive and arresting artistic events, which fascinated, and often appalled, a rapt audience. Modernism needs to be understood not as an elite craft refined in secret but as a complex exchange between artists and audiences. Through the last half, and especially the last quarter, of the nineteenth century, a large, literate public found itself entreated and defied, encouraged and repulsed. The revulsion of many prepared the pleasure of some. "Of all the artists of the nineteenth century," wrote one early commentator, "Wagner and Ibsen stand out as the best hated. Byron and Shelley faced abuse only in England; Manet was hated in Paris; the controversy over Nietzsche was comparatively a local affair. But like Wagner, Ibsen received from all Europe fervent praise and bitter blame."[3] The notoriety of these two artists, spreading so quickly, secured the image of modernism as an epidemic.

Always we need to remember the authority of the middle-class settlement, the entrenchment of bourgeois sensibility. The lure of domesticity, the ethic of respectability, the rise of professionalism, the creation of bureaucracies, all helped to solidify the triumph of routine that Max Weber would soon describe. To secure an income, to manage a household, to beget a family, and, perhaps above all, to achieve the ideal of private *comfort* were pervasive goals, pursued by individuals and families and perpetually ratified by the press and by popular art and literature.

The imagery of snugness became conspicuous in the later nineteenth century: the picture of a cozy interiority held in place by a well-administered social world. The clutter of so many middle-class drawing rooms— the engravings and statuettes, the ivory boxes and lace ruffles—constructed the inner space of home as its own dense universe. Yet the middle-class household knew its vulnerability to the world beyond its walls. The ascendancy of domestic comfort coincided with the rise of mass journalism. The arrival of the daily newspaper or the quarterly journal was itself part of the rhythm of middle-class life. Commentators often worried that domesticity would be unsettled by the avid reading of newspapers, but an appetite for news was one of the essential hungers of the bourgeoisie. Indeed, middle-class readers, then as now, feasted on sensations in the press.

George Bernard Shaw wrote short books about Ibsen and Wagner at the end of the century, as his own career in the theater was still forming. At one point he asks why these late-nineteenth-century writers should create such controversy: What, he wonders, has changed?

> Tolstoy and Ibsen together, gifted as they were, were not otherwise gifted or more gifted than Shakespear and Molière. Yet a generation which could read all Shakespear and Molière, Dickens and Dumas, from end to end without the smallest intellectual or ethical perturbation, was unable to get through a play by Ibsen or a novel by Tolstoy without having its intellectual and moral complacency upset, its religious faith shattered, and its notions of right and wrong conduct thrown into confusion and sometimes even reversed.

He immediately adds Wagner, August Strindberg, and Anton Chekhov to the list of agitating artists and then answers his own question by describing a growing seriousness in culture. It is no longer possible to laugh at the world's folly; the craving for amusement now "seems mere cowardice to the strong souls that dare look facts in the face."[4]

Yet the problem was more complex than Shaw makes out. Late-century artists indeed took on new ambition in their work, but so did their audiences. In a modernizing and disorienting world, one response was a more strenuous commitment to the sanctity of routine. It is insufficient, then, to see the conflict as that between revolutionary art and static bourgeois resistance, a struggle between motion and stasis, change and permanence. The dominant middle-class culture was itself a culture of change, thrusting and ambitious in its industry, its technology, its empire. To preserve the continuities (religious orthodoxy, economic efficiency, public decorum, home comfort, often in combination but sometimes apart) could be a challenge as great as that of the radical artists. The agon of modernism was not a collision between novelty and tradition but a *contest of novelties,* a struggle to define the trajectory of the new.

Still, even in the midst of pervasive change, of transformation everywhere, the new art was seen as a rival and threatening modernity. There was novelty on both sides, yes, but modernist novelty was seen as dangerous and contagious. Madness was the favored metaphor (art as lunacy), but that was only one among a constellation of terms. Bodily disease, insanitary filth, and sexual immorality were metaphors often deployed, as in Clement Scott's infamous description of Ibsen's *Ghosts* as "an open drain, a loathsome sore unbandaged, a dirty act done publicly, or a lazar-house with all its doors and windows open."[5] The pursuit of a language of abuse is itself an event in the history of Modernism. Invective has its own modern style, and finding the conclusive dismissal or the definitive caricature became a vocation in its own right. What often haunted the critics was the thought that, within the community of despised artists and their small loyal audience, the "lunatic" utterance was perfectly intelligible—part of an impenetrable language belonging to a community that dared to understand it.

Snugness and shock became intimates within a tight circuit of exchange; the inwardness of home life was interrupted by startling accounts of novelty. The Great Exhibition in London, the series of expositions in Paris, the Jubilees of Queen Victoria, but also the Indian revolt of 1857, the Crimean and Franco-Prussian Wars, the strikes of newly organized working classes, the lives of the dispossessed on the streets—all these intruded upon the closed world of comfort, producing a cadence of fascination and revulsion. Just as artists depended upon a civil society they often despised, so audiences were drawn to the art that frightened them. The effect was to create tense, unsteady relationships between ambitious artists and a middle-class public. It soon became clear that cultural sensation was not an anomaly; rather, a series of spectacles had assumed the persistence of a counterworld. Alongside the daily rituals of work and leisure were indelible signs of another way of life.

Not only particular works but also individual careers became nodes of enthrallment and contention. Byron served as a precedent for the late-century uproar, the revolutionary artist as the dauntless bearer of culture. Thomas Carlyle offered his version of the type in "The Hero as Man of Letters," where he speaks of new sovereign individuals whose power emanates from the act of writing. The "Man-of-Letters Hero must be regarded as our most important modern person. He, such as he may be, is the soul of all. What he teaches, the whole world will do and make."[6] For Carlyle the heroic act was the writer's creation of a text released into a society reluctant to comprehend it. Indeed, part of the essay's interest is that it promotes a new idea of culture as distinct from religion and politics, as a separate vocation.

Yet even as Carlyle was composing his essay, the figure of the artist-hero had begun to change its bearing. The figure of the invisible, neglected, but world-transforming writer gave way to a quite different image: the artist as a conspicuous and culture-dividing celebrity. Not Samuel Johnson in the garret but Wagner at Bayreuth and Ibsen as the scandal of Europe—this was the new tableau. Instead of writing that would yield its secrets only over generations, there appeared the relentless immediacy of spectacle.

Byron created Byronism, much as Wagner produced Wagnerians. But the change in the later part of the nineteenth century came when spectacle was no longer a question of a singular eruption but a succession of controversies. Ibsen appeared alongside Wagner, but then Nietzsche, Walt Whitman, and Émile Zola created their own disturbances, until it seemed that the condition of modernity was its susceptibility to the latest defiant artist. Each of these figures appeared as a solitary provocateur, a strongly marked individual who created a distinctive oeuvre, exciting and dividing the public. But a significant turn occurred when the public was no longer concerned only with demonic genius and its angular creations but with the shifting ground of the entire culture. The exclamation "What does Wagner mean?" gave way to the cry "What is happening to our civilization?"

Nietzsche's *Thus Spoke Zarathustra* marks a telling moment. Appearing in the crucial decade of the 1880s, it is both a denunciation of the rabble and a hymn to individual preeminence. The recurrent chord, as throughout Nietzsche's mature career, is contempt for the democratic multitude, for the "little people" who "all preach surrender and resignation and prudence and industry and consideration and the long etcetera of the small virtues."[7] The chasm between artist and multitude is one of the inciting images of Modernism. No one is more responsible for its prominence than Nietzsche. Yet *Thus Spoke Zarathustra* both repudiates the human mass and calls for transformation. Contempt for the multitude runs parallel to the vision of a new race of Overmen who will have passed beyond the lure of pity and tolerance and who will dance beyond the spirit of gravity. But who are these people? What group or community can withstand Zarathustra's disdain? How can there be Overmen when there is only one Zarathustra?

Much of the force of the book grows from a tension between the one and the several. Nietzsche can easily enough denounce the many. But because he longs for the radical renewal of humanity, he cannot give up the picture of a collective change, something far larger than self-renewal. "I am in the middle of my work," pronounces Zarathustra, "going to my children and returning from them": for his children's sake, Zarathustra must perfect himself (161). He also speaks of his yearning toward "the few, the long, the distant" (289), acknowledging that there are always "a few whose hearts long retain their courageous bearing" (179). The antipathy toward the democratic mass is uncompromising, but *Thus Spoke Zarathustra* balances precariously between the "lonesome" prophet-precursor and the "few" with whom he might share a vocation.

Nietzsche's *Zarathustra* registered an unsteady transition in a developing Modernism. The shock effect of strong individuals was changing into the shock of a collective. The interest of growing audiences in the operas of Wagner and the dramas of Ibsen made radical cultural transformation a living possibility. But it also encouraged alliances among the like-minded. No longer was the model Carlyle's underappreciated man of letters, destined to exert influence only over time and through the invisible workings of a book. Nietzsche's early (though temporary) devotion to Wagner and the support that Ibsen received from Georg Brandes and later from George Bernard Shaw suggested how the banner of the new art could unfurl quickly. The stirrings of a collective aesthetic began to consolidate in the second half of the nineteenth century. The short-lived Pre-Raphaelite Brotherhood appeared in Britain in the 1850s, generating early controversies—the high dudgeon of critics, the passionate support of admirers—that became characteristic of the avant-garde. Impressionism became a visible movement in the 1870s when Claude Monet, Camille Pissarro, Berthe Morisot, Alfred

Sisley, and Jean Renoir painted their way to outrage. Other challenges followed quickly.

In the view offered here, the emergence of Modernism was not just the result of provoking artifacts and not just a succession of individual careers. Neither a collection of forms and styles nor an array of geniuses, Modernism was a heterogeneous episode in the history of culture. It depended as much on its enemies as on its proponents, on audiences as much as on artists, on a network of little magazines, on the attentions of reviewers in the mainstream press, on patrons as well as on publishers. Had there merely been a parade of audacious works that stirred attention and passed away, that created the tremor of novelty and then subsided, that created a glamour for various nonintersecting careers—in short, had there been a time like the beginning of the current millennium—it would be difficult to justify the term "Modernism." The decisive event was the emergence of an oppositional culture. It was only when singular disturbances—the spectacle of Wagner, the shock of Ibsen, the scandal of Charles Baudelaire—became connected to one another that modernity recognized Modernism, and modernists became conscious of their historical possibility. There was no Modernism without individually audacious artifacts, but equally there was no Modernism without relationships among artists, their works, and the institutions and audiences that encircled them.

Is the life of the arts a rarefied and disengaged realm of its own? Is it a sphere of contemplation? Are its sensations precious only insofar as they are unique and unassimilable? The terms that I have just been developing suggest that we should turn from viewing the arts in terms of *experience* to recognizing them as a *practice*. Any encounter with an artwork occurs within a social world, a world vastly larger than a momentary contemplation. It takes place within a network of activities: making, exhibiting, publishing, performing, selling, discussing, viewing, debating, studying, quoting, parodying.

This book contains many brief readings of texts and images, but Modernism here is not treated as a set of solitary encounters with formidable artifacts. Art, we might say, is instead a social practice of culture. As one of the practices, it is a self-consciously post-traditional activity whose value is internal to the vocation of practicing it. Modernity comprises a field of great social practices, chief among them religion, politics, science, and art, each taking on new form in a later age. Modernist art is no more determinate, nor more autonomous, than the other social practices. Its boundaries were insecure, even permeable, its separate identity always in question. An abiding struggle of modernity is the competition among the practices. Each offers a vocation, a conviction, a framework of meaning, a social world. Each vies with the others, and through the course of the past two centuries, right up to our present, their struggles have been ongoing and unresolved. My claim is not that these practices are new—of course not—but that they take on new aspects in an age of revolution and modernization.

Modern art is a perpetually contested practice. It marks out no single zone of value, no single pattern of experience. It is an ill-defined collection of acts and responses—representation and abstraction, engagement and abstention, fascination and detachment, contemplation and critique—that has offered not one value but a region of commitments. In this sense, the emancipatory project of the arts runs in specific parallel to the emancipatory project of politics. Both are fated to engage in conflict, negotiation, rapprochement, and refusal, and each is fated to have the same complex struggle with religion and science.

All these transactions unfold under the banner of the New, which was not itself new in the epoch of Modernism but which took on a strikingly different character in these decades. Reinhart Koselleck has argued that by the year 1800, Europeans had become conscious of living within "new times" (*neue Zeit*). Now the present was experienced not as a stable historical period, the latest in a succession of periods, but as something unprecedented, characterized by the "expected otherness of the future" and the "alteration in the rhythm of temporal experience: acceleration, by means of which one's own time is distinguished from what went before." The result was that "lived time was experienced as a rupture, a period of transition in which the new and the unexpected continually happened."[8] Koselleck is centrally interested in time, whereas my interest here is on the side of the New, the rise of novelty as an essential category of experience. The word (the concept) is another technology: a generating force in nineteenth- and twentieth-century life. Notably, the omnipresent term began to crowd out other terms—for instance, "original" and "originality." The two latter words cluster around individually radiant works or radiant individuals, whereas the New tends to describe supra-individual episodes and events, collective fashions and fascinations, or social or institutional events: new imperialism, New Woman. And the art of the period—art in the wide sense—became a magnet for the word.

The discourse of the New was secured over a surprisingly brief period in the 1890s. Here is Joseph Conrad in 1902, when, at a moment of difficulty in his early career, resisting demands from agent and publisher that his novel be completed soon, he insisted that he must take as long as the formidable work demanded. "I am *modern,* and I would rather recall Wagner the musician and Rodin the Sculptor who both had to starve a little in their day—and Whistler the painter who made Ruskin the critic foam at the mouth with scorn and indignation. They too have arrived. They had to suffer for being 'new.'"[9] The use of the word "modern" here, as well as "new," is illuminating. At a moment of emergency, Conrad reaches for these terms. He identifies them as a feature of his vocation and as events in the world, events specified by proper names (Wagner, Rodin, Whistler) that point to a historical shift.

In modernist studies, we need to engage the extension of the field; we need to be theoretically aware; and we need a subtle understanding of relations between texts and contexts. Within the limits of my expertise and stamina, I aim toward these goals. No book on Modernism can ever be ambitious enough; there will always be much more to say and to write. I am convinced that we have reached a moment when many self-contained and specialized studies can be brought together, and my hope is to stimulate more synthetic thinking. But this is not to say that we should aim toward a new coherence for Modernism. The varying pace of change in nations and regions, the uneven development in different media, modes, and genres, the sheer diversity of artifacts, and the contradictions in the self-understanding of individuals and movements all need to be respected. Rather than presenting an argument for an encompassing framework or a set of governing techniques, the book has an emphasis on intersections and transitions, moments and phases, continuities and interruptions.

No study can reach as far as it should geographically. While my aim in this book is to represent the life of Modernism within transatlantic and cross-Channel perspectives, important texts and episodes are inevitably left for other scholars to engage. I have stretched my arms as wide as my training, my reading, and my energy allow, but my eyes can see beyond the waggle of my fingers on these keys. In the first chapter I propose a new history of the avant-garde up to the moment of the First World War. There follow three chapters on each of the major genres within the context of social and intellectual life, a retelling of the crucial decades from the perspectives of different affiliations and legacies. In a fifth chapter I consider the circumstances of Modernism after the war, and the book ends with reflections on the afterhistory of the movement. A guiding assumption is that the period before 1914 requires a far more sustained encounter, be-cause here, rather than in the canonical works of the 1920s, is where the history and the meanings of Modernism stand most in need of revision. The synthesis of chapter 5 depends on the more patient acts of recovery in the chapters that precede it. I also assume that any useful new history must be comparative (from Baudelaire to Stein, from Dada to Joyce, from Russian Ego-Futurism to the Harlem Renaissance) and contextual, and that it must offer both readings of individual works and synthetic judg-ments, ambitious and skeptical.

1

the avant-garde in modernism

The account of the avant-garde here builds upon assumptions laid out in the introduction, above all the conviction that the tumultuous events of cultural modernity appeared not merely as a succession of disturbing artifacts or critical provocations but as constituents of an oppositional social milieu, as a radically alternative practice that presented a counterhistory for modernity. In this view, the telling events were not the text, the painting, the film, or the quartet, no matter how extreme, but the artifacts as emblems of a widening counterworld. The growing perception, as conspicuous in the dominant press as in the avant-garde journals, was that these formidable artifacts exemplified rival forms of life, other styles of thinking and feeling.

EXPERIMENT AND ANTIPATHY: ART, POLITICS, AND THE CONFLICT OF CULTURES

The dislike of the new art, so marked in the epoch of Modernism, is not surprising, but the extent of the revulsion and the fear that civilization was at stake continue to startle. Enemies of experimental culture were numerous and stubborn; their charges—of madness and insurrection—were extravagant. The background to the furor lies first of all in the political struggles of the nineteenth century. From the middle of the century a subversive art often appeared as a reflection of revolutionary politics, with the small sect of embattled artists, no matter what their stated views, seen as comrades of anarchists, socialists, feminists, vegetarians. In 1871, at the Paris Commune, artists stood alongside workers at the barricades. Out of the violent events of these months, including the bloody catastrophe at its end, came a multitude of artworks, especially paintings and engravings, that secured a connection between art and revolutionary politics. The political desire to transform society met the aesthetic desire to *represent* and to *circulate* the signs of transformation. For many figures of the period, the Paris Commune took on the aspect of a glimpsed utopia; over succeeding decades it lingered as an image of the union of aesthetics and politics. But even in the absence of overt alliances between artists and revolutionaries, even, indeed, when artists disdained the aims of politics, the threat of social insurrection was part of the connotation of new aesthetic forms. The fear of the revolutionary political sect was quickly displaced by the fear of the radical artist. If politics seemed a more urgent threat, art was often taken as the determinative index of crisis.

On the side of the artists, the connection to insurrection was more uncertain than their critics suggested. A rejection of the prevailing order often became opposition to the entire field of social and political relations, as well as the dominating bourgeoisie. Revolutionary politics could appear as tainted as the bourgeois alternative. An early expression of this attitude appeared in Symbolism, which played a leading role in the history to follow. On one side, symbolist poets, critics, and dramatists repudiated the coarse materiality of everyday social life, progressive or reactionary; on the other side, they pursued an aesthetic vision—the "ideal" or "super-sensible" world —available only to initiates. The symbolist salon with its select company and its obscure ceremonies may seem to stand as far as possible from political engagement. But late-nineteenth-century realism also frequently separated itself from mass politics even as it identified itself with social liberation. The realist estrangement was not in the name of the invisible truths of the symbolists but in blunt refusal of democratic judgment and insight. Even Ibsen, in his most socially committed phase, defended the preeminence of "that minority which leads the van and pushes on to points the majority has not yet reached."[1] And Shaw, Ibsen's most eager expositor, put the claim still more harshly: "If 'Man' means this majority, then 'Man' has made no progress; he has, on the contrary, resisted it. . . . The majority of men at present in Europe have no business to be alive; and no serious progress will be made until we address ourselves earnestly and scientifically to the task of producing trustworthy human material for society. In short, it is necessary to breed a race of men in whom the life-giving impulses predominate."[2] The artist as "enemy of the people" appears sometimes in the guise of a fastidious aristocrat, a dandy, a relic of fine responsiveness; but at least as often, as here in Shaw, the artist is portrayed as a portent of the future, an Overman, who opens possibilities without precedent. Through

the 1880s, Nietzsche offered both the philosophic justification and the imagery for the last figure. But for all his importance, Nietzsche belongs within
a wider field of modernizing pressures.

The emergence of modernist art as "one of the practices"—I have proposed this phrase as a way to place aesthetic activity within a network of
activities: making, exhibiting, reading, debating, viewing, reviewing.[3] Acknowledging that such networks had no determinate origin, we can nevertheless argue that by the last third of the nineteenth century a recognizably
distinct artworld had appeared, with a web of practices separate from politics and religion. The crucial event was not an inward turning, a cult of
ornamental form and a narrowing to an initiated elite, although contraction was indeed a tendency. More significant was the establishment of art
as the practice of a broadening subculture.[4] The career of Gustave Flaubert
was a paradigm and a lingering memory. Despite his famous agonies ("It's
pleasure and torture combined. And nothing that I write is what I want
to write"), Flaubert understood his labor as fully justified.[5] What justifies
the work is not only the satisfaction of having wrought an artifact but the
conviction that it will be sanctioned by artistic comrades, that it will be
published and reviewed, and that it will exert a force, however indeterminate, upon society. Flaubert was sustained by the thought of the encounter
between his books and the world.

The growth of art as a self-conscious practice rarely implied indifference to the social realm. Rather, it suggested that aesthetic labor had a distinctive, not an autonomous, character. Its formal features aside, what gave
it distinctiveness, I argue here, was the presence of an artworld as complex
as the political culture with which it vied. Moreover, as I have suggested,
it need not have vied with politics. Much like the career of Flaubert, the
events of the Paris Commune hung over later Modernism as a memory. For
a period of months in the French capital, it seemed possible to invent new
social forms; it also seemed that two great social practices could converge.
We need only think ahead to the connection between Modernism and the
Russian Revolution, or between Dadaism and postwar political insurgency,
or between Bertolt Brecht and revolutionary theater, to realize that the period 1870–1940 saw recurrent episodes of intensely politicized art. But
it was the radical undecidability of the tie between aesthetics and politics
that became an abiding mark of Modernism. Social transformation and the
transformation of art were concurrent possibilities: they knew one another;
the dialogues between them were as telling as their separate monologues.
When Shaw offered a view of Ibsen's work as part of a revolutionary social

movement and described him as a Socialist, the *Daily Chronicle* printed an interview purporting to show Ibsen renouncing the political affiliation. There followed a revealing letter from Ibsen himself.

> Where the correspondent repeats my assertion that I do not belong to the Social-Democratic party, I wish that he had not omitted what I expressly added, namely, that I never have belonged, and probably never shall belong, to any party whatever. I may add here that it has become an absolute necessity to me to work quite independently and to shape my own course. What the correspondent writes about my surprise at seeing my name put forward by Socialistic agitators as that of a supporter of their dogmas is particularly liable to be misunderstood. What I really said was that I was surprised that I, who had made it my chief life-task to depict human characters and human destinies, should, without conscious or direct intention, have arrived in several matters at the same conclusions as the social-democratic moral philosophers had arrived at by scientific processes.[6]

The incident highlights the uncertain boundaries between modernizing art and modern politics. In much writing on the subject, social urgency is seen as making demands on an uncommitted art. But demands come from both sides. Even as activists in the midst of political struggle called on art to make common cause, so artists demanded that politics recover its radical inspiration. Modern politics has followed an arc of hope and disenchantment, and in the periods of disenchantment—after the revolutions of 1848, the Paris Commune, the Russian Revolution, the First World War—it was art that often assailed compromise, convention, and weak will and that summoned politics back to its radical vision.

Ibsen speaks of his surprise that his independent course as a dramatist converged with revolutionary politics "in several matters." We can take this as a sign of the separation of these two great modern practices: their separation, but also their competition and intense mutual consciousness. At the end of the nineteenth century Ibsen saw his art as at once separate from politics (he did not belong "to any party whatever") and, at the deepest level, concerned with the same questions: "human characters and human destinies." The correspondent for the *Daily Chronicle* wanted to fan the coals of competition, but Ibsen refused the invitation; at the same time he defiantly held to the integrity of his vocation.

During times of political impasse and disorientation, as in the last third of the nineteenth century, newly confident artists saw themselves assuming the mantle of radicalism. Like the political revolutionaries, they deplored the complacency of the public and the widespread blinkered surrender to cliché and fantasy. As long as the political struggle remained in deadlock, artists could claim the central role in rousing a dormant modernity. Ibsen accepted it as his task "to awaken individuals to freedom and independence —and as many of them as possible."[7]

Such independent radicalism of the arts found one epitome in Sté-phane Mallarmé's notorious utterance "Let man be democratic; the artist must separate and remain an aristocrat." Art, he writes, "is a mystery acces-sible to the very few."[8] Here appears a view of the artist as the only living relic of hierarchical society, the one who sustains high values within a level-ing age. The dandy is related to this figure of the aristocratic artist, who caresses difference, even eccentricity, in a bid to preserve a threatened zone of culture. Raymond Williams persuasively sees the artist-aristocrat as one of the roles that will remain continually available to modernists.[9] Yet we need to distinguish this rearguard gesture—the effort to preserve old val-ues and old mysteries—from another lineage of oppositionalism, exem-plified in the career of Arthur Rimbaud. The life (and legend) of Rimbaud is that of the modernist who leaps into culture without warning, who pro-duces unprecedented verse that breaks long-standing conventions, and who embodies a principle of artistic/sexual/political radicalism.

For Rimbaud the crucial gesture was not to withdraw in order to pre-serve threatened values; it was to enter the world in order to break through. His poetic seer is precisely not one who tends the ancient mysteries; the seer is a thief of novelty, and he steals by submitting to the most strenuous psychic regimen. "The poet makes himself a *seer* by a long, involved, and logical *derangement of all the senses*. Every kind of love, of suffering, of mad-ness; he searches himself, he exhausts every possible poison, so that only the essence remains. He undergoes unspeakable tortures that require com-plete faith and superhuman strength, rendering him the ultimate Invalid among men, the master criminal, the first among the damned, and the supreme Savant! For he arrives at the *unknown!*" Again: "The poet is really a thief of fire." This dramatic rendering of the artist aligns with Nietzsche's portrait of the Overman, and such images—vigorous, sensuous, unrepen-tant, unconstrained—stand against the stately ceremonies of Mallarméan aristocracy. Marjorie Perloff has located a root division in modernist po-etry that begins with the late-nineteenth-century struggle between the open forms of Rimbaud and the exquisite music sought by Mallarmé.[10] This contrast will return in the discussion of the modernist lyric. At the moment, though, the careers of Mallarmé and Rimbaud open to another distinction.

From one historical perspective, the avant-garde has always seemed an affair of elites. Mallarmé, for instance, has been taken as a paradigm of the refined artist with rarefied sensibilities, whereas part of the legend of Rimbaud is that of the poet who came from nowhere. Living far from privileged metropolitan circles, he read the poems that came to him and invented the terms of his own transformation. Granted, Rimbaud sought out Paul Verlaine and made his way to Paris; granted, too, his work became indispensable to the revolutionary generation in the capital. Yet it is also true that he soon left Paris, with its select company of published poets and its emerging avant-garde, that he prized his independence from even the most advanced movements, and that his sense of extremity brought him to abandon the making of art. The example of Rimbaud was a challenge to the milieu of the Parisian salons—and continues to challenge a view of Modernism as exclusively the production of metropolitan elites.

From the 1880s on, the sheer proliferation of forms, movements, manifestos, and experimental works indicated an openness to novelty that was itself a form of social insurgency. Despite the tendencies toward closed circles of aesthetic initiates, the new conditions defied insularity and created a rapid traffic in artistic provocation. Aspiring artists came from many places and conditions; they were women as well as men, provincials as well as metropolitans. Certain individuals and groups may have perpetuated attitudes of aristocratic disdain, but no one was able to police the boundaries of innovation. From the 1880s until the First World War, the life of public culture was wider than the intentions of any artist; it was an ongoing eruption whose leading effect was an expansive field for experiment. Everywhere you looked a new magazine was in sight, or a shocking image, or a poem that would not scan.

CHANGING FACES OF PROVOCATION—CONCEPT, IMAGE, WORD

In 1913, in a new edition of *The Quintessence of Ibsenism,* and earlier, in a preface to *Major Barbara,* Shaw evokes the international character of the shock effect. He notes that after he published his book on Ibsen in 1891, a German reader announced that all his ideas came from Nietzsche's *Beyond Good and Evil.* "That was the first I heard of Nietzsche," rejoins Shaw. "I mention this fact, not with the ridiculous object of vindicating my 'originality' in nineteenth century fashion, but because I attach great importance to the evidence that the movement voiced by Schopenhauer, Wagner,

Ibsen, Nietzsche, and Strindberg, was a world movement, and would have found expression if every one of these writers had perished in his cradle. . . . The movement is alive today in the philosophy of Bergson and the plays of Gorki, Tchekov, and the post-Ibsen English drama."[11]

It is important to recover the force of this moment. The names in Shaw's list are all familiar, but now, at the beginning of the twenty-first century, none of them stands as a central representative of Modernism. They characteristically appear instead under the heading of "precursor" or "context." But Shaw's remarks remind us, first of all, that Modernism has become circumscribed as a history of techniques, a species of formalism in which the figures he names here are typically set aside. Second, and more important, these remarks show that a sense of transformative change preceded the works and artists now canonically marked as high modernist. Through the first decade of the twentieth century, sensations and tremors were associated with each of the artists mentioned by Shaw. His partiality aside, we can agree that the succession of texts—works of philosophy as well as works of art—created the perception of a "world movement," though nothing as coherent as a "program" or a "zeitgeist."

The differences among the figures are as striking as their similarities: a long passage separates Wagner from Anton Chekhov and Nietzsche from Henri Bergson. Still, the artists shared an adversarial temper; they resisted the complacency of official culture that dominated the publishing industry, the venues of performance, and the pages of the mass circulation journals and newspapers. Most significantly, their challenge was fundamentally *discursive*, the challenge of propositions, ideas, and theories. Even in the midst of the sensuous and sometimes overwrought artifacts of August Strindberg or Wagner, or within the subtle game of perspectives in Chekhov, or in the complex rhetoric of Nietzsche, the discursive "idea" remains prominent. The discussion play of Ibsen was a vivid paradigm. But the works of all those named by Shaw initiated a play of ideas, and there can be no doubt that audiences engaged with the discursive, ideological incitement before all else. What the plays "proposed" and "argued" was what attracted the rapt attention and the splenetic rebuttal. Elsewhere in *The Quintessence of Ibsenism*, Shaw makes the brazen claim that "modern European literature and music now form a Bible far surpassing in importance to us the ancient Hebrew Bible that has served us so long. . . . There comes a time when the formula 'Also sprach Zarathustra' succeeds to the formula 'Thus saith the Lord,' and when the parable of the doll's house is more to our purpose than the parable of the prodigal son" (236). Modern culture is a scripture. It is biblical in its force and its authority—or, according to Shaw, it should be. Its lessons are parables open to committed interpretation. The new culture is portrayed as a usurping discourse, which achieves its power by generating more discourse.

In the narratives to be developed here, Shaw's cohort of revolutionary figures deserves prominence because we need more acknowledgment of a "philosophic" modernity that challenged the self-understanding of the greater public. Those resonant late-nineteenth-century ideas—atheism, socialism, the war between the sexes—were more than fashionable subjects of conversation: they were sources of instability and instruments of change. By any fair reckoning, the metropolitan cultures of Europe and North America endured a crisis of ideology in the last decades of the nineteenth century. The public discourse was rife with signs of anxiety; to see the signs as superficial or inconsequential is to miss the role of legitimating propositions within modernization. Richard Rorty has developed the notion of a "final vocabulary": the "set of words which [people] employ to justify their actions, their beliefs, and their lives." This vocabulary is "final," suggests Rorty, "in the sense that if doubt is cast on the worth of these words, their user has no noncircular argumentative recourse. Those words are as far as he can go with language; beyond them there is only helpless passivity or a resort to force."[12] At the end of the nineteenth century many metropolitan citizens had their final vocabulary cast into question and struggled to preserve the arguments, concepts, and words validating their lives.

Yet the challenge, despite all its disruption, belonged to a recognizable current of public conversation. The debates over Charles Darwin and evolution or Ibsen and marriage epitomize the culture of metaphysical crisis. A threatening proposition is advanced, and a counterargument is proposed; experts and authorities weigh in on both sides. The dangerous thought is at the same time a rich journalistic opportunity; indeed, the convergence between the shocking theory and the apparatus of the media was speedily achieved. In this respect, *discursive Modernism* was at once unsettling and continuous with the circuitry of intellectual exchange. The challenges to religious faith, to marriage, and to bourgeois respectability were substantial and far-reaching. But they were also assimilable to the protocols of public conversation.

The art that came out of the Paris Commune—the paintings, illustrations, and engravings—remained within a broadly realist tradition. The most ambitious pieces memorialized the events of the political struggle, reproducing momentous scenes soon after they occurred. Alongside the large canvases came the plentiful ephemera, including images in the press that offered the aura of authenticity.[13] To sustain reference to historical reality was at once the motive and the effect of these pieces. We should connect the engaged realism that came out of the Commune with the range of realisms and Naturalisms that became controversial at the end of the nineteenth century. As Ibsen recorded: "The world events around us are taking up a great deal of my thoughts. The old illusory France has been smashed to bits, and when the new, *de facto* Prussia is also smashed, we shall enter the age that is dawning with one leap. Oh, how our ideas will come crashing down around us! . . . What we really need is a revolt of the human spirit."[14] The socially charged incidents at Paris and elsewhere nourished an increasingly militant art. Tones and techniques varied, but they converged in the staging of evocative representations designed to provoke agitated conversation. A discursive Modernism of ideas and theories most often appeared within the conventions of an aesthetic realism that needs to be preserved in any full account of the period.[15]

At this point, however, a notable development must be registered, namely, a different style of provocation, which takes on a double aspect—first as what we may call the *transgressive tableau*. When the paintings of Gustav Klimt began to appear in the 1890s, when Zola described the naked Nana, or, for that matter, when Thomas Hardy's Angel Clare carried milkmaids across the muddy lane, the reaction was not to an insurgent idea but to an unacceptable image. Swinburne, in repudiating Zola, spoke of details that "might have turned the stomach of Dean Swift" and scenes that newspapers would consider "too revolting for publication in our columns."[16] The issue was not censorship. Even though some editors declined to publish risky work, the texts remained available to those keen to find them. Hardy, for instance, took out passages too delicate for the *Graphic* and published them instead in the *National Observer* and the *Fortnightly Review*. In the case of Zola's, Huysmans's, and others' "dirty" French books, enterprising English readers could find copies either just across the Channel or in the hands of friends. The striking part of the controversies is that they cast the challenge of these books in such intimate (domestic and personal) terms. Beyond the question of what beliefs to hold was the question of what images to permit within one's mental theater. The private, even involuntary, character of imagination now became part of the cultural risk. The fear was of an apparition that would unsteady the work of reason: if there was no control over what could be represented in print, then the anarchy of fantasy seemed limitless. The problem was typically put in terms of the vulnerability of the young and the female, but in Britain and the United States the anxiety was more radical: it was a concern about the contagion of imagery. Once pictures from the sewer began to multiply, how would a tainted imagination ever come back to health?

The second aspect of provocation, equally liable to arouse public sensation but perhaps even more pointed, was the taboo word. The word "syphilis," which hovered over *Ghosts*, the word "shift" (referring to a woman's underwear) in J. M. Synge's *The Playboy of the Western World*, the insolent coinage "merdre" (a misspelled "shit") at the opening of Alfred Jarry's *Ubu roi*, even the word "pure" applied to Hardy's *Tess*—each became a node of contestation. A brief sound, a terse inscription, the single transgressive word, was enough to excite scandal. But the paradox of the word-as-taboo is that it resisted the circulation that it provoked. Particularly with sexual epithets, appearing or intimated in "French novels," there was a frantic comedy, a mix of indignation and silence. The words could not be repeated, which would compound the insult, but expressing proper outrage required that they somehow be indicated—indicated but not uttered.

Sigmund Freud, too, soon encountered the paradoxes of speech and silence. Psychoanalysis relied on letting patients find the names for repressed desires and objects; it also relied on speaking those names within its founding texts. In *Fragment of an Analysis of a Case of Hysteria*, the case known as "Dora," Freud anticipates the reaction to his plain speaking; he notes that "in this case history . . . sexual questions will be discussed with all possible frankness, the organs and functions of sexual life will be called by their proper names, and the pure-minded reader can convince himself from my description that I have not hesitated to converse upon such subjects in such language even with a young woman."[17] Freud denies that the charged words create any sexual excitement, but he knows that the concern exists, that people fear the indelible stain caused by a word (as by an image)—and they fear that its very sound can be a lure to danger. In *The Importance of Being Earnest*, Oscar Wilde plays waggishly with the Victorian obsession with that respectable adjective. As the name for all that is good, respectable, and marriageable, as, indeed, the required name of Gwendolen's husband, "Earnest" is a parodic reversal of the taboo word. It can be recited tirelessly, in a chorus of affirmation and in a refuge from filthy speech. But an effect of the play's comedy is to suggest that the overly moralized investment in the word "earnest" mirrors the secret of the wanton word, the dissolute phrase.

This movement from the *brazen idea* to the *transgressive tableau* or the *scandalous word* registers a significant change in the development of a modernism. Confronted with poetry like this—

C'est elle, la petite morte, derrière les rosiers.—La jeune maman tré-
passée descend le perron—La calèche du cousin crie sur le sable—
Le petit frère—(il est aux Indes!) là, devant le couchant, sur le pré
d'œillets

(Rimbaud, Illuminations)[18]

(There she is, the little dead girl, behind the rose bushes.—The young
dead mother descends the flight of steps—The cousin's carriage cries
on the sand—The little brother—(he's in India!), there, before the sunset,
in the meadow of carnations)

—or a stage direction like this, "The fountain sobs strangely and expires"
(Maurice Maeterlinck, *Princess Maleine*),[19] or Gustav Klimt's poster for the
first show of Secessionist artists in 1898, a common response was to feel
that a dangerous threshold had been crossed (fig. 1). Havelock Ellis, who
translated *Germinal* in the early 1890s, recalled that the "accredited critics
of the day could find no condemnation severe enough for Zola. Brunetière
attacked him perpetually with a fury that seemed inexhaustible; Schérer
could not even bear to hear his name mentioned; Anatole France, though
he lived to relent, thought it would have been better if he had never been
born."[20] Here we read the distinctive rhetoric of the outraged, who trade in
images of purging and extinction.

The problem of art in modernity is often cast in terms of significance,
as in the recurrent disputes over whether a work had *meaning*. And yet for
most works the question of meaning never arose. Symphonic music, for
instance, was not typically valued because of its "meanings"; the novels of
Dickens and the paintings of Frith were enjoyed and discussed, but not
usually in terms of what they meant—which was most often taken for
granted. The question of meaning and unmeaning always belongs within
a wider context; and with a great many artifacts, including music and popular fiction, the chatter they stir is not an act of interpretation but a much
more heterogeneous activity of exchanging enthusiasms, filling in contexts
(including biographical contexts), noticing details, making associations,
ruminating without a directed goal. What sustains the social practice of art
is miscellaneous and inconclusive talk. To say that a work lacks meaning
is often just to say that we cannot assimilate it to our ongoing dialogue of
art-speech; we cannot put it into conversational play. Not meaning alone,

not even meaning especially, but a whole range of interests are put in jeopardy if silence greets a work. Points of comparison are lacking; it stirs too few associations; it fails to enter the improvised circuit of exchange. The key event, then, occurring repeatedly at the end of the nineteenth century, was the *interruption of discourse,* a break in the continuity of thought, that we can reasonably regard as a fracture in the coherence of culture. In the face of certain objects, the public no longer knew how to conduct its discourse. Reviewers kept writing, but they often talked about not knowing what to say.

A culture of opposition that breaks the continuity of public discourse —this is one useful way of characterizing the late-nineteenth-century practice of Modernism. Although this moment has precedents, it has its own distinction. Modernism, it is true, is scarcely conceivable without the discontinuities of class society. Karl Marx wrote in *The Eighteenth Brumaire of Louis Bonaparte,* "As long as the rule of the bourgeois class had not been organized completely, as long as it had not acquired its pure political expression, the antagonism of the other classes, likewise, could not appear in its pure form."[21] The divisions of class society set a framework for conflict in culture. At the point of social division is where the practices of art and politics intersect and where an invitation to alliance is historically conditioned. The despised artists and the oppressed classes could, and sometimes did, see themselves as merely occupying different places within the same struggle. But cultural revolt, in its specificity, had an unsettled correlation with social struggle. The break with public discourse—the recourse to scandalous speech and transgressive tableaux—was not only a refusal of bourgeois respectability; it was also a challenge to the reasoned speech of revolutionaries. The conjunction of oppositional culture and discontinuous discourse placed an emancipatory Modernism in an unstable relationship with liberationist politics.

THE SYMBOLIST AVANT-GARDE: DREAM AND DEPORTMENT

After such stirrings as the Pre-Raphaelite Brotherhood in Britain and the impressionists in France, the historically defining event was the appearance of Symbolism in the 1880s. This is when the more radical artistic techniques and the new publishing initiatives assumed a shape that would appear around the world in countless iterations. Symbolism was a many-sided episode; even its name, the outcome of flurried negotiation, was always on the point of being lost under the rubric of "decadence." The manifestos of Jean Moréas in the mid-1880s, Verlaine's edition of contemporaries in *Les*

Poètes maudits, and the publication of Joris-Karl Huysmans's *À Rebours*—these sharply different texts forced the perception of a growing, indeterminate cultural eruption. As one historian of the movement has put it, "Never was there a year like 1886 for the appearance of new talents, for the ferment of activity in poetic circles, for the founding of new magazines, and for the creation of new manners in expression."[22] It was the year, for instance, when free verse became a widely visible technique. For all of the inner contradictions of Symbolism, its practitioners established a matrix of confrontation that became nearly definitive of the avant-garde: a few leading ideas, some exemplary works, and the public gestures of collective identity.

As has often been observed, many of the defining works of Symbolism appeared before the movement had a name, indeed, before it knew itself as a movement. Rimbaud's *Une Saison en enfer* and major poems of Mallarmé and Verlaine were published in the 1870s. But only in the flurry of the next decade did the terms of defiance emerge. Two leading ideas, the "symbolic" and the "accursed," the first from Moréas and the second from Verlaine, vigorously converged. Around the notion of the symbol clustered images of the "ideal," an abstraction that was still compelling enough to be a rallying cry. It worked as a point of resistance both to Naturalism and to the Parnassians. The ideal was opposed to documentary literature—indeed, to all art that took constatation of the real as its motive. At the same time it was opposed to the formalism of the Parnassians, the enshrinement of craft and verbal precision. In 1894, Gustave Kahn described Symbolism as "antinaturalism, antiprosaism in poetry, a search for freedom in the efforts in art, in reaction against the regimentation of the Parnasse and the naturalists."[23] Within the triad of terms (Naturalism, Parnassian formalism, Symbolism), the symbol marks out an indeterminate space, neither real nor merely formal, beyond the reach of all such "regimentation." Though defined negatively, it comes to imply a positive realm of beauty, significance, and ultimate value.

Mallarmé's celebrated aphorism "To *name* the object is to destroy three-quarters of the enjoyment of the poem" was an influential dictum and an epitome; it also suggests the double extremity of this moment.[24] As Naturalism became more visible and insistent, with its claim that no social fact is too sordid for representation and no taboo too coarse to be named, Symbolism pursued the opposing vision: a refusal of reference and specificity. The conflict between the two unfolded within the new condition of "manifesto culture," that is, at a time when a distinctive type of document—the short public assertion of shared values, promulgated in extravagant rhetoric—

was becoming an indispensable aspect of art. The manifesto, whether naturalist or symbolist, should be seen as partly a defense against attacks and partly an attempt at self-comprehension. But from the moment of conflict between Naturalism and Symbolism in the 1880s, a recognizable dialectic governed the critical exchange.

First, the artists saw themselves as belonging to movements, to larger-than-individual pursuits guided by articulated principles. Naturalism was not merely a collection of works by Zola and the Goncourt brothers, Edmond and Jules, but a mode of aesthetic practice that could be summarized in essays, prefaces, and epigrams and embraced by others. So, too, with Symbolism, which was identified through certain resonant poems by Moréas, Verlaine, and, above all, Mallarmé, but which also offered memorable utterances that could be accepted as a code of ongoing practice. Second, the groups became conscious not just of themselves but of one another. What was made visible in the 1880s became pervasive in the decades to follow: artistic movements set in opposition both to the dominant culture and to rival movements. The analogy with revolutionary political factions is clear, and as with political factions, the dialectic drove toward extreme positions. Why this was the case is more difficult to say. Some of the reasons are undramatic: the glamour of the absolute and the appeal of conceptual purity. But part of the explanation must be that modernity itself appeared extreme and seemed to require extreme responses. The effect of a rapidly modernizing social world (Darwin, railroads, revolution—many examples will serve) no doubt encouraged the aesthetics of ultimacy.

Symbolism played a crucial role in the dialectic of extremity. As I argue in this chapter, the challenge of Naturalism, even at its most radical, remained intelligible and therefore open to familiar styles of rebuttal and critique. But the symbolists changed the terms of contention. The goal, as Mallarmé put it, was "to paint not the thing, but the effect the thing produces."[25] But how do you paint an effect? The provocation of Symbolism began, but did not end, with the break between language and the world, with the turn away from reference and toward internal relationships among words. At least as challenging was the labor of "suggestion." René Wellek has described symbolist poetry as "poetry of the predicate": "It speaks of something or somebody, but the subject, the person or the thing, remains hidden."[26] But even this formulation mutes the challenge. In many symbolist poems, the problem is not that something is hidden but that there is no "thing" to be identified. "Suggestion" was not simply an indirect approach to content. It was a wholesale break with the idea of determinate reference;

in place of such reference was the evocation of "mystery" or "atmosphere." The turn of symbolist lyrics toward musical forms reflected the evocative indeterminacy of music, as well as a care for aural textures. The initiated delight of some and the angry bewilderment of many others became typical reactions to the avant-garde. Symbolism offered its first distinctly modernist incarnation.

Here, though, we need an enlarged sense of the practice of symbolist poets, critics, and readers. Two remarkable poetic artifacts—Mallarmé's "Hérodiade" and "L'Après-midi d'un faune"—helped to shape a literary movement, but they did not limit its reach. Precisely because the poems worked through evocation and aimed beyond words toward the effect of words, the works could be completed only through the lives of their readers. Symbolism divided its fascination between the flawless crystalline work and the misty associations stirring beyond it. "Words," as Arthur Symons would write, "are of value only as a notation of the free breath of the spirit." That is, the movement saw both the creation of formidable artifacts and the begetting of attitudes, predilections, sensibilities. A memorable description of Mallarmé—"a little bit of priest, a little bit of dancer" ("un peu de prêtre, un peu de danseuse")—captures the importance of personal style, of physical bearing. Symbolism can be preserved only partly through its texts and forms, since it was equally a matter of forms of life.[27]

In this regard, the significance of Huysmans's *À Rebours* (1884) is difficult to overstate. The book is nothing like a tract of Symbolism; it was more important for confirming the movement's possibility than for defining its terms. Its publication has been taken as one of the precipitating causes of the new aesthetic and as the reason for Mallarmé's rise to fame. But these effects appear only through the presentation of a character for whom the form and style of a life is the single object, an object requiring infinite care, taste, time, and wealth. Even as *À Rebours* devotes itself to exquisite artifacts, it pursues Duc Jean Des Esseintes himself as an exquisite object. Why not take one's own life as the object of art? This is the question that Walter Pater had carefully insinuated into British consciousness. Within *À Rebours* this question takes on its most prominent and extravagant aspect.

Early in the work Des Esseintes seeks to prove that ingenuity and persistence can create "imaginary pleasures similar in all respects to the pleasures of reality": "The main thing is to know how to set about it, to be able to concentrate your attention on a single detail, to forget yourself sufficiently to bring about the desired hallucination and so substitute the vision of a reality for the reality itself."[28] This theory of artifice has a vivid career in the fin de siècle, but Des Esseintes goes further in the pursuit of the exact sensation and the ideal mental state. At the beginning of the fifth chapter we learn of his search for images that will blot out sordid contemporary society in favor of "erudite fancies, complicated nightmares, suave and sinister visions" (50). The state of mind of the viewer becomes an artifact as complex as any other; indeed, it could be the supreme artifact. Late in the novel Des Esseintes realizes that in order to attract him:

> a book had to have that quality of strangeness that Edgar Allan Poe called for; but he was inclined to venture further along this road, and to insist on Byzantine flowers of thought and deliquescent complexities of style; he demanded a disquieting vagueness that would give him scope for dreaming until he decided to make it still vaguer or more definite, according to the way he felt at the time. He wanted, in short, a work of art both for what it was in itself and for what it allowed him to bestow on it; he wanted to go along with it and on it, as if supported by a friend or carried by a vehicle, into a sphere where sublimated sensations would arouse within him an unexpected commotion, the causes of which he would strive patiently and even vainly to analyse. (165)

The more extravagantly Des Esseintes seeks to extend the life of sensation, the greater the risk that the work will dissolve among the sensations. As if in acknowledgment of the risk, Des Esseintes holds to the value of the work "in itself" even as he recruits value as a stimulus. But the whole of À Rebours serves to tease out the possibility that the *experience of aesthesis* might come to replace the *aesthetic object* and that painting, literature, and music might become no more important than other stimulants. Des Esseintes experiments with perfumes—"pure spirits and extracts" and "compound scents"—aspiring to an arrangement of smells so subtle that it would give the satisfaction of a work of art (105). He plays as well with the tastes of liqueurs, linking each with a musical instrument, until he can transfer "specific pieces of music to his palate, following the composer step by step, rendering his intentions, his effects, his shades of expression, by mixing or contrasting related liqueurs, by subtle approximations and cunning combinations" (46). At times he goes still further, inventing his own music on the palate.

To arrange sensations into an aesthetic dream-state, to live in a state of perpetual responsiveness, to compose oneself into a work of art—these practices of the symbolist vocation become questions of reverie and sensation, of conversational habit, of dress. The effect of *À Rebours,* as well as an effect of Pater's writings, was to promote new styles of life, as well as new works and new opinions. The practice of metropolitan experience was also part of the symbolist avant-garde.

When Des Esseintes constructs his palace of sensation, he describes himself as "exhausted by life and expecting nothing more from it." Like a monk, "he was overwhelmed by an immense weariness" (63), and from Verlaine's poetry he achieves "a languor made more pronounced by the vagueness of the words that were guessed at rather than heard" (71). The cultivation of a swooning lethargy, a weary torpor as one drifted along the currents of sensation, became pervasive among the symbolist generation. Mallarmé's faun is a poetic epitome. He contemplates the surge of passion, "purple and already ripe," but turns immediately away from the exciting image.

> Sans plus il faut dormir en l'oubli du blasphème,
> Sur le sable altéré gisant et comme j'aime
> Ouvrir ma bouche à l'astre efficace des vins!

> (enough! on the thirsty sand, forgetful of
> the outrage, I must sleep, and as I love
> open my mouth to the powerful star of wine!)[29]

The faun sinks back from desire into languor, a gesture that becomes a bodily signature in the later 1880s and 1890s. In the poem's final line, he bids the nymphs farewell in a last exhalation: "I shall see the shades you become" (54–55). The arrival at luminous reverie—as the dozing faun watches images flit across the brain—exemplifies the symbolist state. Physical activity suspended, the faun prepares to be moved by what will appear in his dream. It is as if the subject has detached itself not only from surrounding events but also from its own sensations. This is what Huysmans's Des Esseintes also achieves after his patient and fastidious arrangement of colors, tastes, scents, or lines of poetry: a release into weary passivity, a swooning lassitude that allows him to surrender to the processions of imagination.

Although the new movement resisted the name "decadent" in favor of "symbolist," the public and the critics saw these figures under the "double name of decadents and symbolists," as Kenneth Cornell has pointed out.[30] The struggle over the proper name marked a turn in the politics of culture, suggesting the diversity of cultural vocations now in contention. Whether the poetry was an index of decline or of long-delayed renewal, this polemic was sustained as long as the movement itself. Where "Symbolism" suggested a coherent method along the lines of "Naturalism," the tag "decadence" was open to censure, which came quickly. Huysmans, in turn, denounced the society that repudiated him, describing it as a grotesque combination of "idiotic sentimentality" and "ruthless commercialism." He praised Mallarmé for completing the work of decadence "in the most consummate and exquisite fashion."[31] The success of À Rebours was a milestone in the formation of Symbolism, which could be seen, by both partisans and opponents, as the beautiful efflorescence of decay.[32] Soon Arthur Symons introduced the symbolist poets to the English-speaking world along these very lines: as the blazing symptom of the end. Both writers emphasized, and celebrated, the lure of sensation and passivity.

And yet as Mallarmé came to predominance in the later 1880s, he appeared not as a character in Huysmans's fiction but in another aspect. Although his poems might be seen to invite a languid swoon, he cast his ambitions in exacting terms. As a writer of essays, reviews, and increasingly difficult poems, Mallarmé was not the sensualist so much as the theorist—though often a theorist of the senses. As Symons revised his views, he came to recognize precisely that. Mallarmé, he wrote, "was not a mystic, to whom anything came unconsciously; he was a thinker, in whom an extraordinary subtlety of mind was exercised on always explicit, though by no means the common, problems."[33] The legend of Mallarmé's mardis, his Tuesday evening salons, conveyed this image of intelligence and self-consciousness in pursuit of the most difficult questions in aesthetics.

The contrast here—between the cult of sensation and the demands of lucidity—provides one way to think about the terminological struggle between decadence and Symbolism. The "decadent" portrait of the sensationalist, "too languid for the relief of action," must be set against the figure of the "symbolist" artist as the theoretically self-aware architect of intricate designs.[34] The latter figure was, after all, one of the novelties of the cultural moment, suggesting as it did that the practice of the arts required high critical intelligence. The unfolding of Symbolism revealed that the work of theory was not prefatory or supplementary to the making of artifacts but constitutive. Mallarmé's career remains the defining example. His failure to produce the great work that he projected can be read, and has been read, as the tragedy of self-consciousness. He knew too much; he thought where he ought to have dreamed. But even in his lifetime another view arose, which saw the incompletion of his oeuvre as the truth of authentic art. If

Mallarmé left only fragments and was condemned to theorize about an achievement that eluded him, this result was not the consequence of incapacity; rather, it was the enactment of the contradictions of modernity. That the totality of modernity could be glimpsed only through its fragments, that labor on the artifact must be endless and must be conducted with unrelenting lucidity—these hard truths condemned (or exalted) the poet who accepted the impossible vocation.

Here we arrive at two closely related points about the history of the movement. The first concerns the prominence of the individual within the avant-garde collective. If, as I have suggested, the history of Modernism involved a transition from the solitary genius to the loosely bound collective, what now remained for the singular figure, the particular career? In 1887 the poet Émile Verhaeren wrote, "At this moment there is only one true Symbolist master in France: Stéphane Mallarmé."[35] Whatever else was in dispute, Mallarmé's oeuvre could be seen as exemplary, his critical utterances as canonical. This pattern became familiar within the avant-garde. Movements that were fundamentally collective in inspiration nevertheless became identified with individual careers. The relations of center and margin, leader and followers, were not unique to the cultural avant-garde. Political and religious sects, especially in this period, often enacted the same ambiguity. What was distinctive in the arts, however, was a more insecure balance of values. Did individuals work for the broader aims of the movement? Was art justified only to the extent that it belonged to a broad cultural transformation, or was the final justification the radiant work? the individual career? Did the flurry of manifestos and polemics exist in order to bring forth the singular achievement? When Ezra Pound spoke of T. S. Eliot's *The Waste Land* as the "justification of the 'movement,' of our modern experiment, since 1900," he was answering yes to the last question.[36] But from Symbolism onward, the question remained open, creating strain and uncertainty within the avant-garde.

The second question in the history of Symbolism concerns its social engagements. The movement is often seen as an essentially defensive action, a flight from late-century modernization with its consumerism, its cheap journalism, its dirty cities, and its noisy transport. When Verlaine in the mid-1880s speaks of "accursed poets" ("les poètes maudits"), he is characterizing a generation of writers who have been derided and dismissed and who must withdraw from the uncomprehending crowd. Huysmans's *À Rebours,* which offered an extravagant vision of withdrawal, held up Mallarmé's poetry as a refined pleasure available only in aesthetic seclusion. But this view of Symbolism cannot stand without important qualification.

UBU ROI, YEATS, AND SYMONS: WEARINESS TO WILL

In the years immediately after *Les Poètes maudits* and *À Rebours* appeared, Mallarmé's preeminence was consolidated, and as he developed his difficult theories, he thought increasingly about the theater. Although his ideas were often hypothetical and beyond the reach of any real performance, they inspired the work of a younger generation who looked to bring Symbolism onto the stage. An account of this turn belongs in a later chapter. Here the point is the changing physical and social scene of the literary movement. When Maeterlinck's first plays appeared on the Parisian stage in the early 1890s, and when Auguste Villiers de l'Isle-Adam's *Axel* was staged in 1894, Symbolism was no longer a lyric event contained within "accursed" pages. The social forum of the theater enlarged the force of challenge. The plays themselves often rehearsed themes of withdrawal and escape, spectacularly so in the case of *Axel*. But the act of production was a return to the world, a deliberate provocation of the public. After a performance of Ibsen's *Enemy of the People* in 1893, Parisian anarchists rioted in the streets. Three years later the first performance of Jarry's *Ubu roi* incited a chanting, howling uproar that marked a defining moment in the rise of the avant-garde. Those in attendance, including William Butler Yeats and Arthur Symons, reported twenty minutes of pandemonium, which subsided slowly to let the pandemonium resume on stage. Symons offers this description of the scene that confronted the audience: "[The] scenery was painted to represent, by a child's conventions, indoors and out of doors, and even the torrid, temperate and arctic zones at once. . . . On the left was painted a bed, and at the foot of the bed a bare tree, and snow falling. On the right were palm-trees, about one of which coiled a boa-constrictor; a door opened against the sky, and beside the door a skeleton dangled from a gallows.[37] Against this background, the masked figure of Père Ubu swelled into the monstrosity of a pure appetite, which wants to ingest everything (food, royal power) but no more than it wants to expel everything (insult, humiliation, flatulence). Ubu moves through his imaginary Poland as instinct unleashed, a human effigy, bobbing between pleasure and violence and always tending to the place where pleasure meets violence: "Bring up the first Noble and pass me the boat-hook. Those who are condemned to death, I shall push through this trap door. They will fall down into the bleed-pig chambers, and will then proceed to the cash-room where they will be debrained. (To the Noble) What's your name, you slob?"[38]

Part of what gives force to Ubu is that he stands as a target of satire—the coarse seeker of power who shows humanity at its lowest—but also as the embodiment of a liberating anarchic will, who erupts against all civility, much in the spirit of his author: he is at once authority and revolutionary. Ubu plotting, Ubu murderous, Ubu triumphant, Ubu defeated, marked a new stage in the culture of novelty. The play flaunts its anachronism—guns firing in the year 1000—and its disdain for coherence. With its romping frantic action, its startling masks, its rude shouts and gestures, *Ubu roi* created a legend that persisted through the next decades of aesthetic experiment. It was impulsive, eruptive, and absurdist—an impudent affront to realism.

It was no less an affront to Symbolism. Although *Ubu roi* came out of the symbolist milieu of the 1880s and 1890s, and although it was produced in the temple of theatrical Symbolism, Aurélien Lugné-Poë's Théâtre de l'Oeuvre, it struck an early death-knell to a movement that was still taking form. It defied the method of evocation; it showed no interest in a supersensible world. *Ubu roi* brazenly confronted viewers; its noisy gestures made a mockery of Maeterlinck's call for a theater of haunting silences. Peter Brook was surely right to say that the challenge of the play is that there is no psychology, no conventional reference, nothing that lets one know how to penetrate behind or within the text.[39] Jarry refuses to imply that meaning is elsewhere or anywhere; the demand is to confront what is present, not what is absent. In place of ritual, there is carnival.

In *The Trembling of the Veil,* Yeats memorably recorded his response to the *Ubu* eruption that he had witnessed in the company of a friend (Arthur Symons) from the London Rhymers' Club.

> I go to the first performance of Alfred Jarry's *Ubu Roi,* at the Théâtre de l'Oeuvre. . . . The audience shake their fists at one another, and the Rhymer [Symons] whispers to me, "There are often duels after these performances," and he explains to me what is happening on the stage. The players are supposed to be dolls, toys, marionettes, and now they are all hopping like wooden frogs, and I can see for myself that the chief personage, who is some kind of King, carries for Sceptre a brush of the kind that we use to clean a closet. Feeling bound to support the most spirited party, we have shouted for the play, but that night at the Hotel Corneille, I am very sad, for comedy, objectivity, has displayed its grow-

ing power once more. I say, "After Stephane Mallarmé, after Paul Verlaine, after Gustave Moreau, after Puvis de Chavannes, after our own
verse, after all our subtle colour and nervous rhythm, after the faint
mixed tints of Conder, what more is possible? After us the Savage God."[40]

Yeats's tone is apocalyptic, but the unfolding history justified the rhetoric.
For Symons as for Yeats, as for their precursors in Paris, Symbolism had
appeared as a definitive Modernism. It completed and corrected the destructive work of realism; in so doing, it elaborated an aesthetic that could
resist the failures of modernity and at the same time could assume the vocation of religion. Yeats saw the confluence of symbolist artists as "the only
movement that is saying new things."[41]

The cultural opening offered by *Ubu roi* was not widely exploited for
some years, but even suspended as a model, it participated in the broad
transformation that Yeats glimpsed. Here again we confront the importance of Nietzsche. The appearance of his work was more than a philosophical event; his philosophy quickly became a source of aesthetic change.
The texts of the 1880s—*Thus Spoke Zarathustra, Beyond Good and Evil, On
the Genealogy of Morals, The Anti-Christ, Twilight of the Idols*—were translated and quickly disseminated. The books were abused and eagerly used.
They were repositories of scandalous aphorisms—"God is dead"; "Man is
finished when he becomes altruistic"—but they also outlined a sustained
critique of modernity. Nietzsche's hatred of any system was itself part of his
legacy. And yet from within the epigrams, the fragments, and the parables,
his early admirers were able to extract a loose diagram of convictions that
could justify the revolts of the avant-garde.

Nietzsche's leading early theme was that our debased lives were the effect of a failed history, a complete deliquescence of social life, hastened by all
the "softening customs" of the modern world: compassion, self-suppression,
equality. Democracy and liberalism represented the institution of weakness. Christianity was itself a long decadence; it was a "fictitious world" in
which the weak became dominant. The envious rabble, who encumbered
the earth, promulgated a poisonous doctrine of equality, which was itself
a decadent outcome of Christian pity: "Pity stands in antithesis to the tonic
emotions which enhance the energy of the feeling of life: it has a depres-
sive effect. One loses force when one pities."[42] The only way out of the impasse of modern life was a reassertion of instinct, the "wholesome, healthy
selfishness" of a "powerful soul."[43] "Wherever the will to power declines in
any form there is every time also a physiological regression, a *décadence.*

The divinity of *décadence,* pruned of all its manliest drives and virtues, from now on necessarily becomes the God of the physiologically retarded, the weak. They do *not* call themselves the weak, they call themselves 'the good.'"[44]

The last point, central to the Nietzschean revaluation of all values, became a rich resource for an oppositional culture that not only repudiated the forms of life constituting modernity, but also contested the rights to the *names* of value: "good," "healthy," "just." The victory of the rabble brought the claim to dictate a moral vocabulary. Nietzsche's insurrection involved usurping the language of evaluation and laying claim to an ethic of power.

> What is good?—All that heightens the feeling of power, the will to power, power itself in man.
>   What is bad?—All that proceeds from weakness.[45]

The mastery of the flourishing self includes power over language, the power to discard the inherited fictions of Christianity, democracy, and liberalism and to invent new names for value.

Before all else, the exercise of the assertive will is Nietzsche's legacy to modernist aesthetics. Peter Nicholls is surely right to argue that his work made available a "concept of the heroic will with which to overcome the pessimism and inaction" of the late nineteenth century and a "fundamental redefinition of the self as active, dynamic, and confrontational."[46] At stake was a difference in the most immediate reflexes of sensibility and style. The posture of languid elegance, with the passive body waiting to receive subtle sensations, gave way to vigorous gesture and an appreciation of strenuous mobile forms. Mallarmé's faun piped lazily in the heat, postponed the fulfillment of desire, and drifted into sleep and dream. It is precisely this icon of weariness that was challenged by Nietzschean will.

Under the title "A Symbolist Farce," Arthur Symons elaborates his first reactions to *Ubu roi.* That he insists on identifying the play as "symbolist" is itself revealing. Symons recognizes that Jarry's work erupted from within the movement that it disclaims, and like Yeats, Symons sees it as an ominous sign of change. Most startling is the "insolence with which a young writer mocks at civilization itself, sweeping all art, along with all humanity, into the same inglorious slop-pail."[47] *Ubu roi,* he writes, represents the "brutality out of which we have achieved civilization" (377); its author is "a young savage of the woods" (371); its hero remains no more than a "monkey on a stick" (376). Identifying Jarry's play as a dangerous regression, Symons joined many of the early critics in expressing his foreboding, but

what is shrewd is how he links *Ubu roi* to a transition of literary generations. Its lesson is that "a generation which has exhausted every intoxicant,
every soluble preparation of the artificial, may well seek a last sensation in
the wire-pulled passions, the wooden faces of marionettes, and, by a further illusion, of marionettes who are living people; living people pretending to be those wooden images of life which pretend to be living people"
(374).

Even before Symons had published *The Symbolist Movement in Literature* he glimpsed the terms in which the movement would come undone.
Although the tone of his brief review of *Ubu roi* is elegiac, he is prescient in
identifying the self-canceling logic of Symbolism. Pursuit of the exquisite
leads to the last expenditure of sensibility, or, as he neatly puts it, "the artificial, when it has gone the full circle, comes back to the primitive; des Esseintes relapses into the Red Indian" (376). He elaborates: "In our search for
sensation we have exhausted sensation; and now, before a people who have
perfected the fine shades to their vanishing point, who have subtilised delicacy of perception into the annihilation of the very sense through which we
take in ecstasy, a literary Sans-culotte has shrieked for hours that unspeakable word of the gutter" (376–377).

The tone of doom had already been rung over the accursed poets that
Symons enshrined. For him to sound the same tone was briskly ironic. The
symbolists had been received with distaste and mockery; they had been
called lunatics and revolutionaries; and now Symons transfers the epithets
to the young Jarry. The encounter marks a resonant moment in the history
of Modernism. Root disagreement over the goals of art and a sharp parting
of ways will become recurrent scenes within the avant-garde ("After us the
Savage God"). As Symons and Yeats sensed, the performances of *Ubu roi*
were an early battleground. In the space of an evening Symbolism witnessed the scene of its death. Even as Symons deplores the play, he offers a
persuasive account of how Symbolism will end, how it will exhaust itself
and prepare for its opposite. From his perspective and that of Yeats, Jarry's
play abandons the modern mission of symbolist poetry and returns to primal savagery. The terms of this critique will become familiar: the latest
novelty is seen, and sometimes sees itself, as deliberate brutality and willful
primitivism.

Both Yeats and Symons located the *Ubu* outburst in an eternal cycle—
Yeats saw the return of objectivity and comedy; Symons, the turn of the
wheel from civilization back to the primitive. Yet one reason that Jarry's
play became legendary was that its absurdism, its rudeness and violence,

broke with the figure of cycle or wheel and generated what was seen as radical novelty: the creation of the never-before-seen. *Ubu roi,* of course, did not stand alone. The scandal over Edvard Munch's exhibition in Berlin in 1892, the rioting over Ibsen, the splutter over the novels of Zola—these, too, created the aura of scandal, of unprecedented provocation. The result was an emphatic shift from the transhistorical temporality of Symbolism— Symbolism as a permanent possibility through the ages—to the temporality of the New, the unanticipated, the unexpected, the unforeseen.

FROM THE LYRIC TO THE STAGE

How was *Ubu roi* able to make its way in the first place? How did it receive a hearing, and a stage, in the face of a Symbolism that it would help to dislodge? Here we need to appreciate the accumulating force of the social practice of modern arts. Paris preeminently, but not Paris alone, had become the site of artistic innovation and outrage. The ongoing sequence of events—the works of Ibsen, Mallarmé, Zola, Maeterlinck, and now Jarry— was only one element in that culture. There was also, as I have emphasized, an active public discourse, most visible in an expanding journalistic field, which fed on the art that revolted it. Moreover, and decisively, by the time of Lugné-Poë and the Théâtre de l'Oeuvre, there was an audience that recognized itself as a loosely arranged but exuberant community. The hundreds, not thousands, who followed the new art were numerous enough to consolidate a subculture of novelty. Those who cheered during the opening riots of *Ubu roi* were no doubt also applauding themselves, and those who chanted and hissed were also indispensable partners in the entrenchment of the New. If Lugné-Poë was willing to take a risk on the young Jarry, that was surely because the conditions of novelty, like the demands of fashion, not only prepared for continual experiment but were beginning to require it. From the perspective of Yeats and Symons, *Ubu roi* may have been the antithesis of a properly modern art, but from the standpoint of others, including the audience, the play belonged to an ongoing practice of innovation.

Indeed, that it was a *play* is itself telling, for reasons that we have begun to see. Within just a few years the cinema would become a rival site and institution, but in the last decade of the nineteenth century, the theater was where the public could recognize the emergence of a new art. Modernism developed unevenly. Just as it did not move at the same pace through all countries, the practice of experiment did not move simultaneously through all the arts. Although Symbolism required a public forum to constitute itself as a movement, its initial impetus remained within the constrained circumstances of private life. Even as Mallarmé began to project his future as a poet, he described the narrow physical, as well as social, conditions of imagination. He lamented the demands of his schoolteaching in a provincial town: "And what's more I'm suffering in my home! As yet I have only half an apartment, and will come to life only when I have my own room, where I can be alone surrounded by my thought, the windows bulging with my inner Dreams like the drawers of precious stones in a rich piece of furniture, and the hangings falling in their familiar folds. I would like, even just to write you this letter, to create a few lines of poetry in this temporary corridor I live in, just as one burns a scent jar, or alternatively wait a year, by which time my solitude will have had time to recompose itself within these walls."[48] We may take this as a characteristic image for Symbolism: the hard-pressed and enervated poet who, though obliged to struggle for money and a writing desk, nevertheless sees imaginative flight as compensation and escape. All that Mallarmé requires, like Virginia Woolf after him, is his own room, and even within his "temporary corridor," he can envision the sprouting of verse.

This tableau remains a compelling story of the origins of the avant-garde. The "inner Dreams" of the symbol require no more than a narrow corner: from there, they can rise limitlessly. Raymond Williams thought of Symbolism in primarily defensive terms, as one among various late-nineteenth-century movements that "sought to protect their practices within the growing dominance of the art market and against the indifference of the formal academies."[49] His insight is important, but it needs to be complemented by a recognition of the *activity* of Symbolism, even within the scene of limitation. On one side, there is a withdrawal into a private space—one's room, one's inner dreams—but on the other side stands the projection of an alternative universe. When Yeats speaks of making a "new religion" of his own, he, too, displays an active, not merely defensive, posture.[50] For Yeats, as for Mallarmé, the invention of the dream-universe is more than an act of self-protection; it offers itself, although it is not always accepted, as a radical remaking of modernity. Yet Williams is surely right to see Symbolism as hemmed in by material pressures and institutional constraints. The new poetry depended on the dissemination and discussion of its texts. The circle of initiates widened, but it was never large. Mallarmé's Tuesday evenings evoke an image of a small interior containing a few sympathetic writers who keep faith in the transcendence of verse. Even when the manifestos began to circulate, poetic Symbolism retained its narrow scale.

Indeed, the distance between small-scale intimacy and transcendent vision became a central subject of the movement.

By the mid-1890s the locus of radical literary experiment had turned from lyric poetry to the stage. But this historical turn was complex. We have already seen how the theatrical provocations of Wagner, Ibsen, and Strindberg created the conditions for an oppositional culture. It is difficult to overestimate Wagner's importance to the symbolists, and equally difficult to overestimate Ibsen's contribution to a culture of sensation and scandal. Still, *Ubu roi* changed the terms of confrontation. The challenge that Symbolism had made to the discourse of meaning—its refusal to offer paraphrasable content or to specify an ethical or political vision—became in Jarry a more extravagant gesture, at once rudely physical and incontestably social. In the open space of the theater, in the presence of an engaged or suspicious audience and a cadre of journalists, *Ubu roi* offered a celebration of audacities: the infinite appetite of Ubu himself and the insistent gestures of aggression in a play that itself rejected all conventions of meaning. It made clear how theatricality could be seen not just as a question of dramatic *representation*, scandalous or otherwise, but as an *event*, a punctual eruption in space-time whose force depended on the immediacy of heightened response.

PAINTING THE PRIMITIVE

Because of the furor associated with *Ubu roi* and the other challenges of the 1890s, the course of avant-garde experiment was broken and uneven for several years. Roger Shattuck has observed that "just after the turn of the century, the major literary and artistic movements had come to a standstill. Impressionism in painting, Symbolism and Decadence in poetry, Naturalism in the novel had all run their course."[51] Shattuck is right to see a prevailing fatigue, which was partly a result of the accident of life histories, with the deaths of Mallarmé (1898), Zola (1902), and Ibsen (1906) suggesting a mortality in the campaigns they had led. And yet the late-nineteenth-century movements did not end. Symbolism and Naturalism, above all, continued their development into the twentieth century even as they became conspicuous targets of the campaigns of the next generation. Yeats in Ireland and Alexander Blok in Russia were two preeminent figures who carried the banner of symbolist poetry through the first decade of the twentieth century. Then, too, in the years just after 1905, several new provocations appeared across Europe. In 1907, Strindberg finally established the Intimate Theatre that he had envisioned for so long: a small performance space holding just over 150 spectators and designed to "avoid all ostentation, all calculated effects, milking of applause, showy roles, solo numbers."[52] Here is where Strindberg's late "chamber plays" were produced, among them *The Ghost Sonata,* a work that would be a major influence upon the new "Expressionist" drama emerging in Germany. In 1908, Arnold Schoenberg began his experiments with atonality that crystallized in such early landmark works as his Second String Quartet and the piano piece Opus 11.

The most visible manifestations of the avant-garde between 1905 and the First World War, however, came in the work of young painters. The group that came to be known as "les Fauves" (wild beasts)—including André Derain, Maurice de Vlaminck, and, above all, Henri Matisse—strikingly deepened the resources of color, especially nonnatural hues applied in bright bands and curves, colors celebrating their independence from the natural world. In such works as *Portrait of Mme. Matisse* (1905) and *The Young Sailor* (1906), space is flattened, while vivid reds, blues, and greens appear as expressive powers set free from the constraints of realism. After the brief period of Fauvism, Matisse pursued still more extreme innovations, as in *Harmony in Red* (1908) and *Music* (1910), paintings that open up broad fields of contrasting shades, absorbing human gesture (and dress) into the life of colors.

At the very moment that Matisse was developing a revolution in color, Picasso was reimagining the fate of the line. Although this puts the comparison too neatly, there can be no doubt that these two figures, intensely aware of one another, offered transformational gestures from distinct directions. Even as Matisse painted masses of color spreading out ever more broadly, Picasso began the great venture of analysis, dissection, and fragmentation. It was Matisse who suggested the name "Cubism" when he described the work of Georges Braque, Picasso's close collaborator, as made of "little cubes" (fig. 2). In the years after 1905, the pace of cubist experiment quickened, leading to Picasso's astonishing succession of works after the breakthrough of *Les Demoiselles d'Avignon* in 1907 and then a succession of riskier experiments: the *Bather, Woman with Pears,* and the portraits of Vollard, Uhde, and Kahnweiler (fig. 3).

At the center of these experiments was Picasso's encounter with the sculptures of Africa and Oceania. His first view of the pieces in the Old Trocadéro in 1906 has become a cherished piece of modernist lore, a revelatory moment when the young European artist looked beyond an inherited tradition and glimpsed another form of life and art. But that event also belongs to the complex (and vexed) history of modernist primitivism. The movement of Europeans around the world—as missionaries, as imperialists, as anthropologists, as tourists—meant that a vast repository of non-European artifacts (bought, looted, or exchanged) steadily accumulated in the museums of the West. The objects became part of a narrative of development often used to defend imperial domination and racial hierarchy; the pairing of "primitive" and "civilized" came to offer a contrast more pointed than the one between modernity and tradition. "Tradition," especially the Greek and Roman tradition, retained an aura of eminence, but when the contrastive term was "primitive," the arguments for modernity appeared self-evident.

Then, among the artists, a change occurred. Apollinaire, in "Exoticism and Ethnography" (1912), wrote that until recently African and Australian objects "were collected only because of their ethnographic interest. Today, art collectors regard them with the respect that used to be accorded only to the art works of the so-called superior peoples of Greece, Egypt, India and China."[53] Here is a direct challenge to the developmental figure that draws an arc from low primitive to high civilized. When Picasso painted an African mask onto a woman in the brothel of *Les Demoiselles d'Avignon,* he not only confirmed the power of the non-European figure but also disrupted the narrative of art history, bringing "ethnographic" or "prehistorical" specimens into the artistic present. As William Rubin has remarked, the discovery of this art was not sudden, since the materials had been available in the museums of Europe for a generation; it was rather a change in the meaning of the objects.[54] For Vincent van Gogh and Paul Gauguin the idea of the "primitive" indicated a whole range of non-European cultures, including those of Egypt, Persia, India, and Japan. Picasso, specifically through the painting of *Les Demoiselles,* helped bring about a transformation: now the "primitive" came to signify works from Africa and Oceania. Rubin usefully opposes John Ruskin's opinion that no genuine art was to be found "in the whole of Africa, Asia or America" to Picasso's view that "primitive sculpture has never been surpassed."[55]

In the twenty-first century, we see that modernist primitivism has assumed a too-predictable aspect. Simon Gikandi, working to refresh our view of it, has argued for a distinction between Africa—its people and their living bodies—and the African artifacts brought to ethnographic collections in the North. For an artist like Picasso the stimulus came from the objects, not from the culture that produced them or the artists who created them. Primitive art became a resource for modern European self-recognition, "a conduit to understanding 'civilized' man, art, and poetry, not an endpoint in itself; there was no incentive to understand the Other unless it would lead to an understanding of Western civilization either in its 'childhood' or moments of crisis."[56] So at a critical moment in Conrad's *Heart of Darkness,* Marlow sails up the Congo river to find "a glimpse of rush walls, of peaked grass-roofs, a burst of yells, a whirl of black limbs, a mass of hands clapping, of feet stamping, of bodies swaying, of eyes rolling under the droop of heavy and motionless foliage. The steamer toiled along slowly on the edge of black and incomprehensible frenzy. The prehistoric man was cursing us, praying to us, welcoming us—who could tell? We were cut off from the comprehension of our surroundings; we glided past like phantoms, wondering and secretly appalled, as sane men would be before an enthusiastic outbreak in a madhouse."[57] Here is the ethically compromised view of black Africans as savages untouched by the work of civilization: Gikandi is surely right to emphasize the European blindness toward these non-European lives. But in Conrad's passage, alongside the blindness stands a critique of European complacency and cruelty—and a demand to recognize the continuities that interrupt the contrast.

The savagery of the natives is African and Other, but Conrad suggests that it is also European and Same. I have described this view elsewhere as the "beyond within," a phrase meant to suggest how the "primitive" served as an essential trope for Modernism, how it became an up-to-date resource for artists pursuing an *outside* that was *inside* bourgeois modernity. In *Les Demoiselles d'Avignon,* the prostitutes stare toward the place where a bourgeois viewer would stand, and as the spectator returns the gaze, the shock does not emanate so much from the tableau of naked bodies, which are, after all, clichés of transgression, as from the large African mask, which is far more mysterious than the naked woman it (partially) covers. The "primitive" generates its effects because it is temporally and spatially outside Europe, but also because it has entered a European matrix of possibilities. The outside/inside ambiguity is crucial. The primitive is the distant, external perspective that has entered European culture, but even absorbed there, it remains a sign of the unassimilated, unaccommodated Other.

Early in D. H. Lawrence's *Women in Love,* Gerald Crich encounters an African carving in a London flat. He recoils from the image of a woman in labor, "dark and tense, abstracted in utter physical stress," while Rupert Birkin gazes with interest.

"Why is it art?" Gerald asked, shocked, resentful.

"It conveys a complete truth," said Birkin. "It contains the whole truth of the state, whatever you feel about it."

"But you can't call it *high* art," said Gerald.

"High! There are centuries and hundreds of centuries of development in a straight line, behind that carving; it is an awful pitch of culture, of a definite sort."

"What culture?" Gerald asked, in opposition. He hated the sheer barbaric thing.

"Pure culture in sensation, culture in the physical consciousness, really ultimate physical consciousness, mindless, utterly sensual. It is so sensual as to be final, supreme."

But Gerald resented it. He wanted to keep certain illusions, certain ideas like clothing.

"You like the wrong things, Rupert," he said, "things against yourself."

"Oh, I know, this isn't everything," Birkin replied, moving away.[58]

The passage pries open an ambivalence. Through Birkin, Lawrence defends the integrity of the so-called primitive work; he asserts its embeddedness in a rich culture and the truth of its vision, which appears as a vision of life in utter physical sensuality. The novel uses the carving as a weapon against bourgeois illusions, those "ideas like clothing." Although the object is the product of an ancient culture, its truth belongs to the present, and it is exactly to the extent that the carving discloses a modern "culture in sensation" that it takes on power in the novel. Any refusal to grant the truth of the sculpture is a refusal to see the sensual truth that bourgeois modernity conceals from itself. For Lawrence, however, the test of a flourishing life depends on overcoming the present truth contained in the ancient object. The fact that the sculpture "isn't everything" is crucial to the thematic work of *Women in Love,* in which Lawrence tries to imagine overcoming the "single impulse" in favor of the "desire for creation and productive happiness" (249). But the carving is also a revealing instance of modernist primitivism, which offers a forceful instrument of critique but which is then overcome, or set aside, in favor of contemporary debates.

Willa Cather located the force of the primitive, not in the spaces of a southern hemisphere marked by racial difference, but in the American heartland. Her early career registered all the pressures of modernization—the spread of transport, the reach of commerce, and also the refinements of polite culture—while sustaining the presence of the antimodern, the rooted, and the unrefined. In an early story, "A Wagner Matinée," the narrator (Clark), living in Boston, receives a visit from his aunt, who had introduced him to the mysteries of culture. Thirty years earlier she had taught music in Boston, had married after a whirlwind romance, and then had gone to build a homestead in Nebraska. Now Clark means to please her with an afternoon in the concert hall, but her reaction exceeds, and undoes, his bland idea.

> The first number was the *Tannhauser* overture. When the horns drew out the first strain of the Pilgrim's chorus my Aunt Georgiana clutched my coat sleeve. Then it was I first realized that for her this broke a silence of thirty years; the inconceivable silence of the plains. With the battle between the two motives, with the frenzy of the Venusberg theme and its ripping of strings, there came to me an overwhelming sense of the waste and wear we are so powerless to combat; and I saw again the tall, naked house on the prairies, black and grim as a fortress; the black pond where I had learned to swim, its margin pitted with sun-dried cattle tracks; the rain-gullied clay banks about the naked house, the four dwarf ash seedlings where the dishcloths were always hung to dry before the kitchen doors. The world there was the flat world of the ancients; to the east, a cornfield that stretched to daybreak; to the west, a corral that reached to sunset; between, the conquests of peace, dearer bought than those of war.[59]

As the concert ends, the aunt, overwhelmed, sobs and pleads, "I don't want to go" (109). The nephew writes that he now understands her agony: "For her, just outside the door of the concert hall, lay the black pond with the cattle-tracked bluffs; the tall, unpainted house, with weather-curled boards; naked as a tower, the crook-backed ash seedlings where the dishcloths hung to dry; the gaunt, molting turkeys picking up refuse about the kitchen doors" (110).

Here is Cather's rendering of the American national primitive: the austere landscape of the plains and the hard living required. But the story lays out the doubleness that runs through much modernist primitivism. On the one hand, as the first passage suggests, modern art appears as the recovery of archaic truths, of powers (and pains) that civilized moderns prefer to forget. Like many works at the turn of the nineteenth century, the story enshrines Wagner as the figure of a proper Modernism (well beyond the "old *Trovatore*"; 109), which creates radical novelty by summoning the "world of the ancients." From this perspective, modern art releases the truth of the primitive: Modernism and primitivism are deeply congruent, in some respects merely two aspects of the same practice.

On the other hand, as the last lines of "A Wagner Matinée" suggest, the primal landscape appears as the antithesis of culture, as the permanent exterior to refined art. The final image of the Nebraskan landscape—spare, harsh, and unconsoling—resists the grandeur of Wagnerian opera. When the aunt weeps with her desire to stay in the concert hall, she measures the distance between culture (modern or traditional) and nature, between art and mortal hardship, between Boston and Nebraska. Here is a second valence in the modernist encounter with ancient cultures. Alongside the acts of appropriation—"primitive art" as model, stimulus, or incitement— stands the other recognition: the premodern or antimodern as the sign of a limit to modernity, unassimilable and distant.

What makes Cather an illustrative example of modernist primitivism is that her "primitives" dwell in the heartland of the nation, not across its borders and boundaries or in remote imperial outposts. Still more complexly, they are often immigrants to the United States, who have traveled long distances toward the geographic interior and who undertake the construction of the modern nation. Jim Burden, the narrator of *My Ántonia*, praises the immigrant girls who had "been early awakened and made observant by coming at a tender age from an old country to a new" but who were "considered a menace to the social order. Their beauty shone out too boldly against a conventional background."[60] In the novel's last lines Ántonia is identified as one who "lent herself to immemorial human attitudes which we recognize by instinct as universal and true," one with "a rich mine of life, like the founders of early races" (926). The provocation of the novel is to insist that a generative novelty depends on the *internal* labor of these outsiders. The longer-established Americans, trying to settle quietly in new western lives, avert their eyes from the truth of things. "Their guarded mode of existence was like living under a tyranny. People's speech, their voices, their very glances, became furtive and repressed. Every individual taste, every natural appetite, was bridled by caution. The people asleep in those houses, I thought, tried to live like the mice in their own kitchens; to make no noise, to leave no trace, to slip over the surface of things in the dark. The growing piles of ashes and cinders in the back yards were the only evidence that the wasteful, consuming process of life went on at all" (851). The immigrants, who are repudiated as coarse and unrefined, are the ones who meet the primal motions of life—desire, need, play, waste—and who wrest modernity from the soil.

The struggles of Cather's Nebraskans, the frenzy of Conrad's Africans, the sensualism of Lawrence's sculptures, the shock of Picasso's masks—

these examples remind us that primitivism was a resource for extremity. The artifacts came to suggest the modern world itself was a form of primitivism, as a mad modernization or a dissolute sensuality. As Rubin notes, they allowed Picasso to break out of the "etiolated" and "hypertrophied" forms of Symbolism, the tense, elusive images of the Blue and Early Rose Periods.[61] In fact, he broke from but also broke toward. For Picasso, as for Conrad, Lawrence, and the expressionist painters, the primitive was at once a rejection of symbolist transcendence and a transformation in European self-understanding, a forced recognition of repressed impulses and a demand for a more comprehensive, encompassing life.

FUTURISM NOW

We come to a startling convergence. Just after Picasso's new work began to attract wider attention, a quite different tremor passed through Paris when, in February 1909, *Le Figaro* published "The Founding and Manifesto of Futurism," by F. T. Marinetti, on its front page. This brief text should stand alongside Ibsen's *A Doll's House* (or *Ghosts*), Picasso's *Les Demoiselles,* and Jarry's *Ubu roi* as one of the landmark events around which both cultural fable and new artistic practice grew. Indeed, Jarry was an inspiration for Marinetti, who had spent his early years as a late symbolist poet. The first futurist manifesto represented a break in Marinetti's career; more significantly, it launched a movement that has rightly been taken as a paradigm of the twentieth-century avant-garde. The memorable manifesto in *Le Figaro* was both a short (very short) story and a list of demands. The story tells of a night of carousing for Marinetti and his friends that culminates in a wild ride in a car. The lure of speed, the fascination with machinery, the tone of aggression—these are the elements of the tale, which terminates in a series of famous/notorious pronouncements, among them these numbered demands:

1. We intend to sing the love of danger, the habit of energy and fearlessness. . . .

4. We say that the world's magnificence has been enriched by a new beauty: the beauty of speed. A racing car whose hood is adorned with great pipes, like serpents of explosive breath—a roaring car that seems to ride on grapeshot—is more beautiful than the Victory of Samothrace. . . .

7. Except in struggle, there is no more beauty. No work without an aggressive character can be a masterpiece. Poetry must be

conceived as a violent attack on unknown forces, to reduce and prostrate them before man. . . .

9. We will glorify war—the world's only hygiene—militarism, patriotism, the destructive gesture of freedom-bringers, beautiful ideas worth dying for, and scorn for woman.

10. We will destroy the museums, libraries, academies of every kind, will fight moralism, feminism, every opportunistic or utilitarian cowardice.[62]

Marinetti's genius for publicity had much to do with the rapid success of Futurism. He produced a series of public events, almost all staged to outrage traditionalists. In Venice, in Berlin, in London, in Saint Petersburg, he declaimed his manifestos, stirred the interest of the press, and worked to bring converts to the cause. That the past was inferior to the future was the cultural axiom of Futurism, an axiom from which flowed an unbroken series of gestures, performances, texts, paintings, and sculptures, and always more manifestos. Marinetti offered a Modernism no longer conceived as a refusal of modernization but now pictured as its emanation. A properly modernist art would coincide with technological progress and would live up to the achievements of industrial capitalism. At the moment when the automobile became the index of modernity, Marinetti made it a sign of futurist liberation. Soon he turned to the airplane with the same exhilaration.

The orientation toward the future and the celebration of the New appear in clear contrast to modernist primitivism, which matured at nearly the same time. The differences are notable and indicate the diversity of experiment at this striking moment in the history of Modernism. Despite the evident contrasts, however, the "primitive" and the "futurist" both offered the resources of distance. The images of an archaic (or exotic) past and the inspirations of the latest machine promised a disruption of the habits of complacency. Furthermore, a primitive Modernism and a mechanical Modernism came into surprising convergence in aesthetic forms. Each promised a break with the conventions of realism; each suggested antinaturalist styles, in which the body, freed from cozy roundness, could appear in terms of a stylized geometry with harsh lines and stiff angles (figs. 4–5).

Marinetti's key and consequential insight was that the allure of the new technologies—speed, power, simultaneity—could be the basis for an aesthetic around which many art forms could gather. Painting that depicted bodies in rapid motion, poetry that broke through syntax, sculpture that resembled machinery—in each case Futurism offered a sharp critique of outmoded forms and suggested styles more appropriate to the present.[63] For several years after Marinetti published his manifesto, he moved through the major capitals of Europe, creating astonishment and winning important allies but also inciting vehement reactions that were themselves productive cultural events. In London the writers and artists around Wyndham Lewis and Ezra Pound organized as "Vorticism," a movement intent on marking its difference from Futurism. The vorticists refused the embrace of technology, machinery, and speed and denounced what they saw as looseness of artistic form. But like artists in other capitals, they were bound to recognize the force of Marinetti's polemic. To the extent that Futurism implied the "renovation of art" and "rebellion against the domination of the past," Lewis accepted its goals.[64] And Pound admitted that as far as the basic futurist dictum was concerned—"on ne peut pas porter *partout* avec soi le cadavre de son père" (you cannot carry the corpse of your father *everywhere*)—then "we are all Futurists."[65]

The case of the Russian avant-garde is especially interesting. Young Russian poets, in their own revolt against Symbolism, launched experiments that were nearly contemporaneous with Marinetti's first futurist initiatives. As early as the spring of 1910, poets, painters, and critics were campaigning together for a post-symbolist aesthetic that would accept the demands of modernity (fig. 6). Over the next several years such figures as Velimir Khlebnikov, Vladimir Mayakovsky, Elena Guro, and Aleksei Kruchenykh found common ground with others and published a series of anthologies of their controversial work. Khlebnikov's poem "Incantation by Laughter" (published in 1910) was one early sign of the new audacity; another was the manifesto "A Slap in the Face of Public Taste," which includes pronouncements such as these:

> We alone are the *face* of *our* time. Through us the horn of time blows the art of the world.
>
> Throw Pushkin, Dostoyevsky, Tolstoy, *etc., etc.,* overboard from the Ship of Modernity. . . .
>
> We *order* that the poets' *rights* be revered:
> [1] To enlarge the *scope* of the poet's vocabulary with arbitrary and derivative words (Word-novelty).
> 2) to feel an insurmountable hatred for the language existing before their time.[66]

These assertions, though given a vivid rhetorical turn, clearly owe a great deal to Marinetti's Futurism. Yet, as Vladimir Markov has shown in detail, the Russians retained a disdainful and adversarial relationship with Marinetti.[67] On the one hand, the artists were eager to take on the name "Futurist." On the other hand, they insisted on giving it meanings of their own. Marinetti visited Russia at the beginning of 1914, soon after Mayakovsky assailed Italian Futurism and defended an independent Russian program. The accounts of the visit indicate its tense course. As Marinetti proceeded on his lecture tour, the Russian Cubo-Futurists kept up a steady and vehement attack. Khlebnikov and his ally Benedikt Livshits lampooned the Italian effort to put the "noble neck of Asia under the yoke of Europe" and satirized the toadying hosts who "prostrate themselves before Marinetti."[68] The Russians claimed that their futurist experiments predated the manifesto of 1909, and they insisted on serious points of difference, especially the national character of their campaigns.

MANIFESTO MODERNISM

The ideology of Modernism, especially in the last two years before the war, was an ideology of radical novelty, perpetually self-surpassing. Picasso transformed representation, revolutionizing the space of pictorial illusion; but from the standpoint of the abstractionists, the goal was to transcend representation altogether. The symbolists broke with the "materialism" of realist art, but the futurists saw symbolist poetry as ethereal vaporizing. The 1890s, once the decade of novelty, became in hindsight the decade of exhaustion. Acts of repudiation were grandly performed; recent novelty was reinterpreted as obsolescence. Each school and sect of the avant-garde justified itself as the one true novelty because the New was the anchoring principle for all of them. From our own standpoint a century later, the passion over small differences can seem comic. The sheer multiplication of groups—the parade of isms in every capital—is easy to deride. The old passion can also seem cynical because the cannier leaders of the avant-garde—Marinetti, Pound, Apollinaire—so clearly understood the tactics of publicity. They saw that the culture of modern journalism fed upon sensation, and also upon the circulation of named and "branded" values. Still, the spread of isms also had an artistically productive character. The name, the manifesto, the compendium of principles, provoked debates among the artists and often clarified their purposes both to audiences and to themselves.

From the time of Marinetti's futurist manifesto of 1909, the avant-garde pervasively (and contagiously) became a manifesto Modernism, a series of collective movements sealed under the weak constitution of a founding document. The phrase "weak constitution" is meant to suggest the peculiar force of the founding documents. A manifesto offered itself as both an index of collective identity and as a warning and instruction to the audience, as a digest of aesthetic values and a handbook of techniques.[69] Manifestos typically released a thunderous and assaultive rhetoric and were sanctioned by the signatures (or printed names) of a small group of individuals; but their strong tonality notwithstanding, they remained always weak enough—necessarily weak enough—to allow for dissent and apostasy. As a result, the history of the early-twentieth-century avant-garde is strewn with factions breeding smaller factions, with repudiations and excommunications and active realignments of group identity.

Manifesto Modernism, which flourished between 1909 and 1916, required new codes of reading for its first audiences. The playfulness of the typography and the aggressiveness of the rhetoric were inseparable from the radicalism of the proposals. What did it mean for Lewis and his friends to "Blast" humor and sport? What did it mean for Marinetti to call for the destruction of museums? Asking whether they were serious is to confront the complex tonality of the manifesto form itself. The teasing and the taunting, the comic affronts, are modes of play that cannot be disentangled from the earnestness of avant-garde ambition.

As opposed to a preface, a text that typically justifies, explains, and defends the challenge of the substantial work it introduces, the freestanding manifesto has a defiant relation toward its temporality. In one aspect, it is firmly oriented toward the future, a not-yet, a still-to-come. But even as it projects a coming epoch of imaginative liberation, the manifesto repeatedly turns back to the repudiated past. Lewis borrowed his "Blast and Bless" from Apollinaire, offering what would become a standard dyadism, a rigorous discontinuity between a tainted (Blasted) history and an emancipated (Blessed) future. An essential element of the labor of novelty was this attempt to secure a contrast between past and future. The third dimension of time also played a role, less visible but ultimately perhaps more significant: the manifesto continually enacted conflict in the present tense, especially conflict with the manifestos of rival movements. We are still accustomed to seeing the avant-garde in historically progressive terms, as a break in the temporality of culture, a resistance to a constraining past. But the history of the avant-garde is horizontal at least as much as it is vertical—at once concerned to make a break in cultural (vertical) time and engaged in (horizontal) struggle within the present, with rival and resistant parties.

Differentialism is constitutive of the avant-garde under Modernism. Born as an episode in faction, such sectarianism is neither incidental nor contingent. What manifesto discourse provoked was an intensifying self-consciousness, cast in the harsh light of publicly competing principles, tactics, and tones. Circulating manifestos produced a theoretical aware-ness of otherwise tacit assumptions; they incited a rich diversity of often-contradictory commitments; in so doing they produced an array of possi-bilities for Modernism. Was Modernism still to be based on representation? Was it the leading edge of modernization—especially the modernization of new technologies of machinery and speed? Was it committed to broad social change or to narrowly focused ambitions of art? These questions were loudly enunciated not only to an audience for the new art but to the artists themselves, artists who were encouraged, sometimes obliged, to think in new terms, conceptual and theoretical as well as practical and technical. The mania to establish differences—between, say, static and dynamic im-ages in painting or between "transrational" and representational poetry—meant that the new art kept extending the reach of experiment, pursuing unprecedented styles, and creating an astonishing diversity of artifacts in these few turbulent years. These considerations suggest that the opposi-tion between Modernism and the avant-garde, much emphasized since the appearance of Peter Bürger's work, needs to be rethought. The idea of an aesthetic Modernism, committed to the autonomy of art, and an aroused cultural activism, of which Dadaism is the cherished example, obscures the ongoing intersection of act and artifact, form and cultural force.[70]

TOWARD A TAXONOMY OF THE AVANT-GARDE

To conclude this chapter let me propose a flexible taxonomy to distinguish among the groups that proliferated in the years and months before the First World War. Cubism was, first of all, a founding experimental movement within twentieth-century visual art, but one whose practice preceded the explosion of theory that ultimately surrounded it. Moreover, the work of Picasso and Braque began without the formality of the weak constitution, of the manifesto as founding text. Cubism stands, then, as an example for the avant-garde of a focused trajectory of experiment outside the terms of an originating theory. During its epoch of transformation between 1906 and 1913, cubist painting can be seen as a research program that embed-ded its concepts within a visual field continually remade and readjusted. These years saw a studied testing of formal problems, a concentration on the artifact, and a self-conscious effort to move along an arc of develop-

ment. There was repetition even as there was change: technical possibilities were broached, refined, refigured. In this aspect Cubism represents an
exemplary modality: the avant-garde movement as a rigorous practice of
art making in which the field of work is carefully delimited—the canvas,
and later the objects that stand out of the canvas—and in which the challenge is extreme (a new style of representation, a new way of seeing) and
determinate (in specific artifacts, the paintings, located in specific settings,
like studios and galleries) while remaining independent of the sanction of
manifesto.

Futurism, by contrast, is the abiding example of a manifesto Modernism that not only depends on the circulating text but makes the text, the
manifesto, a leading form of imaginative production. The manifestos
anticipated and solicited works of art that would be conducted beneath
its slogans, and as works began to appear under its rubric and banner,
Marinetti continually produced new manifestos with new demands in
new typography. Futurism gives particular force to the avant-garde as a
movement—partly because of its swift circuit across national boundaries
and partly because its theorists and practitioners aggressively sought to
draw new adherents to its campaigns. It performed as a "movement" by
refusing either a narrowly determinate aesthetic or a delimited field of
action. It included works of painting, sculpture, drama, music, and poetry
that had only loose and evocative relations with one another.

As Marinetti traveled across Europe, and as artists working in a variety
of media committed themselves to the cause and the spectacle, Futurism
became the inclusive, even encompassing movement, whose very name laid
claim to the banner of the New. Far from taking the focused trajectory of
Cubism, with its research program within a specified field, Futurism assimilated styles and artifacts that had been devised within separate national
milieus and in diverse media. The many texts and objects displayed as futurist and harking back to futurist manifestos remain impossible to reconcile, as are the fiercely competing groups in contention for the futurist
name. But what can be seen as a conceptual or aesthetic weakness was
plainly a strength within the politics of culture. Perpetually extending and
absorbing, Marinetti and his allies captured the initiative toward the New
in its broadest aspect, and forced other groups to respond to the futurist
campaign.

Cubism and Futurism make a dyad, but we need to dislodge this binary
twice over, first because Expressionism changes the terms of understanding. For a long while, what became Expressionism did not know itself as a

collective initiative or a shared style. In the decade before the war, a range of artists, musicians, and writers—Ernst Ludwig Kirchner, Wassily Kandinsky, Arnold Schoenberg, August Stramm—often working in ignorance of one another, produced works (and manifestos) that were only later, and slowly, brought within the reach of the term "Expressionism" (fig. 7). Unlike early Cubism, these works were frequently accompanied by self-conscious theory, but neither the works nor the justifications offered themselves as part of a unified program. When the movement-concept of "Expressionism" began to circulate just before the war, earlier works were retrospectively gathered within its boundaries. Over the next several years the varied artifacts were collected within the space of anthologies and galleries, and within the frame of a theory.

Even the best historians of Expressionism continue to struggle over agreed-upon criteria for a movement in which works preceded manifesto and artists preceded the named identity by which they would be known. The episode was still more complex, because by the end of the war, when "Expressionism" became a secure unit of discourse, and was established within the matrix of the avant-garde and given the integrity of a manifesto, it lived on vividly—for instance, in films of the 1920s (those of Robert Wiene and Fritz Lang). A name and a series of features—stylized representation in nonnatural spaces, primitive or archaic iconography, extravagant physical gestures—gave the fragile coherence to artists and their artifacts that is often all that a "movement" requires. In these respects, Expressionism is like Modernism itself: it is a cultural episode of great diversity that received its name only retrospectively and poses vexing problems for literary historians who look to find signs of common styles, shared principles, parallel lives.

Dada gives a last challenge to the dyad of Cubism and Futurism. Peter Bürger was surely right to emphasize that Dada has no style, that it neither aimed toward nor enforced a common aesthetic, and that it allowed, even aggravated, differences among its partisans.[71] "DADA MEANS NOTHING," Tristan Tzara liked to say, and even though others thought that Dada meant *something,* the group itself roundly denied the coherence of a movement.[72] The comic insurrections at the Cabaret Voltaire—the costumes, the improvisation, the double chanting of nonsense poems and nonsense songs, the assault on the audience—were directed both against the forces of modernization that brought about the war and against the affirmative modernisms (especially the works of those artists who were beginning to be called expressionists) and the high missions that animated them.

The manifestos of Dada are as anarchic and theatrical as any others. Significantly, they mark a full self-consciousness of manifesto activity that is detached from the serious labor of concept, proposition, argument, and theory (fig. 8). With Dada the manifesto becomes another space for radical play—play that promotes a disdain for program as well as an indifference to style, that encourages improvisation but permits rivalry, that stimulates antic gestures of any kind or magnitude but only poorly attends to its own survival.

1. Gustav Klimt, Poster for the first Secessionist exhibition, 1898. 25 x 18 7/16 in. Wien Museum Karlsplatz, Vienna, Austria.

2. Georges Braque, *Man with a Guitar,* 1911-1912. Oil on canvas, 45 3/4 x 31 7/8 in. The Museum of Modern Art, New York, NY. Acquired through the Lillie P. Bliss Bequest. © 2010 Artists Rights Society (ARS), New York / ADAGP, Paris.

3. *right, top* Pablo Picasso, *Les Demoiselles d'Avignon,* 1907. Oil on canvas, 96 x 92 in. The Museum of Modern Art, New York, NY. Acquired through the Lillie P. Bliss Bequest. © 2010 Estate of Pablo Picasso / Artists Rights Society (ARS), New York.

4. *right, bottom* Umberto Boccioni, *Dynamism of a Soccer Player,* 1913. Oil on canvas, 76 1/8 x 79 1/8 in. The Museum of Modern Art, New York, NY. The Sidney and Harriet Janis Collection.

5. Gino Severini, *Visual Synthesis of the Idea: "War"* (*Synthèse plastique de l'idée: "Guerre"*), 1914. Oil on canvas, 36 1/2 x 28 3/4 in. The Museum of Modern Art, New York, NY. Bequest of Sylvia Slifka. © 2010 Artists Rights Society (ARS), New York / ADAGP, Paris.

6. Kazimir Malevich, *Untitled*, ca. 1916. Oil on canvas, 20 7/8 x 20 7/8 in. The Solomon R. Guggenheim Foundation. Peggy Guggenheim Venice, Acquisition confirmed in 2009 by agreement with the Heirs of Kazimir Malevich. 76.2553.42.

7. Ernst Ludwig Kirchner, *Potsdamer Platz, Berlin,* 1914. Pastel with black chalk on dark cream laid paper, laid down to a thin wood pulp board (mounted overall); sheet: 26 1/4 x 19 3/4 in.; mount: 29 11/16 x 23 3/8 in.; frame: 32 15/16 x 26 15/16 x 1 1/4 in.; sight: 25 5/16 x 18 3/4 in. Harvard Art Museum, Busch-Reisinger Museum, Association Fund, BR50.616.

8. Marcel Duchamp, *Bicycle Wheel,* 1951 (third version, after lost original of 1913). Metal wheel mounted on painted wood stool. 51 x 25 x 16 1/2 in. The Museum of Modern Art, New York, NY. The Sidney and Harriet Janis Collection. © 2010 Artists Rights Society (ARS), New York / ADAGP, Paris / Succession Marcel Duchamp.

9. Pablo Picasso, *Gertrude Stein,* 1906. Oil on canvas, 39 3/8 x 32 in. The Metropolitan Museum of Art, New York, NY. Bequest of Gertrude Stein, 1946 (47.106). © 2010 Estate of Pablo Picasso / Artists Rights Society (ARS), New York.

2

narrating modernity:
the novel after flaubert

In 1884, Henry James published "The Art of Fiction" in *Longman's Magazine,* an essay marking a decisive stage in the self-understanding of modern narrative. Three years earlier, with *The Portrait of a Lady,* James had widened his ambition; the later essay reflects a maturing of literary historical consciousness. The English novel, he writes, until recently "had no air of having a theory, a conviction, a consciousness of itself behind it—of being the expression of an artistic faith, the result of choice and comparison."[1] A self-aware art, holds James, came late to England from across the Channel, and this notion of English belatedness became a recurring conviction. In the next generation, Ford Madox Ford elaborated the claim, proposing that the art of the novel had begun in England with Samuel Richardson, then crossed over to the Continent. Ford suggests that it matured in the hands of Gustave Flaubert, Guy de Maupassant, and Ivan Turgenev and has just returned to England, "having been born to consciousness with the year 1892 or thereabouts."[2] Ford gives one date; James's essay marks another. But it is clear that at some point in the 1880s a concerted effort arose to articulate a self-conscious theory of the novel. At the same time, the symbolists were recognizing themselves, and becoming recognized, as a distinct cultural formation: an aggregation of individuals, poetic strategies, and critical tenets. The coincidence of these two events—a movement of radical poetics and a less radical polemic about the future of the novel—marks the advent of a self-conscious literary culture. From this point forward, the activity of making new art would be linked to theory—that is, to reflection on its origins, its internal complexity, its social effects. Earlier movements were also connected to acts of theory, but it is fair to say that for Modernism

the workings of creation and criticism often grew so close as to be inseparable. In this chapter, the subject of transformative and self-conscious
prose fiction will be placed alongside a range of writings—psychoanalytic,
anthropological, sociological—that participate in the changing narratives
of modernity. The perplexities of life-in-time pervaded the period.

Gustave Flaubert broaches the problem with brisk effect; for him the
tasks of narrative inevitably provoked theoretical reflection. The most interesting remarks, although they appear in private letters, show a keen
consciousness of the stakes of realism—the stakes, but also the risks and
impasses. In the fall of 1868, during the composition of *L'Éducation senti-
mentale* (The Sentimental Education), Flaubert wrote to Jules Duplan asking for help. He had suddenly realized that there was no train between Paris
and Fontainebleau in 1848, which meant that a detail in his manuscript was
false and that he must now "scrap two passages and begin afresh": "You
can't imagine what a nuisance this is for me. So—I need to know: 1. how,
in June 1848, one went from Paris to Fontainebleau; 2. perhaps *part* of the
line was already in use? 3. what coaches did one take? 4. and what was their
terminus in Paris?" Then he puts one more question to Duplan, "Can you
recall what the ambulances looked like?"[3] As with James Joyce, two generations later, Flaubert feels the lure of minute and ephemeral details, which
must be respected simply because the world contains them. Beyond the
reach of any reader's interest, he preserves the sanctity of precision, even
excessive precision, and takes pleasure in the reproduction of reality. His
letters continually make clear that he sees "realism" as the outcome of arduous labor and obsessive research.

Flaubert describes his new novel to George Sand around the same time,
remarking, "The patriots won't forgive me this book, nor the reactionaries
either." Her response is worried and cautious—"You disturb me when you
say that in your book you'll blame the patriots for all that went wrong. Is
that really true? . . . I trust you to be generous"—to which Flaubert replies
in turn: "I expressed myself badly if I told you that my book will 'blame
the patriots for all that went wrong.' I don't recognize my right to blame
anyone. I don't even believe that the novelist should express his opinion on
matters of this world. He can communicate it, but I don't like him to state
it. (Such is part of my poetics.) Thus I confine myself to describing things
as they appear to me, to expressing what seems to me to be true. Hang the
consequences. I want to have neither hate, nor pity, nor anger. As for sympathy, that's different" (118). Here is a memorable statement of Flaubertian
detachment, but here, too, are signs of its instability. The author should

suppress judgment, should record the truth of events without the drapery of emotion or opinion. This credo has a long afterhistory. It inspired Chekhov; it invigorated Hemingway; Joyce's Stephen Dedalus made it central to his aesthetic philosophy in *A Portrait of the Artist as a Young Man*. As the formula "A writer should show but not tell," it has become a classroom adage. Yet here, as on many other occasions in Flaubert, the canons of objectivity are ambiguous.

The unsteady relation between truth and judgment is the crux. On the one hand, Flaubert has just written that the patriots (like the reactionaries) will never forgive him; on the other hand, he vows to express only truth, not opinion. He reserves the right to "communicate" his views without "expressing" them. The pressure of these different imperatives—truth, not opinion; communication, not expression—yields a volatile mix, shown in another remark to George Sand: "What is the best form in which to express one's opinion, occasionally, about affairs of this world without risking being taken later for a fool? It's a difficult problem. It seems to me that the best way is simply to depict the things that exasperate you. Dissection is revenge" (113). Any prospect of realism as a neutral or "objective" rendering of the world is undone in these succinct phrases. Realism is a motivated assault, a finely managed critique. The image of dissection puts it well. The novelistic subject resembles a cadaver on the table; it is for the writer to cut and carve in the spirit of revenge. And yet Flaubert remains committed to the abstention of the author. Even when the time comes to dissect one's enemy (in this context, the politician Thiers), there must be no overt moralizing. The act of critique stands at a remove. It lies in the suggestion of exposure, which speaks for itself and keeps the author free from stain. A *detachment* that is at once a *judgment*—this is Flaubert's momentous legacy. But we still need to ask about the basis of such judgment. Where does Flaubert stand at the dissecting table, and where is the reader located? How does clinical exposure produce the withering critique? What is this modernity that he eagerly carves to bits?

SENTIMENTAL EDUCATIONS: ART BETWEEN POLITICS AND LOVE

Modernist art, as "one of the practices" and "one of the vocations," had politics as the chief of its rivals. During the nineteenth century, both appeared as post-traditional activities; increasingly through the course of the century, they presented themselves in revolutionary aspects. *Madame Bovary* has a distinguished place in the history of Modernism, but *The Sentimental Education* is the work of the mature Flaubert, written when he was fully engaged in the agon of politics and aesthetics. This complex, not always pleasing novel offers the failed revolution of 1848 as the truth of modern history and puts forth art as the alternative to politics and other forms of social hope.

The sentimental education of Frédéric Moreau ends so badly that it is easy to forget how brightly it began. Frédéric advances into the 1840s with hopes for love, art, wealth, education, and social change. The movement toward social revolution seems to coincide with private desire: to live fully is to swim in the currents of modernity moving through Paris and to mix personal interest with public life. The friendship of Frédéric and Charles Deslauriers is the partnership of writer and social actor, both of whom expect harmony between their two pursuits. In 1844, Frédéric still sees the future as "nothing but an unending procession of years brimming with love."[4] When the revolutionary months of 1848 begin, his hope at first persists.

Flaubert's answer to George Sand's plea for generosity ("Have pity! There were so many splendid souls even so") was not to withdraw his critique but to extend it. "I told you," he wrote in September 1868, "that I don't flatter the Democrats in my book. But I assure you the Conservatives aren't spared either." His letter lays out a formal/political figure crucial to his novel, the trope of *false antithesis*. The first days of revolution seem an ecstatic wedding of opposites: "Everything is going well! The people have triumphed! The middle classes and the workers are embracing each other" (285). But for Flaubert the joyful advent of change is a trap set by history. From this point forward, the paired opposites will recur, now in the aspect of diabolical marriage. After the counterrevolutionary revenge enacted by the National Guard, we read that "equality (as if to rebuke its defenders and taunt its enemies) emerged triumphant—an equality of brutish beasts, a common level of bloodstained savagery. For the fanaticism of the rich was as great as the frenzy of the poor, the aristocracy was a prey to the same madness as the rabble, and the cotton nightcap proved as hideous as the revolutionary bonnet" (330). The device of false antithesis first converts plurality into duality—sometimes into workers and bourgeoisie, sometimes into rich and poor, sometimes into aristocracy and rabble or conservatives and socialists—and then reveals both sides to be equally corrupt and destructive. Deslauriers "preached brotherhood to the conservatives and respect for law to the socialists, so the former had tried to shoot him and the latter had brought a rope to hang him with" (360). The once-hopeful

Dussardier comes to a despairing insight: "The workers are no better than the bourgeois!" (391). Social upheaval brings no shift in power, not even a new phase of history. On the contrary, revolution is a false infinity that exposes an empty balance of opposites.

Another trope, however, gaining in prominence as the novel goes on, is as important as false antithesis. This is the figure of *succession,* which typically appears in the form of a list. Near the novel's end, the reader is told that Deslauriers "had been, successively, a director of colonization in Algeria, secretary to a pasha, editor of a paper, and an advertising agent, and had ended up working in the legal department of an industrial organization." A few sentences later, we learn that Pellerin "after dabbling in Fourierism, homeopathy, spiritualism, gothic art, and humanitarian painting had become a photographer" (417). These are just two examples of a recurrent pattern, the movement of characters through sequences of failed possibility— occupations here, but elsewhere love affairs and political adventures. Of the opportunistic and wealthy Dambreuse, Flaubert writes that "he had acclaimed Napoléon, the Cossacks, Louis XVIII, 1830, the workers, every regime in turn, so in love with Power that he would have paid to sell himself" (370). The novel represents history as serial possibility, the potentially infinite movement from one contingency to the next. The pursuit of personal happiness, like that of social revolution, is hollow, because love and power have no destination, no more than history does. Succession, then, stands with false antithesis as an essential figure in *The Sentimental Education*—as if to say that the only thing worse than a paralysis of contraries is the endless series.

In writing "About Flaubert's Style," Marcel Proust celebrates the use of the imperfect tense in *The Sentimental Education*. According to Proust, Flaubert's imperfect is no mere grammatical form; it is "a newcomer to literature," which "entirely changes the look of people and of things." It envelops them in a "continuous and homogenous vision"; in which time is not composed of punctual moments, discrete events, but of an unending flow, overwhelming any fixed points. The "use of the imperfect serves to narrate not only people's words, but their whole lives," writes Proust, and elsewhere he describes Flaubert's greatest achievement as the "masterly manner in which he managed to produce the effect of time *passing*," so that "time ceases to be a matter of mere successive quarters of an hour and appears to us in the guise of years and decades." The effect, although Proust would not put it like this, is to defeat history through time. The imperfect tense and its effect of enduring time erase the distinctions of history; they immerse separate events (political, romantic, vocational) in an unending temporal flow.[5]

In fact, *The Sentimental Education* contains many discrete events and separate incidents. F. W. Dupee describes it as a novel built "out of an accumulation of anecdotes," a view that seems to be the reverse of Proust's. Dupee emphasizes the extended tableaux: the outbreak of revolution in Paris and the failed encounter between Frédéric and Madame Arnoux, each recorded in abundant detail. But we can put these two ideas together by seeing how the novel allows singular events to luxuriate and ramify, only to dissolve them beneath onrushing time—a point Dupee acknowledges when he writes that "each episode extracts from the situation a maximum of irony" and is then "caught up in the furious current of the enveloping narrative."[6] It is worth noticing how heavily the novel relies on the locutions "one day" and "one afternoon" when introducing major anecdotes. As the narrative moves forward, the imperfect produces an ongoing duration, the ceaseless time of decades and generations, and then it abruptly pauses "one evening" to allow an incident to expand. But when the incident concludes, the imperfect inevitably returns, again releasing the time of duration and continuity, of "usually" and "routinely." Proust is surely right to appreciate the force of passing time in *The Sentimental Education,* but its force is more striking when we recognize that its flow is constantly interrupted. The events of personal and public history are dense and resistant, and the work of time is to show both the weight of particular incidents and their ultimate dissolution within "imperfect" time.

We should see an alignment, a rhyme, between these views of narrative temporality—the stasis of incident, the flow of duration—and the figures of antithesis and succession. Flaubert invents a matching pair of catastrophes. In one perspective, revolutionary history arrives at a moment of climax, time slows down, and the events unfold their dense, secret meaning, which is precisely the secret of a false antithesis (workers as bad as the bourgeoisie). What had seemed an alternative is a mirror image. Then, in the other aspect of the critique, time begins to flow again, but with the destructive force of the imperfect; it moves through a succession of possibilities that are revealed as nothing but temporary investments, one ardor succumbing to the next.

Unlike more sentimental "sentimental educations," the novel does not offer an escape from history to private life. *The Sentimental Education* presents subjectivity as hemmed in by historical pressures; it is neither refuge nor sanctuary. Here is Frédéric in the midst of revolution: "The crowd swayed to and fro in constant eddies. Frédéric did not move; he was trapped between two dense masses and, in any case, fascinated and enjoying himself immensely. The wounded falling to the ground and the dead lying stretched out did not look like real dead and wounded. He felt as if he were watching a play" (281). Frédéric's euphoria is the private counterpart to the ecstasy of revolution. But for Flaubert, a chasm opens between subjectivity and history. Frédéric's fate is to pass through the convulsion of politics, but always at a remove. At the end of the novel, we find that he "was so preoccupied with his own affairs that those of the nation meant nothing to him" (409). Yet, ironically, the arc of personal life in *The Sentimental Education* follows the trajectory of political history: from ecstasy to disillusionment, and from earnestness to irony. No matter how detached Frédéric feels from social and political life, he is condemned to repeat its logic.

Like the history that surrounds him, Frédéric Moreau is caught up in the futility of endless succession. He aspires to greatness but has "endless projects" (127). He holds to the thought that "one of these days he would do something decisive. He dreamed of a different life, which would be pleasanter and nobler in every way" (356), but in the novel's famous coda, he discovers that his only happy time came at the very beginning. Once he enters the milieu of modernity—that is, Paris—he finds that one "desire awoke another" (132). As a lover, Frédéric gives way to the same serial movement that governs public life. His own "revolution of '48" has been his dream-love for Madame Arnoux, continually postponed and corroded by his infatuations. When she finally approaches him, years too late, he finds himself trapped in the impossibility of desire.

In their long-deferred encounter, when Madame Arnoux removes her hat and reveals white hair, "it was like a blow full in his chest" but to "conceal his disillusionment he fell to his knees beside her" (414). Frédéric speaks to her tenderly, she accepts his adoration, and "intoxicated by his own words, [he] began to believe what he was saying." In a ghastly play of spectral desire, they approach one another: "Once again he was seized by a furious, ravening lust, stronger than any he had known before. But he felt something inexpressible, a repulsion, and something like the dread of incest" (415). He holds back, anticipating disgust, reluctant to coarsen the "ideal." Finally, he turns away and rolls a cigarette while Madame Arnoux thanks him for his chivalry. When they part, she kisses him "like a mother" (416). Mother-lover is the impossible antithesis, transferred now to private life. Just as Frédéric witnesses the convergence of workers and bourgeoisie, so he now encounters the repellent union of maternity and romance. The long-nurtured dream of another life, a refuge from failure, dissolves like the rest.

Notoriously, the novel ends when Frédéric and Deslauriers meet again: sitting together, they "summed up their lives" (418). Admitting undeniable failure, "they blamed chances, circumstances, the times they were born in" (419). Then, in a last devastating irony, the narrator records a memory of their early years: a first and unsuccessful visit to a house of prostitution. On a Sunday while the community attends vespers, the boys bring flowers to the women, but under the shock of the encounter, Frédéric flees. Deslauriers, with no money, is forced to follow.

> "That was the best time we ever had!" said Frédéric.
>
> "Yes, you may be right. That was our best time!" said Deslauriers.
>
> (420)

So the novel ends with nostalgia for the time when desire confronted its first impossibility, but also before it brought a fall. It offers a portrait of subjectivity as absence and emptiness: all that private life can imagine is the rapture of unattainable love. Romantic love remains as phantasmagoric as political revolution.

The Sentimental Education enforces a double catastrophe: the failure of history and the wreck of subjectivity. Its intricate formal designs—the false antitheses and endless successions, the contradictory events and the ongoing imperfect tense—perpetrate revenge upon modern practices and vocations. Politics and love are placed in careful counterpart: both endure the corrosive power of the form; both are exposed as futile. The novel is not only an exemplary work that loomed over the careers of subsequent novelists; it also represents a telling stage in the conflict of modern practices, the struggle among vocations. Early in the novel, when Frédéric first sees Madame Arnoux, he watches as she reads "a thin book with a gray cover. Occasionally, the corners of her mouth curled up and her face lit with pleasure. He was jealous of the writer whose work seemed to absorb her" (12). We may take this as a prideful moment, when Flaubert contemplates the power of literary fascination—and the experience of art as the alternative to failed modernity.

Set against the disarray of politics and the incoherence of romantic love is the austere practice of a modern art. It must be austere—too austere for these characters, who are incapable of resisting immediate temptation. *The Sentimental Education* suggests that art can stand against corrupt politics and sentimental love only by practicing the exacting precision of the realist method—this is what the novel shows without saying. The text is a rejoinder to its characters. Where they yield to doomed fantasies, the novel offers itself as astringent speech that refuses departure from the truth as severely as it resists looseness of style.

CROWD, MOB, MASS

The Sentimental Education remains a novel of character. Its large cast of individuals belongs to a recognizable tradition; the narrative follows the life trajectory of characters with separate histories and proper names. A sentimental education is something that happens to one person and then to another: the disillusionment of Frédéric Moreau, the helplessness of Rosanette, the hardening of Madame Dambreuse, the drift of Arnoux. Central to the project is this compound of specificity and diversity. But another figure erupts in the middle of the novel, nameless and formless. It is heard before it is seen, but once seen, it cannot be forgotten: "It was the mob. It rushed up the staircase in a dizzying flood of bare heads, helmets, red caps, bayonets, and shoulders, so impetuously that people disappeared into the swarming mass that still swept upwards, like a river forced back in its course by a spring tide, with a long roar, driven by an irresistible impulse" (282). Here is the revolutionary mass that overwhelms Paris in 1848, and the appearance of this great collective subject—crowd, mass, mob—is one of the chief events in the history of modernity. The year 1789 witnessed its awakening to revolution, and 1848 saw its impatience to complete the work. By the middle of the nineteenth century, the crowd was recognized as a transforming agent that explodes the categories of social life. Its power to devastate boundaries (physical and legal) and to discover its own desires becomes an abiding spectacle.

At the same time, the representation of the crowd is one of the tasks of nineteenth-century narrative. The novel is a form that came into being as a vessel for individuals, a history of named characters. But it is also a form committed to the arena of social life. This double investment created an enduring novelistic paradigm: the entry of characters onto the social stage, the transaction between sociality and individuality, and then the reassembly of individuals within the confines of private space. From Frédéric young to Frédéric old, *The Sentimental Education* follows this long-standing trajectory. Yet the force of the novel is precisely to show how attenuated the traditional archetype has become. Individuals remain the focal points of the narrative, but they lose many prerogatives of agency. Desire is thwarted, and intention is confounded. For characters to undertake projects is simply to begin an arc of disillusionment. The crowd, on the other hand, appears as a creature whose objects of desire are always close, therefore always inciting dreams of fulfillment. After the throne is hurled through a palace window,

> there was a frenzied outburst of joy, as if a future of boundless happiness had appeared in place of the throne; and the mob, less from a desire for vengeance than from a wish to assert the fact that they were in possession, broke and tore mirrors, and curtains, chandeliers, sconces, tables, chairs, stools, all the furniture, even sketchbooks and embroidery baskets. Since they had gained the victory, they had a right to amuse themselves, hadn't they? The rabble decked themselves mockingly in laces and cashmeres. Gold fringes were tied around smock sleeves, ostrich-feather hats adorned the heads of blacksmiths, sashes of the Legion of Honor became belts for prostitutes. Everyone followed his own whim; some danced, others drank. (283)

How to devise conventions to represent the mass became a leading question for a modernizing literature. Here Flaubert invents a rhetoric that others will share. First, there is a constellation of names for a collective subject—mob, crowd, mass, rabble, throng—frequently cast as a physical/biological unity, a force moving like fluid, flame, or wind. Then, in a second movement, the collective is articulated into parts, sometimes through categories of work (blacksmiths, prostitutes) but often through the abstract labor of pronouns: everyone, some, others.

Georg Lukács's influential essay "Narrate or Describe" begins with a well-known contrast between two scenes of horse racing, the first from Émile Zola's *Nana* and the second from Leo Tolstoy's *Anna Karenina*. Zola, writes Lukács, lays out a freestanding panorama of the social scene: "Every possible detail at a race is described precisely, colourfully and with sensuous vitality. Zola provides a small monograph on the modern turf; every phase from the saddling of the horses to the finish is investigated meticulously. The Parisian public is depicted in all the brilliance of a Second-Empire fashion show."[7] In *Anna Karenina,* on the other hand, the race marks a crisis in the lives of two lovers, Anna and Vronsky; his fall sets in motion a fateful sequence of events: "The race is thus no mere tableau but rather a series of intensely dramatic scenes which provide a turning point in the plot." For Lukács the difference is fundamental; it epitomizes the contrast marked in the essay's title. "In Zola the race is *described* from the standpoint of an observer; in Tolstoy it is *narrated* from the standpoint of a participant" (111). As Lukács builds his picture of nineteenth-century fiction, he offers Sir Walter Scott, Honoré de Balzac, and Tolstoy as historically progressive novelists, engaged with the evolution of social life. Flaubert and Zola, on the other hand, who stand outside events and regard them from a distance, represent a disenchanted post-1848 bourgeois sensibility. They inhabit a settled bourgeois society, and in their bid to sustain integrity, they become "specialists" in the art of writing (118), compensating for the loss of social engagement with the virtuosity of craft.

This account captures a genuine change in nineteenth-century fiction. In particular, it clarifies the movement toward a more self-conscious objectivity in the second half of the nineteenth century. But other questions are worth asking about the turn. For Lukács the notable event is the loss of experience and participation; the detachment of both Flaubert and Zola deprives individual characters of their centrality and their agency. But instead of seeing this only as the novel's loss of history, we should also take it as a change in the historical object. Both Flaubert and Zola, like others who came to wear the name "naturalist," took the creation of mass society as a leading concern. Henry James describes Zola's attempt "to deal with things almost always in gregarious form, to be a picture of *numbers*, of classes, crowds, confusions, movements, industries."[8] The individual life, he continues, "is, if not wholly absent, reflected in coarse and common, in generalised terms" so that "the most characteristic episodes affect us like the sounding chorus or procession, as with a hubbub of voices and a multitudinous tread of feet" (431). It is easy to see what James means. Zola seeks to represent history as a larger-than-individual process; he understands modernization as the life of populations. No one character can signify the movement of mass society. The burden, then, is to narrate the lives of collectivities because they are the motor forces of history.

To put it this way is to change the terms of Lukács's critique. Zola indeed challenges the privilege of the individual participant in history, the agent immersed in events, Vronsky in the middle of the race. Instead, he sees history as the effect of broad, often-invisible forces (heredity, economy), manifested in the movements of the mass. For Lukács the strength of realist fiction—narratives that had not succumbed to the post-1848 pessimism—lay in the coherence and purpose of deliberate actors. But for Zola, the telling incidents were the swarming of multitudes in closed courts, the rush of carriages through the streets, the array of strikers outside a factory. These were the salient events of modernity, which overwhelmed the minor bustle of individuals. Walter Benjamin has memorably written that "of all the experiences which made his life what it was, Baudelaire singled out his having been jostled by the crowd as the decisive, unique experience."⁹ For others besides Charles Baudelaire an encounter with the crowd became a condition of modernity—sometimes traumatic, sometimes utopian, often mixed and indeterminate.

In the last paragraphs of *Nana,* when the Second Empire is tottering and the catastrophic war with Prussia is beginning, the urban throng moves through the city. "Torches were still being carried past, throwing out sparks; in the distance, the groups of people were rippling in the gloom like long flocks of sheep being led by night to the slaughter, and this confused whirling mass of people streaming by created a feeling of terror and immense pity for the massacres to come. They were bewildered, their voices cracking in the frenzy of their intoxication as they hurtled towards their unknown fate beyond the dark wall of the horizon."¹⁰ The crowd enjoys the dubious privilege of uttering the novel's final words: "From the boulevard below there came a great desperate gasp, making the curtains billow: On to Berlin! On to Berlin! On to Berlin!" (425).

For the sociologist Gustave Le Bon, collective humanity was a new organism, demanding a new science.¹¹ Opaque, limitless, and threatening, it will now determine the course of history. Following its own unconscious logic, the crowd possesses the inferior mental capacity of women, children, and primitive men; it obeys fantasy and desire, not reason, and it yearns for domination by a strong leader. In this guise, the crowd is the bearer of mass hysteria, the antithesis of the rational liberal subject. Partly, the fear is that the multitude will swamp individuality, bringing the terror of oceanic immersion and the loss of autonomy. A myth of the French Revolution, active for instance in Charles Dickens's *A Tale of Two Cities,* renders the mass as a universal solvent that melts boundaries around the self and releases an inhuman force. In the aftermath of 1848 the crowd appeared to be always threatening to overwhelm public spaces, as in Matthew Arnold's evocation in *Culture and Anarchy* of a crowd eager to make "Hyde Park a bear-garden or the streets impassable." Arnold spoke of the masses as asserting "an Englishman's right to do what he likes; his right to march where he likes, meet where he likes, enter where he likes, hoot as he likes, threaten as he likes, smash as he likes." Once these private rights are made collective, they produce "anarchy," the enemy of culture.¹²

But in another body of thought and practice—in Marxist theory and working-class struggle—the massing of human beings is not the sign of anarchy but of a formidable coherence. In *The Communist Manifesto,* Karl

Marx and Friedrich Engels describe how the working class begins as "an incoherent mass" but how through the logic of capitalism, it "not only increases in number; it becomes concentrated in greater masses, its strength grows, and it feels that strength more."[13] The result is that the proletariat becomes the first organized and the first universal collective in history: "All previous movements were movements of minorities, or in the interest of minorities. The proletarian movement is the self-conscious, independent movement of the immense majority, in the interest of the immense majority" (21). As the working class became larger and more insistent, the fearful vision of the chaotic crowd, jostling and leering, met the contrasting image of a disciplined and rational collectivity, intent on wresting history from the hands of the bourgeoisie. This double valence, falling along well-marked political lines, plays a significant role in modernist representation.

The problem of crowd versus collectivity takes on yet another aspect when the issue is no longer the mass of physical bodies with their demands and desires but rather mass opinion and mass media. The consolidation of a newspaper society in the nineteenth century, culminating in wide circulation dailies, meant that "public opinion" became a dominant force and, further, a subject of representation. The realist novel was often seen as an alternative to the power of the commonplace, with Flaubert again marking a threshold. In his *Le Dictionnaire des idées reçu* (Dictionary of Received Ideas) he identifies the public mind as a nest of clichés, including these:

> HOME Always a castle. However, the police can enter whenever they please. Home, sweet home. No place like it.

> ORIGINAL Make fun of everything that is original, hate it, jeer at it, and annihilate it if you can.[14]

Flaubert sees the life-draining tyranny of received ideas as a bourgeois phenomenon, the effect of a complacent middle class and a pandering journalism. As such, it makes the bourgeois distinct from both the organized working-class and the anarchic urban crowd. A developing Modernism confronted these different aggregates, which created an unsteadiness in the aims of any oppositional culture. Modernist artists and thinkers consistently took the "bourgeoisie" and its shared clichés as a powerful, though dull, enemy. Far less consistent, as we have seen, was the new art's relation to the working class, regarded sometimes as an ally and sometimes as another mass obstruction to art. Yet, even though these collectivities divided on class lines—the crowd of workers, the orthodoxy of the middle class—

they converged at decisive moments. Especially in the mobilizations of wartime, the cliché and the crowd met. To think of Modernism as an oppositional culture is to acknowledge this complex basis for resistance and attraction.

NANA, STATISTICS, AND SINGULARITY

If we take mass society as at once resistance and stimulus to Modernism and if we take an encounter with the collective subject—groups, classes, crowds, clichés—as a provocation to modernist narrative, we need now to turn the provocation on its head. Modernism experienced an enthrallment with, and revulsion from, mass society and, at the same time, a fascination with the special case, the eccentric, and the exception. Just as narrative had to devise conventions to represent the crowd, so, too, it had to invent forms for individual eccentricity and extreme pathology.

Zola gives a point of entry to the problem. In *Nana,* the eponymous heroine is called into being by the lust of society. Before we see her, we meet the strength of shared desire, largely, but not exclusively, male, privileged and louche alike. By rumor, Nana is the invention of the theater manager Bordenave, but the novel shows how the entire social world constructs the object of its desires: "Nobody knew Nana. Where on earth had she sprung from? People were telling each other stories. Jokes were being exchanged in whispers. The name sounded endearing, it had a nice familiar ring, everybody liked pronouncing it; merely saying it made the crowd cheerful and sympathetically inclined. Paris society was being gripped by a typically feverish curiosity, a sudden stupid craze. People couldn't wait to see Nana" (6). She was an emanation of urban modernity. Without the hunger and fascination of the public, she would be lost in the lumpen mob, but once summoned into focus, she becomes both an object of need and the register of social failure. *Nana*'s strongest political modality lies in a transparent allegory. The young girl from nowhere, the body susceptible to sex and therefore sexualized, the actress, prostitute, and kept woman, performs the decline of Second Empire France. The trajectory is visible and unavoidable: individual decay is the sign of social catastrophe.

All this is clear. But even as the novel aligns protagonist and nation, the contradictions of the allegory disclose themselves. In developing the principles of his Naturalism, Zola pondered the relations between two orders —social world and physical body—casting the distinction as that between environment and heredity, insisting that these two forces were of "equal importance." Yet, when he turns to an example, Balzac's *La Cousine Bette,* the balance is undone. According to Zola, Balzac's novel shows how "an entire family is destroyed, all sorts of secondary dramas are produced, under the action of Hulot's amorous temperament. It is there, in this temperament, that the initial cause is found. One member, Hulot, becomes rotten, and immediately all around him are tainted, the social circulus is interrupted, the health of that society is compromised."[15] Nana, too, inherits the poison of her family, and like Hulot, she distributes the corruption to all within the reach of her eroticism. In both these respects, the dangerous precipitating cause erupts from an individual "temperament."

How shall we understand the relation between these orders of experience? How does the inherited poison of hypersexuality bear on the social will that summons Nana as an image of desire and destruction? To insist, as Zola does, on their equal importance—to emphasize the "reciprocal effect of society on the individual and the individual on society"—is not to solve the problem. As he frankly acknowledges, the path of science is uneven. Physiology will "someday" explain the mechanism of thoughts and passions; then "we shall know how the individual machinery of each man works." But that day is not now. Zola asserts the truth of determinism, "an absolute determinism for all human phenomena," even as he admits that its pathways are unknown.[16] The result is that a gap opens between individual and society, heredity and the environment. Each can be the initiating cause; each can modify the other; but they remain discontinuous and, at least for now, irreducible to one another. If the gap is a dilemma for the unity of science, it is more immediately a puzzle in Zola's fiction.

Two comments, collected by Philip Walker, bear on the issue, and each belongs to Zola's early anticipations of *Nana*.

> The philosophical subject is this: a whole society racing after a piece of ass. A pack behind a bitch, which is not in heat and doesn't care a bit about the hounds pursuing her. *The poem of male carnal desire,* the giant lever that moves the world. That's all there is, just ass and religion.

> The poignant drama of a woman destroyed by her appetite for luxury and easy pleasures.[17]

The first comment gives the naturalist reduction—"That's all there is"—which offers the novel as the unmasking of the motives that drive a decaying society. The second remark preserves the skepticism, but it also unsettles the perspective. As long as Zola pictures society as a desiring-machine or, to change the image, as a horde of beasts acting on their appetites ("ass") and their fears ("religion"), then he can sustain his determinism. The difficulty is his turn to individuality. Destroyed by her own taste for her pleasure and seen from the outside, Nana is only another beast. But as the second quotation suggests, the novel does not preserve the outside view.

As a theorist, Zola asserts a parallelism between heredity and the environment: both are determinisms; the body and the social body are equally law-governed. The difficulty is that they follow independent paths, and within *Nana* the gap between them reappears. The novel offers a view of social decline, with the central character standing as a blazing symptom. It also gives an account of Nana as a specific physiology, a singular individual in a line of inheritance. But the breach in the novel is still more radical. Apart from these two parallel determinisms, which can never meet but which always remain allegories of one another, there is a rupture between determinism-as-such and what we can best think of as Nana's "phenomenology."

The history of the novel, we might say, encourages the production of phenomenology—encourages, that is, the representation of lived experience, the texture of sentience, the perspective of subjectivity. In canonical ways, *Nana* gives its heroine a point of view. To adapt Thomas Nagel's phrase, there is something that it is *like* to be this woman.[18] But more is at issue than the conventions of the novel. In the eighth chapter, Nana takes up with the actor Fontan, even though it will mean sacrificing money, luxury, and protection. The affair quickly begins to languish; Fontan cadges off her, beats her, and betrays her. Nana, lost in love, submits to the abuse. Soon she has returned to the sordid past, selling herself to keep him. Toward the end of the chapter we read that she took "a bitter enjoyment in her crazy, heroic infatuation which made her, in her eyes, a very noble woman, capable of great love. Ever since she'd been going with other men in order to provide for Fontan, she loved him all the more" (242). The language of love and satisfaction, fatigue and disgust, exists outside the determinist vocabulary of blood and environment. The book presents Nana not simply as a nexus of cause and effect but also as an irreducible subjectivity, seen from the inside. She looks out on the forces that construct her and remains fascinated by what she has become: "She was always curious to find something new whenever she looked at herself" (191). True, she does not preserve her subjectivity for long. The novel returns to the detachment of mechanism and the working of political allegory: Nana soars and falls as a counterpart to social catastrophe. Yet the breach remains. In the extent of her decay, in the sheer extremity of "being Nana," she ceases to be only a symptom.

The logic of Zola's Naturalism is part of a broader logic in Modernism. The extreme is the true. The attempt to comprehend modernity produces not merely the statistics of mass society but also, repeatedly, a portrait of the special case, the singular instance. Nana can reveal the essence of a barren modernity precisely because she carries it to an extreme. But in reaching ultimacy, she becomes as much exceptional as representative. In death (her face a "shapeless, slushy grey pulp") as in life (with her "full curves and deep creases"), she is a spectacle that enthralls and repels (425, 192). For other characters, as for the novel's readers, what she *means* is intelligible, but what she *is* becomes insupportable. The pathology of the individual exceeds the mass society that spawns it.

HARDY'S *TESS:* NATURALISM AND RESPECTABILITY

In 1890 and 1891, while struggling with *Tess of the d'Urbervilles*—partly because of the refusal of cautious magazine editors to publish certain sequences of the novel and partly because of a personal decision to allow a tamer version to appear—Thomas Hardy wrote two short essays that extend the problem we are following here. The first, "Candour in English Fiction," is a sometimes bitter, sometimes sorrowful account of the constraints on the British novelist at the end of the nineteenth century. Although Hardy chooses not to mention his own case, his struggles to publish *Tess* lie everywhere behind the argument. The magazines and the circulating library "have arrogated to themselves the dispensation of fiction."[19] Because books are not sold directly to the public but are read in journals or borrowed from libraries, authors are at the mercy of these institutional gatekeepers. And because editors and librarians dread scandal, they enforce the "censorship of prudery" that inhibits serious fiction. Suppose a narrative begins in a magazine, writes Hardy, and then suppose that as the chapters unfold, artistic honesty drives the novelist toward an unmentionable subject. "The dilemma then confronts him, he must either whip and scourge those characters into doing something contrary to their natures, to produce the spurious effect of their being in harmony with social forms and ordinances, or, by leaving them alone to act as they will, he must bring down the thunders of respectability upon his head, not to say ruin his editor, his publisher, and himself" (130). The outcome is that "puerile inventions" and "false colouring" now dominate the British novel and make honest representation nearly impossible (127).

The effect in Hardy's case is that when *Tess of the d'Urbervilles* had its first serial publication, some sanitized chapters were published in the *Graphic,* while uncensored versions appeared in the *Fortnightly Review* and the *National Observer*. These "trunks and limbs," as Hardy called them, were then stitched back together to create the book that was published in late 1891, complete with an explanatory note in which Hardy anticipates the rage to come. He insists that the book was written in "all sincerity of purpose" and asks the "genteel reader" to remember a sentence from Saint Jerome: "If an offence come out of the truth, better is it that the offence come than that the truth be concealed."[20] Hardy recognized that the forces of respectability were not simply timid matrons covering the eyes of children; they were also a band of editors, writers, publishers, and politicians who resourcefully orchestrated a moral reaction that he had reason to fear.

Hardy wrote a second, less well-known essay in this period, which appeared in the *New Review* under the title "The Science of Fiction." Can fiction be a science? is Hardy's blunt question. He answers that indeed it can, as long as by "science" we mean the "comprehensive and accurate knowledge of realities," the law of "things as they really are."[21] But art is more than such accurate knowledge; it is science plus psychological insight and subtleties of form. A great error of the day, suggests Hardy, is to identify art with science and to see it as mere "copyism," as if the reproduction of reality could satisfy our needs. Here he makes a revealing turn toward Zola. Hardy reads the theory of the experimental novel as exactly a theory of "copyism" (136) and then suggests that the theory is contradicted by the practice: the novels of Naturalism inevitably show the workings of art. Yet Hardy is unsettled by Zola—and not simply because theory and practice fail to correspond. In "Candour in English Fiction" he deplored "developments of Naturalism in French novelists of the present day";[22] now in "The Science of Fiction" he regrets the confusion caused by the word "realism," which, on the one hand, suggests accuracy but, on the other, the excesses of "prurience."

At the end of his essay on candor, just before he again condemns "English prudery," he makes a concession to the partisans of respectability: "Were the objections of the scrupulous limited to a prurient treatment of the relations of the sexes, or to any view of vice calculated to undermine the essential principles of social order, all honest lovers of literature would be in accord with them" (131). It is a striking statement. It suggests that despite Hardy's resistance to the constraints of prudery and despite his defense of the offensive truth, he, too, worries about the immorality of realism. He distinguishes carefully between "copyism" and "prurience," but beneath his distinction runs the fear that the terms will meet and that the scientific ambitions of Zola's Naturalism will sooner or later lead to indecency.

The revealing assumption is that realism inevitably meets the disturbances of sexuality. Life being a "physiological fact," the one thing that any honest representation must include are the "relations between the sexes" and the "catastrophe[s]" of the "passions." But Hardy resists the loss that scientific Naturalism encourages. "The higher passions," he had written in 1888, "must ever rank above the inferior—intellectual tendencies above animal, and moral above intellectual—whatever the treatment, realistic or ideal," and he warned against any "system of inversion" that would emphasize appetites over aspirations.[23]

Hardy resisted the sentimental evasion of English prudery, but no more than he resisted the prurient brutality of French Naturalism. His reactions belong to a wider binational negotiation on the future of modernity. We have seen how, especially in England, Zola came to typify an unspeakable literature of the gutter. But there was contempt on both sides of the Channel. At a key moment in Huysmans's *À Rebours,* Des Esseintes comes to an aesthetic impasse. Unable to decide which art to admire most, he tries to soothe himself with a "course of emollient reading" in Dickens.

> But the Englishman's work produced the opposite effect from what he had expected: his chaste lovers and his puritanical heroines in their all-concealing draperies, sharing ethereal passions and just fluttering their eyelashes, blushing coyly, weeping for joy and holding hands, drove him to distraction. This exaggerated virtue made him react in the contrary direction; by virtue of the law of contrasts, he jumped from one extreme to the other, recalled scenes of full-blooded, earthy passion, and thought of common amorous practices such as the hybrid kiss, or the columbine kiss as ecclesiastical modesty calls it, where the tongue is brought into play.[24]

The satire of Dickensian sentimentality is not only a Continental indulgence. But cast in the figures that Huysmans favors, the passage shows how cross-Channel conflict became an instrument of modernist self-definition. "English" and "French," "Dickens" and "Zola," gave names to the antagonism. The assertion of morality against sexual nihilism, the disdain for repressive sentimentality—these became leading antitheses at the turn of the century.

Between sentimentality and Naturalism is where Hardy found himself in the 1890s, and these pressures converged violently in *Tess of the d'Urbervilles:* "He was inexorable, and she sat still, and d'Urberville gave her the kiss of mastery."[25] The chain of circumstances that brings Tess to

Alec d'Urberville is not drawn as inevitable: a string of accidents, a "mesh of events," including a mishap along the road (59), joins the contexts of history (rural poverty, a failing aristocracy, the status-purchasing bourgeoisie) and the demands of nature (especially the demand of desire). Alec is represented as a man so impelled by unconscious causes, inner and outer, that his sexual violence defies moral judgment. Tess, who might have blamed him, blames herself instead. In a much-quoted passage, she is said to feel shame "based on nothing more tangible than a sense of condemnation under an arbitrary law of society which had no foundation in nature" (306). The difficulty, often seen by readers of the novel, is that if moral norms are arbitrary, then what basis remains for distinctions of value? Specifically, we can follow Marjorie Garson in asking how we can reject Alec's brutality if our only resource is an "arbitrary" law.[26]

Within the dialectic of the novel, all readers recognize Angel Clare as the counterpart to Alec d'Urberville. Angel is the Shelleyan seeker, whose love is "ethereal to a fault, imaginative to impracticality" (272). Where Alec presses Tess downward—toward desire, the body, the ground—Angel's motions are upward-tending: toward purity, dignity, the ideal. Tony Tanner's efficient summary lays out the canonical form of the opposition. Both men, writes Tanner, drive Tess toward death, "Angel by his spiritualised rejection, Alec by his sexual attacks." While Angel "wants her spiritual image without her body," Alec "wants only her body and is indifferent to anything we might call her soul, her distinctly human inwardness."[27]

Without pressing too far, we can recognize analogies between Tess's double bind and the predicament of the modern novel as Hardy understood it. Alec d'Urberville is not only a romping bourgeois with a "bold rolling eye" for women (67) but a motive-reducing naturalist. His nihilism accepts just two basic impulses, sex and money; he sneers at the self-deception of those who claim loftier motives; he wants to bring Tess down to the circuit of coarse desire. Angel Clare, on the other hand, fashions himself as a humanist, freed from the limits of family orthodoxy. But as events unfold, Angel becomes the inflexible moralist, who refuses to hear Tess's confession and who, when she insists on speaking, condemns her utterly. He shows himself to be, after all, another voice of respectability.

The plot of Tess of the d'Urbervilles thus reenacts the cultural dilemma that Hardy articulated in his essays. The impasse of the novelist, caught between prudishness and brutalism, sentimentality and science, reproduces itself in the situation of his heroine, who, like the novel she inhabits, is assailed from two sides. We need not see this allegory as part of Hardy's pro-gram. But we have good reason to believe that the obstacles to his fiction—obstacles both to imagining an acceptable story and to publishing and circulating the text—left traces on the plot and that the external narrative of the novelist caught between prudery and prurience intersects with the internal narrative of Tess caught between Angel and Alec. In the charged sequence before the wedding, she tries to make a clean break and to tell her story honestly. But the opportunity passes: "She had not told. At the last moment her courage had failed her, she feared his blame for not telling him sooner; and her instinct of self-preservation was stronger than her can-dour" (217). It is impossible not to recall Hardy's plaint in "Candour in English Fiction." Tess stages the tableau of obstructed speech. Faced with the same "censorship of prudery" that constrains the novelist, she sup-presses the truth until guilt is overbearing. But when she finally tells, she faces ruin and the "thunders of respectability" that Hardy had forecast for the plain-dealing novelist. After she confesses to Angel on their wedding night, she is "awe-stricken to discover such determination under such ap-parent flexibility. His consistency was, indeed, too cruel. She no longer ex-pected forgiveness now" (270).

Although Alec and Angel press from opposite directions, they share the desire for power that lies deeper than the contrasts that separate them. Alec exerts the pressure of physical mastery, but Angel, too, for all his gentleness, exerts a "will to subdue" (273). Furthermore, and despite appearances, Alec and Angel are both creatures of modernity: the modernity of a skepticism (Alec) that sustains no faith to resist animal desire and the modernity of humanist morality (Angel) not yet free to accept the life it pretends to cel-ebrate. What, we can ask, does this mean for Tess herself? And in our wider context, What does it mean for a nascent modernist conception of charac-ter, personality, identity, selfhood?

Here we should recall that Tess enters the plot as "a mere vessel of emo-tion untinctured by experience" (41), who, at the moment of Alec's assault, is still "practically blank as snow" (103). Both images are charged, since the traumatic events have precisely the effect of filling the emotional vessel and coloring the "blank of snow." Kaja Silverman has persuasively described Tess as "a surface upon which a pattern is imposed": through the relentless course of the book she is a site on which experience gathers and concentrates into an overwhelming density.[28] Indeed, the word "experience" becomes a leading character in the novel. The narrator observes that her "turbulent experiences" have yet to demoralize Tess: "But for the world's opinion those experiences would have been simply a liberal education" (128–129). Since she must live in sight of the "world's opinion," however, Tess falters under the accumulated weight of judgment. Angel Clare's light relation to her burden unfits him to understand Tess's melancholy, because he fails to remember that "experience is as to intensity, and not as to duration" (154). When Tess longs to confess her secret, Angel misses the resonance of the word.

> "And I will give you a complete answer, if you will let me go now. I will tell you my experiences—all about myself—all!"
>
> "Your experiences, dear; yes, certainly; any number." He expressed assent in loving satire, looking into her face. "My Tess has, no doubt, almost as many experiences as that wild convolvulus out there on the garden hedge, that opened itself this morning for the first time." (206)

"Experience" is Hardy's term for the relentless agglomeration of marks, stains, and traces that make "character." Experience is scored onto Tess's body, inscribed in her memory and into the structure of the novel, whose most striking formal feature is the accumulation of predicates—emotions, sensations, memories—appended to the name "Tess." The protagonist is made to signify everything she has endured. Tess becomes the fully ravaged heroine, and here we should connect her to Zola's Nana. Both are figures of scarcely assimilable density. Nana is marked and scarred as the corrupt woman of modernity; she is "poisoned," whereas Tess remains "pure." Partly, the difference belongs to that broader contrast between France and England as two polarities within modern culture. But both Nana and Tess are products of a late-century realism in which character is submitted to the deformations of the world. No self can be protected by the veneer of moral categories or literary conventions. The formal-philosophic decision in each novel is to create conditions of endurance/experience, in principle without limit. What more could she withstand? This is a question forced upon every reader of *Nana* or *Tess of the d'Urbervilles*. It reflects a moment in the history of characterization when selfhood is no longer understood as a repertory of dispositions—benevolence, ambition, egotism, jealousy— but as an effect of what Hardy calls "the harrowing contingencies of human experience, the unexpectedness of things" (263). Tess, like Nana, is exposed to the inscription of events; the traces of experience are written all over the two characters. By the end of their histories, they exist not as stable conditions, pure or poisoned, but as unsustainable accumulations of contingency.

CHARACTER AND CASE HISTORY

In 1894, Strindberg wrote an essay entitled "Character a Role?" in which he asks, What does it mean "to be at one with one's character? Is it not the case that we continually adapt ourselves to people and to circumstances, that reality, so varied and shifting, makes us changeable, and that we play along in the comedy of life without knowing it?" He presses his point through a series of vignettes: a trusty servant in his parents' house who suddenly became a drunkard; a sensual nun; a miser transformed into a spendthrift.

> It would appear that character is not as stable a thing as people would like to believe. That is why I do not undertake to classify Characters: people cannot be classified. Every time I choose to study a man, I find I end up thinking the object of my studies mentally deranged. So incoherent is the way people think and act if one follows closely the restless movements of their souls. Record from day to day their expressions of opinion, their fixed ideas or their passing fancies, and one discovers a hotchpotch that does not merit the term 'character.' Everything has the appearance of inconsequential improvisations, with man himself the greatest liar in the world, continually at odds with himself. The simplest bourgeois will emerge as the most complex of individuals; after a while you will be obsessed by him, and in the end you will be convinced that this man is concealing something, and that he is making fun of you and your interests.[29]

What Strindberg articulates here, and what Hardy and Zola implicitly attest to, is the undoing of a system of conventions. It is not that a traditional system disappears. Older typologies continue to inform modernist narrative. Yet self-conscious refusal like Strindberg's—"people cannot be classified" —now becomes widespread. But if character is seen as radically contingent, it is not obsolete; rather, it is recast as a conundrum: character as case history.

In its modernist aspect, case history resists classification according to type and class; it moves instead toward the Strindbergian recognition: that existing categories (such as "character") cannot account for the *indeterminacy* hidden beneath a proper name. We can begin to speak of the modernist case, I propose, when the self defies canons of intelligibility in much the way the passage suggests. The *specification of a conundrum*—the obscurity of motives, the demand for new methods of understanding, the shock effect of newly disclosed habit and appetites—is the project of modernist case study, which lives on the border between art and the sciences (and pseudosciences) of human behavior.

The publication and extraordinary success of Richard von Krafft-Ebing's *Psychopathia Sexualis*—issued first in 1886 and then in new editions almost every year until his death in 1902—marked a threshold not only in psychiatry and sexology but also in modern narrative. The sheer number of case histories and their wide circulation opened an unknown world to view. Stories never told before appeared in profusion. Revealing so many unacceptable tastes and compulsions—the taste for taboo objects and parts of the body, the compulsion to perform transgressive and illegal acts—Krafft-Ebing's dramatis personae were repellent and fascinating to the reading public. Memoirs make clear that *Psychopathia Sexualis* was one of the great forbidden books at the turn of the century, pored over by anxious readers: the young, the uncertain, the agitated, and the desperate. On the borderline between pornography and science, it introduced new characters and plots to its avid audience.

> CASE 66. X, age thirty-eight, engineer, married, father of three children, married life unmarred. Visited periodically a prostitute who had to enact, previous to coitus, the following comedy. As soon as he entered the compartment she took him by the ears, and pulled him all over the room, shouting: "What do you want here? Do you know that you ought to be at school? Why don't you go to school?" She would then slap his face and flog him soundly, until he knelt before her begging pardon. She then handed him a little basket containing bread and fruit, such as children carry with them to school. He remained penitent until the girl's harshness produced orgasm in him, when he would call out: "I am going! I am going!" and then performed coitus.[30]

> CASE 99. X, aged twenty, inverted sexually. Only loved men with a large bushy mustache. One day he met a man who answered his ideal. He invited him to his home, but was unspeakably disappointed when this man removed an artificial mustache. Only when the visitor put the ornament on the upper lip again, he exercised his charm over X once more and restored him to the full possession of his virility. (241)

The content of such stories would have been familiar within the various subcultures, especially urban subcultures, that nourished the "contrary" desires catalogued in *Psychopathia Sexualis*. But the book's wider significance lay in the universalizing language of science brought to bear on minority desires. The short case studies, rarely more than a few sentences long, offered an affectless and usually nonjudgmental account of intimate desire: its objects and its orbits. In later editions, Krafft-Ebing translated many sections into Latin to discourage prurient interest; he always kept up the tone of medical expertise, but he quickly became aware of the thirst of his public. Harry Oosterhuis has recently collected some of the massive correspondence that the book attracted.[31] Readers who had suffered in solitude looked to Krafft-Ebing as a first sympathetic voice. Their letters were often expressions of gratitude, but were also new accounts of sexual experience, and many of them found their way into later editions. The result, as Oosterhuis emphasizes, is that the book became an ongoing collaborative venture in which Krafft-Ebing adjusted his view to the impassioned writings of his correspondents.

The force of *Psychopathia Sexualis* lies in its presentation of character as case, developed through a series of micronarratives built upon a few revelatory events. The case studies are histories of extremity, of eruptive gestures and unrelenting obsessions. In this respect, the book belongs to the moment of *Tess of the d'Urbervilles* and *Nana*.

When Hardy projected a future for the novel, he foresaw a revival of tragedy. Within the cycle of culture, literature would now recover an ancient possibility. Law and custom ("social expedients") merely disguise deeper tragic truths, in particular "the triumph of the crowd over the hero, of the commonplace majority over the exceptional few." What Hardy casts as the return of tragedy, we should recognize as a condition of modernity. It is true that the agon of the crowd and the exception is as old as agon itself. But it is equally clear that modernity brought a hardening and a sharpening of each term. The crowd now appears not merely as social background (urban or rural), subjugated population, or human average. It now stands as an ever-present agitation, which at any moment—through strikes, through street demonstration, through political action, or through the chances of street life—can become insurgency. In another perspective, as we saw in Flaubert, an organized collectivity appears within the middle classes. Public opinion represents a less physical but no less effective aggregate. When Hardy identifies respectability as his opponent, he understands it as an ensemble: a network of publishers, editors, librarians, and readers who enforce limits on literary speech. On the other side, the exceptional one is now less likely to be identified as a besieged and noble hero than as a freak or a monstrosity, one who must be mastered by an administrative apparatus: the school, the military, the prison, or the asylum.

Collectivity and exceptionality are not merely distant principles within a rigid social frame. They are mutually constitutive and reciprocally adaptive. The perception of monstrosity was (and remains) an incitement to mass reaction. What gave this distinctively modern perception form was the circulation of image and anecdote by the press, especially the illustrated press. Whether the item was a medical illustration of the Elephant Man or a cartoon of Louis Bonaparte, the public came to know itself by hooting at a monster.

But we need to see monstrosity as itself encouraged, and often produced, by mass society. Bureaucracy, as Michel Foucault has shown, created new compartments for aberration. A system of grading and classifying kept a logical space (and a physical location) for the exception. Still another, equally notable reason for the production of aberrant lives was the massification of urban life, which created interstitial places where nonnormalized desires could pursue satisfaction. The rise of prostitution in a growing urban economy and the proliferation of subcultural communities with coded forms of communication meant that desires, which might have been repressed or unfulfilled, could sustain a life for themselves. We should recognize *Psychopathia Sexualis* as itself promoting opportunities for subcultural experiments. From the responses that Krafft-Ebing received, we have reason to believe that the text was mined for clues and that it suggested how a life of fantasy might lead to an active practice of desire—a turn that gratified some and brought guilt to others. And yet even those who could satisfy their desires (and invented ways to live beyond the norm) displayed the pain of the human anomaly. The correspondents record the acute sense of their exceptional position and their victimization, and while neither they nor Krafft-Ebing sees their lives as high tragedy, they do endure the everyday pathos of exclusion.

Psychopathia Sexualis offered itself as a contribution not only to psychiatry but also to public policy, especially in relation to the laws of sexual crime. Krafft-Ebing argued that many cases of "aberrant" sexuality should be treated by doctors, not by judges, because often the "offender is merely an automaton" (549). The aim of the book was not to resist the law but to shift the terms of debate. What it offered was not a theory but a multiplication of cases. In an early commentary, Havelock Ellis described it as opening "a great neglected field of morbid psychology" and "a vast mass of detailed histories."[32] Indeed, Krafft-Ebing thinks in terms of cases. Faced with a conceptual challenge, he always responded by introducing a new example; the social effect of his work was due to the disclosure of a new population not only to respectable society but also to the "inverts," the "fetishists," the sadists, and the masochists themselves. As vividly as any work of the period, *Psychopathia Sexualis* established sexuality as an inescapable topos of modernity. The growing population of Krafft-Ebing's "deviants" must be placed alongside the provocative artworks with which they are linked and which increasingly took sexual pathology as their content.

The other, greater figure in this lineage is Sigmund Freud, whose founding of psychoanalysis is unthinkable apart from the reinvention (and intensification) of case study. His research, therapy, and writing all depended on encounters with the individual-as-conundrum, especially the individual-as-sexual-conundrum. But unlike the encyclopedic method of Krafft-Ebing —sexuality as a compendium of brief examples—Freud's cases were few, intricate, and sustained. He was himself surprised by the genre that his methods brought into being, almost against his better judgment.

> Like other neuropathologists, I was trained to employ local diagnoses and electro-prognosis, and it still strikes me myself as strange that the case histories I write should read like short stories and that, as one might say, they lack the serious stamp of science. I must console myself with the reflection that the nature of the subject is evidently responsible for this, rather than any preference of my own. The fact is that local diagnosis and electrical reactions lead nowhere in the study of hysteria, whereas a detailed description of mental processes such as we are accustomed to find in the works of imaginative writers enables me, with the use of a few psychological formulas, to obtain at least some kind of insight into the course of that affection.[33]

The great psychoanalytic case histories of the early twentieth century —"Dora," the "Wolf-Man," the "Rat Man"—established a form of writing acutely conscious of its novelty and its difficulty. Early in the study called *From the History of an Infantile Neurosis* ("Wolf-Man"), Freud writes, "I am unable to give either a purely historical or a purely thematic account of my patient's story; I can write a consecutive history neither of the treatment nor of the disease, but I shall find myself obliged to combine the two methods of presentation."[34] The formal challenge of the case history—its failure to follow either linear chronology or causal sequence—is a convergence of two conditions: the neurosis of the patient and the demands of treatment, especially its demanding temporality. From early attempts at a rapid cure, especially through techniques of hypnosis, psychoanalytic technique

> has been completely revolutionized. At that time the work of analysis started out from the symptoms, and aimed at clearing them up one after the other. Since then I have abandoned that technique, because I found it totally inadequate for dealing with the finer structure of a neurosis. I now let the patient himself choose the subject of the day's work, and in that way I start out from whatever surface his unconscious happens to be presenting to his notice at the moment. But on this plan everything that has to do with the clearing-up of a particular symptom emerges piecemeal woven into various contexts, and distributed over widely separated periods of time.[35]

No one event, memory, or symptom can illuminate neurosis. The relevant contexts are spread over many years; therapy takes time; psychoanalysis, in short, becomes narrativized. A self is the intersection of many stories, and psychoanalytic treatment involves the reconstruction of their plots. Neurosis is itself a pathology of narrative, an incapacity to give a coherent account of one's life. A sufferer loses memories or distorts the past, overvalues certain incidents while repressing others. During treatment, "the patient supplies the facts which, though he had known them all along, had been kept back by him or had not occurred to his mind." The gaps and distortions of memory are gradually overcome, with the result that "it is only towards the end of treatment that we have before us an intelligible, consistent and unbroken case history" (32).

The patient who talks without premeditation or self-censorship (the "fundamental rule" of therapy); the analyst who occasionally offers commentary and interpretation; the case history that follows neither the life-course of the patient, nor the arc of treatment, nor the sequence of interpretations—the result of these is a network of intersecting trajectories, whose intricacy places the case studies among the experimental narratives of the early twentieth century.[36] As Peter Brooks has persuasively said, "In a manner yet more radical than Mann's or even Proust's—perhaps more nearly approaching Faulkner's—Freud's case-history involves a new questioning of how life stories go together, how narrative units combine in significant sequence, where cause and effect are to be sought, how meaning is related to narration."[37] These are all central modernist concerns.

At the same time, the case histories change the terms in which character is understood. Krafft-Ebing saw his patients as a collection of new dispositions, as anomalous but relatively fixed structures of desire. For Freud, however, human beings live through a complex drama of development, and characters are (re)formed through unfolding negotiations between desire and the world. To attain a release from suffering, more must be uncovered than the structure of desire; it is necessary to disclose the close intricacy of neurosis, its history, its ruses and guises, the meaning of its various symptoms and their changes over time. A dream can be interpreted again and again for many years; a memory can be recast; a stubborn image can take on new significance during therapy. But beyond the demands of treatment, psychoanalysis offers, in effect, a new metaphysics of character. Character is the precipitate of fantasies, desires, and dreads; it is an overlay of past and present; it possesses an inexhaustible convergence of meanings. Freud writes that "a single symptom corresponds quite regularly to several meanings *simultaneously,*" and "in the course of years a symptom can change its meaning or its chief meaning, or the leading role can pass from one meaning to another." The most trivial gesture can summon the most ancient desire.

Sexuality's location at the base of these meanings is what made a scandal of psychoanalysis. In the case study known as "Dora," Freud wrote that he was eager "to show that sexuality does not simply intervene, like a *deus ex machina,* on one single occasion, at some point in the working of the processes which characterize hysteria, but that it provides the motive power for every single symptom, and for every single manifestation of a symptom. The symptoms of the disease are nothing else than *the patient's sexual activity.*" But while Krafft-Ebing followed the compulsions of sex in the byways of psychopathology, Freud made no exemptions for the "healthy." In the account of perversion in *Three Essays on the Theory of Sexuality* Freud insists that "the sexual life of healthy people" also shows elements of perverse desire.[38] "Normality" cannot keep itself aloof from taboo desires—that is one stinging challenge. The other is that the pervading pressure of sex erodes our pride in self-mastery.

Freud is often connected with Marx and Nietzsche in a modernist triad credited with dissolving the privilege of the Cartesian self and bringing about a decentering of subjectivity. Certainly the abrasion of the rational ego is a marker of high Modernism. But Freud himself linked the advent of psychoanalysis to two other assaults on human pretension. The first was the astronomy of Nicolaus Copernicus, which showed that "our earth was not the centre of the universe but only a tiny fragment of a cosmic system of scarcely imaginable vastness." The second was the biology of Darwin, which "destroyed man's supposedly privileged place in creation and proved his descent from the animal kingdom and his ineradicable animal nature." Now "human megalomania" will receive its "third and most wounding blow" from psychoanalysis, "which seeks to prove to the ego that it is not even master in its own house, but must content itself with scanty information of what is going on unconsciously in its mind."[39] What distinguishes Freud's contribution from the precursors he names, but also from Marx and Nietzsche, is that the *dislocation* of the rational ego, its loss of mastery in its own house, accompanies a massive investment of force elsewhere in the psyche—not within the self-understanding of consciousness but in the great reservoir of the unconscious. Rationality endures limits while arational instincts take on new depth and significance.

The challenges of Marx, Darwin, and Copernicus depended on locating selfhood within an encompassing context that overwhelms its claims of authority. Nietzsche stands closer to Freud in seeing the modern wound as *internal* to character. He, too, describes the ferocity of a psychic conflict between such forces as pity and power, will and resentment, weariness and laughter. Freud owed much to Nietzsche. But where he differed was, among other things, in the systematic aspect of his theory and in his respect for the singularity of case history.

The last two points are at odds. Psychoanalysis, both as theory and as institution, projected the universalizing claims of a new science. But the course of therapy, as revealed within the case histories, displayed individual life as intricate and unrepeatable. The tales of Dora and the Wolf-Man may read like late gothic novels, but their lives are unhappily their own. Freud's promise was that even obscure and atypical neuroses would eventually be revealed as intelligible and that the most eccentric conduct would fall within the laws of the psyche. Although he held to the vocation of science and resisted "wild psychoanalysis," his work was an invitation to other uses, with the case studies encouraging a view of selfhood as deep, extravagant, and desirous. Furthermore, the celebrated central technique of therapy— the free associations of the patient—was a spur to narrative experiment. Freud rigorously demanded the application of law-like principles, but for many artists, writers, and musicians, the great example of his work was the image of life beyond the law. In the 1920s, the surrealists took Freud as an inspiration for their use of dreams and automatic writing as essential

sources of artistic creation. But well before Surrealism emerged, psychoanalytic ideas (and images), especially where they converged with the anti-
rationalism of Nietzsche, suggested the power of singularity rather than the
force of law.

MANN, KAFKA, LUKÁCS

Thomas Mann's protagonist in *Death in Venice* (1910), the writer Gustave
von Aschenbach, enters the work as the perfectly successful artist, feted and
petted at the summit of fame. His life has been one long effort to marry
discipline to sensuousness, form to pleasure, the voice of the father to the
warmth of the mother. And then there comes the abrupt thought, emerging as if from nowhere: What if a lifetime's heroism of the will should sink
into will-lessness? What if classical form should suddenly seem a repression
and a constraint? What if the man of discipline should release his grip?
Stimulated by both Freud and Nietzsche, Mann imagines art undoing its
sublimations, the artist returning to the sensations that he had made it his
vocation to control.

Aschenbach's impossible love for the beautiful boy Tadzio in diseased
and decaying Venice is the culmination, but also the justification, of self-
abandonment. The artist allows art to mix with life and then lets art abase
itself before life. Such living is also a way of dying. To abandon the discipline of form is to enter the circuit of ripeness and decay. On the point
of succumbing—to Tadzio, to psychic dissolution, to physical disease—
Aschenbach has a "thought of returning home, returning to reason, self-
mastery, an ordered existence, to the old life of effort." But the thought
fades against the prospect of what "chaos might confer," the "visions of a
monstrous sweetness," when reason gives way and passion swoons.[40]

In many respects, the milieu of *Death in Venice* belongs to the fin de
siècle culture of weariness, with its gorgeous lethargy and its release into
sensation. But the formal event of *Death in Venice,* which separates it from
its precursors in the 1890s, is the rigor of its third-person perspective,
which stays near to the protagonist but never swoons with him. The narrative voice records Aschenbach's drift through desire to death, almost always
seeing through his eyes and most often speaking in his tones. It perfects a
free, indirect discourse that coincides with him. Yet it also refines an irony
that preserves distance between narrator and character. Crucially, the narrator stands outside to watch Aschenbach's painted face when he tries to
attract the fourteen-year-old Tadzio, and again to watch his corpse while it
still sits at the seaside gazing out.

Aschenbach, too, is a case study, the case of the artist as solitary ("our solitary" is the narrator's epithet for him). As the lone artist, he must live out the extreme fate of doubleness: "Solitude gives birth to the original in us, to beauty unfamiliar and perilous—to poetry. But also, it gives birth to the opposite: to the perverse, the illicit, the absurd" (24). Form itself, which seems the alternative to chaos, also has two aspects: it is "moral and immoral at once," and in its essence it is "indifferent to good and evil" (13). To call this a Freudian (or Nietzschean) perspective, however indebted the story is to both, is to miss the specificity of Mann's project. *Death in Venice* displays, and enjoys, the spectacle of art making enthralled by its own mythology, its ambiguous appeal, and its contradictory sources. But the story shows what it refuses to tell—namely, that the case of Aschenbach does not exhaust the possibilities for art. The narrator who stands so close to the character steps away just far enough to indicate the coherence of an outside view. A story that displays the fatality of art—its complicity with chaos— offers itself (its own shape, its lucidity, its control) as an alternative to what it records.

It was otherwise with Franz Kafka. By his account, he composed his brief story "The Judgment" over the course of a single night in September 1912, recording the creative convulsion in his diary.

> I wrote [the story] at one sitting during the night of the 22nd–23rd, from ten o'clock at night to six o'clock in the morning. I was hardly able to pull my legs out from under the desk, they had got so stiff from sitting. The fearful strain and joy, how the story developed before me, as if I were advancing over water. Several times during this night I heaved my own weight on my back. How everything can be said, how for everything, for the strangest fancies, there waits a great fire in which they perish and rise up again. How it turned blue outside the window. A wagon rolled by. Two men walked across the bridge. At two I looked at the clock for the last time. . . . The conviction verified that with my novel-writing I am in the shameful lowlands of writing. Only *in this way* can writing be done, only with such coherence, with such a complete opening out of the body and the soul . . . thoughts about Freud, of course.[41]

He had thoughts about Freud no doubt because "The Judgment" records a violent contest between father and son, but also because it has the aspect of dream or hallucination. It begins with banal incidents in everyday tones. Georg Bendemann, living with his father after the death of his mother, sits at home, composing a letter to an old friend who has moved to Russia. He drifts in reverie, thinking of his friend's failures abroad and then of his own success in business and his happy engagement to a well-off young woman. The daydream having ended, Georg enters the bedroom of his weakened father, who has been failing since his wife's death. Here the story first breaches its plausibility. The father, "still a giant of a man," rises to meet the son, but no sooner does he hear about the letter to Russia than he denies the existence of Georg's friend. Soothingly, the son lowers the father back to bed, draws the blankets ("Don't worry, you're well covered up"), only to find him jumping up in the next minute, throwing off the blankets, touching the ceiling with his hand, and saying, "You wanted to cover me up, I know, my young sprig, but I'm far from being covered up yet. And even if this is the last strength I have, it's enough for you, too much for you. Of course I know your friend. He would have been a son after my own heart." There follows a taunting, mocking pantomime of the fiancée, accusations that Georg has dishonored his mother, has only posed as a business man, and has in fact become "a devilish human being." Then comes the irresistible paternal edict: "I sentence you now to death by drowning!" Without hesitation, Georg runs from the house, dashes across the road, and jumps from a bridge into a river.[42]

The eruption of another order of reality, the passage from the ordinary to the ultimate, the exchange of roles between weak and strong, the shift from slow rhythms to the quick pulse of disaster—these are often-repeated scenes in Kafka. They confirm a central pattern of relationship. The protagonist (here Georg Bendemann) wants to live in the light of the everyday and looks to grow toward the common pleasures of friendship, work, and love. For a time, these goals seem near. Then all at once they are shown to be illusory, paper-thin. An older power has been lying in wait, ready to reveal that nothing has changed, that a flourishing life is as remote as ever, even more remote now, because everything has been revealed for what it is. The authority of the father is intact; the weakness of the son is permanent. Nothing is left to do but to complete the reversal, through submission to the ultimate judgment.

The "Kafka effect" is to show that simplicity—simple words, clearly drawn events—is a property of both the banal and the catastrophic. The reading of a letter and the headlong rush to suicide can both be told in the same straightforward prose. This recognition may be the closest link between Kafka and Freud: not the schematic rendering of the Oedipal conflict but the continuity between everyday life and extreme states, between familiar gestures and uncanny outcomes. The deadpan of Kafka's prose never breaks, no matter how extraordinary the turn of events. One of its effects is to remove the possibility of a properly external point of view, like that of Mann's narrator, who emerges just enough to become distinct from Aschenbach. Kafka asks us to live without the contrast between internal and external, between character and narrator. There is only the even prose, which moves from breakfast to suicide without changing tone.

The "expressionism" of Kafka—the rending of a familiar context with an abrupt gesture of extremity, the intimation of the violence lurking within the everyday, the sudden discontinuity or sudden convergence between levels of reality (rational and irrational, intelligible and incoherent, plausible and inconceivable)—has made his work a paradigm of Modernism-as-conundrum. The fiction inevitably solicits, and resists, interpretation. It invites an allegorical reading that it never satisfies. The aura of mystery remains incongruous with the bland acceptance of the characters who move through the strange world. In all these respects, Kafka's stories and novels serve as epitomes of the modernist masterwork, of the work as an object of insatiable fascination, endless in its implications.

Lukács was no doubt right to insist that the way of Kafka, which he considered the way of "blind and panic-stricken angst," would not exhaust the field of modern possibilities or limit the scope of literary history. For Lukács, Mann offered a vigorous alternative: a "fruitful critical realism" that saw beyond anxious immediacy and that sustained detachment, selectivity, and, above all, perspective.[43] Kafka, too, as Lukács observes, depends on the refinements of the realist method, even as he turns the banality of the everyday toward the abyss of strangeness. As an increasingly elastic concept, realism continued to attract critique—it was rejected as formulaic or archaic, or as mere copyism—but it lived on within the milieu of experiment and cultural opposition as an evolving style.

JOYCE, JAMES, CONRAD: WORD, WORLD, MIND

The next turn in this account of Modernism is also an opportunity for some acts of synthesis and consolidation. I begin with a passage from late in *A Portrait of the Artist as a Young Man,* where Stephen Dedalus meditates on the sources of his vocation in language.

> Words. Was it their colours? He allowed them to glow and fade, hue after hue: sunrise gold, the russet and green of apple orchards, azure of waves, the greyfringed fleece of clouds. No, it was not their colours; it

was the poise and balance of the period itself. Did he then love the rhythmic rise and fall of words better than their associations of legend and colour? Or was it that, being as weak of sight as he was shy of mind, he drew less pleasure from the reflection of the glowing sensible world through the prism of a language manycoloured and richly storied than from the contemplation of an inner world of individual emotions mirrored perfectly in a lucid supple periodic prose.[44]

These questions occupy Joyce for the rest of his career, but they also belong to the wide milieu of twentieth-century Modernism. Where does the force of language reside? Does its power come from the "glowing sensible world"? In resisting this thought, Stephen Dedalus refuses to justify art in terms of representation, imitation, or association ("associations of legend and colour"). But the refusal leaves alternatives open. Is it language itself that thrills the writer and justifies the work—the words themselves, their balance and rhythm? Or is it the inner life of the artist, the "inner world of individual emotions," the sensations and perceptions that seem prior to language? Early in the novel, recalling a nursery rhyme, the young Dedalus had wanted to cry quietly, "but not for himself: for the words, so beautiful and sad, like music" (22). Joyce is consistently drawn to the idea that language is independent of both world and self, that it contains a force and a form beyond the reach of any individual. We can use language, but language, as it were, has already used us. Martin Heidegger wrote that "language remains the master of man. . . . For strictly, it is language that speaks. . . . Language is the highest and everywhere the first."[45] Yet for all the attraction of this thought within Modernism—that a supra-individual network of signs precedes and exceeds any speaker, any artist—the other image remains: the foundational power of selfhood (the "inner world of individual emotions"). Here the emphasis falls on private consciousness, not on the collective and anonymous force of language. While later thinkers will contest the distinction, arguing, for instance, that consciousness is an effect of language, modernists like Joyce preserved competing origins that offered different paths to the new art.

The three possibilities offered by Stephen Dedalus can be seen as a later articulation of the aesthetic positions that emerged in nineteenth-century France, which I described earlier under the headings of Naturalism, formalism, and Symbolism. By the time we reach the first and second decades of the twentieth century, each of these broader attitudes has been transformed. Even as Joyce celebrates the self-sufficiency of language, he (intermittently) accepts the claims of realism and its crystallization in Naturalism. For him it was Ibsen above all, but also Tolstoy, Maupassant, and Gerhart Hauptmann, who offered rich invitations to the Real. Especially in the early years, Joyce defended his art in defiantly realist terms, as in his celebrated remark about *Dubliners:* "I have written it for the most part in a style of scrupulous meanness and with the conviction that he is a very bold man who dares to alter in the presentment, still more to deform, whatever he has seen and heard."[46] The austerity of direct presentation ("scrupulous meanness") and the value of the world as experienced ("seen and heard") belong to a realist/ naturalist moment.

At the same time, aesthetic formalism was radicalized. The pleasures that the Parnassian poets took in verbal technique—the control of rhythm, the precise diction, the taut rhymes—have now become more abstract satisfactions. Form inheres in the deepest structures of the work. Joyce's later fiction, like Gertrude Stein's, will imply that narrative must surpass the privilege of character and event and instead enact form—not merely as local felicity but as the achievement of total synthesis, a pattern of the whole. As Stephen Dedalus puts it, you "apprehend [the work] as balanced part against part within its limits; you feel the rhythm of its structure" (Joyce, *Portrait,* 249).

The third term in the triad, Symbolism, underwent the most striking changes. We have already met resistance to the symbol—namely, distaste for its ineffable elusiveness. Marinetti, we recall, was outspoken in repudiating the ethereal symbolists, who had been his early inspiration. Pound tersely commented that the "natural object is always the *adequate* symbol."[47] Throughout the decade before the First World War, young voices of critique pressed the claims of the visible world and lampooned the dream of a symbolist Elsewhere. In the stiff words of Joyce's Dedalus in *Stephen Hero* (an early version of *Portrait of the Artist*), "Art is not an escape from life. It's just the very opposite. . . . An artist is not a fellow who dangles a mechanical heaven before the public. The priest does that."[48]

The attack on Symbolism was often made in the name of realism. The refusal of vagueness, of hints and glimpses, of languid dreaming and sumptuous ornament, had an influence across the arts. Nevertheless, symbolists enjoyed a productive afterlife in later Modernism, perhaps most surprisingly in the modernist novel, a point that can be approached by way of Henry James. When he looked back on the career of Flaubert, James generously acknowledged the magnitude of a founding project. Flaubert had introduced precision and the dignity of craft to the vocation of prose fiction. But despite this indispensable accomplishment, James regretted a fatal weakness that showed itself, above all, in *The Sentimental Education*. There, Flaubert had painted upon an intricate historical canvas and had refined the precision of style, but he had placed the burden of narrative on Frédéric Moreau, a prop far too weak to bear its weight. Moreau, with no distinction of mind and no gift of responsiveness, remained a dull instrument, inadequate to the ambitions of the novel. For James it can never be enough to deploy the intelligence of the author, and this, he thought, was Flaubert's error: to keep the powers of discrimination and responsiveness for himself and to leave his characters as no more than marionettes. In James's own fiction, the assumption is that events will not speak for themselves; they must be addressed and interpreted by alert fictive respondents who are capable of assigning meanings to their experience. Elsewhere I have traced the longer lineage of this idea, which has cardinal nodes in the work of Matthew Arnold, Walter Pater, and T. H. Huxley.

Here I propose that we recognize continuity—and also significant change—between Symbolism and the turn to subjectivity in modernist fiction. As we have seen, the symbolist attempt to evoke a supersensible world was always bound to the author's and the reader's states of mind. Mallarmé's meticulous descriptions of the scene of reading, Huysmans's fascination with the exquisite moment, and Yeats's pursuit of a receptive attitude are notable examples. Symbolism was no more concerned with the supersensible Beyond than it was with the subjectivity of a this-worldly reader, listener, or viewer.

The central registering intelligence of modern narrative—from James's Maggie Verver to Woolf's Lily Briscoe, from Conrad's Marlow to Proust's Marcel, from Ford's John Dowell to F. Scott Fitzgerald's Nick Carraway— should be linked to the symbolist refusal of externality. But for these novelists, the emphasis falls on the inward universe of consciousness, which becomes its own vast and subtle region. They are often aggressively dismissive of a spirit-realm. In Conrad, Joyce, and Woolf, the prospect of nihilism, of life without the sanction of God, is a terror but also an impetus, as human subjectivity assumes the signifying burden. But the language of spirituality does not disappear for these writers. However secular James's plots, his metaphors enact a logic of redemption and salvation, and we have seen how Woolf defends the new fiction in terms of "spirit." Then, too, the word "soul" plays a role, especially in Joyce's work, which often acknowledges its indebtedness to the Catholic theology that it repudiates. The assimilation of religious language indicates that religious concern has not disappeared from the work of even some avowedly skeptical writers. But the religious temper almost always appears within secular subjectivities.[49]

James is rightly acknowledged as the great novelist of consciousness, where consciousness is both a vocation for his characters and a formal resource. He repeatedly invents figures—such as Ralph Touchett in *The Portrait of a Lady,* Fanny Assingham in *The Golden Bowl,* and, more complexly, Lambert Strether in *The Ambassadors*—whose task is precisely to abstain from the circuit of desire and quest and instead to accept the responsibilities of knowledge and interpretation. There are events, and then there is the significance of events. James insists on the labor of meaning as indispensable to the dignity of a properly self-conscious novel. In the ambitious works at the end of his career—*The Ambassadors, The Wings of the Dove, The Golden Bowl*—stormy desires still course through the events. But the plot is always a drama of recognition, of agitated, prolonged movements of mind that create the terms for meaning. Without the intervention of consciousness, narrative is only a play of instinctual reflexes.

Joseph Conrad was James's near contemporary, his admirer, and in many respects his ally in this campaign. In a review of Conrad's novel *Chance,* James praises the virtuosity of its technique as "the prolonged hovering flight of the subjective over the outstretched ground of the case exposed."[50] The image here indicates a point of convergence between these two leading novelists. For Conrad, too, the task of modern fiction was to overcome the muteness of events by way of an active, restless, meaning-giving subjectivity. His invention of the narrator Marlow, who comes into his own in *Heart of Darkness* and *Lord Jim,* is closely parallel to, and owes much to, James's device of the central consciousness. Marlow assumes a similar burden of interpretation—sifting, deliberating, revising, speculating—but he acknowledges the skeptical implications of the subjective turn more than his Jamesian counterparts do, and he tests the limits of first-person narrative. James had held back from the looseness of the first person, but Conrad sees the narrating "I" as attractive just because it breaks loose from older certainties. As he worked through its effects in practice, he approached recognitions that were made fully explicit only by his collaborator Ford Madox Ford.

When Ford came to write a memoir of Conrad, he suggested that the two writers accepted the name "Impressionist" because they "saw that Life did not narrate, but made impressions on our brains." Earlier he had explained the principle through this anecdote.

Life does not say to you: In 1914 my next door neighbour, Mr. Slack, erected a greenhouse and painted it with Cox's green aluminium paint. . . . If you think about the matter you will remember in various unordered pictures, how one day Mr. Slack appeared in his garden and contemplated the wall of his house. You will then try to remember the year of that occurrence and you will fix it as August 1914 because having had the foresight to bear the municipal stock of the city of Liège you were able to afford a first-class season ticket for the first time in your life. You will remember Mr. Slack—then much thinner because it was before he found out where to buy that cheap Burgundy . . .[51]

Less picturesquely, Ford said that impressionism confines itself to the "impression of the moment," not to a "sort of rounded, annotated record of a set of circumstances."[52] As a frank subjectivism, then, literary impressionism bears comparison with impressionist techniques in other arts, especially painting. When Claude Monet responded to critics by saying, "Poor blind idiots, they want to see everything clearly, even through the fog," he was asserting a parallel principle. His haystacks, cathedrals, and water lilies are portrayed not "in themselves" but as they appeared to a finite and changing perception.[53]

The logic that drives Modernism from realism toward subjectivism is deep within the epoch. Inevitably, it raises a question of skepticism, which erupts in the fiction of Conrad and Ford. The paintings of Gustave Courbet and the fiction of Flaubert and George Eliot asserted the radicalism of representing the world as it is: the real set free from the gauzy drape of the ideal. This radicalism was itself radicalized by the generation of naturalists, who saw the real as law-governed, inexorable, and open to a precision as rigorous as that of science. But the attempt to record the world-as-it-is changed steadily into an effort to express the world-as-it-appears. This circuit of ideas is familiar in philosophy, as it is in the fine arts. What gave it force in the later nineteenth century was that a skeptical subjectivism coincided with the crisis of faith. In the decades after Darwin, the skeptical drift—from world to self, from object to subject of perception—suggested a risk of essential loneliness within a world that was itself absent of meaning. In an often-quoted passage from early in his career, Conrad imagined the nihilistic universe.

There is—let us say—a machine. It evolved itself (I am severely scientific) out of a chaos of scraps of iron and behold!—it knits. I am horrified at the horrible work and stand appalled. . . . And the most withering thought is that the infamous thing has made itself; made itself without thought, without conscience, without foresight, without eyes, without heart. It is a tragic accident—and it has happened. You can't interfere with it. The last drop of bitterness is in the suspicion that you can't even smash it . . . it is indestructible! It knits us in and it knits us out. It has knitted time, space, pain, death, corruption, despair and all the illusions—and nothing matters.[54]

The creators of modernist narrative built fictions that unfolded within a godless universe. In that context, the burdens of subjectivity assume new significance: the extraordinary valuation of consciousness in James can be seen as compensation for the loss of divine sanction. Confronted by "mere bald facts," the fretful acts of interpretation project meaning and value onto the blank world.[55] In so doing, they offer affirmation on the far side of skepticism—a hope that meaning is within the compass of our talents and our will.

STEIN, PICASSO, AND THE PORTRAIT AS CASE STUDY

At a moment of transition in Modernism, Gertrude Stein played a central role in the staging of the case study, as both object and subject, specimen and maker. Picasso's portrait of her in 1905–1906 marked a decisive point in his career, and Stein's own near-contemporaneous work on *Three Lives* approached a first limit in experiment. Taken together, these acts of portraiture changed the terms by which character and form were understood; they also prepared for a more focused stage in the relation between Modernism and its audiences. As Stein and Picasso put radical questions to the conventions they inherited—What is a sentence, after all? A character? What is a space or a face?—they prepared for a new spectacle in Modernism. *Three Lives* and *Portrait of Gertrude Stein* brought their art to the edge of extremity.

From late 1905 and then into the autumn of 1906, Picasso struggled over his portrait of Stein (fig. 9). He had met her and her brother, Leo, in Paris, had visited their salon, and had begun painting her soon thereafter. Stein sat for Picasso more than eighty times, and then, at a crisis in his work, he painted out the head that he had carefully composed, creating instead a flattened face, deprived of the usual marks (tone, contour) that give the signature of identity. The final facial image, usually spoken of as a mask, shows the rigidity and impassivity that Picasso developed to great effect in the next few years. But, as Michael North has shown, what makes the portrait uneasy in itself and resonant in his career is that it is neither face nor mask but suspended in between.[56] The nose, the upper lip, and the wrinkling between them retain the texture of personality, as does the expressiveness in the gaze. But that gaze emerges from eyes that have already taken on the symmetry, especially of upper and lower eyelids, that will become a sign of the impassive, unreadable face. The helmet of hair, the almost sheer tone of the forehead, the artificial color and shape around her left eye, the draining of blood from the lips and cheek, the nearly featureless ear, the bounding line along the left of the head—these create a detachable prop of a face. Gertrude Stein remains identifiable, just as the chair and the room do. But the portrait stages a conflict between the fineness of feature by which we understand individuality and the bluntness of shape which offers a view beyond personality. The hunch of Stein's shoulders—beneath a coat that seems as much an animal skin as a garment—gives her the solidity of a ritual object and leaves her no more a person than a statue.

The escape from organic forms, including an escape from smooth transitions and curvilinear drafting, breaks open the image to multiple contradictory significations. One eye does not correspond to the other; they seem not only to be gazing in different directions but to belong to different orders of style. The dignity of the molded and shaded nose plays against the stubby fingers. The shading beneath the right eye has a human character, but as the cheek recedes, it meets the neck and ear, and all three darken into a patch of color (bounded by an arbitrary horizontal at the bottom) that begins to absorb the body into a pictorial style indifferent to the look of nature. Character is not defunct; this is still a portrait. But from the time of this painting, character for Picasso was not something rendered as a unit or a whole. Rather, it was open to as many perspectives as the painter could find gestures to make. Parts of the body have entirely different vocabularies of meaning, just as space, volume, and color can generate separate ideas and emotions that never converge.

In reflecting on the breakthrough in her fiction, Stein declared her debt to modernist painting, to Picasso most immediately, but to Paul Cézanne no less significantly—though again, and revealingly, she remembers the literary precedent of Flaubert.

> Everything I have done had been influenced by Flaubert and Cézanne, and this gave me a new feeling about composition. Up to that time composition had consisted of a central idea, to which everything else

was an accompaniment and separate but was not an end in itself, and Cézanne conceived the idea that in composition one thing was as important as another thing. Each part is as important as the whole, and that impressed me enormously and it impressed me so much that I began to write *Three Lives* under this influence.... I began to play with words then. I was a little obsessed by words of equal value. Picasso was painting my portrait at that time, and he and I used to talk this thing over endlessly. At this time he had just begun on Cubism.... You had to recognise that words had lost their value in the Nineteenth Century, particularly towards the end, they had lost much of their variety, and I felt that I could not go on, that I had to recapture the value of the individual word, find out what it meant and act within it.[57]

Stein's eagerness to align herself with Cézanne and Picasso reflects the early-twentieth-century preeminence of painting. Within the uneven development of Modernism, post-impressionist painting had taken the place of drama as the most visible sign of an adversary culture. The reshaping of representation, the assault on the integrity of the body, the refusal of one-point perspective became shock effects attracting a familiar reaction: outrage and defiance, repudiation and solidarity. Stein—like Guillaume Apollinaire, like Pound—self-consciously aimed to bring the radicalism of painting into literature, and although she emphasized the connection between her work and Picasso's, it is clear that the literary project confronted separate difficulties. The directedness of language toward the world was the frame within which Stein pursued a formal abstraction in literature. The first notable result came in "Melanctha," the long middle story in *Three Lives*.

"Melanctha" is an act of verbal portraiture that follows its heroine from early life to her death. But to describe it this way is already to be misleading. Even as Stein threads the tale of Melanctha's life—with its charged episodes of friendship, desire, romance, loss, and loneliness—her story pictorializes narrative. It slows events down and then abruptly shifts attention. It flattens the significance of incident so that climax is always deflated and major and minor events attract the same attention. Melanctha's romantic/erotic history is achingly prolonged; the erratic path of love becomes a repetition of possibility and impasse. Its end is sudden, leading to Melanctha's sharp downward arc.

As Melanctha's friend Rose Johnson abandons her, leaving Melanctha to languish and die, Rose complains, "You certainly never can learn no way

Melanctha ever with all I certainly been telling to you, ever since I know you good, that it ain't never no way like you do always is the right way you be acting ever and talking, the way I certainly always have seen you do so Melanctha always."[58] These lines display the most distinctive formal audacity of the story—namely the audacity in language. Stein uses everyday words but not in everyday syntax. The repetition of phrases and the distended rhythms create the uncanny speech of the story. At the same time, she places ordinary words in new contexts until many of them become part of a special vocabulary, an internal language that seems to belong to this story alone. So Melanctha "wanders"—"From the time that Melanctha was twelve until she was sixteen she wandered, always seeking but never more than very dimly seeing wisdom" (97)—where the word suggests the course of her desires but also extends beyond eroticism to suggest curiosity, improvisation, aimlessness, a lack of discipline, and also a refusal of orthodoxy. The special vocabulary of the story includes insistently repeated words such as "wisdom," "always," "certainly," and "real" ("realler," "really"). Even prepositions become instruments of this dislocation whereby common words are reframed, giving the reader a continual experience of meanings at once preserved and evacuated, sustained but altered.

> Melanctha Herbert somehow had made him feel deeply just then, what very more it was that she wanted *from* him. Jeff Campbell now felt *in* him what everybody always had needed to make them really understanding, *to* him. Jeff felt a strong disgust *inside* him; not *for* Melanctha herself, *to* him, not *for* himself really, *in* him, not *for* what it was that everybody wanted, *in* them; he only had disgust because he never could know really *in* him, what it was he wanted, to be really right in understanding, *for* him, he only had disgust because he never could know really what it was really right *to* him to be always doing, in the things he had before believed in, the things he before had believed in *for* himself and *for* all the colored people, the living regular, and the never wanting to be always having new things, just to keep on, always being in excitements. All the old thinking now came up very strong *inside* him. He sort of turned away then, and threw Melanctha from him. (155; italics mine)

The rhythm coincides with and then defies the rhythm of ordinary speech; the repetitions repeat; the precision becomes excessive. Like Picasso's portrait of Stein, "Melanctha" still presents its subject matter. It is possible to follow the fate of its characters and to accept the story as about desire, race, and the struggle between the sexes. But the attractions of words back toward themselves unsettles Stein's boundary between language and object, sentence and character.

The tradition of *le mot juste*—the right or exact word, discovered through arduous imaginative labor—derived from the example of Flaubert. But a signal passage in modernist history is the transition from hard-won precision—the word that would mirror the world or express the soul—to the word before, or beyond, the act of reference. This movement of sensibility is also a conceptual shift. It stands in rough parallel to the shift from realism to impressionism, from the world-as-it-is to the world-as-it-appears. As such, it, too, can take on an aspect of skepticism: doubts about the possibility of linguistic reference can correspond to doubts about the objectivity of the world. But as new paintings—the work of Kandinsky, Robert Delaunay, and Picasso—exuberantly showed, the relinquishing of reference need not appear as skeptical withdrawal. Rather, it might release the fullness of the sign, the plenitude and pleasure that the sign offers, quite apart from the usual labor of meaning. The aural satisfactions of verbal music and the visual satisfactions of verbal sculpture were pronounced in modernist poetry—in Apollinaire and in E. E. Cummings, for example—but they also belonged to experiment in the novel. Like Stein, Proust and Joyce, Woolf and Faulkner, and Dorothy Richardson, among others, understood the invention of new plots, new trajectories for human life, as closely tied to experiments with a nonsignifying language. Though connected, plots and words remain in tension: the desire to record new events often strains against the impulse to set language free from the claims of event.

The contest between formalism and fictive character is unresolved in "Melanctha." Even as Stein's story extends the literature of the case study, it makes character strange and distant. Melanctha is named and placed by a constellation of adjectives: pale, yellow, mysterious, pleasant, strong, sweet, patient, submissive, soothing, untiring, subtle, intelligent, attractive. These terms unfold and repeat, but they never settle into personality. Characterization is an excess and an indeterminacy. Either there are too many traits to make a single person, or the traits contradict one another, as in the description of Melanctha as "always seeking peace and quiet" while always finding "new ways to get excited" (92). This last example suggests a psychological diagnosis in the manner of Freud, but for Stein, the problem was always more linguistic than psychological. Language does build pictures of characters that are tense and evocative, but the pictures are the result of what Stein called "composition," the artificial workings of style, which she saw as a more radical act than any psychological judgment.

MODERNISM AS RACISM: STEIN'S "MELANCTHA"

"Melanctha" was a breakthrough work for Stein and for modernist formalism, but it is also an exemplary case of Modernism as racism. Michael North's description of the story as a "mixture of aesthetic experimentation and racist crudity" is incontestable.[59] The narrator speaks early of the "simple, promiscuous unmorality of the black people" (96), and beyond the staccato of racial epithets is the detachment of a roving eye that regards the black population of Bridgepoint as a collection of specimens to be fixed in a phrase; repeatedly evoked, for instance, is "the wide, abandoned laughter that makes the warm broad glow of negro sunshine." The narrator speaks casually of the "better sort of negroes" (96) and just as casually describes how the women enjoy a "good warm nigger time with colored men" (209).

Modernism had racism coursing through its development. A pervasive race-consciousness was partly due to the conditions of modernity (understood as the experience of new times) and modernization (the external habitus of change), which were themselves bound up with racism. The resurgent nationalism of the late nineteenth century brought hardening boundaries and exclusion: the making of new nations relied upon a hierarchy of races. Race was also constitutive to ideas of modernity, especially ideas of the primitive and the civilized, which helped to create the temporality of the modern. At the same time, whites considered nonwhite races to be raw material, meant to be organized by the administrators of the new economy, who often assigned skills according to racial and ethnic categories. Although such race-thinking was conspicuous in the United States, it appeared throughout the modernizing world. But Modernism itself, as an oppositional movement of culture, also turned to racism in many of its founding gestures. The separation from the corrupting clichés of journalism and the coarseness of middle-class opinion was also a separation from the discourse and habits of liberal tolerance. As the unfolding of the movement made clear, a progressive political disposition was not a natural concomitant of the adversary culture. The radicalism in the refusals of the adversary culture invited artists to entertain extreme social fantasies on both left and right.

Precisely in aiming toward an outside, toward an exotic site or a distant historical period, Modernism inevitably took up attitudes of distance, detachment, and fascination toward racial difference. Here the emerging discipline of anthropology played an important role. The writings of anthropologists brought the non-European world into the outside consciousness of the modernists; it drew the attention of artists to other Others. But anthropology produced complex effects on modernity. Partly owing to the spread of empire and partly owing to early missionary work, anthropology depended on the movements of Europeans around the world; in this respect it was entangled in the practices and often the assumptions of empire. Yet it was the armchair anthropology of James George Frazer that had the most immediate influence on the course of modernist culture.

Frazer's collocation of myths of the dying god, his proposal to connect those myths to early vegetation rites, his gift for assimilation, and the elegance of his prose all prepared *The Golden Bough* to become a major reference point and also to stimulate new tropes and new narratives.[60] It is clear, however, that the stimulus of *The Golden Bough*, as for much of the anthropology that surrounded it, worked in multiple directions. On the one hand, the tales of human sacrifice and primitive ritual confirmed a narrative of progress, the "toilsome ascent from savagery to civilisation," a long advance from superstition to rationality; Frazer's triadic scheme of magic, religion, and science could be taken as a shorthand summary of the upward course of enlightenment.[61] On the other hand, the link between Christianity and pagan ritual, though understated, was everywhere apparent. As John Vickery has written, *The Golden Bough* was "consciously directed to showing how the uniqueness of Christianity is dissolved in its emergence from primitive fertility cults."[62] In this way, the book laid the groundwork for a radical reinterpretation of progressivist history ("savagery to civilisation"). As more myths and legends were assimilated in each succeeding edition, evidence grew for the plurality of cultures and the relativity of beliefs. Within *The Golden Bough*, a narrative of enlightenment culminated in the anthropologist, a figure with a clear-sighted and comprehensive view of culture, but the skeptical force of cultural relativity soon became a corrosive instrument.

Anthropology incited a reinterpretation of the bases of modernity. It suggested innovations in form (patterns of speech and dialect, pictorial and sculptural styles), but it also helped to ensure that race was an inescapable presence for many artists and often an indelible stain on their art. Stein's coarseness in "Melanctha," the anti-Semitism of Pound and Eliot, the racism in Conrad's rendering of the Congo and Southeast Asia, are not to be explained away. Even more ambiguous examples, such as Synge's rendering of the Irish and Picasso's appropriation of African sculpture, display the centrality of race-thinking to modernist experiment.

What makes the issue most difficult is that the race-thinking of Modernism is often at one with its liberatory possibilities. Paul Peppis notes that "Melanctha" has been taken as both a landmark work of literary feminism and an object-instance of race-thinking and that its "rac(ial)ism" is "inseparable from and formative for its modernism."[63] This insight applies equally to other major modernist works. Chinua Achebe has made it impossible to ignore the racism of Conrad's *Heart of Darkness*—the absence of speech among the Africans, their reduction to little more than "black shapes," "black shadows of disease and starvation." [64] Conrad's entanglement in racialism is unmistakable, and yet *Heart of Darkness* does not leave race where it finds it. When the steamer moves upriver toward Kurtz, Marlow watches the "whirl of black limbs" of the natives on shore and describes himself as moving along "the edge of a black and incomprehensible frenzy." But it is at just this moment, he tells his listeners, that he also comes to "the thought of their humanity—like yours—the thought of your remote kinship with this wild and passionate uproar." The connection here is fragile; the kinship, after all, is "remote." But this encounter with racial Otherness prompts Conrad's Marlow to one of the most resonant sentences in turn-of-the-century Modernism: "The mind of man is capable of anything—because everything is in it, all the past as well as all the future" (38).

The democracy of impulse, the acknowledgment that every human gesture inheres in each psyche, and that what we call Other is always also within—this recognition is a foundational thought for Modernism. *Heart of Darkness* does not leave its race-thinking behind, but the acknowledgment of kinship suggests the surpassing of objectivity in favor of an incipient intersubjectivity. Race was an invitation to objectify the excluded human beings, especially those caught in the imperial network. But, as we have seen with Picasso's *Les Demoiselles d'Avignon,* the workings of Modernism contained another invitation—namely, a call to ponder the subjectivity of the race-marked individual. G. W. F. Hegel's massive insight is required here: "*Self-consciousness achieves its satisfaction only in another self-consciousness. . . .* A self-consciousness exists *for a self-consciousness.* Only so is it in fact self-consciousness; for only in this way does the unity of itself in its otherness become explicit for it."[65] The complex process that he describes unfolds within much work of the modernist epoch. A clinical detachment studies its human objects so precisely that it is compelled to realize (or to invent) their inwardness, agency, and will.

Stein's "Melanctha" continues to avail itself of racist categories and epithets, especially in relation to the faithless friend Rose, whose failings are always tied to her blackness. Yet the story also unsettles the categories that it exploits. It would be wrong (and sentimental) to suggest that the novel overcomes its race-thinking by adopting the standpoint of the racial Other, but the concentrated study of the fictive object that is Melanctha undoubtedly summons a complex subjectivity. The story invites the puzzle of racialized identity into its center, where Stein also meditates upon the vagaries of desire and the incoherence of personhood. The intersection of these questions destabilizes categories of race as much as it does those of subjectivity. Melanctha is repeatedly referred to as half-white and as having white blood, even as she is said to be the child of a black father and a "pleasant, pale yellow, colored woman." This contradictory identity, discussed by Corinne Blackmer, epitomizes the confusion of race in "Melanctha": a mixing of attributes that corresponds to a mixing of the blood and that blurs the color line at the heart of the story.[66]

MASS AND CASE, CLOSE-UP AND CROWD

Here we return to the mass, that other prominent incarnation of modernity, standing as counterweight and Other to modernist subjectivity and the case study. By the time of the First World War, film had become the most culturally important medium for the staging of mass collectivity. Nineteenth-century photography had helped to invent the self as the object of the case study, not only within the tradition of the family portrait but also for the marking of individuals as candidates for supervision and discipline. (An early use of the camera was to make a photographic record of those admitted to prisons and asylums.) The early opportunities for larger-than-individual photographic tableaux were real but limited. Movies, on the other hand, brought the crowd into the visual field, even as it created a new collective experience for its audiences. The appearance of feature-length films from 1913 on securely established the crowd as one of the chief protagonists in the new form.

D. W. Griffith's *Judith of Bethulia* (1913–1914) was the first American four-reeler and also Griffith's last work before he left Biograph for Reliance-Majestic Studios. The visual ambitions of the director, freed in a film of convention-breaking length, helped create a theater for the masses. In Bethulia—the hilltop town guarding a passage to Jerusalem—the townspeople swarm through narrow streets, exchanging goods in the markets, tending the fields, and fetching water according to the usual daily rhythms until they are attacked by marauding Assyrians. In representing the invaders, Griffith is faithful to the image in the Apocrypha: "A great number also of sundry countries came with them like locusts, and like the sand of the earth: for the multitude was without number"—there were so many that they seemed to "lick up the face of the earth" (Judith 2:20). The multitudes clash. Assyrians approach to destroy or to scale the walls of the town. The Israelites panic, recover, and organize a response. As the equally matched forces reach an impasse, Holofernes prepares for a siege and the inexorable work of starvation.

The film loosely follows the biblical narrative as it had been recently retold—in verse and then on stage—by Thomas Bailey Aldrich. But the narrative was also a pretext for an exercise in form: the staging of the multitude to create a kinetic fascination as it gathered and dispersed, charged and faltered, moved as a swarm of insects or as a tribe of stick figures, perpetually making and undoing shapes on the screen.

Judith is the solitary figure beyond the mass. Above the street, apart from the roiling crowd, kneeling in prayer or lost in meditation, the widow of Manasses is intact and separate. The camera loves, and lingers over, her. The shots of the lone Judith, reverential and beautiful, mark a telling stage in the history of close framing and the close-up. Lit in high contrast, with whitened face against black robes, she is preserved from scenes of frenzy and kept for the private gaze of the camera. Griffith describes the visual logic that brought about the close-up: "When you saw only the small, full-length figures, it was necessary to have exaggerated acting, what might be called 'physical' acting, the waving of hands and so on. The close-up enabled us to reach real acting, restraint, acting that is a duplicate of real life."[67] Judith is marked out and separated from all others, her whitened face above black robes, then above a sackcloth, and finally above the plumed costume of seduction, the "garments of gladness." Even within the terms of the silent era, this film is noisy with scenes of aggression and panic, open mouths and frantic bodies. But Judith remains an image of quiet on a different visual plane.[68] Set against the exteriority of the crowd, she appears capable of inwardness, reflection, and thought. Much of the labor of the film is to establish the eminent individual, the heroic woman, as both self-contained and expressive, as a fully integral person even when others come near, and as an inviolate body that protects the inner life that shows through the eyes. Judith, as the Bible teaches, is inviolate. A widow, who knows the ways of carnal desire, she can entice the Assyrian warrior Holofernes into passion, drunkenness, and senseless stupor. ("Her sandals ravished his eyes, her

beauty took his mind prisoner, and the fauchion passed through his neck";
Judith 7:4). When she beheads him and carries the prize back to Bethulia,
she completes the work of an individual that can save community.

The film's narrative records the struggle between two peoples, Assyrians and Israelites, but the visual form stages a different struggle: between
the furious mass surging across the screen and the radiant individual in
close-up, each a distinctive spectacle of the young medium. From this perspective, the real triumph is not the resistance of the Jews but the heroic
resistance of the sharply visualized individual, the celebrity actor, her inviolate separate shape. The two contending masses are in this sense just a
single mass, the cinematic multitude, while Judith represents the other landmark, the indomitable self as expressive, distinct, luminous.

High modernists in the years before the First World War often saw
themselves in urgent struggle against the multitude. They asserted the rights
of experiment in the face of a resistant citizenry (Joyce's "rabblement") that
was given to lower pleasures and held in thrall by the new mass journalism
and mass entertainment. Modernist narrative emerges in large part through
a negotiation between the pressures of the collective and the claims of exceptionality. The acceptance, and even the cultivation, of difficulty is one
conspicuous sign. The difficulty of the new works received many aesthetic
justifications, but no justification could conceal the social effects: the creation of a widening gap between the initiated and the benighted.

Between the case study and the mass is where Modernism so frequently
found itself, and before the war its practitioners' most frequent impulse
was to pursue the case study and to parry the challenge of the mass. In the
"War-Number" of *Blast*, Wyndham Lewis began his unfinished story "The
Crowd Master," set during the days of mass mobilization. Its protagonist, a
man called Blenner, wanders through a London dominated by the human
mass, which moves as a single organism, a "huge indefinite Internment."[69]
The sketch turns on the encounter—stark, ineradicable—between the Ego
and the Crowd, a distinction that becomes the final truth of experience.

THE INDIVIDUAL and THE CROWD: PEACE and WAR.
Man's solitude and Peace; Man's Community and Row. (94)

Within the dreamscape of imminent war, the crowd stretches its "thick
well-nourished coils all over the town" while Blenner fortifies himself with
a book he has found on Charing Cross Road, *The Crowd Master*, whose
author he then improbably meets.

THE CROWD MASTER. What might that mean? His bright astonished eyes fixed on the words, drinking up a certain strength from them.

An opposition of and welding of the two heaviest words that stand for the multitude on the one hand, the Ego on the other.

That should be something! (99)

In a painting called *The Crowd*, which can be seen as a companion piece to the unfinished tale, Lewis constructed a large grid of unbroken rectangles, several of which contain tiny humanoid figures crawling upon one another (see fig. 11). The figures are securely enclosed within the boxes that surround them; the herd of featureless individuals is segmented and controlled, trapped in the stiff geometry of the grid. Here, in visual space, Lewis repeats the gesture performed in the story: the artist circumscribes, and thereby dominates, the crowd.

"The deepest problems of modern life derive from the claim of the individual to preserve the autonomy of his existence in the face of overwhelming social forces of historical heritage, of external culture, of the technique of life."[70] These are the opening words of Georg Simmel's influential essay "The Metropolis and Mental Life," in which the author unhesitatingly takes up the problem of modernity from the standpoint of the individual. Simmel might, after all, have identified the central agent as the family, the couple, the community, or the class, each of which also struggled for existence against the same demanding social forces. But if Simmel's focus on the autonomy of selfhood seems narrow, it conforms to many of the prewar narratives with which it is contemporaneous. The escape from the conventions of the marriage plot, the Nietzschean call for an Overman, the Freudian excavation of density within the psyche, the Carlylean image of the writer as hero, and the lineage of strong selves inside and outside artworks (Napoléon, Byron, Madame Bovary, Walt Whitman, Nora, Rimbaud, the suffragettes), but also the passive and weary selves of decadence and the humiliated selves collected by Krafft-Ebing and Freud—all converge in a narrative project that became vastly ambitious just before the war.

Still, it should be clear that for all the labor of self-making and all the formal virtuosity in rendering consciousness, these works remain haunted by powers that exceed the individual. The crowd will not be mastered by a single story or painting; the desire that intensifies the sense of solitude also drives the self toward an Other; the voice that refines its own singularity is interrupted by shouts in the street.

3

the modernist lyric "i":
from baudelaire to eliot

In Paris in the 1880s, in salons and literary reviews and steadily in the wider press, an early epitome of a modernist circle found its shape. A series of extreme gestures—prophetic, obscure, insinuating—emanated from a loose confederation of poets. Baudelaire, recently republished and recently dead, became the cherished precursor, even as his enthusiasm for Poe was revived. Poets who had worked separately came to acknowledge one another, and when Verlaine christened them "poètes maudits" (accursed poets), they assumed, whether they chose it or not, the look of a collective insurgency.

REALISM, FORMALISM, SYMBOLISM

The emergence of Symbolism, a history that we rejoin here, should be placed against the double background of realism and formalism. On one side, a succession of novels—by Flaubert, the brothers Goncourt, and Zola —pressed the claim for unrelenting realist austerity. It would expose the lies of sentimentality and romance; it would display the truth of individual desire and class conflict; it would not hesitate to use rude names for coarse reality. On the other side stood the virtuosity of the Parnassians (among them Charles-Marie-René Leconte de Lisle and Théodore de Banville), who admired Théophile Gautier in his resistance to both utilitarian practicality and visionary Romanticism. Parnassian formalism developed under the banner of Gautier's overcharged slogan, "Art for art's sake," a defense of the beauties of the verbal surface, of musical design and lyric precision— the poem as a self-warranting and self-legitimating form. Tautly burnished verse was its own justification, because the vocation of poetry was the perfection of craft, not the summons of infinity. The Parnassians joined the realists in refusing the mystifying rhetoric of Romanticism and its soaring ideals.

The terms "Romanticism," "realism," and "Parnassianism" are notoriously broad, and yet early modernist history unfolded beneath these rubrics. They became instruments of self-definition, often by way of negation. The repudiation of Romantic excess was one aspect of the history. A second, intersecting tendency was a critique of both Parnassian formalism and realist representation. Symbolism belonged to this second moment. Without calling for a return to Romanticism, its leading voices contested the terrain of the New. The symbolists saw both the visible word of realism and the perfect rhyme of Parnassianism as narrowly confining domains. In response, they espoused suggestion, evocation, and music—for the conjuring of a world beyond everyday practice and perception. We recall Mallarmé's dictum: "To *name* the object is to destroy three-quarters of the enjoyment of the poem."[1] The poetic Symbol could be a sound, a scent, or a memory, incarnating the invisible meanings of the world or intimating a mystery beyond the senses. Yet the Symbol was not a return to romantic vision. Even as it refused the sordid world and the limits of form, it remained within its own cherished circumscription. It was not a public utterance. It was esoteric and partial rather than accessible and total.

Nevertheless, the affinities between Symbolism and Romanticism are deep and intricate. Even as many symbolist poets gave up the grandeur of prophecy and the lure of an encompassing myth, they shared a romantic disdain for mere matter and settled social habits, a desire to transcend empirical knowledge, and a pursuit of new sensations as signs of a new form of life. Symbolism can be seen as a Romanticism obliged to live after the advent of militant realism, formalism, and historical defeatism. As we have seen, there was a defensiveness in its early posture, a sense of writing in the face of overwhelming encroachments. On one side, Symbolism faced the industrializing economy and a political impasse; on the other, it confronted the successes of realism and the prestige of Parnassian craft. In these circumstances, a return to Romanticism was inconceivable.

BAUDELAIRE AMONG THE APPARITIONS

The career of Baudelaire took place during the decades of late Romanticism, the Parnassian reaction, and the publication of Flaubert's fiction. The poet took all these events into account, commenting often on the contradictions of his milieu, alternately deploring and applauding the modernizing pressures that surrounded him. Baudelaire was among the first to make modernity a subject of reflection, which is partly why he has been so fertile a subject for theorists and historians. His essay "The Painter of Modern Life" memorably asserts, "Modernity is that which is ephemeral, fugitive, contingent upon the occasion; it is half of art, whose other half is the eternal and unchangeable."[2] Baudelaire refuses the dominance of classical beauty and timeless norms and defends the claims of the present, insisting that "a love of universal beauty, as expressed by the classical poets and artists, is no excuse for ignoring particular beauty—the beauty of the occasion, and of day-to-day existence" (23). The attention to the fleeting, contingent, impermanent character of the new times became a cardinal tenet of cultural modernity.

Yet Baudelaire's resistance to a theory of Modernism should not be ignored. Even as he vindicates the rights of the fugitive present, he upholds the dignity of a classical past. He makes modernity only "half of art," asserting that "every old-time painter had his own modernity" (37). This is as much as to say that *every* present tense has the same claim upon art and that the modernizing forces of the nineteenth century are not distinctive despite their speed, their commodities, their decadence, their masses. As Marshall Berman points out, such a position "empties the idea of modernity of all its specific weight, its concrete historical content. It makes any and all times 'modern times'; ironically, by spreading modernity through all history, it leads us away from the special qualities of our own modern history."[3]

Still it is not hard to see why Baudelaire is often regarded as an originating modernist. He is the one, in Walter Benjamin's insightful reading, who experienced the shock effect of modernity and who connected that shock to the metropolitan crowd. Yet Benjamin, like Berman, acknowledges the double valence of Baudelaire's modernity. Baudelaire submits himself to the new age—its jolts, its agonies—but often seems to adore the world that undoes him. Berman emphasizes the poet's apparently sincere embrace of the bourgeoisie and its thrusting material progress, the fitful moments of revulsion against the world that he elsewhere claims to love. These are unreconciled contradictions. Rather than see them as mere personal inconsistencies, we do better to locate them within the conditions of Baudelaire's career and his strategies of response.

In the more than a hundred poems of the second edition of *Les Fleurs du mal,* Baudelaire invents both a lyric "I" and a world of apparitions, which alternate in precedence. Sometimes the "I" commands a poem from the start and devises the strange pageant. At other times the world shows itself first, spreads itself out as in a theater, and then is suddenly revealed to be not a world in itself but only something conjured in verse. These two regions, the "I" and its apparitions, come as close to each other as possible, but they rarely meet. Equally spectral, they can pass through one another. The principle is enunciated in "The Painter of Modern Life" where Baudelaire, speaking of the visual art of Constantin Guys (but revealing himself), writes of the artist-flâneur, whose vocation is "to behold the world, to be in the midst of the world, and yet to remain hidden from the world" (33).

The virtuosity of the Baudelairean "I" is that it can generate the phantasms that then turn back upon the "I." "Un Voyage à Cythère" (A Voyage to Cytherea) summons an idyll—"Le navire roulait sous un ciel sans nuages" ("The ship was rolling beneath a cloudless sky")—only to let it dissolve into abomination.[4] Cytherea, by legend "Belle île aus myrtes vertes" ("Beautiful isle of green myrtle"; 207), transforms into a dismal island where birds feed on a corpse rotting upon a gibbet. The vision rises to a pitch of horror —eyes becoming black holes, intestines falling to the thighs—at which point the perspective suddenly shifts:

> Ridicule pendu, tes douleurs sont les miennes!
> Je sentis, à l'aspect de tes membres flottants,
> Comme un vomissement, remonter vers mes dents
> Le long fleuve de fiel desire douleurs anciennes;
>
> Devant toi, pauvre diable au souvenir si cher,
> J'ai senti tous les becs et toutes les mâchoires
> Des corbeaux lancinants et des panthers noires
>
> (209)

> (Ridiculous hanged man, your sorrows are mine!
> I felt, at the sight of your drooping limbs,
> Like vomit, rise through my teeth
> The long bilious river of my ancient sorrows.
>
> Before you, poor devil so dear to memory,
> I felt all the beaks and all the jaws
> Of the raging crows and the black panthers)

And then in the final stanza we read

> Dans ton île, ô Venus! je n'ai trouvé debout
> Q'un gibet symbolique où pendait mon image . . .
>
> (209)

(On your isle, O Venus, I found standing
Only a symbolic gallows, where my image hung.)

Here is the unstable circuit of "I" and apparition. The voice projects an
unreal, uncanny scene, which assumes the power of objectivity. It becomes
a dreadful fragment of the universe that can be walked around, inspected,
and suffered. Then, in another turn, the objective apparition dissolves and
shows itself as a phantom of the self. The poem projects the image outward,
releasing it into a public space where the reader, too, can sniff and suffer,
and only then reappropriates and internalizes it.

The place of the reader is telling. As the poems shift between inner and
outer worlds, marking distinctions only to erode them, they intimate a
similar fate for us. In the indelible lines from the volume's opening, "Au
Lecteur" (To the Reader), we helplessly read:

Tu le connais, lecteur, ce monstre délicat,
—Hypocrite lecteur,—mon semblable,—mon frère!

(7)

(You know him, reader, this fastidious monster,
—Hypocritical reader,—my fellow,—my brother.)

Simply by understanding the words in sequence, the reader becomes the
figure invented by the poet. We readers play the part of an objectivity seized
by the speaker in the poem and recruited as props in his drama. Much of
the scandal of Baudelaire's poetry was inflamed by its refusal to stand apart
as marginal, eccentric, or lunatic. The address to the reader insists that we
will not be able to keep ourselves apart. If nothing can prevent the poet
from imagining us, how can we protect our own imaginations?

But Baudelaire's "I" possesses its greatest strength in weakness. The
moments of assertion are only a flaring within a scene of abandonment. By
presenting itself as a compound of vices, defects, and terrors, the voice becomes a force of contagion, as if the best way to erase distinctions between
Self and Other is not to batter the fortress of the moral reader but to imply
the intimacy of low desire. Part of the giddy subversion of *Les Fleurs du mal*
is to build a community of those who know in spite of themselves: "Tu le
connais"—you know it, as I know it. Another name for that community is
Paris, which appears as a web of consciousness-in-degradation; Baudelaire
recognizes himself as a product of the modernizing city as much as its poet.
This is what gives the work its eerie oscillation. The "I" continues to sum-

mon a world even as it offers itself as an effect of that world, an emanation from powers beyond its control.

Les Fleurs du mal shows that all sensations are aftereffects, dependent on the contingencies of history. If the poems undo the naïveté of self-will, they also show disenchantment as itself a kind of naïveté. Horror is no more stable than paradise. It, too, lives in changing times that it cannot command. Much interpretation of Baudelaire's urban modernity has rightly stressed the role of accident and chance. But there is still another specter. Living through 1848 and its aftermath, enduring the Second Empire and the transformation in Paris, Baudelaire had good reason to see the city as rife with plots and plans, the streets as scenes of chaos, looming faces, and receding backs, but also rife with malevolent intention. In part, he is responding to imperial politics and revolutionary resistance, each of which eyed the other suspiciously while concealing its own designs.[5] But in Baudelaire the emphasis falls on the designs of the dispossessed: the gamblers twitching with hopes around the gaming board, the ragpicker with grand plans ("glorieux projets"), the wine drinker scheming for a glass. These figures incubate their intentions and create a counterforce to chance. The world may not be graced by a divine plan, but it is saturated with local intrigue.

The most charged manifestation of intention/intrigue lies in the erotic spectacles of the poems: the desires of a lover but also the stratagems of a prostitute. The fascinations and revulsions of sexuality occupy the center of the Baudelairean universe, but they too are effects of the discontinuous city. Inward spaces—rooms and tombs, as well as the inwardness of subjectivity—interrupt the network of streets. *Les Fleurs du mal* moves abruptly from the promenades of the flâneur to the interior scenes of ceremonial, often-debased desire. Here the sensation lies not in the apparition of a swan or an old man but in the slower rituals of baffled desire.

> La très-chère était nue, et, connaissant mon coeur,
> Elle n'avait gardè que ses bijoux sonores.
>
> *(261)*

> (My cherished one was naked, and, knowing my heart,
> She wore only her reverberant jewels.)

"Les Bijoux" begins with this tableau of the naked lover arranging the stretch of her body and revealing her jewels, whose display gives her a conquering air ("Dont le riche attirail lui donnait l'air vainqueur"). As so often in Baudelaire's poetry, the lyric opens on a scene of enthrallment, where fascination overwhelms the speaker. Indeed, the shiver lies exactly in a self-forgetting, an inability to say "I." But even as the speaker neglects to speak, he quickens at the prospect of being spoken for—at having all his desires known, his pleasures anticipated. Intention and action belong to her because she has absorbed his desires, the run of his fantasy.

> Et son bras et sa jambe, et sa cuisse et ses reins,
> Polis comme de l'huile, onduleux comme un cygne,
> Passaient devant mes yeux clairvoyants et sereins.
>
> *(261–262)*

> (And her arm and her leg, and her thigh and her loins,
> Polished like oil, swaying like a swan,
> Passed before my eyes, clairvoyant and serene.)

The space between the bodies, the gap between two subjectivities, the distance between desire and object, and the reversal of agency—this is the field of Baudelairean eroticism. The thrill resides not in reciprocity but in unequal power, as in "La Géante," where "I" imagines a leisurely passage along her momentous forms ("Parcourir à loisir ses magnifiques formes") and a nap in the shadow of her breasts ("Dormir nonchalamment à l'ombre de ses seins"; 35). But in "Les Bijoux," such a vision of paradise is interrupted by the upsurge of desire. The lover can always rouse herself, refuse to stay in place, break the enthrallment. In the sixth stanza, after posing and stretching, she moves toward "I" and shatters the enclosure of the dream. Here is the self-erasing logic of fantasy. The sinuous ("onduleux") dance of arms and legs breaks the reverie and leads toward sexual contact, as if it were impossible to preserve the spectacle of a daydream; sooner or later it had to become the embrace of bodies.

> Et son ventre et ses seins, ces grappes de ma vigne,
>
> S'avançaient, plus câlins que les Anges du mal,
> Pour troubler le repos où mon âme était mise,
> Et pour la déranger du rocher de cristal
> Où, calme et solitaire, elle s'était assise.
>
> *(262)*

> (And her belly and breasts, clusters of my grapevine,
>
> Came forward, more seductive than the Angels of Evil,
> To trouble the rest where my soul was set,

And to disturb the crystalline rock
Where, calm and solitary, it had taken seat.)

Freud writes that sooner or later all desire makes an image of its fulfillment. Baudelaire explores the reverse proposition: that an image will eventually create the desire that undoes it. Contemplation, then, is always aesthetic/ erotic, and in "Les Bijoux" (The Jewels) the invisible line between image and desire is drawn only to be crossed. As the lover comes close to the speaker, he makes a new design ("un nouveau dessin"; 262), but the body— with its waist, hips, and rouged face—breaks the clarity of line.

The poem elides the act of lovemaking. Its last stanza depicts the aftermath, when the quiet body of the lover is again available to form, and open to calmer vision, as the speaker watches her body under the flickering light. The violence in the figure—the lamp washes with blood the skin that is the color of amber ("Il inondait de sang cette peau couleur d'ambre"; 262)—is the violence of formal mastery reasserting its claim. It is also a return to the distance of spectacle. Although the lover is as close as possible, she recedes to an absolute distance, becoming something to be gazed upon and then ornamented in language.

"Les Bijoux" has the recurrent Baudelairean rhythm: it begins by evoking a spectacle in the world; then, under the pressure of desire (or aversion), the vision compels a response in the "I," which often appears only in the middle of a lyric; and finally, the agitated "I" withdraws again, left to contemplate the ruins of spectacle. The unit of Les Fleurs du mal is the single reverie (the unfolding of a self-contained tableau, the staging of a desire, the course of a fantasy). This reverie, whether as mood or experiment, is not sustained beyond the miniature. Even a scene of ultimacy, as in "L'Héautontimorouménos" ('The Self-Tormentor'), comes to conclusion quickly and leaves no traces.

One effect of the miniature scale is that subjectivity has no career. In place of continuity, there is the erratic reappearance of a pronoun. This "I" remembers having lived before but assumes no responsibility for its precedents, nor does it take on the burden of self-narrative. Each new flower of evil finds the "I" responsive again but no more capable of mastery. In "Le Cygne," this condition is explicitly announced: "Paris changes! but nothing has shifted in my melancholy!" ("Paris change! mais rien dans ma mélancolie/n'a bougé!"; 151). We may take this as a central state of Les Fleurs du mal. The world is inconstant and impulsive; the city alters, and so do the performances of eroticism. Paris with its new palaces, scaffolding, and blocks ("palais neufs, échafaudages, blocs"; 151) and the body with its invitations create a universe writhing beyond the self. The fugitive city repeats and resembles metamorphic sexuality.

And yet the "I" that encounters these two heaving immensities (body and city) remains in a circle of repetition. When Baudelaire sighs that his melancholy has not changed, or when he greets his boredom again, he suggests that modernist subjectivity has a formidable posture—namely, that it attains certain extreme states (ecstasy, melancholy) whose challenge is that they recur *in the same aspect*. The poems of *Les Fleurs du mal* achieve an extraordinary variety, but not through the shape of the "I." Indeed, the shock of the poetry lies often in a return of the same desperation, the same terror, for an "I" that cannot transcend its immediacy. The first-person verbs tend to be simple and bald—I love, I see, I breathe, I smell—even as the objects of perception become breathtakingly intricate.

The depthlessness of subjectivity creates an uncanny effect. "I" appears as a screen or membrane, as if its inner world has been depleted, eviscerated by ennui or melancholy. It looks within, and finding only a stock language for understanding its sensations (boredom, melancholy), it is driven outward to engage phantasmagoria. "They march ahead" ("Ils marchent devant moi"; 71) begins one lyric; "The deafening street shrieked around me" ("La rue assourdissante autour de moi hurlait"; 161) begins another. In significant ways, these lines describe the condition of all of *Les Fleurs du mal*. The swarming object-world is rich, dense, diverse, and theatrical, whereas selfhood dwindles to an invisible point. But even as subjectivity abandons itself to others (to their accidents, intrigues, desires), it retains the claim of verse. The speaker suddenly rouses himself and puts a frame around the world that has framed him. The effect, distinctive and influential, is that the lyrics hover between sensation and object. The lyrics project themselves outward, toward a world that remains at a distance, spectacular and seductive but always on the point of dissolving into the sensations of the depthless "I," which reserves the final privilege of bestowing aesthetic form.

MALLARMÉ'S LEAKING CRYPT

The relationship between Baudelaire and his later readers is as complicated as the dance between the "I" and its lovers. Much of the force of the poetry was posthumous. Baudelaire achieved significant recognition in his lifetime, but the low value bestowed on lyric poetry, the eminence of Victor Hugo, the censorship of several of Baudelaire's poems, and his personal struggles deferred the provocation of *Les Fleurs du mal*. The revival of lyric poetry achieved by Symbolism in the 1880s marked a decisive moment. It brought prominence (even reverence) to Baudelaire; but even as members of the symbolist movement enshrined his work, they often considered it a cherished precedent, belonging to a superseded past. Having defiantly testified to the lure of the senses, Baudelaire still appeared encumbered by the worldliness that Symbolism looked to escape. So Arthur Symons, an early and influential proponent of his work, could write, "Even Baudelaire, in whom the spirit is always an uneasy guest at the orgie of life, had a certain theory of realism, which tortures many of his poems into strange, metallic shapes, and fills them with imitative odours, and disturbs them with a too deliberate rhetoric of the flesh."[6] Baudelaire became part of a modernist narrative in the generation of the symbolists, but he was to have a greater effect on the next generation.

Stéphane Mallarmé appears here as the author of formidable poems that still resist reading, and as a second, comparably mythologized figure of an emergent lyric Modernism. His career makes a strange sequel to Baudelaire's. Mallarmé's early poems were written under the shadow and inspiration of *Les Fleurs du mal,* but they reinvented the sources they acknowledged and reinterpreted Baudelaire's project even before it had taken on shape and definition. As understood here, that project was the fate of lyric subjectivity in conditions of extremity, and Mallarmé's innovation was to pursue such states through exacting impersonality. Here is how he cast the question in a haunting letter of 1867.

> I've just spent a terrifying year: my Thought has thought itself and reached a pure Concept. All that my being has suffered as a result during that long death cannot be told, but, fortunately, I am utterly dead . . . I confess, moreover, but to you alone, that the torments inflicted by my triumph were so great, I still need to look at myself in that mirror in order to think and that if it were not in front of this desk on which I'm writing to you, I would become the Void once again. That will let you know that I am now impersonal and no longer the Stéphane that you knew,—but a capacity possessed by the spiritual Universe to see itself and develop itself, through what was once me.[7]

"What was once me"—this is the charged utterance capturing the self-estrangement and self-overcoming of Mallarmé's work. Baudelaire achieved many of his most unsettling effects by representing a lyric "I" that may, or may not, be understood to stand for the poet. *Les Fleurs du mal* heightens and stylizes the real; none of its events can be taken as straightforward testimony. Yet, as "Baudelaire" became the name for a principle of modernity, the lyrics were inevitably read as signature events in the life of the poet. Mallarmé, on the other hand, insisted on a rigorous depersonalization that refused biographical transitions between a lyric and its author.

Begun in 1864 and published in *Le Parnasse contemporain* (1869–1871), "Hérodiade" was the first crystallization of Mallarmé's rigorous initiative. As he labored on the poem during the next thirty years, it took on an overture and then a concluding canticle. But in its first publication, the entire poem was its "Scène," the dialogue between Hérodiade and her nurse, which opens as follows.

> N.
> Tu vis! ou vois-je ici l'ombre d'une princesse?
> A mes lèvres tes doigts et leurs bagues et cesse
> De marcher dans un âge ignoré . . .
>
> (Are you a living princess or her shadow?
> Let me kiss your fingers and their rings, and bid you
> Walk no longer in an unknown age . . .)
>
>
> H.
>   Reculez.
> Le blond torrent de mes cheveux immaculés
> Quand il baigne mon corps solitaire le glace
> D'horreur, et mes cheveux que la lumière enlace
> Sont immortels. O femme, un baiser me tûrait
> Si la beauté n'était la mort . . .
>
>   (Forbear.
> The blond torrent of immaculate hair
> Bathing my lonely body, freezes it
> With horror, and my tresses laced with light
> Are deathless. A kiss would kill me, woman,
> If beauty were not death . . .)[8]

Hérodiade is fierce in the service of her intactness and apartness. She folds back into herself, gazes in the mirror, and draws away from touch, all the while discoursing on hatred, boredom, horror, and bitterness. The poem is a monument of self-constitution. "I love the horror of virginity," says Hérodiade ("J'aime l'horreur d'être vierge"); and she asks, "Who would dare

touch one of the lions left alone? / I want nothing human" ("qui me touch-
erait, des lions respectée? / Du reste, je ne veux rien d'humain"; 33). She has
been called "perhaps the supreme expression of narcissism in modern literature, but a Narcissus intellectualized, tormented and maddened in her
intoxication before the mirror, yet finding in this torment the fullest pleasure that life can hold."[9] Making a fetish of herself and her body, she invents
a rhetoric of "je" and "me" (I and me) that makes the pronouns into characters in their own right.

Oui, c'est pour moi, pour moi, que je fleuris, déserte!

(Yes, it's for myself, for myself, that I bloom, deserted!)

(33)

The repetition—"pour moi, pour moi"—is like the mirror at which she
gazes. It lets her dwell, lovingly, hatefully, on the sign of the self: word, image,
body. At the same time, the division prepares for a more profound transaction in the poem.

Mallarmé's early hope was to see "Hérodiade" performed in a theater,
and in evident ways, the plan seems absurd. The poem is built on word, not
gesture; its images are elusive, its rhetoric sumptuous, its conclusion obscure; it offers none of the satisfactions then available on the Parisian stage.
Yet Mallarmé's fascination with the theater reflects the inescapably dialogic
subjectivity of the poem. If Hérodiade is a narcissist, her narcissism has to
be recovered from entanglement in the not-self. The Nurse begins the scene
with a startled recognition: "Tu vis! ou vois-je ici l'ombre d'une princesse?"
("Are you a living princess or her shadow?" 29). Hérodiade's response, "Re-
culez," establishes both the drama of the poem and the labor of narcissism.
There can be no caressing of subjectivity. Even to possess a voice is to enter
into a strenuous transaction with another. Meanwhile, the Other, the Nurse,
assails Hérodiade, lays siege to her self-devotion. The Nurse attempts to
kiss her—"A mes lèvres tes doigts" ("Your fingers to my lips")—then offers
her perfume, and finally reaches for her hair. Each time Hérodiade recoils
and refuses the advance. Here is the insight that no doubt attracted Mallarmé to the theater: that perfection of the self can be achieved only through
traffic with another, including the other of oneself. As the poem ends, "I"
and "you" become confused. All Hérodiade can do is fabricate subjectivity
from within self-estrangement.

"As far as I am concerned," Mallarmé remarked in an interview, "the
situation of a poet, in this society, which does not allow him to live, is that

of a man who isolates himself to sculpt his own tomb."[10] The evocative image resonates through the history of Modernism. But it also has an immediate bearing on "Hérodiade." The poem aims toward the consummation of finality. The heroine's body reflects the body of the poem: both aim toward self-containment unbetrayed by any stain. During the long period of composition, Mallarmé wrote that "the subject of my work is Beauty and its ostensible subject is merely a pretext for approaching Beauty."[11] His letters refer continually to the "beloved torture" of "Hérodiade," to the compound of pleasure-pain that describes the labor of writing and the fate of the heroine. As both a formal and a psychological enactment, "Hérodiade" stages the quest for a perfect self-possession. As Mallarmé dreams of the fully corrected poem with no more errors, so Hérodiade exerts a will to sustain herself without the imperfections of others. In both aspects, the poem is the building of a crypt.

Nothing is more striking than the failure of the project. The self-enfolding artifact (psyche, body, poem) fails to secure impenetrability. The crypt leaks. In one sense, this is because subjectivity is disclosed as riven from the start: it can never secure its integrity. The Nurse is the pressure that emanates from others; to turn away from the Nurse is only to find the outside already within. As the "Scène" ends, Hérodiade is left in swarming bewilderment, her narcissism scattered into fragments of past and future, body and consciousness.

In the midst of writing "Hérodiade," Mallarmé broke off to write his summer poem, "L'Après-midi d'un faune."[12] On the surface, the two poems are contraries. The young woman who would possess herself and repulse every desire stands against the avid Faun, who longs to tumble with nymphs. This is indeed a significant contrast that will unfold through the history of gender in Modernism. But it is also an unstable opposition, masking an identity. Our Faun asks, "Aimai-je un rêve?" ("Did I love a dream?"; 38), and every word in the utterance claims an emphasis and opens an uncertainty: Was it a *dream* that I loved? Was it *love* that I felt? Was that *I*?

It is right to say, as is often said, that the poem performs the sublimation of desire into art. The Faun summons images of the two nymphs he would like to "perpetuate" ("je les veux perpétuer"; 38), but when they are gone, he can find no murmuring apart from the blowing of his pipes—the visible, serene, and artificial air ("Le visible et serein souffle artificiel"). A trajectory that Freud will extend is lightly sketched here. When desire surrenders (or is forced to surrender) its objects, then the pleasures of form can be achieved. But Mallarmé offers no straightforward diagram of sublimation. The Faun is in search of reeds for his pipe when he first glimpses "animal whiteness" ("une blancheur animale"; 39). Art, or the will to art, *precedes desire.* When he begins playing, he achieves no aesthetic distance, no escape from the body and its sensations. The arc of the poem is not toward the ascendancy of art but toward the permanence of the art-desire circuit. In the poem's last phases, the Faun surrenders the nymphs to pursue more visions. "Others will lead me to happiness" ("vers le bonheur d'autres m'entraîneront"), he remarks; and as he drifts toward languid sleep, he prepares to love another dream.

> Sans plus il faut dormir en l'oubli du blasphème,
> Sur le sable altéré gisant et comme j'aime
> Ouvrir ma bouche à l'astre efficace des vins!
>
> Couple, adieu; je vais voir l'ombre que tu devins.
>
> (And so, let me sleep, oblivious of sin,
> Stretched out on the thirsty sand, drinking in
> The bountiful rays of the wine-growing star!
>
> Couple, farewell; I'll see the shade that now you are.)
>
> *(41)*

These two lyric scenarios, conceived at the beginning of Mallarmé's career but prolonged through revision, constitute archetypes of modernity: the languorous male, swollen with desire, and the overwrought female, tense and wakeful. The weary Faun sinks into the eternal swarm of desire ("l'essaim éternel du désir"; 41); Hérodiade remains vigilant, proud, and unreconciled. These two figures collide and diverge through the last third of the nineteenth century. They establish the terms for the revaluation of sex and gender, and at the same time they furnish topoi for modernist representation.

What they share is the incompletion of "I." The protagonists of both poems live in the ruins of subjectivity. The Faun wants to hold and clutch and penetrate the nymphs, who disappear (were they ever there?) and who can now only exist, only be "perpetuated," in the Faun's dreams of the swooning creatures. Hérodiade wants to keep others away from her self-regard; she clutches an essential selfhood, but the more firmly she holds it, the more thoroughly she is dispersed. In each case the "I" fails to coincide with itself, to possess itself, or to discharge its desires. It divides within, through either dream or self-objectification, even as it is vulnerable to disturbances from outside (the solicitation of the Nurse or the apparition of the nymphs).

Mallarmé is at once the exemplar and the theorist of autonomy, and he is a central case for later claims that Modernism makes a cult of the autonomous artifact: self-contained, self-justifying. "The pure work," he wrote, "implies the elocutionary disappearance of the poet, who yields the initiative to the words."[13] The art-object as a system of internal relations, generating its meanings from within, indifferent to the biographical artist and audience—this is the epitome of autonomy. Beyond the autonomous work, there is the notorious question of *Le Livre* (The Book), the inclusive volume that would justify the life of the poet. A letter of 1867 not only discloses Mallarmé's own aspiration but also describes a recurrent dream of Modernism.

> I've worked infinitely hard this summer, on myself first of all, creating, through the most beautiful synthesis, a world of which I am the God,— and on a Work which will result from that world, and will be, I hope, pure and magnificent. . . . I'm allowing twenty years to complete it, and the remainder of my life will be devoted to an Aesthetics of Poetry. Everything is in draft form, I've only to determine the place of certain internal poems, a place which is predestined and mathematical. My entire life has its *idea,* and all my minutes work toward creating it. I am planning to publish everything together and to detach fragments of it only for my close friends.[14]

Recall Mallarmé's memorable sentence: "Everything in the world exists to end in a book."[15] And consider his testimony to Verlaine, where again he speaks of his life's work as the creation of "a book, architectural and premeditated, and not an anthology of random inspirations, however marvelous. . . . The orphic explanation of the Earth is the sole duty of the poet."[16] The total work will justify the whole life. Moreover, once the world exists in the book, it will surrender its independence and live only within the autonomous work that completes it.

This vision of totality, self-sufficiency, ultimacy—literature as the secular Bible—loomed over Modernism. The autonomous *Livre,* the book of the world, the complete unity of text and career, remained an ideal for others, a modernist blazon, carried forward into the twentieth century. But the incompletion of the project is an equally important legacy. Mallarmé wrote occasional poems, among them acts of homage to Baudelaire, Verlaine, Poe, and Wagner; he wrote translations, essays, and prose poems; for a time he produced regular journalism. Alongside these slighter works, he continued to devise his plan for the *Livre,* the pure poem that would justify the world. The sketches that survive are evocative and absorbing, in large part exactly because they are broken, obscure, and incomplete. Even as we hold to a picture of Mallarmé as the apostle of autonomy, we need to see him as living (and writing) within contingency and impurity. To Verlaine he confessed that he did not expect to complete the entire work—"you'd have to be I don't know who for that!"—just to disclose "a fragment which had been created, and in making glorious authenticity shine in one place, and in indicating in all its entirety, the rest, which would demand more than one lifetime."[17]

If *Le Livre* remained ideal and hypothetical, posterity made important use of the poems that did reach publication despite Mallarmé's hesitations. Among the many after-effects of "Hérodiade" and "L'Après-midi d'un faune," the one worth emphasizing is the change in the referent of "I." Different as the two poems are, they both rewrite subjectivity as a suprapersonal condition. Mallarmé evokes characters who belong to no secure historical reality but occupy an imaginary region where subjectivity is free to challenge the contradictions of its being. The first person in Baudelaire's *Les Fleurs du mal,* I have argued, often vanishes before the objects of its perceptions, and its anguish is cast within the concrete metropolitan circumstances of mid-nineteenth-century Paris. Mallarmé's poems, on the other hand, invent a nonhistorical realm; they are stimulated by metaphysical possibility (perfection, selfhood, beauty) and the accumulating connotations of their words; but their force depends on inventing a no-place beyond history where the "I" can aspire and fail, fail and aspire.

SYMONS AND SYMBOLISM

Arthur Symons has already appeared in another strand of this history, as one whose encounter with Jarry's *Ubu roi* marked a collision between a "culture of weariness" and an emergent "culture of will." As we traverse the 1890s through the terms of lyric poetry, we again find Symons playing a leading role in a cross-cultural transition. In 1889 and 1890 the young poet visited Paris and met prominent figures in the literary world, including Mallarmé and Verlaine. The encounters led not only to developments in his own poetry but, more notably, to a series of published judgments that stimulated the diffusion of Modernism and encouraged its maturing self-consciousness. Despite his marked idiosyncrasies, Symons can stand as an exemplary late-century figure, who looked to define the New by finding some principle of stability within late-nineteenth-century culture. His loss of faith, his reading in Walter Pater, his responsiveness to difficult French

writing, his career divided between poetry and journalism—all these prepared him for the task of synthesis and popularization. He was a border-
crossing aesthete and a shrewd journalist who quickly recognized the
transnational reach of the new art and saw an urgent need to spread the
news. He described Pater to his French acquaintances, as he later described
Mallarmé to the English.

In 1893, Symons published an essay called "The Decadent Movement
in Literature." The choice of name is again revealing. Symons begins with
ruminations on terminology, noting that the recent movement in European literature "has been called by many names, none of them quite exact
or comprehensive—Decadence, Symbolism, Impressionism, for instance."[18]
He is caustic about the flurry of terms, calling them "the badge of little
separate cliques, noisy, brainsick young people who haunt the brasseries
of the Boulevard Saint-Michel, and exhaust their ingenuities in theorizing
over the works they cannot write" (96). But even as he disengages himself
from the noisy polemic, Symons recognizes that he, too, must play the
game of name and manifesto. He announces that his chosen term will be
"Decadence," which he describes as "an intense self-consciousness, a restless curiosity in research, an over-subtilizing refinement upon refinement,
a spiritual and moral perversity" (97). Like Huysmans before him, Symons
welcomes what others will see as a frightful contagion; indeed, he speaks of
decadence precisely as "a new and beautiful and interesting disease" (97).
The brothers Goncourt offer examples of the decadent style, with its "fe-
verishness" and its "sharpness of over-excited nerves" (102). But for all its
sympathy and critical appreciation, "The Decadent Movement in Literature" keeps its distance from the events it describes. Mallarmé, the "prophet
and pontiff of the movement" (106, 107), appears as a poet reaching after
impossibilities: "in his latest period he has succeeded in becoming absolutely unintelligible" (108); the recent work has become "a jargon, a mas-
sacre" (109). Symons deplores the pursuit of "singularity for singularity's
sake" among Mallarmé's epigones: "These people have nothing to say, but
they are resolved to say something, and to say it in the newest mode" (111,
112). He ends by celebrating Pater at the expense of the French, Pater who
avoids the violent excesses of the Goncourts, who has mastered the art of
reticence, and who knows what to omit.

Soon after Symons articulated this view of decadence, he began to
change his mind. His association with Yeats explains part of the change,
as does his revaluation of what he had read and seen. Over the next few

years, he compiled a series of chapters on French writers from Balzac to Jules Laforgue, now grouped beneath the rival term, "Symbolism." At the turn of the century he published *The Symbolist Movement in Literature,* a book that belongs as much to Yeats's career as to Symons's and that helped to transform the early poetry of T. S. Eliot. Symons gives up more than the name "Decadence"; he abandons the historical picture that cast the new literature as a sign of overrefinement, disease, and decline. The specific adjustments are striking. Now the Goncourts appear as precursors, not exemplars; the critique of Mallarmé and his disciples disappears; Verlaine ceases to be the ideal. Tellingly, Symons no longer describes the movement as a willing perversity. In his introduction he explains that decadence is the name for only a minor literary interlude (when "perversity of form" met "perversity of matter"), which distracted critics—although he neglects to name himself as one of these critics. All the while, he says, a more profound movement, Symbolism, was taking shape. The triumph of the word "Symbol" registers the new view of literary modernity.

The narrative that Symons devised has in many respects remained a standard account even up to the present. As he revised the book in the twentieth century, he more explicitly specified the false path of modern literature, the unavailing turn toward realism of Flaubert, the Goncourts, and even Baudelaire. These writers, distinguished though they were, gave way to the pressures of modernization, to "the age of Science, the age of material things."[19] What preserved their art was the conversion of reality into form, with Flaubert standing as the most eminent case, especially the Flaubert of *The Sentimental Education,* who carried realism as far as it "can go without ceasing to be art. . . . Everything is observed, everything is taken straight from life: realism sincere, direct, implacable, reigns from end to end of the book. But with what consummate art all this mass of observation is disintegrated, arranged, composed! with what infinite delicacy it is manipulated in the service of an unerring sense of construction!" (177).

This remark, standing at the center of Symons's revised edition in a chapter called "A Short Note on Zola's Method," lays out a critique of Naturalism on which both symbolist and post-symbolist theory relied. "There is a certain simile in *L'Assommoir,*" Symons writes, "used in connection with a bonnet, which seems to me the most abjectly dirty phrase which I have ever read." But Symons is careful to explain that he objects to the fiction, "not as a matter of morals, but as a matter of art" (171). The problem with Zola is not what he says, but the gracelessness of his method of saying it. Zola becomes for Symons, as he would be in very different respects for Lukács, the clinching example of the naturalist failure: description unredeemed by form.

This determined and polemical rejection of Naturalism raised an immediate question. On what basis could there be an alternative Modernism? Realism-as-Naturalism had laid claim to modernity, offering itself as up to date and scientific, unsentimental and unafraid. The task for Symbolism—the task that Symons took upon himself—was to formulate an alternative Modernism, one that acknowledged and then surpassed the claim of realism. For the Symons of *The Symbolist Movement in Literature,* the achievement of Flaubert resembles that of the poet Gautier; both writers undertook a labor of realism that was at the same time a triumph of form. A formal realism and a realist formalism—Symons admits the power of the confluence.

But as his attitudes develop, Symons insists on the limits of Flaubert and Gautier. The convergence of realism and form is both an achievement and a failure. Even as their works achieve breathtaking precision of detail, they set boundaries upon themselves: "they express definite things, definite ideas, definite sensations" (112). Exactitude is circumscription. Gautier "had no moods, was not to be distracted by a sentiment, heard no voices" (98); his forms closed in upon themselves. The symbolists, too, make the beauties of form a high value, but they see another value as higher still. In Symons's formulation, "there is such a thing as perfecting form that form may be annihilated" (8). The transcendence of a *self-extinguishing form* is what Symons came to mean by Symbolism.

Mallarmé, no longer regarded as the author of impenetrable texts, becomes the symbolist visionary, the one who has most clearly seen beyond the "mere literature of words. Words, he has realised, are of value only as a notation of the free breath of the spirit; words, therefore, must be employed with an extreme care, in their choice and adjustment, in setting them to reflect and come upon one another; yet least of all for their own sake, for what they can never, except by suggestion, express" (194). These canonical formulations are part of what made Symons's book important. He added little to Mallarmé's own utterances, but he organized and simplified them, put them into lucid English, and helped to circulate them among young Anglo-American poets. His book crystallizes the triadic negotiations of emergent Modernism, which I have described here as the post-romantic struggle among Naturalism, formalism, and Symbolism—or, as I put it earlier: *the claim of the real, the beauty of verbal surfaces, the pursuit of the un-*

seen. In firmly defending the last of these principles, Symons offered a glowing, accessible picture of the path of modern literature.

> Here, then, in this revolt against exteriority, against rhetoric, against a materialistic tradition; in this endeavour to disengage the ultimate essence, the soul, of whatever exists and can be realized by the consciousness; in this dutiful waiting upon every symbol by which the soul of things can be made visible; literature, bowed down by so many burdens, may at last attain liberty, and its authentic speech. In attaining this liberty, it accepts a heavier burden; for in speaking to us so intimately, so solemnly, as only religion had hitherto spoken to us, it becomes itself a kind of religion, with all the duties and responsibilities of the sacred ritual. (32)

Where Symbolism had appeared as an interesting disease in the early 1890s, it could now claim to be a new religion. Here we turn back to Yeats, who was at once a grateful recipient of Symons's work and an influence upon it. But the significance of Yeats lies not in conforming to a theory of Symbolism but in devising a poetry that both resists and solicits the new categories and new forms.

YEATS: THE SYMBOL, IRELAND, MAUD GONNE

Yeats wrote that he could never know how much his theory and practice owed to the "passages that [Symons] read me from Catullus and from Verlaine and Mallarmé."[20] Still, we know that he did not have to wait for Symons; as Denis Donoghue has said, "He was already half-way toward Symbolist procedures by instinct."[21] The well-known event for Yeats was an encounter with magic and mysticism that began in the mid-1880s, which drew on the popular spiritualism of the decade—the séances in middle-class households, the celebrity mediums, the desperate attempts to contact the dead in drawing rooms. In Yeats's own case, magic was far more than a refuge; at the beginning of his career it was a means of resistance to science, Darwin, and skepticism. He frequented dark rooms, performed rituals, and caressed sacred objects. Irony about these enthusiasms did not wait for a later generation. Yeats knew he was the object of derision, but he was unrepentant and outspoken. In a letter of 1892, he wrote, "If I had not made magic my constant study I could not have written my Blake book nor would 'The Countess Kathleen' have ever come to exist. The mystical life is the centre of all that I do & all that I think & all that I write."[22]

It has become standard to repeat what Yeats himself often implied: that magic gave him metaphors for his poetry. The point is unarguable. But it is also true that magic was a social and collective enterprise for Yeats. He connected the secret lore to a lineage of precursors and also, crucially, to a community in the present. In 1888 he joined the Esoteric Section of the Theosophical Society; two years later he moved from Madame Blavatsky's theosophy to the teachings of the Hermetic Order of the Golden Dawn. Discussion of the levels of spiritual initiation in the Golden Dawn was no doubt different from the conversation in Mallarmé's Tuesday salons, but there exist important relations between the two. The invention of a spiritual discipline with a small group of committed believers belongs to the wider milieu of the avant-garde: it is another sign of the opening toward subcultural forms that pointed, not only to new values in art but also to an alternative practice of daily life.

What distinguished Yeats within a wider Symbolism was that alongside his interest in magic lay an equally ardent concern with Irish legend. He quickly recognized the stimulus of the stories that still existed in popular memory and that became a more immediate source of his early poetry than his experiments in magic. His early two essays in the *Irish Fireside* on the poetry of Samuel Ferguson show him already pondering the resources of national narrative. In the first he calls Ferguson the greatest Irish poet because his work embodies "the Irish character," which for Yeats is a character of lyricism, fantasy, and legend. The second essay on Ferguson is more defiant. Here he assails Irish criticism for its attention to the "faintest echo of English thought"; he deplores cultivated readers who are "servile to English notions"; and he calls on Ireland to free itself from domination: "Of all the many things the past bequeaths to the future, the greatest are great legends; they are the mothers of nations. I hold it the duty of every Irish reader to study those of his own country till they are familiar as his own hands, for in them is the Celtic heart." Yeats concludes with an appeal to young men stirred by patriotism and elevated to the "selfless passion in which heroic deeds are possible and heroic poetry credible."[23] These words also describe his ambitions in "The Wanderings of Oisin," published in 1889.

As Yeats later explains, "When Oisin is speaking with Saint Patrick of the friends and the life he has outlived, he can but cry out constantly against a religion that has no meaning for him."[24] The poem is a manifesto. It stands up for Ireland, for pagan heroism, and for unrepentant will. Yet even as "The Wanderings of Oisin" assured Yeats's early reputation, he was reconsidering his path in ways that would be illuminated in a remark from his *Autobiographies.* There he mentions that when he had finished his tale of Oisin, he was "dissatisfied with . . . all that overcharged colour inherited from the romantic movement" and so had "deliberately reshaped" his style, seeking "an emotion which I described to myself as cold."[25]

This early turn may seem slight, but it had lasting effects for Yeats and Modernism. He might have continued to follow William Morris into epic romance; it was, after all, the tale of Oisin that had won Morris's admiration ("It is my kind of poetry").[26] But it was Yeats's instinct, as well as his historical situation, to keep reacting to his own work and to the world. His significant act was to break up the unity and continuity of legend and to abandon the longer forms of narrative poetry. The first steps appear in the early ballads—such as "The Ballad of Father O'Hart" and "The Ballad of Moll Magee"—which reduce narrative to the most modest scale: an unheroic life condensed to a few rhythmic stanzas. Over the next several volumes, *The Rose* (1893) and *The Wind among the Reeds* (1899), Yeats recasts poetry on the basis, not of grand legend, but of the everyday romance of popular life: the local tale, the fireside yarn, the fable. The shift is nourished by the belief that the "true foundation of literature is folklore"; folklore nourished Homer and Shakespeare, but it "has not been the foundation of more modern writers."[27] Yeats aims to recover what has been lost to modernity. He concludes his essay "The Celtic Element in Literature" by invoking the genealogy of Symbolism that Arthur Symons had offered to him: "The reaction against the rationalism of the eighteenth century has mingled with a reaction against the materialism of the nineteenth century, and the symbolical movement which has come to perfection in Germany in Wagner, in England in the Pre-Raphaelites, in France in Villiers de l'Isle-Adam, and Mallarmé, and in Belgium in Maeterlinck, and has stirred the imagination of Ibsen and D'Annunzio, is certainly the only movement that is saying new things."[28]

Yeats locates the reanimation of Celtic folklore within this genealogy, but more is at stake than he acknowledges. The symbolist pursuit of universal and nontemporal realms had encouraged what became an international style: the style of evocation/suggestion with certain common topoi, such as music, silence, dream, a wafting scent, a glimpse of beauty.[29] But the career of Yeats revealed that Symbolism could have a local habitation through its encounter with specific national conditions. The intersection of symbolist techniques with late-century Ireland marked a signal transition in the history of modernist poetry. Yeats invested the abstract symbol with political and cultural density. "My first principle," he wrote in 1897, "is that poetry must make the land in which we live a holy land . . . I believe that the celtic literature which is now beginning will find it possible to do this, for the celtic races love the soil of their countries vehemently & have as great a mass of legends about that soil as Homer had about his."[30] The volume called *The Rose* contains deep meditations on the symbol ("The Rose of the World," "The Rose of Peace," and "The Rose of Battle"), alongside poems with legendary subjects ("Fergus and the Druid," "Cuchulain's Fight with the Sea"), but it concludes with "To Ireland in the Coming Times," a willful assertion of his double commitment to magic and to his country.

> *Know, that I would accounted be*
> *True brother of a company*
> *That sang, to sweeten Ireland's wrong,*
> *Ballad and story, rann and song;*
> *Nor be I any less of them,*
> *Because the red-rose-bordered hem*
> *Of her, whose history began*
> *Before God made the angelic clan,*
> *Trails all about the written page.*[31]

The argument of the poem is that national life can be redeemed by a symbol-mastering verse. The Irish agony repeats the compulsions of the "unmeasured mind / To rant and rage in flood and wind," while the poetry offers "measured quietude." The commitment to the nation, to its counter-imperial struggle, and to its legendary past depends upon more ancient truth. Although dedicated to Ireland, the poem repeatedly asserts the image with which it ends: "the red-rose-bordered hem" (50).

To contemplate the dark infolded rose and to recover the scenes of old Ireland—these were the twinned convictions of Yeats's early career. Seen from one perspective, the eternal symbol emanates from the Irish nation. Seen from another, national identity depends on magic and incantation. In the face of these grand projects, the lyric "I" recedes. The poems build toward a symbolic scene or a legendary tableau, and yet they acknowledge, though rarely explicitly, that the vision must be partial or flickering or still-to-come. Subjectivity most often shows itself at such moments of concession, sometimes as "I," at other times as "we"; and when "I"/"we" does come forward, it gives itself almost no character or personal history. In this respect, much like the Baudelairean "I," it is absorbed by the scene that it makes and contemplates, as if it could never justify itself, but only be justified by what it glimpses through the symbol.

The aspiration "beyond the senses" was the unremitting regimen of Yeats's early work.[32] It is what he recognized in the symbolist poetry that Arthur Symons brought from France and what animated his adventures in magic as much as it did his experiments in poetry. To mortify the everyday self, to chasten the practices of rationality, science, and habit—these were stages on the way to spiritualized perception. The result was that selfhood was always on the point of disappearing in favor of the symbol or the legend, the rose or the rage of Cuchulain. Subjectivity was bestowed on these others. Yet this disposition of the Yeatsian "I" changed under the double pressure of modern love and modern politics.

For too long Yeats's difficult and unresolved relation with Maud Gonne appeared as a colorful biographical fact. But Maud Gonne was not a distant princess in symbolist raiment. She was an active, ardent Irish nationalist, and just as important, a sovereign agent in her personal life, one who bewildered Yeats by revealing her secret marriage to the Belgian politician Lucien Millevoye and her secret maternity. As R. F. Foster remarks, Maud Gonne was a New Woman of the fin de siècle, who belonged to a wider movement of change between the sexes. Her insistence upon loving on her own terms, like her willingness to take up radical political positions, placed her within a group of women who disregarded the canons of gendered respectability. When she shocked Yeats a second time by marrying the nationalist John MacBride in 1903, as when she maintained her resistance to his projects at the Abbey Theatre, Gonne claimed her right to defiance. The poems that Yeats wrote in response to her life became prominent around the turn of the century. Alongside the invocations to the rose—far-off, secret, inviolate—these poems address another human being—crucially, a human being who refuses the call of love. The earlier lyrics are wistful; they speak of "the pity of love," and "the sorrow of love"; but they also offer simplicity and a release from grand gesture, as in "When You Are Old," which begins,

> When you are old and grey and full of sleep,
> And nodding by the fire, take down this book,
> And slowly read, and dream of the soft look
> Your eyes had once, and of their shadows deep.
>
> (Collected Poems, 40)

The inversion in the last line ("shadows deep"), like the inversion in "The Lake Isle of Innisfree" ("pavements grey"), is a mark of the rhetoric that Yeats was unwilling to surrender, even as the address to Maud Gonne brought him toward a conversational style. Later readers often look back at such moments and puzzle over the slow emergence of a less encumbered voice. Yeats frequently announced a break with his earlier styles. "I hate the soft modern manner," he wrote as early as 1888, regretting the "sedative" tones of the first poems. He declared in 1895 that "all the old things were re-written" and in early 1903 that his poetry "has got far more masculine. It has more salt in it."[33] Despite the repeated assertions that he had achieved a more rigorous style, he continued to write poems (like "Under the Moon") inspired by occult symbology and the romance of Irish legend. It is impor-tant not to fit Yeats's development into a narrative of freedom, in which the poet finally throws off artifice and achieves simplicity of speech. If he repeatedly proclaims his harder, saltier, more masculine manner, it is be-cause another manner still attracts him. He continues his search for a more-than-personal context that will orient (and make meaningful) direct utterance. The Yeatsian atmosphere—of "wave and wind and windy fire," of "elemental powers" that encompass every act, gesture, and emotion— never disappears from his poetry. But those powers began to lose their ethe-real character and become part of the visible world. Maud Gonne herself appears as one of the powers.

In the earlier poems to her, he often takes greater risks in the titles than in the poems standing beneath them: "The Lover Asks Forgiveness Because of His Many Moods," "He Wishes His Beloved Were Dead," "He Mourns for the Change That Has Come upon Him and His Beloved, and Longs for the End of the World." In these and other titles, Yeats tests new feelings and experiments with different rhythms. Addressing himself in the third per-son, he names dissident attitudes that he is still reluctant to include within the verses themselves. But he is surrounded by the assertions of the suf-fragettes and the radical questioning of relations between the sexes, and as his relationship with Maud Gonne changes, the disruptions in voice come down from the title into the texture of the poetry. "No Second Troy" is *about* Maud Gonne, but it inevitably registers the assertions of militant feminism.[34]

> Why should I blame her that she filled my days
> With misery, or that she would of late
> Have taught to ignorant men most violent ways,
> Or hurled the little streets upon the great,
> Had they but courage equal to desire?
> What could have made her peaceful with a mind

That nobleness made simple as a fire,
With beauty like a tightened bow, a kind
That is not natural in an age like this,
Being high and solitary and most stern?
Why, what could she have done, being what she is?
Was there another Troy for her to burn?[35]

When Yeats allows himself to feel antagonistic emotions, the lyric "I" takes on definition through that very antagonism. The next poem in the sequence, "Reconciliation," begins with attitudes of resistance bordering on resentment.

Some may have blamed you that you took away
The verses that could move them on the day
When, the ears being deafened, the sight of the eyes blind
With lightning, you went from me, and I could find
Nothing to make a song about but kings,
Helmets, and swords, and half-forgotten things
That were like memories of you.

(Collected Poems, 89)

That Helen/Maud can be an enemy of poetry, who drives him back to the legends that he believed he had left behind, summons the echoing word "blame," which seems so charged for Yeats. The poem ends by proposing reconciliation: ". . . dear, cling close to me; since you were gone, / My barren thoughts have chilled me to the bone." But the little ceremony of forgiveness notwithstanding, the poem hardly conceals its grievance. Yeats's adversarial love poetry was indispensable to the emergence of lyric subjectivity and to the transformations of voice. The emotions of longing and anger, the invention of a style to accommodate them, the definition of the "I" through the stress of frustration and impatience—these had much to do with how Yeats "entered into myself and pictured myself and not some essence."[36]

If the lyrics in *The Green Helmet and Other Poems* (1910) show Yeats taking on the more definite tones that he thought of as more savory and masculine, they do so in response to the definition of a woman. The emphasis on the ferocity of her will—"high and solitary and most stern"—has its counterpart in the brisk verbal rhythms. The "tightened bow" of her beauty corresponds to the tightened arc of the poem she inhabits. Her ferocity yields his precision. Setting aside a romance of romance, with ideal lovers and nostalgic atmosphere, these scenes depict the reciprocity/ animosity of two equal beings. The woman embodies a relentless demand (a political demand, but also the erotic demand that emanates from her beauty), but at every stage, the language of the poem, with its four questions that frame her challenge, vivifies the presence of the poet. Yeats, in significant part, became a determinate lyric "I" by representing Maud Gonne as another full and willful subjectivity.

POUND'S YEATS, YEATS'S POUND

Ezra Pound sailed to Europe from America in February 1908 at the age of twenty-two, arriving in Britain with two large ambitions: to become a successful poet and to pursue his interest in medieval literature, especially the literature of medieval Provence. These aims were closely related. T. S. Eliot once commented that Pound's prewar literary experiments were essentially critical exercises, and the reverse might be said of his essays: they are imaginative gestures that refuse the conventions of literary criticism and often achieve the concision and power of his poetry. Soon after Pound settled in London, he presented a series of lectures on medieval literature, which became the basis for his first published book, *The Spirit of Romance* (1910).[37] He offers it as a work of critical archaeology, an attempt to recover valuable artifacts buried under the encrustations of Victorianism. Even though his opinions would change, this first work begins a task he never abandoned— namely, the effort to rewrite the history that culminated in modernity and to establish a living tradition beneath a dying one. During this period his poetry attempts to reanimate the rhythms and robust force of the Provençal troubadours. "Sestina: Altaforte," which summons the voice of Bertran de Born, opens without apologies.

> Damn it all! All this our South stinks peace.
> You whoreson dog, Papiols, come! Let's to music!
> I have no life save when the swords clash.
> But ah! when I see the standards gold, vair, purple, opposing
> And the broad fields beneath them turn crimson,
> Then howl I my heart nigh mad with rejoicing.[38]

Direct, vigorous speech is Pound's goal throughout the early work: no mystification, no incantation, but clear images and quick rhythms, often enacted in words of one syllable. Pound develops an aggressive lyric "I" that owes less to Nietzsche than to the troubadours' pleasure in the immediacies of love and war. His academic iconoclasm, a contempt for the cautious understanding of the professors, as well as a self-styled brazen American-ness also stimulate the force of the "I." The short lyric "A Pact" starts with the abruptness that Pound favors.

> I make a pact with you, Walt Whitman—
> I have detested you long enough.
>
> *(New Selected Poems, 39)*

Pound developed his poetics under the banner of aggressive speech, which not only offered the glamour of love and war but also tempted the verse into archaic phrasing ("howl I my heart nigh mad with rejoicing"; 11). Such rhetoric brought a timely rebuke from Ford Madox Ford, an early and important acquaintance. When Pound was working on his third volume of poetry, *Canzoni,* he visited Ford to ask his opinion. As he later recalled, Ford was so appalled with the florid style that he began to roll on the floor—a gesture that "sent me back to my own proper effort, namely, toward using the living tongue."[39] Pound praised Ford as the one who upheld the values of clarity, efficiency, and precision that he now saw as essential to a revolution in modern poetry: the attempt "to bring poetry up to the level of prose."[40] This goal meant clearing away the rot of rhetoric; it meant restoring the privilege of common speech; it meant a commitment to virtues of control and discipline; and most significantly, it meant the embrace of a new realism in poetry which held that the artist must register the data of the world no less precisely than the scientist.[41]

These convictions led Pound to repudiate Symbolism, and soon after seeking out and meeting Yeats, he assumed the role of aesthetic adversary. Modernism continually reenacted the conflict between generations, and it is well to recall that when Pound proposed revisions to Yeats's style, he was confronting an eminent poet nearly twice his age. James Longenbach has persuasively shown the extent of their mutual influence, especially during the winters that they spent together at Stone Cottage beginning in 1913.[42] *Responsibilities* (1914), the volume that appeared during the time of their close relations and that bears the clear signs of Pound's critique, has been taken as the threshold to Yeats's mature style—a style that he had been promising for decades, as we have seen. Pound, who composed a review for *Poetry* magazine under the title "The Later Yeats," loyally called his friend "the best poet in England, . . . assuredly an immortal," and described "a manifestly new note in his later work." Having had so many "mists and fogs since the nineties . . . one is about ready for hard light"—ready, that is, for a poetry that is "becoming gaunter, seeking greater hardness of outline."[43]

Pound's metaphors for the contrast, particularly the celebration of hardness, belong to the change that we approached through Jarry, Marinetti, and Futurism: the turn from languid weariness toward definition and assertion. Although Yeats never fully fits the cut of the metaphors, it is nevertheless clear that Pound is describing a genuine development.

If we ask what opened Yeats to Pound's influence, part of an answer, I suggest, lies in the "adversarial" character of the new poems. Just as Maud Gonne incited the productive clash of personal will, her militant nationalism kept alive Yeats's unsteady relation to politics. Through the 1890s he shared the popular resentment of British colonial rule but was never willing to give up the British cultural standpoint: magic and mysticism, poetry and drama. His work in the 1890s, symbolist and spiritualist, drew skepticism from the nationalists, which blossomed into overt hostility when Yeats began to work earnestly in the theater. The founding of the Irish National Theatre Society in 1903 with Yeats as president and the opening of the Abbey Theatre the following year were momentous occurrences, matched by the dramatic provocations of Yeats, Augusta Gregory, and John Synge.

The climactic event was the first production of Synge's *The Playboy of the Western World*. Yeats later recalled the telegram he received in Scotland while *Playboy* was still in its second act—"Play great success"—and another, more famous telegram that came a few hours later: "Audience broke up in disorder at the word shift."[44] The so-called *Playboy* riots were one of the great spectacles of Modernism. The reaction to the naming of a female undergarment ("shift") is part of its legend, but the struggle over Synge's play had many causes. Joseph Holloway, for instance, objected that *Playboy* was "not a truthful or just picture of the Irish peasants, but simply the outpouring of a morbid unhealthy mind ever seeking on the dunghill of life for the nastiness that lies concealed there."[45] This is another example of the language of disease and excrement aroused by an encounter with a modernist work, but Holloway's remark also establishes the class basis of outrage. Many Irish nationalists and many members of the church saw *The Playboy of the Western World* as grotesque, immoral, and offensive. When Yeats returned to Dublin, he gave an impassioned speech to the audience and also arranged police protection for the theater. The latter act, linking the defenders of Synge's play to the custodians of British domination, incited more controversy.

For Yeats, the uproar over *Playboy* revealed the chasm between the art of the inspired few and the debasement of the modern audience. Synge remained a central figure in Yeats's imaginative life, in his development as a dramatist, and in the casting of his autobiography. But the episode of 1907 also had an immediate bearing on Yeats's poetry—most plainly in the lyric first called "The Attack on 'The Playboy of the Western World,' 1907":

Once, when midnight smote the air,
Eunuchs ran through Hell and met
On every crowded street to stare
Upon great Juan riding by:
Even like these to rail and sweat
Staring upon his sinewy thigh.

(Responsibilities, 40)

The date in the title marks the immediacy of the content. But the poem also displays the signs of Yeats's changing rhetoric: the active verbs, the strong halting rhythms, the massing of stresses in short lines, and the physical language that gathers around the sexualized body ("Eunuchs," "sweat," and "sinewy thigh"). Nietzsche is a likely source of the link between the uncomprehending rabble and the loss of masculinity, but the defense of the artist as potent, alone, and beyond the reach of the masses resonates through the next phase of Yeats's poetry.

The extent of the change can be felt by recalling "The Symbolism of Poetry" (1900), in which Yeats proposed to "cast out of serious poetry those energetic rhythms, as of a man running, which are the invention of the will with its eyes always on something to be done or undone; and . . . seek out those wavering, meditative, organic rhythms, which are the embodiment of the imagination, that neither desires nor hates, because it has done with time, and only wishes to gaze upon some reality, some beauty."[46] The poem on Synge's *Playboy* shows how an exuberant release of indignation changed not only the content but the rhythm of Yeats's verse, so that negative emotion is again a verbal resource. He regrets but exploits the conflicts in culture, convinced, as he put it in the essay on Synge, that "all noble things are the result of warfare."[47] For Yeats, one of those noble things is the brazen lyric "I."[48] "The Fascination of What's Difficult" demands freedom for the "colt" of inspiration, and ends with these tense lines.

I swear before the dawn comes round again
I'll find the stable and pull out the bolt.

(Collected Poems, 92)

The insistence of "I swear" is one sign of directness, but even more striking is the contraction "I'll." Within a body of poetry that had been chary of contractions (no doubt because they seemed too colloquial for a spirit-tending verse), the use of "I'll," like "what's" in the title and first line, represents an engagement with everyday speech as important as the encounter with Irish cultural politics. Between "I will arise and go now" ("The Lake Isle of Innisfree," 1890) and "I'll find the stable and pull the bolt," written two decades later, stands a reconsideration of poetic language that is at the same time a rethinking of the lyric "I" within the public world.

A few years after *Playboy* was performed and booed, another spectacle of art and politics flared in Dublin. Hugh Lane, nephew of Yeats's friend and patron Lady Gregory, had offered to give major paintings from his collection to Ireland on condition that enough money was raised for a suitable gallery. When the project reached an impasse in 1912, Yeats fumed, and in a rage, he wrote a poem that would come to be called "To a Wealthy Man Who Promised a Second Subscription to the Dublin Municipal Gallery If It Were Proved the People Wanted Pictures" (*Collected Poems*, 105). Foster has located a letter from Yeats to Craig that lays out the full vehemence of the poet's anger: "In Ireland we have a most ignorant press & a priest created terror of culture. Lady Gregory & I have lit our little lanthorn & kept the wick a light by solid determination. We would have found a better public elsewhere but we could not have found in ourselves & others this determination which exists for the same reason that our stupid public exists. Ireland is being made & this gives the few who have clear sight the determination to shape it."[49] Yeats names the press and the church as his antagonists here; he is outspoken about the former and usually circumspect about the latter. But from roughly 1908 to 1913 the journalist and the priest are only two of his enemies. Another is the amorphous crowd, the dull public, "The pack" ("To a Shade") in "my fool-driven land" ("All Things Can Tempt Me") where "The weak lay hand on what the strong has done, / Till that be tumbled that was lifted high" ("These Are the Clouds"). Just as often the crowd of fools is the commercial middle classes, "the merchant and the clerk" ("At Galway Races"), who evince the dispiriting forces of religion, mass opinion, and narrow greed that converge in "September 1913."

> What need you, being come to sense,
> But fumble in a greasy till
> And add the halfpence to the pence
> And prayer to shivering prayer, until
> You have dried the marrow from the bone?[50]

The tactic of the poem is to lay claim to "Romantic Ireland," the Ireland of heroic resistance and national assertion, an inheritance that Yeats was not alone in claiming. He often preferred to picture the struggle as between visionary imagination and the conservatism of commerce, journalism, and the church. But far more difficult was the relation of his oppositional art to the already oppositional politics of nationalism—whose adherents were equally intent on claiming the heroic past in the service of Irish regeneration. Yeats's changing poetry (and drama) lived alongside the rapidly changing political struggle: two transformations, each suspicious of the other. Yeats believed the militant nationalists to be caught in the false lures of logic, rationality, and clarity, which could never produce an alternative to colonial subjugation. In turn, the nationalists saw him and his literary allies as lost in a symbolist dream that was as un-Irish as it was unreal. Arthur Griffith, who founded the *United Irishman* in 1899 and helped to begin Sinn Féin in 1905, was often a corrosively hostile opponent of Yeats, whose work he derided as cosmopolitan and elitist. Maud Gonne, among others, was often skeptical of Yeats's poetic summoning of the Irish nation. In the face of resistance, Yeats continued to hold that a cultural nationalism, confirmed by occult vision and poetic symbolism, was the genuinely radical act. When attacked, he was unrepentant, asserting, "I have worked in Ireland for a long time to check the rhetorical writing which our political necessities have developed & to persuade our own not very well educated Irish public to accept literature as literature, & not as partly disguised politics."[51]

Here is the crux. Yeats held firmly to a distinction between art and politics. Yet to speak of his art as "autonomous" merely substitutes a concept for a history. Yeats audaciously claimed that the proud artist, cold in Nietzschean indifference, is nevertheless intimate with the ways of the people. An art that reviles modernity, including its latter-day priests, politicians, shopkeepers, and journalists, can find its way back to the sources of national tradition. He argued that the "poetry of coteries"—the writings of those initiates who make art out of old and secret lore—"does not differ in kind from the true poetry of the people." Both poetries abandon the shallow rationality of the commercial classes in favor of "strange," "obscure," and ancient images. If Ireland was to resist English dominance, Yeats argued, it must no longer discourage a "cultivated minority," alone capable of recovering true nationhood.[52]

In the Ireland of the decade before the First World War, the practices of art and politics met and contended. But the struggle was not between two well-marked positions or two clearly distinct camps. Friends and associates of Yeats—Maud Gonne above all, but also George Russell (A.E.) and Padraic Colum—moved between aesthetic and political initiatives, and Yeats himself could quickly shift emphasis from the defense of literature as literature to a reaffirmation of Irish solidarity. The practices of art and politics were permeable to one another. Both sides regarded cultural life as central to social self-understanding: the nationalists looked to art as a rich source of imagery and affect, while Yeats saw national renewal as the outcome of radical imagining.

The striking change in the poetry, then, was not simply the choice of a saltier and more vigorous speech, which Yeats had pursued for so long. It was an effect of his negotiation with a resistant world. The emergence of a brisk voice, speaking in stiff rhythms and willing to affirm the first person, was fed by the intensity of these struggles, just as it was fed by the contest over Irish drama and Hugh Lane's gift of paintings. The lyric "I" came into full being through opposition, and as Yeats's career unfolded, the "I" took its own earlier incarnations as an adversary.

H.D. AND POUND: THE ART OF LIMITATION

Pound, for his part, while promoting a new, "harder" Yeats, was inciting a broader movement of the young (*les jeunes*), who were more prepared for radical change. Since arriving in London, he had formed connections with established writers like Ford and Yeats, but also with a group of younger poets who met weekly to read their work and to discuss the most advanced views arriving from the Continent. A leading figure was T. E. Hulme, who, under the influence of French theories of vers libre and the philosophy of Bergson, had devised a theory of the Image on which Pound would soon draw. According to Hulme, both the grandeur of classical epic and the perfection of the romantic lyric were now obsolete. Poets should imitate the example of impressionist painters and communicate momentary states of mind, instantaneous perceptions captured in striking images. The Image would replace philosophic declamation and lyric effusion; it would be concrete and direct; it would free poetry from constraining meters and from cliché.

These insights had few immediate results. The young poets abandoned their weekly gatherings—Pound later referred to the group as "the forgotten school of 1909." His search for allies moved to other candidates. By early 1912 he was in close contact with Hilda Doolittle (H.D.), an old friend who had also come to live in London, and with the young English poet Richard

Aldington, who married Doolittle the following year. In the lapidary style of H.D.'s early poetry, with its stark metaphors and its tense rhythms, Pound found the example he was looking for. As the legend goes, he turned one day to his young friends in a tea shop in Kensington and informed them that they were "*les imagistes.*" Doolittle began to sign her poems "H.D., imagiste," while Aldington, though he never generated the same enthusiasm in Pound, closed ranks. Pound, who had recently mocked the Parisian inclination to form "eight schools for every dozen of poets," now launched himself into the cultural politics of faction.[53]

The history of Imagism is, among other things, a locus classicus of the power of modern publicity. Pound was never satisfied to formulate new ideas; he sought to provoke others into a confrontation with novelty. Thus, in announcing Imagism to the readers of *Poetry*, he wrote in typically combative tones that "the youngest school here that has the nerve to call itself a school is that of the Imagistes."[54] He began an active campaign to win adherents to the cause, and in 1913 he persuaded several other young poets, among them D. H. Lawrence, Amy Lowell, and William Carlos Williams, to contribute to an anthology of imagist verse, published in early 1914.

Having coined the term, Pound had to define what it meant. In the March 1913 issue of *Poetry* there appeared the manifesto "A Few Don'ts by an Imagiste," in which he set out his definition of the Image as "that which presents an intellectual and emotional complex in an instant of time." To this axiom were appended three more principles: direct treatment of the "thing," whether subjective or objective; economy of presentation; and rhythm based not on fixed metrical schemes but on musical phrasing. Pound went on to attack the reign of adjectives and abstractions, to defend the legitimacy of free verse, and to refuse the symbolist pursuit of "something that moves beyond the senses," insisting that "the natural object is always the *adequate* symbol."[55] The early imagist propaganda contained an element of posturing, but behind the posturing lay a serious attempt to free English poetry from rhetoric—from sentimentality, ornament, and vagueness—and to restore direct presentation and clear speech. H.D. traveled a long distance from her early imagist lyrics, but her early work displayed the features that Pound celebrated. The first stanza of "Hermes of the Ways" became a portable example of the new technique.

The hard sand breaks,
and the grains of it
are clear as wine[56]

The spareness of the verse, its subtly changing rhythms—from the crisp accents in the first line to the long tone of "grains" and "wine"—and its evocative single metaphor served as defining features of Imagism. Pound described the early poems as "straight talk, straight as the Greek!"[57]

But H.D., as recent scholarship has shown, never fit comfortably beneath the banner that Pound was intent on waving. Even in these early years, she was pursuing a broader lyric ambition that resists the technical/formalist reading that Pound favored.[58] "Hermes of the Ways" exceeds its rigorous Image, moving toward an encounter with a reanimated Hermes—

> more than the many-foamed ways
> of the sea,
> I know him
> of the triple path-ways,
> Hermes,
> who awaits

(37)

And he appears, like other gods in H.D.'s work, not as a literary relic but as a living force, a mythic and coercive emotion. Diana Collecott has established the depth of H.D.'s early commitment to Greek inspiration, especially her commitment to Sappho. Far more than a question of "straight talk," the Sapphic Greek—in Collecott's persuasive words—opened "a place of continual transformation from literal to figurative" that "returned repeatedly to the *radiant, white* centre of emotion, the *white* ash of extreme ecstasy: at once a physical condition and an altered state of consciousness that is a point of infinity for the individual, seemingly between life and death."[59]

At the moment of Imagism, Pound himself kept the emphasis on questions of verbal form. The force of will, and the broader masculinism of Modernism, meant that H.D.'s "Sapphic Modernism" remained marginal to Pound's polemic. Still, a project of technical reform had been set in motion; to the extent that H.D. coincided with the literary program, she was content to publish under its rubric. Her poem "Oread" became a favorite specimen of the new imagist doctrine.

> Whirl up, sea
> Whirl your pointed pines.
> Splash your great pines
> On our rocks.

Hurl your green over us—
Cover us with your pools of fir.[60]

When Pound came to link his literary theory to radical experiments in the visual arts, he proposed that each form use only its primary medium. Painting has its own pure pigments, and the "primary pigment of poetry is the IMAGE."[61] In 1914, H.D.'s "Oread" served as Pound's example of poetry's pigment, its technical essence. To make such a claim was to ignore its other themes and interests. Rachel Blau DuPlessis has written of the contest between "I" and "you" in H.D.'s early poetry, a struggle that here takes on the aspect of "us" and "you"; and Collecott has described the convergence of "sexual desire and the desire for elemental obliteration."[62] For Pound such details were merely distracting when set against the formal achievement— namely, the compression of concept and emotion into one image. His own celebrated example of Imagism, the two lines (and the title) of "In a Station of the Metro," was published in the spring of 1913.

The apparition   of these faces   in the crowd;
Petals   on a wet, black   bough.[63]

Like H.D.'s "Oread," his verse stood then, as it stands now, as a little landmark in the history of Modernism, marking the power of compression. "It is better," wrote Pound, "to present one Image in a lifetime than to produce voluminous works."[64] T. E. Hulme, still an important ally, published his "Complete Works" in 1912, a handful of short poems, under thirty-five lines in total. At the time, Hulme's act could be seen as part literary austerity, part bravado, part joke. After his death in the war, it took on more somber meanings. Hulme's few short poems, like the examples from H.D. and Pound, reflect the aura of modernist minimalism.

The aesthetics of limitation can be seen as unfolding in two phases. First was the symbolist refusal of discursive meaning: the disdain for rational paraphrase and the reliance on incantatory suggestion. Second, however, was the turn against Symbolism. This turn was precisely against the style of evocation, which for Pound and his allies seemed soft, woolly, and imprecise. The purging of excess—rhetorical eloquence, discursive morality, the adjective—was a consuming mission just before the First World War. Images of concentration and purity became prominent; the elimination of lyric waste seemed an urgent labor. But the self-chastening, self-limiting aesthetic of Imagism was never likely to survive for long. To critics of the movement, such as Harold Monro, it was "petty poetry": "Such reticence denotes either poverty of imagination or needlessly excessive re-straints."[65] H.D. and Pound themselves soon felt the constraint of the one-image poem. In "Cities," at the end of her first volume of poetry, *Sea Garden* (1916), H.D. was already pressing toward longer flights. Pound, too, soon broke through the limits of the single image and moved toward the open forms of *The Cantos*.

Nevertheless, the example of Imagism persisted as a resource and leg-acy of Modernism in the form of the small-scale and self-sufficient artifact that offered itself without commentary. A minimal gesture seemed maxi-mally resonant. Even if it could not be sustained as the basis of lyric poetry, the idea of the Image continued to exert pressure on later verse, especially within the Anglo-American context. It encouraged verbal discipline and cast suspicion on what Pound condemned as the lax speech of "perdam-nable rhetoric" and the rhapsody of "emotional slither."[66] More signifi-cantly, it confirmed the strength of epiphanic Modernism: confidence in the revelatory power of a self-contained experience, in instantaneous rec-ognition. The Impression, the Symbol, the Image, the Vortex, the Moment, the Luminous Detail, and the Epiphany differed in many respects, but they converged in the power they granted to the "intellectual and emotional complex in an instant of time."

APOLLINAIRE'S SHALLOW EYE

Across the Channel in Paris, poetic experiment ran in parallel to the cam-paigns of Pound and the imagists. The leading spirit was Apollinaire, whose early work had been *symboliste,* but who, like Pound, made a sudden turn against his poetic fathers. For Apollinaire, too, the impasse of Symbolism came to stand for the exhaustion of the nineteenth century. The speed and the violence of the break, repeated throughout Europe between 1908 and 1912, register one milepost in the history of Modernism.

That Symbolism could be overturned so quickly remains a point worth pondering. Partly, the change was a product of new ways of thinking about modernity, drawn especially from Nietzsche but also from the political radi-calism of Marx, Georges Sorel, Mikhail Bakunin, and others. It reflected as well a change in personal style, habits of living, and patterns of gesture. We have seen the shift from "weariness" to "will." But as the case of Apollinaire makes clear, the arc of change reflected many vectors. Alfred Jarry was a looming precursor for Apollinaire, one whose buffoonery and grotesque comedy had defied symbolist incantation. Even more important was the early work of young painters working in Paris: Picasso, Braque, Delaunay, and others. Along with Gertrude Stein, Apollinaire was among the first to appreciate their body of radical work. Both as a conversationalist in the cafés and as a prolific art critic, he became a persuasive defender of the controversial paintings. Even though the artists sometimes derided his interpretation of their work, there can be no doubt that Apollinaire was indispensable to the early success of Cubism and its successor movements.

Immersed in the avant-garde milieu, Apollinaire called on poets to invent a language for modernity, a language suitable, in Joyce's phrase, to the "velocity of modern life,"[67] specifically one that could evoke crowd and nation as the lyric had not done before. Here, Apollinaire's response was strikingly different from Pound's. Where Imagism aimed toward austere limitation, Apollinaire looked to create open forms—open but resistant to romantic or symbolist transcendence. In place of a vertical relation to supersensible vision, Apollinaire pursued the widest *horizontalism*. He developed a rhythm, tone, and perspective that, in principle, could register anything that passed before the gazing eye, from the neglected gestures of the passing crowd to the vestiges of the past living into the present. The artist with this wide lyric eye blithely and crucially gave up the effort to wrest coherence from the world. The release of experience into heterogeneity and discontinuity—this was the gesture that Apollinaire elaborated in the years just before the war. When he collected a decade's worth of poetry in his first volume, *Alcools* (1913), he opened with the recently published "Zone," which epitomized years of experiment.

A la fin tu es las de ce monde ancien

(You are weary at last of this ancient world)[68]

"Zone" begins with this line addressed by the poet to himself, but as it unfolds, its discovery is the shedding of a century of weariness, and the revival of curiosity.

J'ai vu ce matin une jolie rue dont j'ai oublié le nom
Neuve et propre du soleil elle était le clairon
Les directeurs les ouvriers et les belles sténo-dactylographes
Du lundi matin au samedi soir quatre fois par jour y passent
Le matin par trois fois la sirène y gémit
Une cloche rageuse y aboie vers midi
Les inscriptions des enseignes et des murailles
Les plaques les avis à la façon des perroquets criaillent

J'aime la grâce de cette rue industrielle
Située à Paris entre la rue Aumont-Thiéville et l'avenue des Ternes.

(2–4)

(This morning I saw a fine street whose name slips my mind
New and bright the sun's clarion
Where executives and workers sweet stenographers
Hurry every weekday dawn and dusk
Three times a morning sirens groan
A choleric bell barks at noon
Billboards posters and
Doorplates twitter like parakeets
There is charm to this Paris factory street
Between rue Aumont-Thiéville and the avenue des Ternes.)

The city generates perpetual novelty; it converts ancient images into the furniture of the present tense: Christ becomes the "original airplane" (*premier aéroplane*); remote legends circulate in the crowded streets. Paris is a machine for absorbing everything into modernity; even in the poems that leave the city, the tones of urban vision persist, the onrush of spectacle, the mix of fascination and detachment.

The *shallowness* of Apollinaire's eye is its strength. Baudelaire is the eminent early recorder of the encounter between subjectivity and the city, and Apollinaire has long been seen as a child of Baudelaire, and the one largely responsible for his position as the originary modernist. Unlike Baudelaire, however, Apollinaire rarely staged a drama of self-extremity. Especially as he moved beyond the early verse, he took himself as just another object in the vista. He may be more prominent than other objects; he keeps colliding with himself; but instead of claiming the agon of subjectivity, the poet presents even strong emotions as passing objects in the field of vision. Frequently addressing himself in the second person, this "I" becomes a "you" that can be summoned and dismissed like a stranger. Or as Apollinaire puts it in "Cortège," addressing the gods who made him: "I live only passing by as you passed by" ("Je ne vis que passant ainsi que vous passâtes"; 70). In "Zone" the pronouns alternate until subjectivity is suspended between consciousness and object.

Tu as fait de douloureux et de joyeux voyages
Avant de t'apercevoir du mensonge et de l'âge
Tu as souffert de l'amour à vingt et à trente ans

J'ai vécu comme un fou et j'ai perdu mon temps
Tu n'oses plus regarder tes mains et à tous moments je voudrais
    sangloter
Sur toi sur celle que j'aime sur tout ce qui t'a épouvanté

(10)

(You went on sad and merry journeys
Before growing aware of lies and old age
Love made you unhappy at twenty again at thirty
I have lived like a fool and wasted my youth
You no longer dare examine your hands and at any moment I could
    weep
Over you over her whom I love   over all that has frightened you)

The central and vigorous device is a break with persistence, duration, continuity—with discursive or even musical succession—in favor of half-detached perceptions that move without punctuation and at great speed. The exhilarating recognition is of the world's procession, which must be quickly seen and named. As Roger Shattuck puts it, each line can become "a partially self-sufficient unit which does not depend too greatly upon the succeeding line."[69] Sometimes the units are several lines in sequence, sometimes only a phrase within a line. In either case, the result is a perpetual exposure to new stimulus. The liberation of the (partially) self-contained perception (or memory) stands as a link to Anglo-American Imagism. Apollinaire, too, evokes the resonance of the independent unit, the luminous detail. But he places no faith in the minimalism of a single "intellectual and emotional complex." His individual images are compelling but incapable of standing on their own. The open forms are built from the doubleness of the poetic unit (a short sequence, a line, a phrase): at once self-sufficient and insufficient.

Cubism encouraged the mobility of perspectives in *Alcools,* the rejection of a privileged line of sight controlled by a masterly subjectivity. At least as liberating, though, was the post-cubist painting of Robert Delaunay, who moved toward greater abstractionism than the cubists did and who developed a theory of "simultaneity." For Delaunay, the simultaneous contrasts of colors lay at the basis of all perception; the artist's task was to return art to this primary source. Or, as Apollinaire distilled the point: "Simultaneity is life itself."[70] Clearly, the force of the thought differs in painting and poetry. But just as clearly, Apollinaire wrested a productive analogy from Delaunay's work. As his poems move among perceptions, they assume no logic of narrative: the end does not supersede the beginning. Rather, the verse gives an equality of attention to each line, every event, and all persons, so the poem becomes its own field of coincidence in which the several parts (images, rhythms, rhyme) create the kinetics of simultaneity.

The field of the poem mirrors the condition of personhood as a scatter of relics, scraps, accretions, impulses, desires, regrets. Apollinaire aspires to no heroic selfhood on the model of either Rimbaud or Whitman. In "Cortège" the "I" searches for himself in the endless procession stretching before him.

> Tous ceux qui survenaient et n'étaient pas moi-même
> Amenaient un à un les morceaux de moi-même
> On me bâtit peu à peu comme on élève une tour
> Les peuples s'entassaient et je parus moi-même
> Qu'ont formé tous les corps et les choses humaines
>
> *(70)*

> (All those who arrived and were not myself
> Brought one by one the fragments of myself
> They built me little by little as one raises a tower
> The nations huddled together and I myself appeared
> Formed by all bodies all human concerns)

A subjectivity composed of the universe of people and things—this is the open self that Apollinaire seeks to release. It corresponds to the expanse of verse, which interrupts and prolongs itself. What Apollinaire identified as the engine of novelty was surprise—surprise as the enemy of cliché but also as resistance to coherence, stability, closure.

CENDRARS AND THE ABANDONED "I"

Apollinaire aggressively promoted, and also benefited from, the ideology of the New. His frequent essays on painting and the publication of his poems, culminating in *Alcools,* established him as a center of the Parisian avant-garde, much as Pound became a center of London-based experiment. Yet a telling aspect of the social practice of the avant-garde is that even such articulate impresarios as Apollinaire and Pound never enjoyed incontestable leadership. The culture of opposition, especially in its antagonism to the rival practices of religion and politics, was resistant to structures of discipline. Cultural opposition was often closer to the temper of contemporary anarchism; any voice of authority was liable to be ironized, repudiated, or directly challenged. Apollinaire, for instance, was forced in Paris to take into account the more strictly painterly group around Picasso, as well as the constellation around Gertrude Stein. Pound negotiated with strong-willed Wyndham Lewis, the force behind *Blast* in 1914, and both Lewis and Pound contended with a group of rivals surrounding Roger Fry. Still, to insist on these ambiguities is not to deny the contribution of the fluent impresario. Not just the visibility of movements but the resolve of individual artists often depended on the support of an authoritative rallying cry, especially when the loud cry opened new venues of publication or display. From at least the 1880s, the time of the symbolists, a fluid structure of authority/community emerged that affected the creation and circulation of new work.

One of the most remarkable careers to appear within this context was that of Blaise Cendrars (born Frédéric Louis Sauser). Cendrars was a restless traveler whose first success, *Les Pâques à New York* (Easter in New York), was written in 1912, the product of both his encounter with American urban misery and his discovery of a new lyric tone. Unlike Apollinaire, who devised a resilient avatar that remade itself from the materials at hand, Cendrars developed an "I" that surrendered to the pressures of modernity. After a night's journeying through the streets of dispossession—in the lower part of town ("le bas de la ville")[71] with its parade of drunks, vagrants, prostitutes, and poor immigrants—he appeals to an absconded God.

> Seigneur, je rentre fatigué, seul et très morne . . .
> Ma chambre est nue comme un tombeau . . .
>
> Seigneur, je suis tout seul et j'ai la fièvre . . .
> Mon lit est froid comme un cercueil . . .
>
> Seigneur, je ferme les yeux et je claque des dents . . .
> Je suis trop seul. J'ai froid. Je vous appelle . . .
>
> Cent mille toupies tournoient devant mes yeux . . .
> Non, cent mille femmes . . . Non, cent mille violoncelles
>
> Je pense, Seigneur, à mes heures malheureuses . . .
> Je pense, Seigneur, à mes heures en allées . . .
>
> Je ne pense plus à Vous. Je ne pense plus à Vous.
>
> (Lord, I come back tired, alone, and utterly dejected . . .
> My room is as empty as a tomb . . .

Lord, I'm all alone and I have a fever . . .
My bed is as cold as a coffin . . .

Lord, I close my eyes and my teeth chatter . . .
I'm too alone. I'm cold. I call your name . . .

A thousand tops spin before my eyes . . .
No, a thousand women . . . No, a thousand cellos

I think, Lord, about how miserable I've been . . .
I think, Lord, about all the days that are gone . . .

I stop thinking about You. I stop thinking about You.)

(235, 10)

In the spirit of such resignation/submission Cendrars undertook the audacious poem that he called "La Prose du Transsibérien et de la Petite Jehanne de France" (The Prose of the Trans-Siberian and of Little Jeanne of France). Its frame is the memory of a journey on the Trans-Siberian Railway, when the poet/speaker was sixteen years old, at the time of the Russo-Japanese War. Businessmen, women, and soldiers crowd aboard, as does Jeanne, a young prostitute, the poet's companion, found "in the back of a brothel" "stark naked," because she "has no body—she's too poor" (239, 19). For Cendrars the train journey is an irresistible multivalent figure of modernity. It evokes a blind nihilism, a violent thrusting through darkness, but also an erotic rhythm and the rhythm of poetry. The milieu of war—"La faim le froid la peste le choléra" (Hunger, cold, plague, cholera) —makes this a death train, hurtling toward the end. But it is also a sex train, where men and women tumble and cling. Finally it is a sex-and-death train, where the two climaxes become indistinguishable.

Puis il y avait beaucoup de femmes
Des femmes des entre-jambes à louer qui pouvaient aussi servir
Des cercueils
Elles étaient toutes patentées

(And there were a lot of women
Women with vacant thighs for hire
Who could also serve
Coffins
They were all licensed)

(237, 17)

Under the pressures of impasse everywhere—sex and death, time and space, memory and anticipation—the poem surrenders itself to "The rhythms of the train/What American psychiatrists call 'railway nerves.'" The chronically nervous poem swerves off the rails of plot and rhythm, releasing itself to a global imagination that anticipates a more fully transnational Modernism. At high velocity it moves to Fiji and Mexico and chants the names of paired world cities: "Basel–Timbuktu," "Paris–New York" "Madrid–Stockholm." It reaches its farthest point—"I stepped off the train at Harbin a minute after they had set fire to the Red Cross office" (28)—and then recoils to Paris, "where desires arrive at the crossroads of restlessness":

> Ville de la Tour unique du grand Gibet et de la Roue.
>
> (City of the incomparable Tower the great Gibbet and the Wheel.)
> *(246, 29)*

The extraordinary effect of "La Prose du Transsibérien" comes from the self-abandonment of its "I." This voice claims no command over the profusion it uncovers. It yields to movement like a passenger on a plunging train. Unlike the buoyant voice of Apollinaire, which keeps floating up through the discontinuity, Cendrars offers a speech that persists, but persists without hope. It is the speech of a chastened, baffled self, yet its confusion is precisely what gives it force. To submit to the speed and incoherence of the world, to surrender the impulse to dominate and assert, is also to release new rhythms of experience. The verse is a lyric of failure. In the first lines Cendrars names himself as "already such a bad poet/That I didn't know how to take it all the way" (15). But he soon acknowledges that as "the bad poet who wanted to go nowhere, I could go anywhere" (16). He paints himself as sexually guilty, artistically blocked, and politically impotent, and he renders these failures as the generating cause of his work. Toward the end of the poem a long, suggestive sequence appears.

> J'ai peur
> Je ne sais pas aller jusqu'au bout
> Comme mon ami Chagall je pourrais faire une série de tableaux
>   déments
> Mais je n'ai pas pris de notes en voyage
> "Pardonnez-moi mon ignorance
> "Pardonnez-moi de ne plus connaître l'ancient jeu des vers"
> Comme dit Guillaume Apollinaire

Tout ce qui concerne la guerre on peut le lire dans les *Mémoires de
    Kouropatkine*
Ou dans les journaux japonais qui sont aussi cruellement illustrés
Je m'abandonne
Aux sursauts de ma mémoire

(I'm scared
I don't how to take it all the way
Like my friend Chagall I could do a series of irrational paintings
But I didn't take notes
"Forgive my ignorance
"Pardon my forgetting how to play the ancient game of Verse"
As Guillaume Apollinaire says
If you want to know anything about the war read Kuropotkin's
    Memoirs
Or the Japanese newspapers with their ghastly illustrations
But why compile a bibliography
I give up
Bounce back into my leaping memory . . .)

(243–244, 26)

This is a taunting, flaunting testimony of failure, not unmixed with pride.
Equally revealing is the nod to contemporaries and allies. The mention of
Chagall and Apollinaire, like a later mention of Maeterlinck, locates "La
Prose du Transsibérien" in the immediate context of radical experiment.
This fold of the poem—where it looks back upon itself and back toward the
artistic present—is part of its interest. As the practice of Modernism spread
in the years before the First World War, it began to take itself as a subject in
its own right. A speeding train is one sign of modernity, but so is the network of artists who have labored their way to visibility.

Any close account of Modernism and the avant-garde must come to
terms with rapid changes in very brief periods. Between 1905 and 1914, as
we have seen, a culture of opposition became conspicuous in capitals across
Europe and North America. Even artists like Joyce and Strindberg, who
kept themselves largely apart from the work of groups, were fully conscious
of the activity. So were the editors of established journals and newspapers,
who often took the provocations of art as both newsworthy and scandalous. That Marinetti looked to publish his first manifesto in a mainstream
newspaper is a sign of his eagerness for a wide popular hearing; that *Le*

Figaro was willing to publish the manifesto is a sign of the arrival of avant-garde agitation as an item of general interest.

Roughly speaking, we can distinguish two generations within this short period from 1905 to 1914: the artists who had been working in the years before Marinetti's thunderclap publication of 1909 and who had been committed to earlier styles, and the younger artists who emerged after the sensations of Futurism and had few commitments to revise. Those in the first group, which includes Marinetti himself as well as Apollinaire, Yeats, Stein, and Joyce, underwent some remarkable changes after their practice of an earlier Symbolism or Naturalism/realism. The second group includes Cendrars, who had few earlier poems to disown, and the generation of expressionists and Dadaists whose activity took shape just before and during the war. This later generation came to consciousness when a culture of novelty (and opposition) was inescapable for any young artist in any major capital. Cendrars's poem "La Prose du Transsibérien" appeared early in the twentieth century, but in important ways it was a belated poem that shows how the will to novelty must now contend with a lengthening history of the New. Cendrars wrote within a field already crowded with experimental gestures; part of the interest of his poem is how he turned belatedness to advantage.

Here we come to the most arresting sign of Cendrars's engagement with the wider avant-garde. "La Prose du Transsibérien" appeared not as lines of verse centered between the margins of white pages but as a set of twenty-two folded leaves that opened to a length of six and a half feet. The text appeared in the right column of the fold. Running along the left was a series of designs by the painter Sonia Delaunay, who like her husband, Robert, was developing toward the freedom of visual abstraction. Apollinaire, we recall, had praised Robert Delaunay as the inventor of "an art of pure color," an art that Apollinaire described in the spring of 1913 as the "new tendency of cubism."[72] The images that Sonia Delaunay devised for the poem are examples of the "new tendency" toward nonreferential abstract design. As Marjorie Perloff suggests in her unsurpassable account of the forms of "La Prose du Transsibérien," they also participate in another radical "simultaneism"—namely, the simultaneity of text and image, of visual and textual radicalism that meet in the hybrid object that baffles classification.[73] Or, as Apollinaire wrote the following year, "Blaise Cendrars and Mme Delaunay-Terk have carried out a unique experiment in simultaneity, written in contrasting colors in order to train the eye to read with one glance the whole of a poem, even as an orchestra conductor reads with one glance the notes placed up and down on the bar, even as one reads with a single glance the plastic elements printed on a poster."[74] Even to put it this way is to simplify the novelty. Cendrars's poem, unfolding down the right-hand column, is a virtuoso experiment in typography—varying typefaces, changing sizes, altered justification—that already unsettles textual norms. Furthermore, rather than a book to be circulated, it was designed as a limited edition to be exhibited, as it was, in Paris, Berlin, London, New York, Moscow, Saint Petersburg. Perloff weighs "the effect of this visualisation" and persuasively suggests that it implies "a *mise en question* of the text's lyric frame, its generic identity as lyric poem as well as its semantic coherence."[75]

The unrepentant brazenness of the Cendrars-Delaunay "La Prose du Transsibérien" reminds us that any history of the period must acknowledge the irreducible singularity of its works. When Apollinaire speaks of the "unique experiment" of the piece, he makes that acknowledgment, although he was quick to assimilate it into his campaign for a "new spirit." We again confront the circuitry between works and movements, the individual and the collectivity. No artifact is like "La Prose du Transsibérien," just as no artifact is like *Ubu roi, The Waste Land,* or Stein's *Tender Buttons.* Yet a central aspect of Modernism was the way that singular works implied a lineage and a legacy, the way that even a "unique experiment" suggested a common project.

PAINTING POETRY: THE IMPRESARIOS OF PURITY

In the case of Cendrars, the immediate suggestion that Modernism had a common project implied further convergence between poetry and painting. We have seen how during the decade before the war, the radicalism of painting—the nonnatural colors in Matisse and the Fauves, the challenge to perspective among the cubists, the early works of collage, the approach to abstraction in the work of the Delaunays and Kandinsky—offered the most visible manifestations of the avant-garde. Under the inspiration of these works, a number of poets began to reevaluate their own medium. Pound in London and Apollinaire in Paris remained near the center of avant-garde activity, where they closely watched and eagerly celebrated the work of the young painters. The question was what the new painting could mean to poetry. Cendrars had implied one solution: the hybrid work within which poetry would stand alongside painting and, more strikingly, would take on its own visual aspect. It is this latter possibility that Pound and Apollinaire pursued, though in quite different ways. What drew both poets was the prospect of an escape from representation. In an essay of 1912, "On the Subject in Modern Painting," Apollinaire wrote, "Verisimilitude no longer has any importance, for the artist sacrifices everything to the composition of the picture. The subject no longer counts, or if it counts, it counts for very little." He carries on in a mood of prophecy.

> An entirely new art is thus being evolved, an art that will be to painting, as painting has hitherto been envisaged, what music is to literature.
> It will be pure painting, just as music is pure literature.[76]

The lure of "purity" to this generation of artists was strong. Representation *as such*—the mere act of recording the world according to *any* convention—now seemed compromised. It carried art out of itself, divided its attention, jeopardized the integrity of form. As the British painter David Bomberg wrote, "My object is the *construction of Pure Form*. I reject everything in painting that is not Pure Form."[77]

Here it is worth stressing the rapid shifts as Pound—over a series of weeks—reconsidered the bases of his Modernism. What he had taken from Ford Madox Ford was the vocation of accuracy, which Ford had described as the effort "to register my own times in terms of my own time."[78] Stirred by this thought, Pound defined Imagism as "direct treatment of the thing." Late in 1913 he consolidated his early thinking in an essay called "The Serious Artist," where he calls for an art that is a science "just as chemistry is a science," because for the serious artist, the "more precise his record the more lasting and unassailable his work of art."[79] These realist principles place representation at the center of a new aesthetic. Moreover, they formed the basis for Pound's critical engagement with Yeats, his determination to persuade Yeats to come out of the mists of Symbolism. But as the year 1914 ended, Pound looked more closely at visual art. By February he was already sketching a different position, when in writing on "The New Sculpture," he unambiguously asserts, "Realism in literature has had its run. For thirty or more years we have had in deluge, the analyses of the fatty degeneration of life. A generation has been content to analyse. They were necessary. . . . We have heard all that the 'realists' have to say."[80]

Arriving at a position close to David Bomberg's—in part because he had been looking at Bomberg's paintings—Pound overturns his own realism in favor of the independence of form: "form, not the *form of anything*."[81] Kandinsky had been moving toward fully abstract designs since around 1907. From this point, his paintings begin to absorb referential detail in broad fields of color that overwhelmed the still-recognizable shapes of houses and towns, cars and human bodies. The images lost their depth, and as they became flatter, the color fields broke into small units of form. A new language of shapes—discs, kidneys, ribbons, bands, grids—appeared, and as Kandinsky grew in confidence, he took the last steps toward a pure abstraction, though not without backward glances at the world he was leaving behind. His influential work *Über das Geistige in der Kunst* (Concerning the Spiritual in Art) was translated into English in 1914. Its assertion that the "emancipation from dependence on nature is only just beginning" arrived at a timely moment in Pound's quest for a formalism.[82]

How could poetry give up the world and achieve the pure forms of abstraction? The question preoccupied Pound in the months leading up to the war. After an Imagism of "true witness," how could poetry, too, liberate itself from nature?[83] Pound's response depended on his rapidly shifting interests: from Yeats and Ford to those who were making (and theorizing about) the new visual art now displayed in London, especially that of Wyndham Lewis and Henri Gaudier-Brzeska. Abstract painting and sculpture suggested to Pound that *each art had its essence* and that its most compelling achievements came through manifesting its essential forms, not through the distractions of representation. The poet writes with images, as the painter uses paint: each must stay faithful to the "primary pigment." Poetry can then be as abstract as painting. With that thought in mind, writes Pound, "you can go ahead and apply Kandinsky, you can transpose his chapter on the language of form and colour and apply it to the writing of verse."[84] In the second issue of the vorticist journal *Blast,* Pound offered an example of a poetry of the primary pigment, entitled "Dogmatic Statement on the Game and Play of Chess."

In another context I have emphasized how Pound's poem, which dropped quickly out of his canon, shows the impasse facing the experiment. It evokes the non-representational styles of the new paintings and sculpture—"lines of one colour," "living in form," "reform the pattern"—but it does so by means of representation. It is a poem *about* the new abstract forms, but not a poem *in* those forms. When it first appeared, its subtitle was "Theme for a Series of Pictures," and for all of Pound's talk about the primary pigment of each art, his "Dogmatic Statement" depends on another art, the art of painting, to achieve the illusion of abstraction. The problem, quickly recognized in avant-garde circles, is that the references and connotations of words seem intractable, more difficult to extinguish than the represented world in painting.

Apollinaire, pondering the same questions in Paris, came to different conclusions and opened a more sustained line of experiment. He began with what he called "conversation poems," built from scraps of overheard speech. More provocative works soon followed, poems that Apollinaire called "calligrammes," which followed the typographical audacity of Mallarmé in dismantling the horizontal poetic line in favor of utilizing the full resources of the page. Instead of lines in sequence, the calligrammes offered visual designs: words and phrases arranged in more or less recognizable shapes. There were poems in the pattern of rain, a valley, a snake, two lovers, a mandolin, a carnation, a bamboo. The light wit of the constructions should not imply that Apollinaire took these pieces lightly.

Apollinaire planned to publish the calligrammes under the title "Et Moi Aussi Je Suis Peintre" (And I Too Am a Painter), a resolve which confirms his ambition to invent verbal forms that could live up to the revolution in painting. Much as Picasso and Braque had recently begun to use printed text (and painted writing) on their canvases, so Apollinaire converted text into image. The chief motive was no doubt the ideal of simultaneity that he found in the paintings of Robert Delaunay, the conviction that a modern aesthetic must engage with life's vast, contradictory immediacy. The near and the far, the trivial and the momentous, the artificial and the natural all inhabit the instant of perception—this is the thought animating Apollinaire. To take seriously the mission of simultaneity was to approach a transnational consciousness, to recognize that the instantaneous plenitude includes, in principle, the entire world. The first of the calligrammes, "Lettre-Océan" (Ocean-Letter), published in *Les Soirées de Paris* in June 1914, releases itself to a global contemporaneity. Stamps from Mexico and the United States, a German steamship, images of a wheel and a tower, run at all angles—in slopes, circles, and crescents. The acronym for wireless telegraph, TSF, appears in vertical boldface, and MAYAS stretches in boldface horizontally below, while miniature type breaks apart words referring to both Parisian and transatlantic life.[85] The reader of the calligrammes is placed in the position of a world-gazing eye faced with limitless heterogeneity. There is no one place to begin, no first or last line. The act of reading is as much an act of scanning, with no obvious termination to the act.

TENDER BUTTONS, WANTON WORDS

Gertrude Stein's *Tender Buttons* belongs to the emerging configuration of verbal painting. Published in 1914, the volume paid an acknowledged debt to Cubism, Stein having recently written that she "was expressing the same thing in literature" as Picasso was in his painting. Although the comment cannot be taken at face value, Stein's prewar work was clearly in active dialogue with the new painting. But while Pound and especially Apollinaire tried to uncover a visual power inherent in poetry, Stein's experiment lies fundamentally within, not beyond, language, although *Tender Buttons* does have a self-conscious visual aspect: the three parts of the work—"Objects," "Food," and "Rooms"—lay out short blocks of writing set off by captions (or titles) in the upper case, as in this example.

CARELESS WATER.

No cup is broken in more places and mended, that is to say a plate is broken and mending does do that it shows that culture is Japanese. It shows the whole element of angels and orders. It does more to choosing and it does more to that ministering counting. It does, it does change in more water.

Supposing a single piece is a hair supposing more of them are orderly, does that show that strength, does that show that joint, does that show that balloon famously. Does it.[86]

The provocation of *Tender Buttons* is that such sentences still recall the norms of ordinary language: its syntax, semantics, pragmatics. The words and structures on the page remain haunted by the conventions they refuse. Passages often begin with the sound and rhythm of description; the reader reaches for a link with the caption; a few words seem to promise discursive coherence. Then the links break, leaving a sentence to end far from where its meanings began. Or a rhythm that hinted of closure suddenly changes and carries on regardless. Subjects arrive at predicates that they have never known before, and predicates find objects that flout the canons of sense. It remains central to Stein's project to retain the artifacts that compose the furniture of the world. Often the paragraphs throw brief bright illumination on their ostensible subjects (a food, a utensil), even as they follow the drift of words to distant points. Committed readers have identified some recurrent subtextual threads in *Tender Buttons,* including references to lesbian sexuality and to a philosophy of language. These subjects certainly appear in the work, but they are no more sustained than any other.

Tender Buttons frees itself to be *about* nothing—indeed, to make a mockery of our craving for *about.* The recurrent word "suppose" or "supposing," as in "Careless Water," suggests that the work is animated, not by the purpose-driven force of assertion, but by the openness of supposition, conjecture, and surmise. Amid the chorus of outrage with which the book was received, Sherwood Anderson came to its defense. "There is a city of English and American words and it has been a neglected city," wrote Anderson, and "the work of Gertrude Stein consists in a rebuilding, an entire new recasting of life in the city of words."[87] The image is a compelling one. It captures Stein's sense that language is larger than those sentences we use in practical life, larger, too, than the sentences that have made up literary life. *Tender Buttons* unfolds as if words have relationships among themselves, independent of our will and want. Here is "Rhubarb."

RHUBARB.

Rhubarb is susan not susan not seat in bunch toys not wild and laughable not in little places not in neglect and vegetable not in fold coal age not please. (338)

One way to think about the peculiar effect of *Tender Buttons* is in the terms offered by Susan Hawkins: to see Stein as refusing to quest for the deep interior consciousness that will be one signature of high Modernism and that her work had begun to challenge in *Three Lives.* Stein's technique, suggests Hawkins, "is not primarily concerned with the growth of human consciousness so much as it is to repeat, so insistently, a kind of phenomenological moment in which consciousness meets (but does not process) perceptual reality."[88] The mind continually forgets the act of perception, as it were, and so repeats the activity, but always with the difference that different aspects bring. In this respect, Stein's work resumes the flattening subjectivity that Baudelaire had broached and that Apollinaire had extended: the conversion of psychic depth into a screen that finds its stimulus in the world's abundance.

Yet what is notable (and notorious) in *Tender Buttons* is the way the problem of perception turns into the question of language. The book continually wanders from any focus of attention. Words describe objects, then usurp them. "Every word I am ever using in writing," wrote Stein, "has for me very existing being."[89] Words, that is to say, are themselves objects, rivals to the usual objects of perception. Stein in effect seeks to liberate language so that it can display possibilities repressed within protocols of sense. At various moments she lets words fly and releases them in chants of defiant whimsy.

THIS IS THE DRESS, AIDER.

Aider, why aider why whow, whow stop touch, aider whow, aider stop the muncher, muncher munchers.

A jack in kill her, a jack in, makes a meadowed king, makes a to let. (326)

Passages like these have understandably attracted the charge of "nonsense." But a closer look makes clear that the difficulty is not the non-sense but the looming and fading of sense. Even in disruptive sequences like these, individual phrases are perfectly clear. Similarly, the object world never disappears. Because almost all the captions are the names of things—especially small-scale domestic things—the text continually reminds us of the act of representation that it briefly performs and then strenuously deforms. The frustration for some readers, and the pleasure for others, is that expectations for discursive meaning are not simply baffled but continually half satisfied. Throughout *Tender Buttons*, language briefly settles within the conventions we know. Sense is shown to be a special case inside a universe of near-sense as well as non-sense.

WORDS AT LIBERTY: MARINETTI, LOY, STRAMM, AND DADA

In the years just before the war, lyric poets across much of Europe pursued the most extreme forms of aesthetic radicalism. "Free verse" (vers libre) appeared among the French symbolists at the end of the nineteenth century, but the liberation of rhythm was only a first stage of experiment. Futurist poetry began under the inspiration of vers libre; by 1914, Marinetti aimed to extend the freedom of verse to the freedom of individual words. A manifesto of 1914—"Distruzione della sintassi. Immaginazione senza fili. PAROLE IN LIBERTÀ" (Destruction of the Syntax. Wireless Imagination. Words in Freedom)—proclaimed the new dispensation.

> With words in freedom we shall have: CONDENSED METAPHOR— MAXIMUM VIBRATION—NODES OF THOUGHTS—CLOSED OR OPEN FANS OF MOVEMENT—SHORTCUTS OF ANALOGIES—BALANCE OF COLOURS— DIMENSIONS, WEIGHT AND SPEED OF SENSATIONS—THE PLUNGE OF THE ESSENTIAL WORD INTO THE WATER OF SENSIBILITY WITHOUT CONCEN- TRIC CIRCLES PRODUCED BY IT—REPOSE OF INTUITION—MOVEMENTS IN TWO, THREE, FOUR, FIVE BEATS—ANALYTIC MEANS OF EXPLICATION THAT SUSTAIN THE BUNDLE OF THE INTUITIVE WIRES.[90]

Beneath the uppercase declamation, the central thought was that poetry was still bound in the snares of syntax. Why should the sentence have supremacy? Why should the structure of grammar claim authority? The

"Technical Manifesto of Futurist Literature" (1912) had held that "one must destroy syntax and scatter one's nouns at random, just as they are born" and "one must abolish the adverb, old belt buckle that holds two words together."[91] Here is a translation of Marinetti's poem "Bombardamento" (Bombardment).

> cattle prods carts **pluff plaff** rear-
> ing of horses **flic flac zing zing shiaaak**
> hilarious neighing **eeeeeee** . . . shuffling of feet clinking 3
> Bulgarian battalions marching **croooc-craac**
> (*SLOW TWO TEMPI*) Shumi Maritza
> of Karvarena **croooc craaac** shouting of
> officers slamming like brass plates
> **pan** here **paack** there **ching buuum**
> **cing   ciak   [*PRESTO*]   ciaciaciaciaciaak**
> up down here there around up high watch out
> above the head **chiaak beautiful**   **Flames**[92]

Part of Marinetti's campaign was linguistic, inspired by a view widely shared in his generation: the sense that language was cluttered, that sentences were bloated with an excess of adjectives and adverbs, and that the rigidity of syntax discouraged speed and immediacy. To set nouns free— "cattle prods carts"—and then to allow other words, including nonsense syllables, to follow motions unconstrained by grammar became a concerted, uproarious assault.

In a similarly vehement polemic Marinetti emphasized a different poetic failure: the "I" of the lyric speaker, another relic that futurist poetry would consign to the past. "Destroy the I in literature," writes Marinetti, "that is, all psychology. The man sidetracked by the library and the museum, subjected to a logic and wisdom of fear, is of absolutely no interest. We must therefore drive him from literature and put matter in his place." In place of human psychology, which is exhausted, poetry can substitute the "lyric obsession with matter." Nouns, set free from other parts of speech, will show the accelerating world beyond the "cold, distracted I, too preoccupied with itself, full of preconceived wisdom and human obsessions."[93] Subjectivity adds nothing to the spectacle of modernity.

Mina Loy made an oblique entrance into this scene of lyric radicalism. Beginning a career as both painter and writer just after the turn of the century, Loy left England and traveled on the Continent, where she encountered

an avant-garde already in full upheaval. While living in Florence she met
Gertrude Stein and several futurist artists, including Marinetti (whom she
credited with "waking me up"), and by the time she arrived in New York in
1916 she had assimilated, repudiated, and re-formed a modernist aesthetic
and a lyric technique.[94] Loy's early publication "Aphorisms on Futurism"
responded to Marinetti's publications with sympathy and resistance.

> FORGET that you live in houses, that you may live in yourself. . . .
> WHAT can you know of expansion, who limit yourselves to com-
> promise? . . .
> MAY your egotism be so gigantic that you comprise mankind in your
> self-sympathy. . . .
> UNSCREW your capability of absorption and grasp the elements of
> Life—Whole.[95]

The format is familiar within manifesto Modernism: the sequence of imperatives, the rhetorical extremity, the insistent typography. But the argument significantly revises a futurist position that was becoming prominent.
Loy sets aside the overheated embrace of speed, industrial technology, and
war; she refuses to destroy the "I"; instead, she offers what can be called
a technology of the self. The demand to extend consciousness beyond its
usual limits, including the limits of body, is noisy and relentless. But this
image of enlargement runs alongside another emphasis: namely, the stress
on "intensification," according to the principle that "THE Futurist can live a
thousand years in one poem" and "can compress every aesthetic principle
in one line" (150). The controlling paradoxical image is that ecstatic intensification of the self will explode it into rapturous enlargement.

Apollinaire's poetry is a close cousin to the poetry that grows from
these convictions. Loy, too, turns free verse toward an open expansive form;
the lines of changing length and rhythm allow quick movements between
sensations of the body and reflections of the mind. But the salient contrast
with Apollinaire, as with Marinetti, is that Loy writes as a woman and from
the perspective of the free woman-to-be. Keenly aware of the contrast in
gender, she stages a sexual agon that involves both struggle with a man and
transports of pleasure and love. But she also constantly invokes the separate
being of the female "I." "Parturition" gives a scene of birth that is at the
same time the birth of a female selfhood brought into being through private "intensification," where the transported "I" expresses grandeur in the
face of pain.

I am the centre
Of a circle of pain
Exceeding its boundaries in every direction

(4)

The wavering boundary between body and mind gives one indeterminacy
—Am I my body? Am I my mind? My pain?—which can transform into
the indeterminacy of self and Other, woman and man, in love and in lovemaking. Here is the twelfth lyric from Loy's *Songs to Joannes*, one of more
than thirty in the 1917 sequence.

Voices break on the confines of passion
Desire   Suspicion   Man   Woman
Solve in the human carnage

Flesh from flesh
Draws the inseparable delight
Kissing at gasps   to catch it

Is it true
That I have set you apart
Inviolate in an utter crystallization
Of all   the jolting of the crowd
Taught me willingly to live to share

Or are you
Only the other half
Of an ego's necessity
Scourging pride with compassion
To the shallow sound of dissonance
And boom of escaping breath

(57)

"Go in fear of abstractions," Pound had written. But Loy's self-consciousness, especially her self-conscious ambivalence toward male modernism, destroys the transparency of imagist "direct treatment." Lyric XII
offers its scene of eroticism as a play of both flesh and abstract nouns—
"Desire   Suspicion   Man   Woman"—and it no sooner evokes the clutch
of passion ("Kissing at gasps   to catch it") than it falls into Loy's characteristic interrogative mood. Is the lover the "inviolate" Other brought into "inseparable delight" or only a reflex of the ego's need? The questions appear

not only without punctuation but without answers. Characteristically, Loy moves from "intensification" to expansion, from sensuous experience to the unfolding of a mental conundrum. Loy's "I" tumbles into love and wanders in thought, but "I" also weaves back toward confidence in her or his own powers. The voice of sarcasm and satire, the voice of unembarrassed desire, and, perhaps above all, the voice of proud self-ownership disclose an active female lyric subjectivity, emanating from within a crowd of men.

In 1912, Marinetti visited Berlin, where Herwarth Walden had founded *Der Sturm* as a beacon of German Futurism. Walden became patron and publisher to some of the most audacious new work, including the plays and poetry of August Stramm, whom he met in 1913. Stramm died within the first year of the First World War, but in the short time between his encounter with Walden and Futurism and his death, he offered a reinterpretation of Marinetti's words at liberty. In what came to be called *Wort-Kunst* (word-art), Stramm aimed toward the fullest resonance for each word, often presented in a line of its own, unencumbered by punctuation or syntax, as in the conclusion of the poem known as "Melancholy":

> dying grows
> the coming
> screams!
> Deeply
> we
> dumb[96]

This "word-art" still makes a world-reference: the caressing of the single inscription (its sound, its shape) sustains the labor of meaning. Even if the poet gives up the effort to represent a coherent world, a grammatical sequence, or a complex self, the power of the word still depends on the echo of each. Stramm's lyric evokes the trenches in wartime and the imminence of death; its force is balanced between human violence and the liberation of the word.

Meanwhile in Russia, at this same telling moment of 1912–1913, some of the most audacious poetry and poetic theory appeared. A group of young artists identified themselves as Cubo-Futurists and led a campaign for "The Word as Such." Much in the spirit of Stramm, they held that "the work of art is the art of the word" with its practical corollary that "a poem could consist of a single word, and merely skillful variation of that word"[97] and the further implication, articulated in "Explodity," that existing words, words in known languages, were inhibiting and insufficient, because "emotional experience cannot be put into words (frozen ones, concepts), word-tortures. . . . Therefore we strive for a transrational free language."[98] Trans-rational poetry—*zaum*—refused any obligation to reference in favor of the resources of sound and typography. A poem could be, and was, written entirely in vowels set free from the shells of words.

Across Europe, in the months just before the war, individual artists and small collectives made this defiant bid for the primal word, the word as such. There are distinctions among the poems and the movements, but they shared a vigorous resistance to the web of given meanings, often iden-tified as a journalistic web, a web of cliché, a bourgeois web of hollowed-out language. Young artists celebrated the Edenic word, separate, integral, pres-ent to itself. At its most extravagant, the liberated word was seen as a break-through to new consciousness and a new practice of social life. The experi-ments reached a culminating point at a slightly later moment—in Zurich in 1916, at the Cabaret Voltaire, where a group of exuberant antiwar artists gathered to invent Dada. In those legendary first evenings, they dressed in strange costumes, chanted several poems at once, and obliterated distinc-tions between words and nonsense. Hugo Ball, a founding Dadaist, offered these declarations.

> I don't want words that other people have invented. All the words are other people's inventions. I want my own stuff, my own rhythm, and vowels and consonants too.
>
> The word has become a thing by itself. Why shouldn't I find it? Why can't a tree be called Pluplusch, and Pluplubasch when it has been raining?[99]

ELIOT'S VOICE OF HUMILIATION

T. S. Eliot met Ezra Pound in the fall of 1914. The timing was significant, because it meant that Eliot entered avant-garde circles in London after the new movements—Imagism, Vorticism, Futurism—had already been formed. It was also just after the war broke out. Pound later commented that Eliot had had the tact, or good luck, to arrive in London "with a formed style of his own."[100] After reading "The Love Song of J. Alfred Prufrock" and "Portrait of a Lady," he wrote to Harriet Monroe that Eliot had "modern-ized himself *on his own.*"[101]

As a student at Harvard, Eliot had had a legendary encounter with Symons's *The Symbolist Movement in Literature,* which he found in the Harvard Union and read as a map of discovery. But what he ignored in the book is as interesting as what he found. Eliot kept his distance from the rhetoric of high Symbolism, the call to follow the pathway "leading through beautiful things to the eternal beauty."[102] Instead, the chapter that excited him was a brief discussion of Jules Laforgue, squeezed between Rimbaud and Maeterlinck. For Symons, Laforgue was an aftereffect of Symbolism, a drift from the visionary to the ironic. Laforgue, Symons wrote, so hates rhetoric that he prefers the "ridiculously obvious" with "lips always teased into a slightly bitter smile"(297–298). Laforgue writes beneath a mask that never drops, in an "icy ecstasy," and assumes the figure of Pierrot, comic, sad, cold, "speaking slang and astronomy." But under the force of irony, "everything may be as strongly its opposite as itself, and that is why this balanced, chill, colloquial style of Laforgue has, in the paradox of its intensity, the essential heat of the most obvious emotional prose" (299–300). "Here, if ever, is modern verse," wrote Symons (299), and Eliot must have silently agreed. He passed from Symons to Laforgue himself and began to develop the techniques that would lead to "Prufrock." This is the early lyric "Embarquement pour Cythère," the second in a sequence entitled "Goldfish":

> Ladies, the moon is on its way!
> Is everybody here?
> And the sandwiches and ginger beer?
> If so, let us embark—
> The night is anything but dark,
> Almost as clear as day.
>
> It's utterly illogical
> Our making such a start, indeed
> And thinking that we must return.
>
> Oh no! why should we not proceed
> (As long as a cigarette will burn
> When you light it at the evening star)
> To porcelain land, what avatar
> Where blue-delft-romance is the law.
>
> Philosophy through a paper straw![103]

The title in French, the self-mocking exclamation points, the faux conversational style, the minor contrivances of civilization (sandwiches, ginger beer, cigarettes), create an arch ceremony of the everyday. But the work of the poem, as throughout Eliot's early pieces, is to mark the distance within complicity. The friction of juxtaposition—philosophy and a paper straw—dissolves solidity in irony: every gesture seems a movement in a play. Eliot names his characters "marionettes," leaving the speaking "I" in the guise of Laforgue's Pierrot, just another puppet, but the one saved—and cursed—by self-consciousness.

Those who perform social rituals, especially the ritual of love, are caught in a machinery of insincerity. But though the social realm is hollow and flirtation shallow, the speaker is in the midst of it. There is no retreat. On one side looms the tangle of sociality, and on the other the abyss of thought, as we see in "Prufrock."

> For I have known them all already, known them all:—
> Have known the evenings, mornings, afternoons,
> I have measured out my life with coffee spoons;
> I know the voices dying with a dying fall
> Beneath the music from a farther room.
>   So how should I presume?[104]

Eliot's Prufrock exists within the terms of the impasse; he can neither stay away from, nor coincide with, the world of the drawing-room, the field of impossible desire. Impelled (again) to "prepare a face to meet the faces that you meet," he comes close only to be farther away (4). This is the scene of self-consciousness in Eliot: to be so near to others that you can smell "perfume from a dress" and yet to remain at an infinite distance.

Eliot later wrote that his style developed "from the study of Laforgue together with the later Elizabethan drama,"[105] and Hugh Kenner has persuasively weighed the force of this claim. Elizabethan playwrights such as Thomas Middleton and Cyril Tourneur offered a "grave magniloquence" that corrected for the "bittersweet dandyism" of Laforgue, even as Laforgue's irony opened up the "rant" of the dramatists.[106] The effect is a vibration between irony and conviction. The characters in the early poetry, Prufrock above all, have no foundation on which to bring irony to rest, but they are still capable of intensities.

> And would it have been worth it, after all,
> Would it have been worth while,
> After the sunsets and the dooryards and the sprinkled streets,
> After the novels, after the teacups, after the skirts that trail along the
>   floor—

And this, and so much more?—
It is impossible to say just what I mean!

(6)

Self-consciousness is an eternal restlessness. It can be neither sufficient to itself nor transparent to others. In this respect, Prufrock's condition recalls Mallarmé's "Hérodiade," that other hymn to an agitated self-consciousness trying and failing to keep itself intact. But Hérodiade remains fierce to the end. Prufrock, though he shares the agony, is detached from its claims. How can he be furious when he is also ridiculous? ("Almost, at times, the Fool"; 7).

The force of desire, sexual desire but also the mere desire for acknowledgment by another, keeps the mind in perpetual motion. Every instant of clarity ("I am no prophet—and here's no great matter"; 6) comes undone with the next press of impulse. The unpublished poem "Entretien dans un parc" recounts a moment when

> With a sudden vision of incompetence
> I seize her hand
> In silence and we walk on as before.

> And apparently the world has not been changed;
> Nothing has happened that demands revision.[107]

The eruptive act that ends the trial of passivity but leaves everything where it unhappily was—this is what Prufrock dreads and avoids. It is not, as is often said, that Prufrock is unable to act but that he has already lived through the futility of action. Passivity and activity come to the same end. Between the failure of intersubjectivity and the absurdity of desire, thought can only talk to itself, acknowledge and chasten itself. The speaker in "Entretien dans un parc" dreams of escape: "if we could have given ourselves the slip."[108] But Eliot's career begins by accepting that we cannot slip outside ourselves. Self-consciousness faces an endless vocation of reacting to the world and then, even more strenuously, reacting to itself.

What remains, and what will grow in the later career, is the flicker of another form of life. In "Portrait of a Lady," a sudden break comes in the midst of failed conversation.

> I keep my countenance,
> I remain self-possessed
> Except when a street piano, mechanical and tired

Reiterates some worn-out common song
With the smell of hyacinths across the garden
Recalling things that other people have desired.

(10)

This moment is strained and elusive. It offers no sign of paradise, but it suggests that in the universe of cliché, there will be glimpses of what might have been, and what has been, for "other people." Among the street scenes in "Preludes"—with their "grimy scraps," "muddy feet," "dingy shades," and "sparrows in the gutters"—the speaker withdraws from the sordid world.

I am moved by fancies that are curled
Around these images, and cling:
The notion of some infinitely gentle
Infinitely suffering thing.

(13)

Prufrock, near the end of his monologue, has his version of this fugitive vision. As he imagines aging into insignificance ("I grow old . . . I grow old . . ."), he thinks of "mermaids singing, each to each."

I have seen them riding seaward on the waves
Combing the white hair of the waves blown back
When the wind blows the water white and black.

(7)

The gleam of beauty is only a momentary break in the circuits of futility. We might see it as all that remains of symbolist transcendence. The vision cannot be pursued or sustained: it looms and dissolves. And yet all of the first ambitious poems—"Prufrock," "Portrait of a Lady," and "Preludes"—depend on these moments. Each "I" catches a glimpse of another form of life, only to lose it immediately. As in "Entretien dans un parc," nothing has changed after the recognition. No one has been saved. The redemptive images are brief, hypothetical, and unsustainable. But they are also integral to the work of the poems, not only because they show what is lost or missing, but also because lost possibility is as important as actual experience. The desires that "other people" feel, the mermaids who sing "each to each" but not "to me," the fancy of an "infinitely gentle / Infinitely suffering thing"—these are rebukes to the enclosure of personhood.

The lyric "I" in the early poetry of Eliot is the humiliated "I." It both ironizes and mortifies itself. After the liberated voices of Whitman,

Rimbaud, and Apollinaire, Eliot's poems break open forms only to disclose the self-ravaging mind. The protagonists do not even achieve the right to howl in pain, because they know themselves as open to ridicule. Eliot described Prufrock sometimes as a young, but sometimes as an old, man. If he can seem either, it is because no matter how young he may be, he has already projected the long duration of pain. This is what the conscious "I" does in Eliot: it foresees the course of life ("There will be time, there will be time"; 4), so that at every moment, it is aging as it endures. More than the poems of Laforgue, which helped to incite it, Eliot's early work turns from punctual irony to the long rhythm of self-diminishment: "I should have been a pair of ragged claws / Scuttling across the floors of silent seas" (5).

Yet, as this last image shows, even degradation has its virtuosity. Failure is a spur to attention. It specifies what has been lost; it studies the desire that will never be satisfied; it gazes at what it cannot touch. Conscious failure becomes, then, a last act of resistance, a refusal of the "formulated phrase" (5) that gives only the illusion of being alive. In this respect, Eliot is close to the Cendrars of "La Prose du Transsibérien." Both poets follow the logic of defeat to its end. Both recognize that loss can be an escape (a risky escape) from literary as well as social conventionality. This is not the way of Whitman and Rimbaud, who promote world-conquering desire or incantatory vision, but the way instead of self-critique, self-ridicule, self-relinquishment.

Even to bring Eliot and Cendrars together is to feel the provocation of the prewar moment. Two young poets, each willing to take risks, disrupted conventions and disclosed opportunities within self-abandonment. Yet, the distance between them is just as significant. Eliot continued to negotiate with the traditions behind him, the rhythms of iambic pentameter, the form of the dramatic monologue, the lyric as portraiture. Cendrars not only dismantled the physical frame of the lyric but smashed the coherence of time, space, and personhood. In earlier histories of the movement, these two poets have been considered epitomes of Modernism, on the one side, and of the avant-garde, on the other. To place them in the same paragraph here is to reject the clarity of the contrast. Rather than endure the constraint of rigid terms, we should recognize the sheer spread of experiment on the eve of the war, the living exuberance before the fields of death.

4

drama as politics, drama as ritual

The vorticist journal *Blast* first appeared in June 1914. There would be only one other issue, diminished and chastened by the violence of the war, published a year later. But in that initial unrepentant publication, among the manifestos, poems, and woodcuts, came an open call to the suffragettes.

TO SUFFRAGETTES

A WORD OF ADVICE

IN DESTRUCTION, AS IN OTHER THINGS,
stick to what you understand.

WE MAKE YOU A PRESENT OF OUR VOTES.

ONLY LEAVE WORKS OF ART ALONE.

YOU MIGHT SOME DAY DESTROY A GOOD PICTURE BY ACCIDENT.

THEN!—
MAIS SOYEZ BONNES FILLES!
NOUS VOUS AIMONS!

WE ADMIRE YOUR ENERGY. YOU AND ARTISTS ARE THEONLY THINGS (YOU DON'T MIND BEING CALLED THINGS?) LEFT IN ENGLAND WITH A LITTLE LIFE IN THEM.

IF YOU DESTROY A GREAT WORK OF ART you
are destroying a greater soul than if you
annihilated a whole district of London.

LEAVE ART ALONE, BRAVE COMRADES![1]

During the years before the First World War, the challenge of young artists was preceded and overshadowed by the public action of suffragettes, and the manifesto in *Blast* reveals again the uneasy relation between radical art and radical politics. The formation of the Women's Social and Political Union in 1903, the demands for votes for women, and the series of urban disturbances—including the breaking of windows, the unfurling of banners, and the burning of buildings—indicated not only the strength of political resolve but also a canny understanding of modern publicity. When suffragettes chained themselves to the railings around government buildings, set mailboxes aflame, or paraded through the streets, they were making resourceful use of the power of spectacle. Such tactics are what the modernists also sought. When Marinetti introduced Futurism to Europe, he offered a counterpart to the action of the suffragettes, whose cause he brazenly opposed. Whether meeting in large halls or open spaces, releasing manifestos at a prodigious rate, or giving interviews and encouraging controversy, he saw that the "event" was more sensational than the "text" or the "painting."

POLITICS AND RITUAL

The parallel arcs of feminism and Futurism give a frame for the leading concern of this chapter: the course of modernist drama through public life. Both suffragettes and futurists recognized theatricality as central and indispensable; in this respect the two movements suggest another link between theater and the wider scenes of public tumult, agitation, and unrest. From the revolutions of 1848 onward, the possibility of social upheaval remained a threat to the middle classes. Even after the restoration of government, and even within countries like Britain and the United States that had avoided revolutionary violence, the aftereffects of disruption kept anxiety alive within the popular imagination. Brief eruptions could incite enduring unease. Strikes like those of the London dockers and the match girls at the Bryant and May match factory took on legendary proportions, and toward the end of the century the string of anarchist attacks stirred more public worry. The space of the city became the arena for political conflict, never more extravagantly than in the months of the Paris Commune. Any account of modern theater must sustain its connection to the theatricality of politics.

It must sustain another connection as well. Yeats, in his *Autobiographies,* recalls his first encounters with the spiritualist philosophies that so consumed him. In one passage he describes a meeting of "the hermetic students" led by MacGregor Mathers: "He gave me a cardboard symbol and I closed my eyes. Sight came slowly, there was not that sudden miracle as if the darkness had been cut with a knife, for that miracle is mostly a woman's privilege, but there rose before me mental images that I could not control: a desert and a black Titan raising himself up by his two hands from the heap of ancient ruins."[2]

Stirred by such experiences, Yeats fashioned his vocation as a poet-spiritualist eager to encounter the theosophy of Madame Blavatsky, the mysticism of George Russell (A.E.), and the secret traditions of magic. He had grand hopes for spiritual renewal: "I planned a mystical Order which should buy or hire the castle [Castle Rock], and keep it as a place where its members could retire for a while for contemplation, and where we might establish mysteries like those of Eleusis and Samothrace; and for ten years to come my most impassioned thought was a vain attempt to find philosophy and to create ritual for that order" (204). Yeats turned these fascinations to his own purposes, but his encounter with spiritualism in the 1880s and 1890s joined a wider current within the culture. Alex Owen has recovered the turn to spiritualism in later Victorian life, especially the vogue of drawing-room ceremonies, with their séances and mediums, their dark closets, their mumbled voices and apparitions.[3] We have met before the affinity between the literary practice of the symbolists and the social practice of spiritualism. Like the popular yearning to commune with the dead and the invention of elaborate ceremonies for the attempt, the gatherings around Mallarmé involved expectant moods, a breathless attendance on obscure words, and incantatory recitations.

Here, then, is the second issue emphasized in the chapter: the development of a culture of ritual that stood outside institutional practices of religion. Walter Benjamin argued that under the conditions of modernity, an art founded on ritual transforms into an art based on politics. This claim notwithstanding, we must recognize the abiding place of ritual even within the liberatory contexts of Modernism. Much as modern drama participated in the outdoor spectacle of social agitation, so it also drew upon the domestic ceremonies of the séance, upon ritual as well as revolution.

THE IBSEN REVOLUTION

Ibsen's turn to prose drama in the 1870s stands as a rare definitive mark of change. After the successes in the early verse plays *Brand* and *Peer Gynt*, Ibsen spent much of the next decade developing a dramatic form based on middle-class life as represented in everyday speech. The effort culminated first in *A Doll's House.* But here the clarity of development is already tangled. Produced in 1879, the play created an immediate sensation, but it took another decade for it to move through Europe, and by the time of its legendary premiere in London, Ibsen had changed the terms of his provocation. This is another example of the uneven development of Modernism that is crucial to understanding its complex history. Even as *A Doll's House* and *Ghosts* inspired the campaigns for theatrical innovation, newer work that would unsteady the consensus was under preparation.

The celebrated event in *A Doll's House,* remarked upon since the earliest performances, is the verbal rupture in the third act, when Nora Helmer interrupts the banter of domestic evasion and insists on having a discussion with her husband. Until now Torvald has had an open rhetorical field to indulge himself in long speeches, ornate similes, and ponderous emotionalism. Not only does Nora change the subject, she changes the conditions of dialogue.

> NORA: We've been married now eight years. Doesn't it occur to you that this is the first time we two, you and I, man and wife, have ever talked seriously together?
>
> HELMER: What do you mean—seriously?
>
> NORA: In eight whole years—longer even—right from our first acquaintance, we've never exchanged a serious word on any serious thing.[4]

Speech takes speech as its subject. The two characters debate the meaning of words, with Nora contesting her husband's assured semantics. She denies that she has been happy, and when Torvald questions that judgment, she chooses the word often translated as "lighthearted." "You've never loved me," she says. "You've thought it fun to be in love with me, that's all." They dispute the use of foundational words: "sacred," "religion," "duty," "husband," "wife." The unfolding of the exchange turns repeatedly from the momentous subject—the unsuitability of the marriage—to the act of discourse. "What a thing to say!" (109), comments Torvald, who then remarks, "A young woman your age shouldn't talk like that" (111), then "Be more explicit; I don't follow you." At the telling moment, Nora tells him that "you neither think nor talk like the man I could join myself to" (113).

The event that thrilled and appalled Europe was Nora's departure from her husband and sleeping children. But the shock of rupture needs to be placed within the speech conditions that prepare it. When the dialogue in the third act turns back on itself and confronts the disturbances of conversation, it lays out a challenge as radical as its final event, in some ways even more radical. Nora does not simply leave after speaking; she leaves *because* she speaks. *A Doll's House* displays the transformative act as the intelligible outcome of deliberation, and this fact is central to the political meanings of the work. It suggests that social change can be the outcome of enlightened dialogue and, further, that the achievement of such dialogue is a significant event in modern social history. In this respect, the productions of *A Doll's House* across Europe and the animated conversations in its wake continued the work of the play. Anecdotes abound of quarrels over dinner and demands by hostesses that guests refrain from discussing Ibsen.

One result of the play's delayed appearance in Britain was that it arrived at a moment when questions of gender, sexuality, and womanhood were becoming inescapably linked. Nora's exile from home served less as a conclusion to a play than as a middle act within the unresolved public discourse. Along with other plays to arrive in London in the early 1890s, Ibsen's *Rosmersholm, Hedda Gabler* and *The Master Builder* contributed still more disorienting images of the New Woman. The militant rejection of Victorian domesticity, the call for a new marriage law, and the demand for a transvaluation of romantic love—these supported the controversy that Ibsen's plays helped to incite and to illustrate. In a chapter in *The Quintessence of Ibsenism* entitled "The Womanly Woman," Shaw casts the issue as starkly as possible.

> The sum of the matter is that unless Woman repudiates her womanliness, her duty to her husband, to her children, to society, to the law, and to everyone but herself, she cannot emancipate herself. But her duty to herself is no duty at all, since a debt is cancelled when the debtor and creditor are the same person. Its payment is simply a fulfillment of the individual will, upon which all duty is a restriction, founded on the conception of the will as naturally malign and devilish. Therefore Woman has to repudiate duty altogether. In that repudiation lies her freedom.[5]

Shaw's influence on the reception of Ibsen was immense, and because his promotion of the plays coincided with his own dramatic success, he set the terms for much early appreciation. The revolutionary technique, he contended, was precisely the discovery of "discussion" as the central work of drama. Nora's demand to Torvald—her request to sit down and talk—establishes the new compact. "Formerly," writes Shaw, "you had . . . an exposition in the first act, a situation in the second, and unravelling in the third. Now you have exposition, situation, and discussion; and the discussion is the test of the playwright" (135). Shaw's long-standing success in Britain and the United States sustained the legacy of the discussion play—in which "play and discussion [are] practically identical" and "the spectators themselves [are] the persons of the drama, and the incidents of their lives its incidents"(146). But Shaw also linked Ibsen's breakthrough and the place of women writers: "When Ibsen invaded England discussion had vanished from the stage; and women could not write plays. Within twenty years women were writing better plays than men; and these plays were passionate arguments from beginning to end" (139). Indeed, as the century turned, a succession of New Woman playwrights came upon the London scene. Their theatrical writings appeared alongside the growing militancy of the suffragettes; the plays not only reflected but also incited the public performative aspect of the struggle for the vote. Elizabeth Robins, for example, an American actress who came to London and played Ibsen's leading women during the crucial decade of the 1890s, wrote *Votes for Women* (1907), a work of political drama that destroyed the boundary between declamation in the theater and clamor on the street.

The Ibsen revolution was in every respect a political as well as a literary event. Indeed, in Shaw's strong reading, the plays and their audiences offered a model for political deliberation. They created a flourishing arena for rational discussion based on open exchange and free of fantasy and cliché: "In the theatre of Ibsen we are not flattered spectators killing an idle hour with an ingenious and amusing entertainment: we are 'guilty creatures sitting at a play'; and the technique of pastime is no more applicable than at a murder trial"(146). Here again we recognize an early Modernism whose challenge is not through experiment in form but through discursive, thematic, and ideological contest—through an assault on mystification and a reasoned critique of social failure.

In the case of Ibsen, however, a further complexity remains. In Paris and London, the dominant capitals of Europe, his reputation depended on the two major "social plays," *A Doll's House* and *Ghosts*. But when these plays were followed by *The Wild Duck, Hedda Gabler,* and especially *The Master Builder,* the response changed sharply. These later works unsettled the terms of political debate; their characters were beyond ordinary comprehension. In *The Master Builder* the young Hilda—aspiring, insistent, hopeful—has persuaded the architect Solness to recover his ambition by laying a wreath atop a high tower he has built. All the pressures upon him have been corrosive and inhibiting; the competition with his rival Ragnar and the impasse with his wife, Aline, have aged him. When Hilda erupts into his life, he rediscovers, or thinks he rediscovers, his vocation; he remembers (or imagines) that he is the Master Builder. She solicits his strength, and when he is strong, he reinforces her power. In a dance of mutual affirmation, they enact their ceremony of will. In the last sequence of the play, the crowd watches Solness's ascent to the tower, and then his fall:

MRS. SOLNESS AND THE LADIES (*as one*): He's falling! He's falling . . .

A VOICE (*down in the garden*): Mr. Solness is dead.

OTHER VOICES (*nearer*): His whole head's been crushed—He fell right into the quarry.

HILDA (*turns to* RAGNAR *and says quietly*): I can't see him up there anymore.

RAGNAR: How horrible this is. And so, after all—he really couldn't do it.

HILDA (*as if out of a hushed, dazed triumph*): But he went straight, straight to the top. And I heard harps in the air. (*Swings the shawl up overhead and cries with wild intensity.*) My—my master builder! (383–384)

The play disrupts the categories of social critique and rational deliberation. It conjures a landscape—a house, a garden, a tower in the distance—that becomes less real and more evocative, less public, less intelligible, and more uncanny. Nietzsche, or at least Nietzscheanism, lies behind the performance of will in this last scene, with Solness resolved to climb the tower in spite of his vertigo and Hilda transfixed by the act. That he falls and dies is a catastrophe from the perspective of everyday rationality ("he really couldn't do it"), but from the perspective of self-overcoming will, his death is no failure. Nietzsche's Zarathustra watches a tightrope walker attempt to make his way between two towers. But a jester follows him on the rope and, by leaping over his head, confuses the tightrope artist, who falls to his death. Zarathustra, at whose feet he has fallen, consoles the dying man: "You have made danger your vocation; there is nothing contemptible in that. Now you perish of your vocation: for that I will bury you with my own hands."[6]

Yet Ibsen, working in the same strenuous region as Nietzsche, heightens the ambiguity. Hilda may be the Overwoman, but she may also be the fictionalist who comes to the end of self-belief. The moments of doubt punctuating the play, especially Solness's doubt, leave the conclusion balanced between transfiguring death and self-delusion. The double emphasis in Hilda's last line—"My, my"—suggests both the pride of the visionary and the pathology of infatuation.

The Master Builder mystified much of its audience, but it also confused some of Ibsen's ardent admirers. It yielded no paraphrase; nor did it offer lucid social insight. Seen according to common standards, Hilda is less a visionary than a murderer. Even those willing to follow other standards were hard pressed to link her to the New Woman, whom Ibsen had helped to invent. Kirsten Shepherd-Barr has shown how the play unsettled the "realist" interpretation of Ibsen that was dominant in England and also how it confirmed the "symbolist" reading now favored in France.[7] Within the milieu of Paris, the late plays were seen as evocative rather than demonstrative, suggestive rather than precise, while Maeterlinck's essay on *The Master Builder* secured the assimilation of Ibsen's work to the canons of Symbolism.

THE STRINDBERG REACTION

The difficulty in gauging the importance of Strindberg coincides with his own difficulty in choosing his terms of encounter. Nothing is more striking in his career than its instability. The various media in which he worked—fiction, poetry, history, painting, music, drama—are signs not only of his restlessness but also of the lures and opportunities of the 1880s and 1890s. The experiments of these decades varied widely, as did the theories brought forward to justify them. But they converged to suggest a *general avant-garde,* a perception that all the arts had arrived at emancipation. The recognition of innovation everywhere surely encouraged Strindberg to change the terms of his radicalism so quickly, but also to change his aims. As Otto Reinert has written, "At one time or another, Strindberg occupied just about every . . . position available to a late nineteenth-century intellectual, sometimes returning to positions he had violently abandoned earlier."[8]

Strindberg's success in the 1880s was an episode in the history, and indeterminacy, of the New. At a time when Ibsen's reputation extended throughout Europe, Strindberg appeared as a counter-Scandinavian, an alternative and rival who disturbed an emerging consensus before it had settled. The contrast between Ibsen and Strindberg became (and has remained) a convention of modernist dualism. It stands alongside other overly invested pairings—Picasso and Matisse, Stein and Hemingway, Proust and Joyce—and suggests that one tactic for disarming Modernism has been to arrange it in columns. But seeing this as a late defensive projection would be too easy, since the artists themselves clearly saw the oppositions and also felt some need to devise a coherence. Strindberg can best be seen not as a simple contrast with Ibsen but as someone attempting to radicalize both sides of Ibsen's innovation: the prose social drama and the symbolist vision. When Strindberg became a vivid presence in the later 1880s, the former turn was most notable. He converted the problem into the theater of sex war. Discussion in Strindberg became quarrel; conversation, a form of violence. That language secretes cruelty and becomes an instrument of domination—this insight deepened in the 1880s and extended throughout his career.

The event beginning the apocalyptic course of *The Father* is a contagious thought: the uncertainty of paternity. The Captain and his wife, Laura, struggle over the prospects of their only child, Bertha. Should she stay at home to sustain the traditions of her mother? Or should she follow her father's advice and live in town, learning the ways of a scientific and freethinking modernity? In the midst of their bickering, the Captain interviews a servant charged with fathering a child. But the servant claims to know nothing of the case, and when pressed, he insists that fatherhood is "something a man can never be sure of."[9] Once dropped into conversation, this thought follows a careening arc through the play. Haunted by the idea, the Captain mentions it to his wife, who caresses the doubt, hurls it back at him, and works to claim the daughter for the domestic tradition.

As a self-styled modern man, a scientist who despises superstition, the Captain places his hopes for the future in his daughter. Within his skeptical framework, a child offers the only chance for perpetuity. But in the tightening logic of the play, he is forced to accept that fatherhood is inevitably uncertain and that his paternal hopes are just more empty faith: "What good is anything to me now that you have taken away my hope of immortality, what good is my science and philosophy now that I have nothing to live for?" (70). The loss is not cast as an abstract problem but, significantly, as a problem in the battle between the sexes. The Captain is the strong man, dedicated to the rigors of free thought—the claims of science, the free inquiry of the modern—but he confronts a resourceful woman who discovers how to turn his weapons (evidence, certainty) against him and win the struggle for the daughter.

I say "woman," but as Strindberg draws the portrait, the salient feature is that women, rather than woman, are the destructive agents. "You've too many women running your home," notes the Pastor, and the Captain acknowledges that "Laura has allies" (30, 32). The brisk advent of the sexual agon and the rapid unfolding of events must have contributed to the shock conveyed by *The Father* at the end of the 1880s. Where *A Doll's House* laid the terms for a long cultural conversation, Strindberg presented a contest that was no sooner recognized than it induced catastrophe. During the three short acts of *The Father,* the Captain doubts, resists, strikes out, and succumbs. Between the dawning of uncertainty and his restraint in a straitjacket, no deviation interrupts. Once the logic of the sex war has shown itself, the conclusion is inevitable and near.

But there is a paradox in the workings of *The Father.* If, as Strindberg maintains, the war between the sexes is biologically embedded and inevitable, why should it come into view only late in the nineteenth century, and why so late in the marriage represented in the play? The deathly struggle between men and women was always there: why does it show itself now? The beginning of an answer comes in the preface to *Miss Julie,* where Strindberg suggests how we should understand the roiling unrest of his title character: "Miss Julie is a modern character, not that the half-woman, the man-hater, has not existed always, but because now that she has been discovered she has stepped to the front and begun to make a noise. The half-woman is a type who thrusts herself forward, selling herself nowadays for power, decorations, distinctions, diplomas, as formerly for money."[10] The thought here, one that underlies Ibsen's work as well, is that an ancient problem has at last been recognized, and once forced into consciousness, it has changed and deepened. From one perspective the New Woman is merely the latest incarnation of an eternal type. The prostitute has become the professional. But now that she has been named and known, her effects are unavoidable: "Love between man and woman is war." *The Father* shows a coming to consciousness of this war, whose only outcome can be catastrophe. Late in the play the Captain thinks of what has been lost and asks, "What became of love—healthy, sensuous love? It died, starved." Yet within the terms of the play, healthy sensuality was always based on a deception; it was a dream encasing the violence, "and then we awoke" (60, 74, 61).

For Strindberg, the pathos of the modern is that it reveals what is ancient and abiding, and so it is obliged to play out a fateful conflict. Now that the half-woman "thrusts herself forward," the man is compelled to resist. As the Captain sinks into madness, the women in the house (and the feminized men) bind him in a straitjacket while they quietly assume power. The daughter, Bertha, will remain at home, enclosed within traditional teachings, safe from the enlightenment of town life. The Captain emits the cry of the defeated male: "Strength has been vanquished by craft and weakness!" (75). Within *Miss Julie* the outcome is different on the surface—the man survives while the woman dies—but the conditions of violence are the same.

When Strindberg wrote these plays, he was a champion of the scientific and skeptical questioning that made conflict inevitable—and catastrophic. Although he remarked that "love is like the hyacinth which has to strike roots in darkness *before* it can produce a vigorous flower," he was relentless in the demand for knowledge: "I myself find the joy of life in its strong and cruel struggles, and my pleasure in learning, in adding to my knowledge" (68, 63). Like his Captain, Strindberg stands for the virtues of liberatory knowledge, even though it is rigorous science that brings doubt. Here is the nexus that became fully visible in the 1880s: on the one hand, the demand for an unembarrassed exercise of modern reason, a contempt for super-stition, and the craft of deception; on the other hand, an encounter with the eternal struggle for power, the conflict of men and women. The cult of reason leads to the discovery of irrational conflict. Knowledge leads to doubt. Liberation of thought prepares for a tragic apocalypse. This tense duality was part of what brought Strindberg to prominence, but it also cre-ated a productive uncertainty throughout late-century drama.

SYMBOLIST DRAMA: BETWEEN OPERA AND LYRIC

One further aspect of Strindberg's developing theater in the 1880s should be mentioned here. As he affirmed his dramatic Naturalism and continued to seek the effects of "real life," he laid ambitious plans to reform the mod-ern stage. He deplored the interruption of separate acts and the break in concentration during the intervals. Aiming to create shorter plays that could be seen in a continuous sitting, he hoped for an audience "educated enough to sit through a whole evening's entertainment in one act." If "we could abolish the visible orchestra, with its distracting lamps and its faces turned toward the audience; if we could have the stalls raised so that the spectators' eyes were higher than the players' knees; if we could get rid of the boxes (the centre of my target), with their tittering diners and supper-parties, and have total darkness in the auditorium during the performance; and if, first and foremost, we could have a *small* stage and a *small* house, then perhaps a new dramatic art might arise" (70, 73). The goal of this reno-vation was to create a raptly involved audience, free from the distractions of public entertainment. Strindberg wanted to sustain the "capacity for il-lusion" and to discourage any temptation "to reflect and escape from the suggestive influence of the author-hypnotist" (69).

The images are striking. Instead of celebrating science and reason, drama now emphasizes nonrational experience and the possibility for absorption within the dream-space of the theater. A well-known precursor of Strindberg's imagined theater was Wagner's theater at Bayreuth. In his 1873 report, Wagner offers this description of the experience he sought.

> Once he has taken his seat, [the spectator] finds himself very much in an actual "theatron," i.e. a room intended for no other purpose than for looking in, and, what is more important, for looking straight ahead. Between him and the picture to be looked at there is nothing clearly perceptible but merely a sense of distance that appears, as it were, to float and which is achieved by the architectonic arrangement of the two proscenium arches: it reveals the distant scene to him with the unapproachability of a dreamlike vision, while the spectral music, rising up from the "mystic abyss" like vapours wafting up from the sacred primeval womb of Gaia beneath the Pythia's seat, transports him into that inspired state of clairvoyance in which the scenic picture becomes the truest reflection of life itself.[11]

The name Wagner was an incantation through the 1880s. Quite apart from his place within the history of music is his influence on literary experiment, which can hardly be overstated. The break with the naturalist plots and informal styles of the nineteenth-century theater, the movement beyond history and toward myth, the creation of atmospheric tableaux, orchestral transport, and dream visions—these were inescapable precedents. We have seen how they stimulated many of the lyric projects of Symbolism, but they also encouraged its self-recognition as a movement and as a counterrealism. In the present context, the most notable effect of Wagnerism was its importance for symbolist drama.

Too little has been said about the turn from the grand public contexts of Wagnerian opera to the intimacy of the small-scale lyric opera, from the spectacle of Bayreuth to the compressed text on the symbolist page. At stake was a reimagining of the Wagnerian revolution, not as a public event but as an event in consciousness, as a transformation of subjectivity that requires no actual performance but only a strenuous imaginative act, a heightened state of mind that permits visions to be seen through the miniature.

Mallarmé remarked of *Igitur,* his closet drama, written to be read but not performed: "This story is addressed to the intelligence of the reader staging everything."[12] The reader projects a drama, imagines a gesture, hypothesizes a stage. As Mallarmé pondered his poem "L'Après-midi d'un faune" (The Afternoon of a Faun), he wrote that it was "impossible in theater, but demanding theater."[13] *Impossible in theater:* because no director could stage a scene so elusive, so brief, so intangible; impossible, too, because no producer could afford to stage such a drama, one for which no public could be found and no theater hired. But *demanding theater:* because it was a poem of gesture and ritual, the ritual of desire, that must be seen, if not with the eye, then with the mind's eye.

Symbolism absorbed the ceremony of Wagnerian opera within the confines of lyric poetry. It assimilated the aura of ritual, of sacred gesture, within its small-scale imaginary stage—on the page. Such poetry demands theater, but the theater remains purely imaginary, as far as possible from Wagnerian spectacle, the physical massing of bodies in the opera house, the social provocation of a large audience. Within the radical theory of Symbolism, drama could become nontheatrical. What, after all, did drama really need of the stage, actors, or physical gesture? Haskell Block has discussed Mallarmé's "detheatricalization" of drama,[14] and Martin Puchner, in writing of what he calls "anti-theatricality," emphasizes Mallarmé's "distrust of public audiences." Block notes that "the reduction of the audience, to a single person at its extreme point, went hand in hand with the virtual abandonment of the physical theater and the elimination of the acting group."[15] Within this strain of imagining, drama becomes a mental enactment, purified from the worldly trappings of the stage.

Here we should recall the allure of interior space in late-nineteenth-century life. Partly as a reaction to mass society and urban tumult, but partly, too, as an exercise in bourgeois display, the drawing-room became an overinvested site of cultural meanings. Much as Mallarmé reflected for years on the most emphatic staging of his performances, so middle-class families devoted themselves to the arrangement of interiority. The privately comfortable room, the socially ornate room, but also the expressive and evocative room, the room of the séance, were all settings of aesthetic/social fascination. It is not too much to see the bourgeois room as a little theater and to connect it with the literature of secular ritual.

And yet the remarkable turn at the end of the century was the materialization of the merely imaginary tableau, the staging of the dream. As long as the nineteenth-century stage was dominated by crowd-pleasing commercialism, the drama of symbolist ritual remained merely hypothetical. But in the late 1880s and under the direct inspiration of Mallarmé's poetry and theory, symbolist drama passed from theory to the theater. In 1890 the young poet Paul Fort founded what came to be called the Théâtre d'Art, which began with audacious dramatic productions, including a triumphant staging of Shelley's *The Cenci,* and public readings, among them a reading of Mallarmé's "Le Guignon." A threshold was crossed in the spring of 1891 when the theatre produced Maurice Maeterlinck's play *The Intruder* (L'Intruse), presenting Aurélien Lugné-Poë in the lead role. That the play could fail to offer the satisfactions of commercial theater and nevertheless win a committed audience showed that the hypothetical drama of Symbolism could now in fact be produced—it was no longer just a mental event but again a public ritual.

Maeterlinck's *The Intruder* and the play that quickly followed, *The Blind* (Les Aveugles), took blindness as the condition of insight. The metaphor was, no doubt, always on the point of cliché, as was the theme of death as a looming invisible presence. But the simplicity of Maeterlinck's presentation, the evident strength of the performances, and the uncanny atmosphere made these plays conspicuous and influential. Their force lay in dramatizing what had been a lyric perception. The aesthetic of evocation had seemed the mission of a nondiscursive, nonnarrative poetry dedicated to the suggestiveness of music. It was Maeterlinck's insight, much imitated over the next several years, to recognize that the pursuit of symbolist insight could be a leading subject for the theater.

The Blind offers a subtle and demanding tableau. As twelve sightless individuals struggle with abandonment—the priest who led them into the countryside having died along the way—they show that blindness and insight come in many degrees. A character called the Young Blind Girl says of the priest, "I was aware that he smiled very gravely; I was aware that he closed his eyes and wished to be silent."[16] "I believe there are stars," says the Very Old Blind Woman. "I hear them" (279). Others hear nothing, sense nothing, hope for nothing. They all huddle together and try to understand what has happened. Where has the priest gone? What is the time of day? Is that the ocean they hear? Not until the priest's dog leads them to the corpse do they grasp the situation ("There is a dead man in the midst of us. . . . My God! my God! what will become of us?" (306). Then, even as they realize that no one will be able to find them, they perceive the scatter of leaves, the fall of snow, and, perhaps, the sound of approaching footsteps. The stage directions ambiguously refer to the "direction from which the sound of footsteps seems to come" (316). Among the blind is a "madwoman" with an infant who can see, and as he weeps, the young girl holds him in the direction of the sound and cries out, "He sees! he sees! He must see something if he cries" (316). The blind listen for the approach of footsteps, and as the play ends, the girl turns to the invisible presence and asks, "Who are you?"; the very old woman cries, "Have pity on us!"; and the child weeps "more desperately" (319).

That they are blind and helpless would give them the pathos of victim-hood if only the audience were sure of what it could see. The drama unfolds in obscure light; the sounds are ambiguous. At one point the very old man cries out, "We have never seen each other. We ask and we reply; we live to-gether, we are always together, but we know not what we are!" (291). The play asks us to ask, "What is the reach of this 'we'?" If the audience sees no one arrive at the finale, might this be because it shares the blindness? The entanglement of the spectator in the action of the play soon became a fa-miliar device, but at a moment when the commercial stage offered distrac-tion and reassurance, Maeterlinck's involvement of the audience had great force. The central social provocation of Symbolism had been to imply that what was modern had lost a capacity to see. Both *The Intruder* and *The Blind* brought this contest between blindness and vision onto the public stage, each suggesting that an audience that confines blindness to the char-acters misses the chance to see as a symbolist.

Vision, too, has a form. In Maeterlinck's drama the provoking gesture is to simplify the events and to slow the pace of their unfolding. The ab-sence of a change in scene, the duplications of lines and phrases, and the repeated circling around the same subjects—Who has arrived among us? Where are we now? What can we see?—produce a heightening of emotion, not discharged until the final scene. Maeterlinck spoke of *la tragédie immo-bile* (motionless tragedy) and *le théâtre statique* (static theater), as opposed to *le tragique des grandes aventures* (tragedy of great adventures).[17] This distinction helps make clear that for all the importance of the precedent, his new work of the 1890s was not a return to Wagner. It grew out of lyric experiment; it did not aspire to a structure of myth, nor to grand operatic gestures or great deeds, nor to a synthesis, the creation of a total work of art (*Gesamtkunstwerk*) in which music, drama, narrative, and visual spectacle were united. Rather, the new drama epitomized by Maeterlinck's early plays was small in scale, fragmentary rather than comprehensive, suggestive rather than encompassing: Wagnerian opera passed through the alembic of lyric. Indeed, the progression—from the public spectacle of Wagnerian opera through the intimacy of symbolist lyric ("impossible in theater, but de-manding theater") and then back onto the stage in the smaller ceremonies of symbolist drama—should be taken as one of the leading trajectories in the history of Modernism.

AXEL AND YEATS

The dramatic poems of Mallarmé and his theories of gesture and mystery; the still-looming example of Wagner; the emergence of a symbolist theater in Paris crystallized in the early plays of Maeterlinck; the ambitious stagings at the Théâtre d'Art and then at the Théâtre de l'Oeuvre—all these produced a milieu of ceremony and ritual. The theater stood as an enclosed social space, an alternative to modernizing commerce (on which it nevertheless depended), an interior world that gave privilege to experience rather than to representation. But the theater of ritual has another lineage.

The most celebrated example is *Axel,* the long, fantastic, and obscure play written by Auguste Villiers de l'Isle-Adam and revised up to the end of his difficult life.[18] Both the play and its author became legends in the history of Symbolism, and when, after Villiers's death, the nearly unperformable play was nevertheless performed, it consolidated a phase of the movement. This work about initiation offered itself to initiates. The time is the early nineteenth century, but the whole force of the play is to recover the secret history underlying the emptiness of the present, with its hedonism, its ambition, and its bankrupt politics.

Axel himself represents the passage of the Byronic hero into the milieu of Symbolism. A brooding exile who prefers "silence above all" (46), he lives in his ancestral home, "an impenetrable castle, lying forgotten in the heart of still and awesome forests" (69), where he studies his hermetic books. The crisis comes when his cousin the Commandant learns of the gold that Axel's father hid. The Commandant insinuates and then demands that the gold be recovered. At the center of the drama stands the long conversation between the two men—preparatory to a duel—in which the claims of worldly existence are set against occult philosophy. "My name is *real life,*" announces the Commandant (87). "As for '*me,*'" says Axel, "I am quite simply a dreamer with whom it is rather difficult to deal and whom it might not be wise of your kings to defy" (123). Dream in this play is not a refuge but a militant assertion. Axel disdains the appeal of the "real" Commandant: "Did you think you were touching me when you shook my hand? Or seeing my real face when I smiled at you? As a guest in my home, I had to tolerate your unseemly and impoverished words . . . but within myself, I was listening to voices other than yours" (95). *Axel* flourishes the image of the symbolist as aristocrat. Alongside the languid aesthete, the passive consumer of sensations, there stands this other figure, the blazing initiate, who will have a notable afterlife in early-twentieth-century culture.

After Axel kills his cousin in the duel, he endures a crisis of renunciation. He turns against his mentor, Master Janus, who enters now for the first time, appearing in an archway at the top of the staircase, illuminated by the flash of lightning. His eyes, with their "magnificent expression," seem as if "they must forever oppress the memory of even those who had gazed upon him but once" (127). The austere mage and his fierce disciple perform a long dialogue through the third part of the play. Axel, who feels himself to be waking from a dream, longs to join the world: "Life calls to my youth, stronger than those thoughts that were too pure for the fire that dominates me!" (131). He hears the call of desire, but Master Janus urges him to preserve the hermetic vocation: "Spiritualize your body: sublimate yourself" (133). "The universe," affirms the master, "is merely a pretext for [the] expansion of consciousness" (137). But Axel refuses the impersonality of hermetic truth and chooses the "great crime of loving and living!" (138).

In the final act the play turns the wheel one more time. Sara, the last daughter of the princely Maupers family, "coldly flawless . . . like steel" (10), has made her own renunciation. She, too, had been a student of occult mysteries, and despite the coercion of the Archdeacon and the Abbess, she has refused to relinquish her inheritance ("castles, palaces, woods, and plains"; 5) to the church. Now she makes her way to the castle in the forest, where she meets Axel in the gallery of tombs. Hostility melts quickly; gun and dagger are thrown aside. In the crypt amid the relics, they speak their way into ardent love. But then, as they dream and plan, Axel recalls the vision of the infinite. When Sara looks to the dawn and proclaims that "everything summons us . . . Youth, freedom, the intoxication of power" (181), Axel asks why two such lovers need to bring their beautiful dreams into reality.

"The future?" asks Axel. "We have just consumed the future. All the realities, what would they be tomorrow, compared with the mirages we have just lived?" (182). He continues with a remark that reverberates for the next generation—"Live? Our servants will do that for us" (183)—and unveils his vision. He and his eternal love should die instead of live; they should avoid impurity and corruption and choose the inviolate dream: "Why seek to bring back to life all the intoxications, one by one, whose ideal sum we have just experienced, and why wish to subject our most majestic desires to momentary concessions, detracting from their very essence, which would doubtless be destroyed tomorrow?" (183). Sara resists, but only briefly, and as they prepare to drink the poison from her ring, she utters the final speech: "Now, since the infinite alone is not a lie, let us—forgetful of the rest of man's worlds—rise into our one and the same Infinite!" (189).

Axel stands alongside the *Liebestod* of Wagner's *Tristan und Isolde* as a supreme example of late-century enthrallment to the sumptuousness of death: the beautiful young lovers bid farewell to the sun and to life and, clasping one another, lie down on a gravel path among the tombs. The pleasure taken in the willing choice of death can be seen as a consummation of the culture of weariness. All the swooning and languid dreamers can finally sink down into beautiful dissolution. In this sense, *Axel* completes an affective trajectory for the later nineteenth century: a dream concludes in death. Yet death in the play also becomes a basis for the oppositional culture of the avant-garde. Set against what passes for life, images of death signify the radical artistic counterworld of those prepared to sit through the five hours of the play and make an aesthetic life out of its death-dreams.

Yeats was one. He was in Paris for one of the two productions of the play in February 1894, and although his French was limited, he remembered the event as revelatory. In a chapter on the "tragic generation" in *The Trembling of the Veil,* he describes how he puzzled through the text, reading it "so slowly, and with so much difficulty, that certain passages had an exaggerated importance, while all remained so obscure that I could without much effort imagine that here at last was the Sacred Book I longed for."[19] Elsewhere he speaks of it "as if it were a ceremony in some order or rite wherein I and my generation had been initiated."[20] At a moment when he was struggling to define his own experiments in drama, Yeats looked to *Axel* as archetype and guide.

From that time forward, he developed a deliberate and articulate theory and practice of drama that is as important as his lyric poetry to the history of Symbolism. In a succession of plays before and after the turn of the century, Yeats vigorously repudiated the claims of Naturalism and the temptations of commercial theater. The arrival of demons in the form of merchants (in *The Countess Cathleen*), the power of the faeries to lure a wife from the domestic hearth (in *The Land of Heart's Desire*), the ability of magic to subdue time (in *The Shadowy Waters*)—such tableaux secured affiliations between Yeats's plays and the symbolist dramas on the Continent. At least as important as the plots, almost always tending to the intersection of earthly and unearthly events, were the experiments with acting and staging. Yeats sought a new form for modern theater, one that heightened the incantatory force of ritual.

"Look to the bolt!" says the young wife, Maire Bruin, in *The Land of Heart's Desire*, "because the unholy powers are abroad."[21] She hears the lure of their call. Restless with desire, she is not reconciled to a safe and loving marriage, to the warm hearth, or to the Catholic Church. Here, as elsewhere in his work, Yeats emphasizes the yearning for escape to an unseen world, even as he openly acknowledges the claims of daily and rooted life. Maire Bruin turns from the sternness of her mother-in-law and sighs for the "unholy powers" (247): "Come, faeries, take me out of this dull house! / Let me have all the freedom I have lost— / Work when I will and idle when I will!" (241). The child faery who entices Maire calls on her to ignore the threats of the priest and to accept the call of her longing.

> Stay, and come with me, newly-married bride,
> For, if you hear him, you grow like the rest:
> Bear children, cook, be mindful of the churn,
> And wrangle over butter, fowl and eggs.
> And sit at last there, old and bitter tongue,
> Watching the white stars war upon your hopes.
>
> *(250)*

Wavering between desire and domesticity, this world and that, Maire Bruin dies in the arms of her husband. Father Hart draws a Christian lesson ("Thus do the evil spirits snatch their prey / Almost out of the very hand of God"), but the last words go to the unseen voices who sing, "The lonely of heart must wither away."

Yeats professed ardent solidarity with the drama just then stirring in Paris. He, too, stood firmly against both naturalist theater with its stern plausibilities and commercial theater with its pandering consolations. Like Maeterlinck, he wanted to stage the unseen powers that haunt everyday life, and yet by casting his dramatic subjects, like his lyric subjects, within the frame of folklore, Yeats again changed the terms of the symbolist project. For Maeterlinck, as for Mallarmé, the unseen realm was most often wordless and abstract: we are all blind wanderers, left to fend for ourselves as night falls. For Yeats, however, the other realm possessed vivid detail and bright precision. In his experiments with magic, he looked to the specificities laid out in sacred books, and when his drama turned back to Irish legend, he relied on the textures of folk narrative that had nourished his poetry. The modest success of *The Land of Heart's Desire* confirmed his ambition to create an Irish national theater; he passed the threshold into the new century with drama, not lyric, as his first commitment. His alliance with writers and actors, the support of his friend and patron Lady Gregory, and then the culminating gift from his fellow occultist Annie Horniman led to the formation of the Irish Literary Theatre and then the Abbey Theatre, landmark events in the history of Irish drama and the development of Modernism.

Politics and drama came into open conflict in Ireland, and Yeats's unsteady position between the campaigns of art and nationalism became more visible after the founding of the Irish theater. Should the new theater commit itself openly to the nationalist cause? Should its productions be in the Irish language? Should it be accessible to the widest possible audience? These were immediate and bitter points of debate. Yeats was often outspoken in defense of the national cause, and several of his plays, especially *The Countess Cathleen* and *Cathleen ni Houlihan* (written with Lady Gregory), were offered, though not always received, as contributions to the political campaign. But because his deepest allegiance remained with a literary/spiritual movement, he understood the work of the Abbey Theatre more in religious than in political terms. "The theatre began in ritual," he wrote, "and it cannot come to its greatness again without recalling words to their ancient sovereignty."[22] He firmly located himself within the tradition of Wagner, Villiers, and Maeterlinck and then alongside the visionary stage designs of Gordon Craig, to which we now turn.

CRAIG, THEATRICAL DESIGN, AND THE ÜBER-MARIONETTE

Craig's audacity was to see theatrical modernity as a problem, not of texts and their meanings, but of design and direction. At the turn of the century, while staging operas by Henry Purcell and George Friderich Handel, Craig developed a system of shifting screens to create expressive space, and he produced other new effects through the use of electric light. Christopher Innes describes the production of *Acis and Galatea* in which the "monster Polyphemus appeared only as an enormous shadow projected on to the backcloth, coalescing out of a deep indigo sky to tower menacingly over the 'wretched lovers'; and as the light grew a single fold of purple mantle, sweeping down from the flies, was enough—as one enthusiastic reviewer announced—to evoke the brooking form of 'the only real and impressive giant ever seen on any stage.'"[23] In his journal *The Mask*, in his books, and chiefly in his productions, Craig laid the groundwork for a radical theatricality that became a major influence over the next several decades.

The biting assumption was that the wretched state of contemporary theater was due to the poison of realism; the only way to restore the art of drama was "by banishing from the Theatre this idea of impersonation, this idea of reproducing Nature; for, while impersonation is in the Theatre, the Theatre can never be free."[24] The demand that the audience recognize itself on stage was the great error, because recognition leads only to a portrait of life at its coarsest: "*realism,* the blunt statement of life, something everybody misunderstands while recognizing" (89). "How ridiculous," writes Craig, "to say that the artist exists to copy the defects and blemishes of Nature!" (109) when the result will be a comedy of blemishes. Realism inevitably becomes caricature.

The alternative is the advent of a theatricality that repudiates the "tendency to be 'natural'; to make 'natural' scenes, and speak in a 'natural' voice" (35). The stage is not a window onto the world but a complex and artificial universe justified by revelation, not by representation. In one emphasis, Craig's views led to ever-greater ambitions for stage design, including an apparatus for raising and lowering columns that would combine with screens and lighting to create abstract moving images. The second, and more controversial, emphasis falls on the dispensability of the human figure.

"Acting," Craig uncompromisingly writes, "is not an art." True art is design, purpose, control, and form, whereas human beings are subject to emotion and accident. Furthermore, the actor always seeks realism: he "looks upon life as a photo-machine looks upon life; and he attempts to make a picture to rival a photograph. He never dreams of his art as being an art such for instance as music. He tries to reproduce Nature" (62). Craig's proposal was to discard the acting body altogether: "Do away with the actor, and you do away with the means by which a debased stage-realism is produced and flourishes" (84). What he sought was a reliable figure, one not subject to emotion, one indifferent to realism, impersonal and detached— that is to say, a stage puppet, or what Craig calls the über-marionette. He admits that puppetry has lost its ancient aura, but if we consider the fate of modern theater, we must recognize that the puppet's time has come around again: "To that end we must study to remake these images—no longer content with a puppet, we must create an über-marionette. The über-marionette will not compete with life—rather will it go beyond it. Its ideal will not be the flesh and blood but rather the body in trance—it will aim to clothe itself with a death-like beauty while exhaling a living spirit" (84–85). These über-marionettes, with their "grace," their "beautiful and remote expressions," their "noble artificiality," will be descendants of stone images in temples. In recovering an ancient theatricality, the über-marionette will destroy a debased modern realism.

For Yeats, Craig was both a theorist of anti-naturalist drama and a practitioner who had invented "the first beautiful scenery our stage has seen. He created an ideal country where everything is possible, even speaking in verse, or speaking to music, or the expression of the whole life in a dance."[25] From his first encounter with Craig in 1901, Yeats looked to bring him from London to Dublin in order to elevate the ambitions of the new Abbey Theatre. Resisting the lure of "peasant plays," Craig offered the Irish theater a stage fit for Symbolism. In place of the rigid nineteenth-century stages—where actors declaimed in front of painted scenery illuminated by harsh light—Craig deployed flexible screens, columns, and electric light, which created the evocative atmosphere that symbolist dramatists had imagined but only rarely produced.[26] Yeats arranged to have the screens transported to Dublin and reconceived three of his own plays—*The Countess Cathleen, The Land of Heart's Desire,* and *The Hour-Glass*—for the new stage.

J. M. SYNGE: "REALITY" AND "JOY"

In 1906, at a difficult crossing point in his career, Yeats wrote, "There are two ways before literature—upward into ever-growing subtlety, with Verhaeren, with Mallarmé, with Maeterlinck, until at last, it may be that a new agreement among refined and studious men gives birth to a new passion, and what seems literature becomes religion; or downward, taking the soul with us until all is simplified and solidified again. That is the choice of choices—the way of the bird until common eyes have lost us, or to the market carts."[27] His instinct was still with the bird, but the remark suggests how Yeats was starting to measure the costs of refinement and how he was locating power in the downward arc pointing to simplicity and solidity.

The virtue of moving downward was shown to him by J. M. Synge. When the two met in Paris in 1896, Yeats was already beginning to recognize the predicament of Symbolism. He felt "weary" of the "language of modern poetry" and worried that the occult had "separated my imagination from life." He gave his new acquaintance earnest and urgent advice: "Go to the Aran Islands. Live there as if you were one of the people themselves; express a life that has never found expression."[28] Although Synge took the cue, his engagement with the west of Ireland—with the life of a traditional peasantry and, at least as important, with the Irish language—took him in directions that Yeats had not anticipated but came to admire greatly.

Synge never accepted the Yeatsian harmony among folk customs, occult experiment, and literary symbol. For him, the Irish peasants were not relics of legendary heroes, nor were their customs signs of hermetic ritual. Rather, a first motive in Synge's work was fidelity to the life he witnessed, and in one immediate respect this ambition bound him to late-nineteenth-century realism. Synge locates his plots within determinate settings; he devises everyday social contexts; his characters remain within the embodied world. But the historical force of Synge's "realism" is that it follows the international success of Symbolism, which depended on a refusal of mere photographic representation. At an early moment, Synge's work participates in the complexities of a post-symbolist realism.

To set the 1905 play *The Well of the Saints* against Maeterlinck's *The Blind* is to gauge Synge's resistance to the symbolist theater that he had encountered in Paris. In *The Well of the Saints,* Synge, too, takes blindness as his *donnée,* but he gives up the expressive obscurity of Maeterlinck in favor of bright Irish particularity. Martin and Mary Doul are a "weather-beaten" couple sharing a sightless fantasy, encouraged by the villagers, that they are handsome and beautiful, noble and dignified—even as the audience sees them as haggard, bent, and broken. When a priest, "the Saint," sprinkles holy water on their eyes and restores their sight, they not only witness the truth of their bodies but also see the truth of village life.[29] No longer begging for pennies at the crossroads, they work and hope like those who had once created and mocked their illusions. The new existence is misery for the Douls. Having come late to sight, they see through social pretension and narrowness—"the muck that seeing men do meet" (59)—and also see the trap of clear-sightedness. The lies were cruel, but no crueler than the truth. As Martin Doul puts it, "The devil mend Mary Doul for putting lies on me, and letting on she was grand. The devil mend the old Saint for letting me see it was lies" (68).

When their sight fades again, the Douls are thrown together in their antagonism. But they bicker their way back into agreement and then into hopefulness. Mary projects an old age when she will be a "beautiful white-haired woman," while Martin pictures himself with a "long, white, silken, streamy beard" (73). The Saint returns, offering a second, irreversible miracle. But the Douls refuse. Scorned as lunatics, they turn toward the south, for, as Martin proudly says, "If it's a right some of you have to be working and sweating the like of Timmy the Smith, and a right some of you have to be fasting and praying and talking holy talk the like of yourself, I'm thinking it's a good right ourselves have to be sitting blind, hearing a soft wind turning round the little leaves of the spring and feeling the sun, and we not tormenting our souls with the sight of the grey days, and the holy men, and the dirty feet is trampling the world" (89). They return to blindness, but not to where they began. Not tempted by another "miracle," they now take their bodies—and their imaginations—as they find them. To give up sight is not to be lost in self-deception but to engage the senses more hopefully, and to join reality, and to dream: "hearing the birds and bees humming in every weed of the ditch," "smelling the sweet, beautiful smell does be rising in the warm nights" and also "looking up in our own minds into a grand sky, and seeing lakes, and big rivers, and fine hills for taking the plough" (82–83). The vision of ripe old age is neither idle illusion nor pinched truth, but an imaginative enrichment of the sensory life that remains. It takes the world as it is and describes it in hopeful speech. As Synge says in the preface to *The Playboy of the Western World,* "One must have reality, and one must have joy."[30]

This last remark belongs to his critique of the literature that surrounds him. On one side, he writes, Mallarmé and Huysmans create their elaborate works "far away from the profound and common interests of life." On the other side, Ibsen and Zola offer "the reality of life in joyless and pallid works" (vi). Synge locates joy in the heightening of everyday experience and defends the extravagant speech in his plays by claiming he has used only one or two words that he has not heard in the Irish countryside.

> A certain number of the phrases I employ I have heard also from herds and fishermen along the coast from Kerry to Mayo or from beggar-women and ballad-singers nearer Dublin; and I am glad to acknowledge how much I owe to the folk-imagination of these fine people. Anyone who has lived in real intimacy with the Irish peasantry will know that the wildest sayings and ideas in this play are tame indeed, compared with the fancies one may hear in any little hillside cabin in Geesala, or Carraroe, or Dingle Bay. All art is a collaboration. . . . This matter, I think, is of importance, for in countries where the imagination of the people, and the language they use, is rich and living, it is possible for a writer to be rich and copious in his words, and at the same time to give the reality, which is the root of all poetry, in a comprehensive and natural form. (v–vi)

Language as an abundant emanation, extravagant and copious, rather than refined and spare speech—this is what Synge created through his collaboration with the peasantry. It is commonplace to say that the turn to language was one of the salient events in Modernism. Yet modernist language was an unstable destination. Like Yeats, Synge scorned realists and naturalists because their words served a joyless referent. But he also rejected the Symbolism of Mallarmé, for whom the sacred word was justified only by what it evoked to the initiated few. What made Synge's work important for later writers, for Yeats and more particularly for Joyce, is that he saw verbal extravagance as its own joy and justification—and because he saw humanity as fully achieved only when it expresses itself in speech. Yeats astutely remarked that "all his people would change their life if the rhythm changed."[31] The medium of language is good in itself, because it is in language that human beings are most themselves.

As Synge's first and greatest defender, Yeats traced his "abundant, resonant, beautiful, laughing, living speech" back to Rabelais, Villon, Shakespeare, and Blake: all his characters "pass by as before an open window, murmuring strange, exciting words" (40). But Yeats was still drawn to a view of Synge as another kind of Symbolist. He connects him to Maeterlinck, who offers "persons who are as faint as a breath upon a looking-glass, symbols who can speak a language slow and heavy with dreams because their own life is but a dream." Yeats read Synge as yet another whose characters are at bottom alone, preoccupied "with their dream," like Nora in Synge's *The Shadow of the Glen*, "intoxicated by a dream which is hardly understood by herself, but possesses her like something half remembered on a sudden wakening" (46–47). Yeats was always drawn to a view of art as the "disengaging of a soul from place and history" (191), but Synge himself clearly saw language as animating life within, not beyond, the world.

Certainly, the roiling controversy over *The Playboy of the Western World* reflects a collision between the dreaming self and the society it disrupts. This is true of the world within the play, and no less of the audience outside it. When Christy Mahon arrives in the village, he is a shivering, whimpering wreck, but he is also prepared to reconstruct his life in fantasy. Because he believes he has murdered his father and because the villagers thrill to the story of his crime, he can freely fabricate a heroic selfhood. A comic race unfolds between the credulous listeners and Christy, who is quick to discover that his crime is his glory. As willful Pegeen sets aside her fiancé Shawn and draws toward the newcomer, the play tests the power of words to transform the real into the radiant. By the time Christy and Pegeen traverse their dialogue, a sordid bloody encounter on a distant hill becomes the sign of epic heroism. When she tells him that he must have come from a great family, he is ready to accept the image, and she presses onward.

PEGEEN: Wasn't I telling you, and you a fine, handsome young fellow with a noble brow?

CHRISTY: [with a flush of delighted surprise] Is it me?[32]

His hesitation is brief. If she believes it, and he can say it, then there will be no limits to the remaking of reality. Pegeen, too, watches herself change within the crucible of mutual enchantment: "And to think it's me is talking sweetly, Christy Mahon, and I the fright of seven townlands for my biting tongue. Well, the heart's a wonder; and I'm thinking there won't be our like in Mayo for gallant lovers from this hour to-day" (92).

Through the length of their infatuation, *The Playboy of the Western World* unveils a central modernist insight, which took one form in Nietzsche's claim (there are no facts, only interpretations) and another in Conrad's image (the truth is disclosed in the moment of illusion). The emphases are different. But the thought returns in many places within Modernism. It reflects, on the one hand, a resistance to empiricism, to the authority of science, and to the supremacy of fact; on the other hand, it displays the aesthetic ambition to absorb and surpass religion, taking unto itself the power of miracle. Associations of religion never disappear from *Playboy*: Christy remains linked to his namesake, Christ, even within the worldly terms of the play. Just as important is the play's famous comic reversal, when the merely wounded father arrives to expose Christy as a sham who never killed his father. ("And it's lies you told," says Pegeen, "letting on you had him slitted, and you nothing at all"; 99.) When Christy responds by attacking his father and "murdering" him a second time, the aura is lost. Pegeen draws a bitter antimodernist lesson from the course of events. Far from being enchanted again, she concludes that "there's a great gap between a gallous story and a dirty deed" (107)—as if to say that verbal enchantment will always dissolve when the real comes close. The upsurge of fact constrains free interpretation. The crowd descends on Christy, who is bound and bullied, and then, in a sensational gesture, Pegeen burns his leg.

But in its last movement, *The Playboy of the Western World* turns again, when the still-unmurdered father lurches back onto stage and frees his son, announcing with mockery that "my son and myself will be going our own way, and we'll have great times from this out telling stories of the villainy of Mayo, and the fools is here." Christy accepts the cue and continues his improvisation. He will be "gallant captain" to his father's "heathen slave" (110). As he sends his father ahead, Christy makes a final speech that becomes a signature utterance for Synge and the Abbey Theatre: "Ten thousand blessings upon all that's here, for you've turned me a likely gaffer in the end of all, the way I'll go romancing through a romping lifetime from this hour to the dawning of the Judgment Day" (111). The poet-hero–vagrant-Christ ends with a superb act of refusal, abandoning the community that exalted and then condemned him. The lilting lyric is a rejoinder to fact and legality: Christy's goal is no longer to enhance the real with rich imagining; nor will he accept Pegeen's contrast between the "gallous story" and the "dirty deed." To go "romancing through a romping lifetime" is to assert the self-sufficiency of aesthetic will. He no longer needs either the reality of murder (an ultimate fact) or the legitimacy of shared perception. Christy can make his fantasy real in language. Rich and romping speech is more than a system of representation or communication; it is life itself, because even if speech cannot make the world, it creates the terms in which we know and grasp and love (or deny) it. When Christy has been unmasked, debunked, and diminished, he remembers the power of will, which for him is always verbal will. He does not speak in the stern rhetoric of the Nietzschean Overman, but his departure is a full-blooded repudiation of common life.

The Playboy of the Western World is most often, and understandably, approached from the perspective of its protagonist, and yet it is unhelpful to think of the play as leaving the community benighted while the Nietzschean hero prances off the stage. Pegeen's wail of recognition—"Oh, my grief, I've lost him surely. I've lost the Playboy of the Western World" (111)—is as irreconcilable and inassimilable as Christy's poet-heroism. No viewer can believe that she will make her peace with Shawn and return to domestic tedium, not after having her scalding insight: that joy came near and was refused. Tragedy is not too strong a word for the loss, but it never separates clearly from the comedy that runs everywhere alongside it. Synge defended the "seriousness" of his work—though not in the mode of Ibsen and the problem play, and not by declaring the morbidity of the modern town—insisting instead that in Ireland, drama is serious only to the extent that it is fully and finally humorous.

CHEKHOV, NIETZSCHE, AND TRAGICOMEDY

The mobility of tones and modes—the comic rendering of seriousness, the tragic upsurge within the comedy—has made *The Playboy of the Western World* notoriously difficult to perform. In any production the director will be tempted to overvalue one tone at the expense of another, giving an instability that registers a telling moment in Modernism. Synge cast the problem within extravagant gestures and rhetoric; Chekhov, at least as demanding in his tones, suppressed the artificiality of climax. The difficult question in Chekhov's late plays, as in his stories, was not how the community would acknowledge the Nietzschean visionary, the large-souled Overman and the poet-hero, but how it could survive—if it could survive—without the consolations of vision. The early responses to Chekhov, including Tolstoy's reaction, represented him as another photographic naturalist, an "unflinching realist," to use Leonard Woolf's phrase.[33] Because the major plays end in failure, especially in the devastation of long-cherished hopes, they can easily become emblems of tragic pessimism. Indeed, everything in the plot can be read as preparation for the harrowing recognition that one will never meet in love (as in *Uncle Vanya*), never escape the suffocating provinces (*The Three Sisters*), never return to the ancestral home (*The Cherry Orchard*).

The last play brought about the famous struggle between Chekhov and Constantin Stanislavsky. "Not a drama but a comedy has emerged from me, in places even a farce," wrote Chekhov, while Stanislavsky insisted, "This is not a comedy or a farce, as you wrote, it is a tragedy."[34] Written at the end of Chekhov's life, *The Cherry Orchard* was the last of the four plays produced at the Moscow Art Theater, premiering in early 1904. For all of its success, then and since, it only underscored the difficult ambiguity of the Chekhov oeuvre. In its final act the family prepares for dispersal; the property has been sold to the businessman Lopakhin, once a peasant on the estate and now a man of great means, who plans to cut down the orchard to make room for cottages. The matriarch, Lyubov Ranevskaya, will return to Paris; her brother, Gayev, takes a job in a bank; her daughter is going to study in Paris.

Pervading the activity of the characters, who run on and off the stage looking for objects, money, and one another, is a sense of irrevocability: after this, never again. As characters chatter in groups of two or three, a "sound of axes chopping down trees is heard in the distance."[35] Everything, in short, is in place for wistfulness, resignation, or despair. Indeed, at moments the characters break down. Varya, the adopted daughter, who for so long has been thought of as Lopakhin's destined wife, has a last conversation with him; again he comes to the point of proposal and fails. Accepting that this is the end, Varya sits on the floor, lies on a bundle of clothes, and "quietly sobs" (377). Near the close of the act, Lyubov Ranevskaya finds herself alone with her brother: "As though they had been waiting for this, they fall onto each other's necks and break into quiet, restrained sobs, afraid of being heard" (379). It is not difficult to see how Stanislavsky, who was rapturously enthusiastic about directing *The Cherry Orchard,* read it as a tragedy. What is more demanding is to make sense of Chekhov's claim for comedy.

In *The Cherry Orchard,* Chekhov accepts the logic of modernization and remains severe in unveiling the self-indulgence and self-deception of the gentry, who dally and dither and lose their home. But for all the austerity of its historical sense, the play also records the mournful disappearance of refinement. It invites a nostalgia that is constitutive of modernity. In *The Cherry Orchard,* elite social privilege has neither significant power, nor a glorious tradition, nor the right to persist. But even in its obsolescence, this privileged family looks toward a realm beyond matter and money; it looks back toward sensibility, charm, and taste, which can be seen as the worthy attainments of a dying class. Here we should recall Raymond Williams's discussion of the anti-bourgeois impulse in Modernism that nurtured a defense of cultural aristocracy.[36] Yet, as the work of Chekhov and Yeats (among others) reveals, aristocracy was not just a style adopted by the modernist artist in a gesture of defiance and contempt. Their work also sustained images of rootedness, tradition, dignity, and sanctuary.

The force of *The Cherry Orchard* comes in large part from the way it evokes these "aristocratic" emotions and images, only to make them appear as absurd as they are dignified. Gayev's paean to an old bookcase, which has stood "unflagging in the course of a hundred years, tearfully sustaining through generations of our family, courage and faith in a better future, and fostering in us ideals of goodness and social consciousness" (327) has its genuine feeling clotted by hopeless buffoonery. Lyubov Ranevskaya is often lost in reverie and regret, as incapable as her brother of taking steps to preserve the house and orchard. But modernity has no privilege over nostalgia. Trofimov, the young intellectual pursuing an unknown future, speaks with an eloquence that flares up but then fades away; the cynicism of Yasha, the young manservant, achieves no more authority than any other tone.

Chekhov's importance is most often seen in the austerity of his realism, in his acceptance of unresolved individual projects, in his attentiveness to broken utterances, to the silences and missed communications that constitute quotidian life. No sentimental consolation, no forced coherence— these are the abstentions in what has been called the "final perfection" of modern realism.[37] All this is true. But the shock of the plays, and what distinguishes them from other turn-of-the-century realisms, does not lie in the stringent rendering of unresolved daily life with its eternal aimlessness. It lies in the recognition of life as an inescapable ensemble. No one can avoid the web of sociality, which exceeds and dislocates every individual within it. The social aggregate is larger than the individual; it chastens individuality. Any demand immediately finds itself dealing with a rival. And because the rivalries are not a clash of opposites but a contention with profuse multiplicity, there is no prospect of either synthesis or final contradiction. There is instead a perpetual exceeding of perspectives. Nothing is constant but the activity of the ensemble.

At the beginning of the final act, Lopakhin bids farewell to Trofimov while the axes chop in the background, leading to the next sequence of events, where the motions of the group are as important as anything said. The first speaker is Lyubov Ranevskaya's biological daughter.

> ANYA [*in the doorway*]: Mama asks you not to start cutting down the cherry orchard until she's gone.
>
> TROFIMOV: Yes, really, not to have had the tact . . . [*Goes out through the hall.*]
>
> LOPAKHIN: Right away, right away . . . Ach, what people . . . [*Follows* TROFIMOV *out.*]
>
> ANYA: Has Firs been taken to the hospital?
>
> YASHA: I told them this morning. They must have taken him.
>
> ANYA [*to* YEPIKHODOV, *who is crossing the room*]: Semyon Panteleich, please find out if Firs has been taken to the hospital.
>
> YASHA [*offended*]: I told Yegor this morning. Why ask a dozen times?
>
> YEPIKHODOV: It is my conclusive opinion that the venerable Firs is beyond repair; it's time he was gathered to his fathers. And I can only envy him. [*Puts a suitcase down on a hatbox and crushes it.*] There you are! Of course! I knew it! [*Goes out.*]
>
> YASHA [*mockingly*]: Two-and-twenty Troubles!
>
> VARYA [*through the door*]: Has Firs been taken to the hospital?
>
> ANYA: Yes, he has.
>
> VARYA: Then why didn't they take the letter to the doctor?
>
> ANYA: We must send it on after them. . . . [*Goes out.*]
>
> (371)

The bustle in the final acts of Chekhov's plays indicates a collective activity that always overwhelms any bid for preeminence. Many of the characters evince the self-will and self-infatuation of Synge's Christy Mahon, but before they can begin fabricating grand personhood, they are challenged or silenced or sent off stage. Speeches are short; exits, like entrances, are rapid. Any attempt to find a center to the ensemble is doomed to fail. All of the leading candidates—the romantic Lyubov Ranevskaya, the rising Lopakhin, the overlooked Firs (the elderly manservant), the intellectual Trofimov —limit one another, and in each case the aspirations (or pretensions) of an individual are absorbed within a group that dislocates any center.

The structure of tragedy—loss, guilt, inevitability—remains in place, but if Chekhov can hold to his subtitle, "A Comedy in Four Acts," he does so, not only because of the farcical interludes, but because the work of the ensemble is itself comic. The group, in eluding individual will, makes the will ridiculous: this is the essential comic act. Stanislavsky was not wrong. Audiences have always responded to the tones of tragedy in *The Cherry Orchard;* and as with *The Playboy of the Western World,* the text is balanced so finely that each production can inflect a different emotion. Chekhov and Synge belong to different worlds; their work emanates from specific circumstances in Russia and Ireland; but from these distant points they approach a similar solution to the problem of modernity. They refuse the clarity of mode and offer "tragedy" and "comedy" as floating mobile conventions that enter new relations. The effect is what we now call "tragicomedy," which must be seen as one of the major syntheses of Modernism. In the hundred years since these plays were first performed, tragicomedy has been assimilated to the mainstream stage. But at the turn of the twentieth century it was still an unstable modern form. Audiences, like actors and directors, were unsure how to interpret central events, unwilling to lend emotions to such mixed characters, and uncertain how to link the works to tradition or precedent. In this respect, a new tragicomedy that represents an unfixing of modes is one of the legacies of the period.

At a telling moment in *The Birth of Tragedy,* Nietzsche asserts that "all individuals, taken as individuals, are comic and hence untragic—from which it would follow that the Greeks simply *could* not suffer individuals on the tragic stage."[38] As his attitudes evolve, he comes to accept, and then to embrace, the "untragic" individual, the laughing, dancing Overman, who is not precisely comic but who refuses tragic resignation. Zarathustra declares himself an enemy of the "spirit of gravity."[39] The gaiety of the Overman is another mark of the modernist passage from weariness to self-assertion. In Nietzsche's case the passage is from tragic catastrophe—the dismemberment of the individual—to the laughter of futurity.

Nietzsche, too, can be taken as one of the modern exemplars of tragicomedy. His Overman laughs in the face of nihilism, refusing to embrace a grave earnestness, but also recognizes the tragic conditions of a life without external sanction. Both Synge and Chekhov wrote within a framework (tragic gaiety) that Nietzsche put in brazen and explicit form, and which often appears as an undecidability between the claims of selfhood and the imperatives of collective life. Synge brings Christy Mahon close to the condition of the dying god, the Dionysian hero who must die in communal sacrifice. But when his father's recovery frees Christy from the sadism of the villagers, he steps off lightly as the laughing Overman, while it is left to the community, speaking through Pegeen, to comprehend the tragedy. Chekhov, on the other hand, tends to reverse the valence. Within *The Cherry Orchard,* and often within *Uncle Vanya* and *The Three Sisters,* individuals—a stuttering buffoon like Yepikhodov as well as the rhetorically sumptuous Lyubov Ranevskaya— can approach tragic self-recognition. But the work of the ensemble is to diffuse the tragic aura and move toward the comedy of the collective.

"EXPRESSIONISM" AND THE NEW MAN

Nietzsche, as will quickly become clear, belongs within another moment of modernist drama: the emergence of Expressionism. Here, though, it is Strindberg who offers the most immediate point of entry, the Strindberg who recast his work in the years after the triumphs of the late 1880s and the personal emergency of the mid-1890s. When he came out of his own "inferno," recording the experience in a book with that title, he was no longer the ally of Zola, who was committed to a disenchanted Naturalism affirming the necessities of history and biology. Now Strindberg pursued the vocation of occultism, telling Georg Brandes in 1896 that "we live in the age of occultism; it is occultism that now rules in literature. Everything else is out of date."[40] He defended the significance of hallucination and delirium. Sometimes approaching a Christian vision, more often veering toward a religious heterodoxy drawn from his reading of Emanuel Swedenborg, Strindberg spoke of the unseen Powers that control human destinies.

His transformed convictions belong to the wider turn-of-the-century struggle between science and spiritualism. In Strindberg's case, the break with science had direct literary effects: he now ardently affirmed what he had mocked just a few years earlier. As he later recalled, "When in Paris I came to read Maeterlinck, he was a closed book to me, so deeply immersed was I in materialism. . . . Not until after my *Inferno* years did I read Maeterlinck again, and this time he struck me like a new country and a new age."[41] But the symbolist scene devised by Maeterlinck—the anti-realist drama of intimations—was here given a sharp twist toward psychic trial. Less interested in the atmospherics of mystery, Strindberg absorbed the demonic powers into the agonized self. An unmistakable sign of the change came in *To Damascus*, a dramatic trilogy begun in 1898 and finished in 1901.

To Damascus records the flight/quest and wandering/pilgrimage of the Stranger, an autobiographical protagonist made to live through miseries that resemble those of Strindberg's infernal years. As the play begins, the Stranger meets a married woman, the Lady, who flees with him and tries to save him, but who then, breaking a promise, reads his most recent book. The work is said to teach her the "difference between good and evil," and in so doing, it teaches her how to hate her lover and mentor: "I like torturing and humiliating him."[42] The two reconcile and break apart, circle back to their innocent beginning, and then spiral downward to mutual loathing. When they are distant, they go in search of one another, and when they meet, they bicker and claw.

In those epitomes of Naturalism, *Miss Julie* and *The Father*, two antagonistic creatures, man and woman, performed their necessary violence. The unsteady balance between the enemies, always with more blame on the side of the woman, gave the drama its impetus. But in *To Damascus*, the Stranger, even as he flails at the Lady, who flails at him, takes the blame for the crime and comes to see the catastrophe no longer as a sex war but as the permanent anguish of consciousness-in-doubt: "I've stopped bothering about the others since I saw that the powers that control the destinies of men tolerate no helpers" (167).

The bafflement of selfhood is what *To Damascus* portrays: primal individuality moving through the ruins of faith. How is it possible to live when everything good turns to ash, when love transforms to hate, success to failure, pride to humiliation? The play relentlessly preserves the clarity of its disenchantment, even as it holds to the image of conversion implied by its title. At the end of part II, as the Stranger leaves his Lady and their child, he declares, "I believe nothing any more" (171). At this moment of extremity the Lady concludes, "All he wants is to leave the world and bury himself in a monastery, unhappy man" (173). This is indeed the step he takes, the unstable solution to the problem of the deracinated self: a retreat from the treacherous world and a grasp at spiritual truth. Sometimes that truth is called the Power, at other times the Powers, sometimes God, sometimes simply the Unseen. It is a reconstructed, reinvented, ever-changing spirituality, chiefly but not exclusively Christian in its images. When Strindberg completed the trilogy three years after beginning it, he left the Stranger on the point of undergoing the ritual of obedience at the monastery: he will be covered in a cloth and lie in his coffin. But up to the last minute he is har-ried by a Tempter, who lures him back to the world, parrying every opinion and challenging every hope until the Stranger can say only, "Enough! Or we shall never end" (260). "One knows nothing," he has admitted, "That's why henceforth I am going to *believe*" (196): the only hope is to receive belief as a gift—unwarranted, unjustified, but always longed for.

Not only does *To Damascus* rehearse a transition in Strindberg's ca-reer, but, as much as any single play, it opens toward a deep change in modernist drama. Much as *Ubu roi* exploded the refinements of Symbol-ism and showed the rich buffoonery of absurdism, *To Damascus* carries Naturalism to the limit, where it becomes an Expressionism. It does so by working all the way through Strindberg's abiding naturalist theme: the sex war, the inescapability and impossibility of love between men and women. At the furthest point of agony in marriage, the form changes, and the play exposes the Stranger to the illogic of his emotional extremity. As the Stranger moves through strange landscapes, he suffers the anguish of radical uncertainty: "Where am I? Where have I been? Is it spring, winter, or summer? What century am I in, what continent? Am I a child or an old man, a man or a woman, a god or a devil? Who are you? Are you *you* or are you me? Are these my entrails I see around me, are those stars or the nerves within my eyes, is that a river or my tears?" (168).

The extremity of doubt is an opening to literary experiment. The boundaries between characters drop away: a beggar reappears as a confes-sor, the cuckolded doctor as a priest, and the Stranger is never distinct from any character he meets. At each moment the past might return and familiar scenes abruptly transform to nightmare. The convergence of sharply out-lined reality with a fantastic dreamscape is the signature and legacy of *To Damascus.*

It is also the signature of *A Dream Play* (1902), and in a well-known author's note to this work, Strindberg linked the two dramas in this way:

> In this dream play, as in his former dream play *To Damascus,* the Au-thor has sought to reproduce the disconnected but apparently logical form of a dream. Anything can happen; everything is possible and probable. Time and space do not exist; on a slight groundwork of real-ity, imagination spins and weaves new patterns made up of memories, experiences, unfettered fancies, absurdities and improvisations.
>
> The characters are split, double and multiply; they evaporate, crys-tallise, scatter and converge. But a single consciousness holds sway over

them all—that of the dreamer. For him there are no secrets, no incongruities, no scruples and no law. He neither condemns nor acquits, but only relates, and since on the whole, there is more pain than pleasure in the dream, a tone of melancholy, and of compassion for all living things, runs through the swaying narrative.[43]

This characterization, although it bears on *To Damascus,* fits the new play more closely because Strindberg has radicalized his experiment. The career of the Stranger maintained the integrity of a case study; through all its scenes of nightmare and the merging of characters, the play still evokes the integrity of a consciousness, no matter how anguished and desperate. Even as its movement from despair to belief is halting and unsure, it remains an arc of possibility.

A Dream Play, on the other hand, is the emanation of a selfhood that never appears within the play but can only be projected behind it. No character is named the Dreamer; dream is rather the condition of every character's appearance and every event's performance. The insight in *To Damascus* was that a suffering self, a Stranger, could generate expressive scenes beyond the reach of Naturalism. But the *donnée* of *A Dream Play* is that no Stranger is necessary to defy the canons of plausibility. The daughter of the Hindu deity Indra visits Earth to see whether the planet's wailing sounds of complaint are justified. This is the dream's premise. A succession of visionary scenes follow, sometimes overlapping, sometimes discontinuous: in Strindberg's phrase, "patterns made up of memories, experiences, unfettered fancies, absurdities and improvisations." An officer is set free from a castle and then grows old waiting outside the stage door for the singer Victoria. A lawyer becomes physically ravaged—chalk-white, furrowed, grotesque—because of all the crime and vice he has seen. A poet arrives, staring toward the heavens, while bearing a pail of mud. Ugly Edith watches others dance and endures the despair of solitude. Through all the changes in time and place and through all the blurring of identities, the same refrain sounds: life is evil, and human beings are to be pitied. Because Strindberg evokes the suffering of a *world,* not that of an individual, there is no prospect of monastic retreat as in *To Damascus.* The world cannot retreat from itself. It can only come to know, without self-deception or sentimentality, the truth of suffering.

Transcendental subjectivity is an imposing but accurate description of the dream device—that is, a subjectivity, transcendental in Immanuel Kant's sense, that gives structure to a world without taking the form of personhood:

the condition of experience but not an element within experience. Much modernist innovation relied on investing a fictional character with new ethical/spiritual weight and psychological depth to create the character as the bearer of meaning. In Henry James's view, as we have seen, the supreme imaginative goal was the creation of characters subtle enough and responsive enough to disclose the significance of the world. But *A Dream Play*, much like its successor *Ghost Sonata* (1907), locates its difficult vision not in what any character sees or feels within the play—no matter how striking such moments—but in the workings of the entire strange imaginary universe. The world of the play is itself the register of transcendental subjectivity, which informs the work without having a role or name inside it. In the 1902 dream play, Strindberg held at least to the idea of an unseen dreamer who projected the evocative scenes. But in 1907, when he presented the chamber of horrors of *Ghost Sonata*—a house with a mummy in the cupboard, a predatory cook, a Room of Ordeal, and languishing lovers—he leaves the tableau unanchored by any reference to a dream. It stands as its own unexplained emanation.

We may take this attitude, gradually and unsteadily developed by Strindberg, as a leading source of the movement we know as Expressionism. The German drama collected under that label, like the fiction of Kafka, offered uncanny representations that resist plausibility but that also imply a transcendental vision underlying the strangeness. Strindberg was explicitly acknowledged as an inspiration for these works; Vincent van Gogh, whose late paintings approach the vividness of dream, was another precursor. The temptation has been to diagnose the psychopathology behind such unusual artifacts; and the lives of artists, especially risk-taking artists, continue to absorb us. But apart from the peculiarities of van Gogh's "madness" or Strindberg's "paranoia," the telling event is the convergence of attitudes, instincts, and strategies.

A landmark event in the history of Expressionism was a play by the painter-writer Oskar Kokoschka under the outrageous title *Murderer, Hope of Woman*. First performed in 1910, it offers a ceremony of sex and death in which a Man and a Woman, each surrounded by a tribe of his or her own sex, approach one another, circling, sniffing, and struggling. After the Man is grievously wounded and placed on a bier suspended above the ground, the followers dance and copulate while the Woman approaches the prostrate victim with curiosity and fascination. As she reaches toward him, he revives, stands erect, and begins a murderous slaughter of those around him, restoring his claim to potency and vigor. The abstractness of the events, the stylized arrangement of the stage, and the aura of ritual became exemplary precedents for a young generation of German dramatists.

For Kokoschka, as for Strindberg, a central incitement toward what became Expressionism came from the war between the sexes. So much turn-of-the-century art returned to this struggle. On one side were the claims of the New Woman and the suffragettes for an end to the double standard of male and female desire and for an acknowledgment of the rights of women within the public sphere (the right to vote, the right to hold political office). On the other side stood a male fascination-and-repulsion for sexualized femininity and an aggressive masculinist refusal of gender equality. As Ibsen became identified with the cause of women, Strindberg identified himself as the counter-Ibsen, the Ibsen who "is hated by grown men! That is why I hate him, especially since he caused the young to rebel, together with their equals, the married women, against the lords and aristocrats of creation—men!" He speaks of making war against Ibsenism until "the day The Father kills Hedda Gabler."[44] Again, the texts of Nietzsche can be read as the philosophic justification for a reinvigorated masculinism.

And apart from the ideology of the sex war, there remained the still-influential legacy of fin-de-siècle decadence, with its images of the alluring, dangerous, sinuous woman: Salome and her successors. The paintings of the Viennese Secessionists contained images of women as exotic vessels of desire—near though remote, alluring and destructive—while Aubrey Beardsley tested the limits of taste in his inked illustrations of vamping women, for whom sex is an instrument like any other.

Only a small turn in the male cultural imagination was required to move from these fantasies of female desire to the spectacle of sexual violence in which man must fight for his life. For Strindberg, as for Kokoschka, the struggle for mastery became an invitation to the extravagant deed, the scene of crisis, and the hallucinatory remaking of the real. Kokoschka's *Murderer, Hope of Woman,* as well as the famous posters that he painted for its production, caused a sensation comparable to the one that greeted *Ubu roi* at the turn of the twentieth century and had more immediate effects on other dramatists. Two years after its opening, a series of Strindberg performances won growing attention, beginning with productions by Max Reinhardt and including, most importantly, the trio of late plays, *To Damascus, Ghost Sonata,* and *A Dream Play.* Michael Patterson calculates that in a three-year period, twenty-four of the plays (more than a thousand performances in total) were produced.[45] At a precise moment, Kokoschka and Strindberg created the double precedent of a stylistic revolution enacted through scenes of sexual conflict.

Here, a distinction is worth making. When the plays we call expressionist began to appear in Germany in quick succession just before, during, and after the war, they told of a shift from sexual to generational conflict. It is not that sexuality disappeared as a question and an impetus but that the dominant concern became the resistance of the young to the oppressions of their parents—specifically, the insurrection of sons against fathers. Reinhard Sorge's *Der Bettler* (The Beggar; written in 1912 and produced in 1917) epitomizes this turn and also stands as the inaugurating work of a self-conscious literary movement. In its first act, the young poet (the Poet) asks his patron to sponsor a new theater to present his plays, which are too experimental for conventional taste.

> I want to show you images
> Of coming things, which have in me arisen
> In all splendor, visions that led me on
> To where I am today, and neither love nor lust
> Has hitherto been able to displace them
> Or even for one instant make them dim![46]

But the patron, who wants to consider "only what's realistic," resists the "fantastic" vision (40), leaving the new art at an impasse. When we next meet the Poet, he appears in the guise of the Son, returning home to confront his cruel father, who brutalizes the family in pursuit of lunatic scientific schemes. It is the task of the Son to kill the father (by placing poison in his drink) and to pursue his immense calling: to create an art toward which "people will stream / To be restored and saved" (41). Poet and Son are both names for the missionary calling. To be a poet is precisely to be a son—a son who can assume his vocation only through an act of parricide.

Walter Hasenclever's *Der Sohn* (The Son), written and produced at almost the same moment as *The Beggar,* develops this figure of the insurgent young man who will lead a "nation of sons." The protagonist, having failed his examinations, faces humiliation before the ogre-father, a doctor and a disciplinarian who suppresses his son's slightest tremor of desire. The Son turns mortification into revolt. Repudiating "old age and enmity," the "tyrant's hand," and the "graying hair," he becomes a hero to the next generation, who rally to his League of the Young against the World and accept his message that "the fathers who torture us should all be brought to justice."[47] Fatherhood, here and elsewhere, connotes both the intimacy of domestic oppression and the public realm of professional, state, and church authority.

Ernst Schürer has persuasively described the two poles of Expressionism as "its subjectivity and private nature on the one hand, and its desire for human interaction and public appeal, on the other."[48] Both Sorge's Poet and Hasenclever's Son sprang from psychic depths that left them damp with passion, but they also projected themselves toward a social world that would validate their hectic struggles. More than Sorge, Hasenclever lays out the treacherous ground that enmires the social visionary. The Son enters the public world—an auditorium, where he speaks to the nation of sons—only to find false prophets, tepid allies, and deceitful friends. Before the League can make its revolution, he must face a last encounter. After a fierce final exchange with his father, the Son raises his gun, and the father dies of a stroke. In a last ecstatic speech, the Son vows to step over the corpse to seize absolute freedom.

Both *The Beggar* and *The Son* sculpt versions of the figure who becomes central during the next decade: the New Man, the messianic individual who, through the labor of vehement emotion, strong will, and high rhetoric, can perform (and lead) a mission of liberation. A world captivated by science and technology—as shown in the dangerous fathers of these two plays—requires the transformative will of the New Man. It can only wither and corrode without him. Georg Kaiser's *The Burghers of Calais,* another early and influential expressionist play, presents a moment of historical crisis—the life-or-death threat to Calais made by the British sovereign—when the citizens of Calais are tempted to make a futile self-destructive gesture of resistance. As the leaders hesitate between fear and impetuosity, one of them, Eustache de Saint-Pierre, changes the terms of possibility, offering a path of sacrifice and resignation instead of wasteful violence. He asks the others, Are you worthy to perform a deed "which becomes a crime—unless its doers are transformed? Are you prepared—for this your new deed?—It shakes accepted values—disperses former glory—dismays age-long courage—muffles that which rang clear—blackens that which shone brightly—rejects that which was valid!—Are you the new men?"[49] In the spirit of the new archetype, de Saint-Pierre exemplifies the sacrifice that he teaches: he reappears as a corpse on a bier. Daunted by the power of the deed, the king of England relents, leaving Calais free.

The New Man was a close cousin of the Nietzschean Overman, the being created through the strength of his own will. The New Man, too, undertakes the revaluation of values, renounces assumptions that had seemed invio-lable, and inaugurates a new historical epoch. The community can only gaze and gape because, in the words of one of Kaiser's characters (the Million-aire in *The Coral*), "the most profound truth is not proclaimed by you and the thousands like you—only the single individual ever discovers it."[50] Yet the striking change worked by these playwrights is that the heroic self be-longs fully to the community around him, and he sacrifices himself to the greater good. Nietzsche looked with contempt on the liberal-Christian-democratic milieu of the later nineteenth century; he identified the work of the Overman as a denunciation of the life-denying values of equality, pity, and tolerance and a break with the supine masses who were incapable of transformation. The Overman did not belong to the contemporary world but projected a future beyond the grasp of a meager present. Sorge's Poet in *The Beggar* comes close to this Nietzschean figure, but as the New Man assumes his shape over the next decade, he rejoins the present. He is strong and willful, not in order to break with the society around him but in order to save it. As he appears through a succession of plays, the New Man remains an engaged political actor, increasingly committed to immediate social needs; indeed, much of the energy of expressionist drama can be seen as the attempt to bring the Nietzschean Overman back into the living po-litical moment. Moreover, in central cases the brazen individual act is justi-fied only by the hopes of the masses, whom Nietzsche scorned. As Georg Kaiser puts it, "Whatever happens to me in this time can happen with the same force to each and every other beside me. Then out of one, comes: ten, from ten: ten thousand, and ultimately, an infinite assembly of spiritual beings. I believe that whatever one can do, so can all others."[51]

The affirmative Nietzscheanism of early expressionist drama reversed its pessimistic sources in Strindberg and changed the valence of his late grotesquerie. For Sorge, Hasenclever, and Kaiser (among others), the un-canny and the grotesque were necessary for a progressive art, one that needed to reach the deepest zones of the psyche in order to liberate revolu-tionary images. And as texts came into performance, the act of physically realizing Expressionism on stage became emblematic. As Mel Gordon has put it, "For the Expressionists the new, untested Expressionist actor was not just a symbol of the physical rendering of the New Man. His abilities to transform himself from one soul-state to another, to emote the broadest range of feelings, to express the ecstasy of the playwright, and then to guide the audience made him the New Man incarnate."[52] David Kuhns has recov-ered connections between the yearning for spiritual/political freedom and the specific methods of stage presentation elaborated during the war.[53] Techniques of lighting, movement, and design heightened the affect and intensified the emotional and social stakes. As both Gordon and Kuhns have shown, the new style of performance developed out of the meeting of several currents: the visionary designs of Craig, the theories of physical movement of Émile Jacques-Dalcroze and Rudolf Laban, and the compelling example of Frank Wedekind, both as the author of *Frühlings Erwachen* (Spring Awakening) and as a charismatic actor who made a spectacle of his own body.

At the center of the emerging style was the radiance of the acting body. Paul Kornfeld, author of the early expressionist play *Die Verführung* (The Seduction), composed an "Epilogue to the Actor," in which he embraces the power of artifice: "Let [the actor] dare to stretch his arms out wide and with a sense of soaring speak as he has never spoken in his life; let him not be an imitator or seek his models in a world alien to the actor. In short, let him not be ashamed of the fact that he is acting. Let him not deny the theatre or try to feign reality."[54] Kornfeld here demands the unembarrassed theatricality and grandness of gesture that characterizes much expressionist performance.

One play after another rises to a crescendo, when the young protagonist can express the liberating strength of his will. He must step across the corpse of his father in *The Son;* he must sing out his poetic vision in *The Beggar;* he must denounce national orthodoxy in *The Burghers of Calais*. At these moments of the "Scream" ("Schrei") both individual and national history resolve into intensely concentrated bodily expression. The plays repeatedly build toward such ecstatic spectacles. In Kasimir Edschmid's formulation of 1917, the New Man was "entangled in the Cosmos, but . . . his emotions alone lead him and guide him. Only then can he advance and approach Rapture, where the tremendous ecstasies soar from his soul."[55] The performance of the Scream—the ardent chant of will in all its stylized unnaturalness—offers itself as the symbol of liberation. Behind much of Edschmid's work lies the utopian hope that if drama can summon a profound psychological intensity, if the actor can express deep individuality, then art will reform humanity.

The political engagements of Expressionism—its projection of "spiritual" vision into political life and its link between individual and social liberation—were partly an accident of history. The characteristic dramatic strategies were developed by 1912–1913, but many texts were not performed before 1916, when war was raging. This meant that the early plays inevitably took on a direct political valence. The visionary Nietzschean affirmations in *The Beggar* and *The Son* could now appear as antiwar utterances, as demands for life within a culture of death. When several of the leading artists were killed in the hostilities, the costs of combat (to literature as well as to life) became inescapable. Several important new plays written during the war had politics inscribed in them from the start.

Georg Kaiser's *Gas* trilogy (*The Coral, Gas I,* and *Gas II*) is a schematic history of modernity and a narrative of German national crisis, told through harsh strokes of caricature. In *The Coral,* a Millionaire wants to protect his children from the disasters that threaten them; he protects himself by appointing a double, his Secretary, to impersonate him in the outside world. But his children refuse the circle of immunity. His son runs away to work on a ship and sees the brutality caused by his father's industrial empire: "Like scales it fell from my eyes. All the wrongs we do became obvious to me. . . . We haven't the faintest right to do it—why do we do it?"[56] The Daughter joins the Son in this refusal, demanding that she be allowed to leave her father's yacht to tend the "most wretched of those who lie ill," those who "were injured in your factories" (161). Faced with the collapse of his project, the Millionaire attempts to recover the authentic will he has suppressed. He kills his double and appropriates the piece of coral that was the only way to distinguish the two men. Misidentified as his Secretary and charged with murder, the Millionaire accepts the absurdity of his sacrifice and does nothing to avoid execution. Kaiser is enacting, but also parodying, the first moment of Expressionism: the exalted belief that strong will is itself sufficient.

The force of the trilogy, however, is to carry on past this moment. In a turn toward explicit social address, the second play places the Millionaire's Son in the role of the New Man, who tries to lead the oppressed gas workers to emancipation. But at every stage he confronts rationalist modernization in the figure of the engineer, who proposes purely technical solutions such as producing more gas to save the German state and pacify the workers. A caustic suspicion of machinery—one major contrast between Expressionism and Futurism—runs through Kaiser's trilogy but never achieves resolution. The Millionaire's Son proposes an escape from industrial modernity into a fairer, healthier world—"streets lined with trees . . . lawns luxuriant with plants blooming out of the smooth turf"—where workers "are released from drudgery and profits."[57] But the workers remain transfixed by the promise of science. When his Daughter turns to his Son and asks, "Are you alone?" he answers yes, "ultimately alone, like all who tried to become one with all men" (240). As the play ends, he falters in melancholy wonder: "When will man make his appearance—and call himself by his name— man?" to which the Daughter responds, "I will give him birth!" (241). The prophetic individual above the mass, who teaches it to recognize its broken being and then to remake itself, is both an emblem of expressionist theater and a mark of its vulnerability to political critique.

Kaiser epitomizes the struggle between Modernism and modernization during the crisis brought on by war. His plays cannot offer themselves as a modern solution to the impasse of tradition. The problem they confront is not an immobile orthodoxy but a rival and dangerous liberation. Figures of the new technology, and also figures of cultural sophistication, appear as emblems of debased modernity, gesturing toward a false opening to the future. Hasenclever's Son challenges those who offer false freedom, while Kaiser's New Man contests figures such as the engineer and the curator, whose modern projects obstruct the real revolution, that of the regenera- tion of humanity. Moreover, as the succession of plays unfolds alongside the devastations of war, the affirmative tone breaks. Far from pointing to- ward the grand hopes of just a few years earlier, Kaiser's trilogy moves toward mass catastrophe; it is able to offer only a negative image of an unregenerate world still not ready for the vision of the New Man.

Eugene O'Neill stands in oblique and suggestive relation to these events in Germany, and the work of his early career, especially *The Emperor Jones*, registers the lineage. Aware of the European avant-garde but conscious of peculiarly American conditions, O'Neill conceived a work that has been taken as a breakthrough in national theater but which also looks back (and draws upon) earlier stages in Modernism. It does so, first of all, in its race- thinking. Brutus Jones is an American black man with "typically Negroid" features, though also with "something decidedly distinctive" in his face. A murderer in flight from the law, he finds himself among credulous natives on a West Indian island. Dazzled by his bravado and mystified by his Amer- ican canniness, his docile subjects make him emperor—until, that is, the day the play begins, when his subjects retreat to the hills to prepare for his overthrow. The events follow Jones's flight into the forest, which confuses and then undoes him: it revives the images of those he murdered and re- leases the terror of "Little Formless Fears" to haunt him. Drawn deeper into the forest, Jones finally reappears as a corpse borne by the West Indians who have hunted him down.

Brutus Jones is a black man killed by a tribe of black men. And yet the different register of their situations gives the play both its racial unsteadiness and its uncanniness. Jones is the black man as murderer, thief, and nihilist, but also as the citizen of modernity, of Pullman trains and streetwise shrewdness. Fashioning himself into the imperial lord, he stands in the shadow of Conrad's Kurtz. But when O'Neill places blackness on both sides of power—imperial desire and colonial subjugation—he makes race the stage for expressionist effects. Although there is dispute over when O'Neill first encountered the new German drama, it is easy to see why his work is so easily absorbed within its frame. Stylistic signatures of Expressionism are unmissable, appearing in the extravagant gestures, the externalization of psychic states (guilt, terror), the stylized settings of an unnatural nature (the haunted forest, a road to nowhere), and the relentless pounding of the drums, which accelerates as Brutus Jones moves toward breakdown. (The "faint, steady thump of a tom-tom, low and vibrating. It starts at a rate exactly corresponding to normal pulse beat—72 to the minute—and continues at a gradually accelerating rate from this point uninterruptedly to the very end of the play.")[58]

O'Neill's decision to cast these techniques within a marked racial context raised (and still raises) difficult questions. Partly, the problem concerns the persisting white presence inside the play's darkened world. The "Cockney trader" Smithers is opportunistic, unprincipled, and conspiratorial. A parasite on native life, he mocks both Jones's bid for grandeur and the simplicity of his subjects. Even as the play theatricalizes blackness as primitive —primitive even in Jones's hybrid "primitive-modernity"—it relegates the white intruder to the status of meager witness to forces beyond his comprehension. As he views the catastrophe of the "Emperor," Smithers is betrayed by his fascination: he is "unable to repress the genuine admiration of the small fry for the large" (1035). The stage directions record his fitful motion between irony and awe: "contemptuously," "wonderingly," "with a snarl," "scornfully," "in a tone of frightened awe," "mockingly" (1061). The quickly shifting tones reflect the play's own uncertain race-thinking; it treats Jones as grand and delusional, strong and vulnerable, charismatic and sacrificial. Through all these changes, he remains exotic, someone who can incite expressionist theatricality but who has neither desire nor ability to make a New Humanity.

O'Neill's first significant success had come with *Beyond the Horizon*, an overwrought domestic drama that turned on the self-bafflements of love. On a farm near the sea, two brothers love the same girl. Ruth chooses to marry the frail, dreamy, literary Robert rather than the hearty, rooted Andy, but as the years unroll, the married couple fail to prosper. The farm and the family decay together; Ruth and Robert fall into verbal violence and mutual contempt; their daughter languishes and dies. The hard force of the play lies in disclosing the impossibility of romance—romance as dream-vision and romance as passionate love. O'Neill named Strindberg as his inspiring precursor, affirming in his Nobel Lecture that "it was reading his plays when I first started to write back in the winter of 1913–14 that, above all else, first gave me the vision of what modern drama could be, and first inspired me to write for the theater myself. If there is anything of lasting worth in my work, it is due to that original impulse from him, which has continued as my inspiration down from all the years since then. . . . He remains, as Nietzsche remains in his sphere, the Master, still to this day more modern than any of us, still our leader."[59] The Strindberg who saw life as the biology of power and marriage as one long intractable conflict, the naturalist Strindberg—author of *The Father* and *The Dance of Death*—is a stimulus for *Beyond the Horizon*. But what makes O'Neill such a revealing case is that he so quickly shifts among the lines of his inheritance. The turn from *Beyond the Horizon* to *The Emperor Jones* is, among other things, a choice among Strindbergs, a turn from domestic Naturalism to the anti-realist expressiveness of *To Damascus, A Dream Play,* and *The Ghost Sonata.* Yet the most revealing aspect of the 1920 play is its suspension between the real and the expressive. It deploys experimental forms perhaps more radically than O'Neill will ever do again, but even here, at a moment of formal extremity, it negotiates uneasily with the claims of politics.[60] The program note indicates that *The Emperor Jones* takes place "on an island in the West Indies as yet not self-determined by White Marines." Increasingly in the postwar period, radical form is hemmed in by social urgency.

We may take this politicization as an emergent condition of both Expressionism and the twentieth-century avant-garde. Formal techniques that first developed in confined spheres—the urban street scenes of Kirchner, the early abstractions of Kandinsky, the generational drama of Sorge and Hasenclever—assume an increasingly ambitious scale. Kaiser's plays are again salient here. They exemplify a movement from evocative tableaux to socially engaged work on a widening canvas. Especially notable is the cinematic Expressionism of the postwar years, including such works as *The Cabinet of Dr. Caligari* and *Metropolis,* which sustain the political charge of Germany's wartime theater. These films extend the technical ambitions of the playwrights—the stylized bodies, the scenes of extremity in unnatural spaces, the uncanny representation of dream-states—and also the social ambitions. The struggle against cruel authority (parent, doctor, boss) remains a stimulus to expressionist style and the basis for its politics. But the later artists encounter as well the intractability of entrenched power. The liberating *Schrei* of the early plays becomes a desperate scream against an indestructible death-seeking authority.

It was perhaps the growing pessimism of these works that drove them beyond the drama of "rapture" and "ecstasy." The later pieces still draw on both the formal lexicon of Expressionism and the charismatic power of the New Man. Yet the works belong to a play of ideas as much as to a theater of rapture. In Kaiser's words, "Writing a drama means: thinking a thought through to its conclusion." He goes on. "Man speaks in order to think—and thinks in order to speak."[61] The contrast with Edschmid's view—"emotions alone lead [the New Man] and guide him"—is vivid and suggests how the course of Expressionism brought the ecstatic toward the political, and the emotional toward the intellectual. This turn looks ahead to Brecht, but more immediately to George Bernard Shaw.

SHAW AND THE PHILOSOPHY OF THEATER

Shaw is too often left out of account in the history of Modernism, and the reasons are clear. He did not invent radical forms; did not thrill to the paintings of Picasso or Matisse; did not participate in the collective solidarity of the avant-garde. And yet if we accept the notion of Modernism as an oppositional culture, a heterogeneous minority culture, then we must acknowledge Shaw, who was seen, and saw himself, as an unsilenceable insurgent. His journalism, his criticism, and especially his defense of Ibsen were all attempts to agitate authority. When he followed celebrated criticism with plays of his own, they appeared under the banner of revolutionary culture. In the present context, the best example is surely *Man and Superman*, Shaw's opus of 1903 that consolidates the political comedy of the 1890s and confirms ambitions that dominate the rest of his long career.

Before it was performed—indeed, when Shaw still thought of it as unperformable—*Man and Superman* was published as a book. As Katherine E. Kelly has helpfully shown, Shaw's interest in book publication was itself a significant moment in modernist drama.[62] It created a drama for the page as well as the stage and encouraged the development of a canon of dramatic texts open to interpretation. *Man and Superman* occupies a nodal place in this history. Not only did the play appear in a book, but the text contained a long preface in the form of an "Epistle Dedicatory" to Arthur Bingham Walkley and an afterword called "The Revolutionist's Handbook," which itself included a collection of "Maxims for Revolutionists." The composite character of the text is part of its challenge: it is an intellectually demanding play whose argument is extended in the postscripts and whose meanings are glossed in the preface.

The play begins firmly within the conventions (and spaces) of drawing-room comedy—Who will marry whom? Who is *already* married to whom? Ann Whitefield is an eligible heiress but also a willful, unpredictable woman, who enters the play adored by the sentimental poet Octavius, whom she teases but cannot love. Violet, sister to Octavius, is married to an American, Hector; though pregnant, she conceals first the fact and then the name of her husband in the attempt to ensure that her marriage will bring her a fortune. These strands of plot, which fit easily onto the popular stage, remind us of Shaw's concern to attract the pleasure-seeking audience that he means to denounce.

The work of disruption begins as soon as the focus shifts from event to interpretation. Love, marriage, sex, and pregnancy—what do these words now mean? And what are the most modern, the most progressive views to take of them? The first comic movement in *Man and Superman* is a contest between false and true emancipation played out between Ann Whitefield's two guardians. Roebuck Ramsden is an aging product of the mid-Victorian progressive consensus—an English reformism identified with free trade and moral earnestness. He despises his fellow guardian, John Tanner, with whom he vies for the banner of progress.

> RAMSDEN: You pose as an advanced man. Let me tell you that I was an advanced man before you were born.
>
> TANNER: I knew it was a long time ago.
>
> RAMSDEN: I am as advanced as ever I was. I defy you to prove that I have ever hauled down the flag. I am more advanced than I ever was. I grow more advanced every day.[63]

Roebuck Ramsden, as his name suggests, keeps up the patter of "advanced thought" but reverts to timid respectability at the first sign of challenge (Violet's pregnancy). Tanner, on the other hand, is his author's avatar, the superman of the title, who understands the strenuous terms of revolutionary change. His initial charge is to light the tinder of morality and marriage: he teases, insinuates, derides, denounces.

The subtitle of the play is "A Comedy and a Philosophy," and it is the Superman who keeps pressing the comic toward the philosophic. Shaw took his central insights from Ibsen and reinvented them for himself: theater was a space for debate, for the refining of a philosophy by which modernity might live. The philosophic ambition is visible everywhere. But its most startling appearance is in act 3, "Don Juan in Hell," where the play leaves the plausibility of the drawing-room and enters a new expressive space. Loosely justified as Tanner's dream (dreamt while fleeing from Ann in the Sierra Nevada), the scene replaces Tanner with his better-known predecessor Don Juan, who debates with the Devil; Ann Whitefield and Roebuck Ramsden appear as Mozart's Donna Anna and the Statue. Within the revolutionary cosmology, Hell is the place of endless pleasure and bodily indulgence. Heaven is where "you live and work instead of playing and pretending. You face things as they are; you escape nothing but glamor; and your steadfastness and your peril are your glory" (104). Even as the Devil dangles the prospect of ease without purpose, Don Juan prepares for the hard labor of Heaven, because in this cosmology an individual can choose a realm according to personal ethics.

The philosophy of life adumbrated in this third act, which Shaw called "a statement of my creed," was criticized as a derivative metaphysics, borrowed from the grand Continental thinkers of the nineteenth century. This charge never disturbed Shaw. He insisted, reasonably enough, that if particular ideas came from others, the act of synthesis was an achievement in its own right, and announced in a letter to William Archer that "my business is to fight for the Grand School—the people who are building up the race. My men are Wagner, Ibsen, Tolstoy, Schopenhauer, Nietzsche, who have, as you know, nobody to fight for them."[64] The confrontational metaphysics of the nineteenth century meets in Shaw in a revolutionary synthesis.

Don Juan himself, as Shaw explains, should not be seen as a figure of seduction or even of erotic desire. He is a renegade, a moral outlaw and an intellectual skeptic, less a lover than an anti-lover. Either under his own name or through his avatar John Tanner, he is the Superman. The figure is taken from Nietzsche, and the prospect of revolution is cast as a Zarathustrian passage from meager humanity to the successor-species that humanity invents for itself. But for all the importance of Nietzsche, Shaw remains equally committed to a tradition that descends from Marx by way of William Morris, a socialist lineage that seeks liberation for all. As in political Expressionism, the triumph of the strong individual will bring emancipation to the multitude. A "Democracy of Supermen" (198) is what Shaw (speaking as Tanner) pursues: "an England in which every man is a Cromwell, a France in which every man is a Napoleon, a Rome in which every man is a Caesar, a Germany in which every man is a Luther plus a Goethe" (193). Moreover, he pursues it under the inspiration of Wagner and Ibsen; his ambitious politics finds a home in the public spaces of the theater.

From this matrix of ideas, and especially from the philosophy of Arthur Schopenhauer grafted on to Hegel's, Shaw devises a Modernism too easily dismissed as eccentric. Life struggles to sustain itself; its energy, which he called the Life Force, will press on blindly unless it can come to self-understanding. In the words of Don Juan in Hell, "It needs a brain, this irresistible force, lest in its ignorance it should resist itself" (105). Both timid domesticity and self-satisfied reform ignore this subterranean power, which is why they can never recognize the urgent problems of modernity. But the few strong individuals will accept the double necessity of the Life Force: to perpetuate itself and to know itself. Within *Man and Superman* it is for a woman (Ann Whitefield) to set aside proprieties and to become "Nature's contrivance for perpetuating its highest achievement" (111)— that is, to find the destined man with whom to mate. And it is for a man (Jack Tanner) to become the brain, "by which Nature strives to understand itself" (133). Their marriage gives an intimation of the "Life to Come" (137). The sexual distribution clearly participates in other and older forms of hierarchy: the woman plots to sustain life while the man thinks out its meanings.

The great joke of the play, prolonged through many hours, is that Ann is the predatory sexualist, willing to outrage the norms of respectability— such as truth-telling and female decorum—to snare the unconscious Tanner. He sees himself as a free intellect, but in fact he is the helpless object of relentless pursuit. When an American correspondent described Ann as "bestial," Shaw responded that she was a "breeder of men," and "all the twaddling little minor moralities that stand between her and her purpose —as, for instance, that she must not be a naughty girl and tell fibs, and that she must not be what you (I rub in this reproach purposely) call 'bestial'— all become the merest impertinences. As she says in her transfiguration 'I believe in the life to come.'"[65] Ann is the precursor of the Superwoman, just as Tanner prefigures the Superman. Even if their relationship does nothing to undo the gender hierarchy of brain and body, the power given to Ann —to pursue and also to desire, to transgress, and to mock her pompous fiancé—shakes the conventions that it replicates.

When Shaw identifies his "grand school," he says not a word about Strindberg or Mallarmé, Jarry or van Gogh, whose artistic radicalism is simply left out of consideration. But rather than see this as evidence of Shaw's conservatism, we might better regard it as another sign of the uneven development of Modernism. Earlier I drew distinctions among phases of modernist provocation—including a distinction between the philosophic battle of ideas, epitomized by the controversies around *A Doll's House,* and the confusion stirred by what I called the transgressive tableau and the scandalous word and then later by a challenge to the category of art itself. Shaw was intent on continuing his challenge on the plane of ideas. Well aware of other aesthetic choices—especially in the poetry of Yeats and the drama of Strindberg—he refused the lure of what he called "style." He held to the promise of art as social action, and although the plots often assume the extravagance of carnival, they preserve an engaged vocation of thought.

10. Wyndham Lewis, *A Battery Shelled*, 1919. Oil on canvas, 71 15/16 x 125 in. Imperial War Museum, London. © Imperial War Museum.

11. Wyndham Lewis, *The Crowd,* date unknown; exhibited in 1915. Oil and pencil on canvas, 86 3/8 x 68 1/2 in. The Tate Gallery, London. Presented by the Friends of the Tate Gallery 1964.

12. Yves Tanguy, *Mama, Papa Is Wounded!* 1927. Oil on canvas, 36 1/4 x 28 3/4 in. The Museum of Modern Art, New York, NY. Purchase. © 2010 Estate of Yves Tanguy / Artists Rights Society (ARS), New York.

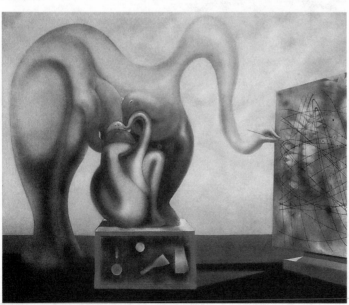

13. Max Ernst, *Le Surréalisme et la peinture (Surrealism and Painting),* 1942. Oil on canvas, 77 x 92 in. The Menil Collection, Houston, Texas, 79-36 DJ. © 2010 Artists Rights Society (ARS), New York / ADAGP, Paris.

5

modernism in and out of war

"Your generation," said a Cambridge undergraduate to his mother, "lost faith in God. Our generation has lost faith in man." The "Religion of Humanity" and its successor, "The coming of the Superman," alike mild reflections of the consciousness of God, have vanished from the public eye in my lifetime. The Great War disgusted every man with its manifestation of human power, which appeared as the Will to Murder.

—*Beatrice Webb*, Diaries

In this chapter I take up another perspective on Modernism, one that recognizes a great change in the movements that we sort under its name. Until this point, I have emphasized the uneven development in the culture of experiment before the Great War. Not only did the spectacles of Modernism move from one capital to another, but the leading impetus shifted from lyric to drama to painting, from novel to film, from the provocation of ideas to that of images and then to the categories of art. In the preceding three chapters, the method of this study has been to approach the unevenness through the separate forms of lyric, narrative, and drama, accepting the distinct character of experiments in these modes even while noting important moments of intersection among them.

An effect of the success of Modernism was that by the 1920s the rights of experiment had been established. Opponents of the new work did not disappear, but the field of novelty had spread too wide to be ignored or denied. All the major modes had undergone radical revision—although traditional or modestly evolutionary styles continued and often flourished —and in this respect, the prominence of experiment brought an end to the sharp unevenness of development. Ambitious works of the 1920s not only drew upon the accumulated force of the prewar achievements, but also reflected a self-consciousness of ambition in other forms. Artists began to borrow more freely from other modes—poets from musicians, painters from photographers, dramatists from composers, Joyce in *Ulysses* from everyone. The best approach to the next phase of Modernism, I suggest, is to acknowledge the rapid mobility among forms and genres and the mixed character of many significant works. Rather than pursue a lineage of separate modes, let us follow the course of simultaneous experiments from the war to the maturity of the later 1920s, when Modernism both established its conspicuous presence and glimpsed the terms of its ending.

ART FOR THE LIVING AND THE DEAD

The outbreak of war in the summer of 1914 was a provocation, a trauma, and a stimulus that changed the course of Modernism.[1] Its first effect was to interrupt the momentum of cultural activity in major metropolitan centers. Partly, this was because artists went off to war, where too many of them died. Partly, it was because the patronage and audience for new artworks swiftly diminished in the face of greater urgency. But less obviously, the war also served as an invitation, even an opportunity, for fresh approaches in modernist projects.

The first issue of the vorticist journal *Blast* appeared just as hostilities were ready to break out, and several of its leading lights, including Wyndham Lewis, Ford Madox Ford, and Henri Gaudier-Brzeska, became soldiers. Before Lewis enlisted, he produced a second number of *Blast* in June 1915, the "War-Number," which was also the last number. It was a willful attempt to confirm the energy of oppositional culture, but in the midst of the violence, its faltering tone is audible. Not only is the issue much shorter, but it also gives up the sharp tone of mockery that had been the journal's keynote. Its manifestos now softened their hostility to English dullness and tried to close the gap between art and politics. Within the perspective of the War-Number, an aggressive Germany stood for "Traditional Poetry and the Romantic Spirit," whereas Vorticism stood for the "Reality of the Present": "Under these circumstances, apart from national partizanship, it appears to us humanly desirable that Germany should win no war against France or England."[2] When news came of the deaths, first of Gaudier-Brzeska and later of T. E. Hulme, the London avant-garde felt the shock keenly. Gaudier-Brzeska, who died in the trenches before his twenty-fourth birthday, had already constructed sculptures that remain nodal points in modernist art.

Pound immediately attempted to memorialize the glory of the brief bril-
liant career and also to consolidate the aesthetics of Vorticism.

In difficult and demoralizing circumstances, Pound stood among
many other modernists who accepted their distance from the cataclysm
and still chose to carry on within the separate vocation of art. Paul Valéry
ended decades of literary silence by publishing his long poem "La Jeune
Parque" (The Young Fate), an elusive meditation on the involutions of self-
consciousness within a desiring body. Although Valéry was working on the
poem during the first long years of the war, its technical intricacies and its
metaphysics of consciousness maintain their detachment from the spectacle of blood and death. For Marcel Proust, the publishing difficulties
caused by war meant that his grand novel À la recherche du temps perdu (In
Search of Lost Time) had years to grow even larger; the initial plan for a
work of three volumes became vastly expanded during wartime; its leading
themes—memory, art, time, love, self-deception—underwent exacting
elaborations, although the noise of guns was not far away.

During the same years Joyce labored at his comparably exacting Ulysses;
asked how he lived through these deadly times, he airily replied, "Oh yes, I
was told that there was a war going on in Europe."[3] Eliot and Pound, left in
London as many of their collaborators departed for the trenches, applied
themselves to a formal problem in modernist poetry. They decided that the
movement toward free verse had gone too far and that a "counter-current"
was now needed. In March 1917—when revolution was spreading in Russia, the Germans were retreating to the Hindenburg Line, and the United
States was on the point of entering the war—Eliot wrote an essay called
"Reflections on Vers Libre" in which he argued that "vers libre has not even
the excuse of a polemic; it is a battle-cry of freedom, and there is no freedom in art."[4] The language of politics and military conflict is brazenly recruited for the purposes of a literary dispute. Pound and Eliot turned back
to Théophile Gautier and the Parnassians, aiming to imitate their regular
rhythms and strophes and to assert the priority of verbal form.

These gestures were acts of defiance. To varying degrees, in making
these assertions they accepted, even courted, the outrage of those who insisted on the absolute priority of the war effort. But their response to the
bloody cataclysm should also be taken as one culmination of the social practice of Modernism. For many artists and their sympathetic audiences, the
question of the independent value of aesthetic activity had now been settled; it would take more than war to undo the change. But let me be clear.
It was not that the artists laid claim, though they sometimes did, to a sphere

of separate value owing nothing to the world beyond its forms. Far more often, this strenuous art was seen as pursuing its own way toward human flourishing. No more than politics was it justified for its own sake. "Independence" meant rather that the artists saw themselves as engaged in their own legitimate, modern vocation, one that challenged rival vocations and practices—politics now especially, in large part because politics was seen as leading to catastrophes like the Great War.

Most of the prewar experimentalists had reached maturity by the time hostilities began; several were in the midst of newly ambitious work and were reluctant to turn all their attention to the war, no matter how urgent or calamitous. The many volumes of Proust's novel and the many episodes of Joyce's claimed an integrity that rebuked a chaotic world. In similar ways, Eliot and especially Pound held to a course of innovation that was well in progress when the war began, which they were unwilling to abandon.

To a younger generation, even just slightly younger, the events of 1914–1918 looked much different. The group of artists who gathered in Zurich in 1916 and who chose to perform under the name "Dada" had no body of experiment to sustain or defend. They began with a perception of a collapsing world and hurled themselves directly at the stupidity of the war in their first performances at the Cabaret Voltaire. The prewar experiments of Picasso and Matisse, Stein and Joyce, and others were often directed at a stagnant and complacent society that felt, in Wyndham Lewis's phrase, "as safe as houses."[5] The radicalism of the Dadaists, on the other hand, came in reaction to a violence that overwhelmed the illusion of safety.

The question of artistic generations is more complicated than it may seem. Even as the prewar modernists strived to preserve the dignity of art, they found the war impossible to ignore: it intruded even into the most regular strophes. The tones of pacifism are marked in the later episodes of *Ulysses*. "How can people aim guns at each other?" asks Leopold Bloom. "Sometimes they go off."[6] Joyce's novel becomes, among many other things, a militant refusal of physical violence, with Bloom declining to use force to regain the rights of marriage. The poem that Pound described as a counter to free verse, "Hugh Selwyn Mauberley," begins as a satire of a debased society that cannot appreciate the glory of the classical past.

> The age demanded an image
> Of its accelerated grimace,
> Something for the modern stage,
> Not, at any rate, an Attic grace;

Not, not certainly, the obscure reveries
Of the inward gaze;
Better mendacities
Than the classics in paraphrase!

These lines follow the rhythms that Eliot and Pound were drawing from Théophile Gautier, and their subject is a familiar pre-1914 theme: the struggle to rouse a society lost in impenetrable sleep. But in its fourth section, the poem breaks its rhythm to evoke those who fought in the war, those who

walked eye-deep in hell
believing in old men's lies, then unbelieving
came home, home to a lie,
home to many deceits,
home to old lies and new infamy;
usury age-old and age-thick
and liars in public places.[7]

When the regular stanzas return in the next section, it is as if they cannot shake the memory of war.[8]

There died a myriad,
And of the best, among them,
For an old bitch gone in the teeth,
For a botched civilization[9]

These lines suggest what made the war such an imaginative as well as a physical cataclysm—namely, the violence of technological destruction, of total warfare, that could kill so many so quickly.

The war was a trauma for Europe and a wound in Modernism. When John Maynard Keynes wrote *The Economic Consequences of the Peace* (1919), his influential account of the meaning of the war, he described it not only as a social catastrophe but also as the dissolution of a world picture. We never noticed, he writes, that what we took as natural and permanent—namely, the peaceful political life of the West in the past fifty years—was in fact "intensely unusual, unstable, complicated, unreliable, [and] temporary." The end of the war exposed the truth: Europe had been living on a "sandy and false foundation." Keynes's "fifty years," it is worth noting, coincided with the emergence of an ambitious, oppositional culture, an emerging modernist culture, that had rejected the stability of bourgeois life. Keynes called this era an "economic Eldorado," a mirage of peace now unmasked by war.[10] The outbreak of violence must be seen, among many harsher things, as an eruption into a modernist aesthetic that had offered *itself* as a form of violence directed against a complacent peace.

When Henri Gaudier-Brzeska arrived on the battlefield, he reasserted his aesthetic principles: form would triumph over violence. In an essay sent back to London for the second edition of *Blast,* he wrote:

> I HAVE BEEN FIGHTING FOR TWO MONTHS and I can now gauge the intensity of Life.
>
> HUMAN MASSES teem and move, are destroyed and crop up again.
>
> HORSES are worn out in three weeks, die by the roadside
>
> DOGS wander, are destroyed, and others come along . . .
>
> *MY VIEWS ON SCULPTURE* REMAIN ABSOLUTELY *THE SAME . . .*
>
> I SHALL DERIVE MY EMOTIONS SOLELY FROM THE *ARRANGEMENT OF SURFACES,* I shall present my emotions by the ARRANGEMENT OF MY SURFACES, THE PLANES AND LINES BY WHICH THEY ARE DEFINED[11]

This document would be poignant and difficult to read even without the knowledge that the writer would soon be dead. Gaudier-Brzeska's manifesto is an assertion of the unrepentant claims of Modernism. Against the unruliness of war and the scenes of bloody death, he offered the "arrangement of surfaces" in painting and sculpture, much as Pound and Eliot looked to the precision of quatrains in their verse. These are signs of an emphatic formalism as an implied critique of the disorderly society that had lurched into war. But when Gaudier-Brzeska's polemic was published in *Blast,* it was set on the page just above a notice of his death in battle. The juxtaposition is one brutal sign of the limits of art. The hopeful attempt to sustain Modernism sooner or later confronted the unpreventable wound. The deaths of young artists were the most unforgettable effects, but another was the challenge to works of art. Could artistic experiment be justified in the face of such violence? Should it be?

The proud initial defense of the rights of art gave way steadily. In the last years of war, and still more in the immediate postwar period, many artists reconceived the bases of their work. Wyndham Lewis had developed a rigorous geometric abstraction in his paintings up to and into the war. But after his experience in battle, he discovered that the course of violence confounded visual geometry. *A Battery Shelled* (1919) opens a dramatic vista almost entirely absent in Lewis's prewar abstract designs (fig. 10). Part of the shock of the image comes from the utter insufficiency of the physical structure at the center, the shattered hut that in another world, a few years earlier, might have suggested the pleasures of form. Here the soldiers, like the painter, claim no mastery over the field of battle; Lewis breaks the surface and opens the long prospect, the endless horizon. The desolation of war is not only mass slaughter. As if that were not enough, it also includes the ravaging of space. Gone are the strong enclosing lines of *The Crowd* (1912) and other prewar abstract arrangements (fig. 11); the war has burst the formal containers, the frames and boxes on an intricate surface. The broken field and unsheltered sweep will leave scarring traces on postwar art, which now endures indelible memories of the open, exposed horizon. From this point forward, many modernists—including Eliot and Woolf—could not suppress pictures of traumatically broken space but were compelled to visualize the outspread, uncontrolled, and perilous terrain: the waste-land. Among other effects, these new images marked a return of the Real.

Part of the argument of this book has been that we need to restore a place for realism within the history of Modernism. Even with the radical formal experiments of the prewar period, the justification for realism was often cast in terms of a deeper truth, a more profound reality. Here, for instance, is Virginia Woolf's celebrated defense of modern fiction in 1919.

> Examine for a moment an ordinary mind on an ordinary day. The mind receives a myriad impressions—trivial, fantastic, evanescent, or engraved with the sharpness of steel. From all sides they come, an incessant shower of innumerable atoms. . . . Life is not a series of gig-lamps symmetrically arranged; life is a luminous halo, a semi-transparent envelope surrounding us from the beginning of consciousness to the end. . . . [Writers like Joyce] attempt to come closer to life . . . even if to do so they must discard most of the conventions which are commonly observed by the novelist. Let us record the atoms as they fall upon the mind in the order in which they fall, let us trace the pattern, however disconnected and incoherent in appearance, which each sight or incident scores upon the consciousness.[12]

Woolf develops a realism of the "halo" and the "envelope," not a false symmetry but the true indeterminacy that stimulated her work in the 1920s. Disconnection and incoherence, the experience of the "ordinary mind on an ordinary day," justified the turn to more demanding forms. Yet the dates of both her essay and her new experimental work remind us that beyond the "ordinary day" were the extraordinary days of violence.

Realism, we might say, followed out a shadow history alongside modernist formalism. Even as rare and outrageous forms appeared in books, on stage, in concert halls, and in theaters, there remained the hovering thought that these images were not merely some fantastic or abstract shapes but were the forms of reality itself. In Keynes's influential book, for instance, the postwar conference in Paris, urgently arranged to secure peace for twentieth-century Europe, was "real" only in the most ghostly sense. Gazing at the faces of the world's leaders, Woodrow Wilson and Georges Clemenceau, Keynes came to doubt whether they "were really faces at all and not the tragi-comic masks of some strange drama or puppet-show." We see that "the nerve center of the European system" was haunted by "dreadful specters."[13]

The war and its aftermath revived the question of formalism and representation. On the one hand, violence made an inescapable claim on many (though not all) aesthetic projects. On the other hand, the aberrant world of war (and also of postwar peacemaking) made reality appear as strange as the shapes of experimental art.

GEOGRAPHIES OF VIOLENCE

Much as Lewis brought abstract design toward culmination before the war, so Ford Madox Ford refined the literary impressionism of *The Good Soldier* just as violence was erupting. Its narrative accepted the disorder of impressions, leapt backward and forward in time, and followed the wanderings of memory. In the years after the war, Ford undertook his most ambitious work, *Parade's End,* a series of four novels appearing between 1924 and 1928, a grandly ambitious project that aimed both to consolidate impressionism and to confront the trauma of violence. Notably, he now sets aside the device of a dramatized speaker (John Dowell of *The Good Soldier,* Conrad's Marlow) and lets the narrative itself perform the complexities once located in a character. Late in his career Ford reflected on the course of the impressionist venture that he had undertaken with Conrad. "That we did succeed in finding *a* new form I think I may permit myself to claim, Conrad first evolving the convention of a Marlow who should narrate, in presentation, the whole story of a novel just as, without much sequence or pursued chronology, a story will come up into the mind of a narrator, and I eventually dispensing with a narrator but making the story come up in the mind of the unseen author with a similar want of chronological sequence."[14] Ford is describing the method of *Parade's End* here, which performs this shift from "narrator" to "unseen author," but what the account leaves out is the relation between form and subject matter.

The tetralogy begins with a modern battle between the sexes. Christopher Tietjens is estranged from his strong-willed wife, Sylvia, and at their moment of crisis he meets the athletic young suffragette, Valentine Wannop, fair and freckled, with whom he falls in love. Yet *Parade's End* only finds its shape when the war between the sexes converges with the war against the Germans. In the third volume of the tetralogy, *A Man Could Stand Up,* we find a searing description of death on the battlefield, dead bodies tangled in wire stretched between the battle lines.

> There were three frosty erections—like fairy sheds, half-way between the two lines. And, suspended in them, as there would have to be, three bundles of rags and what appeared to be a very large, squashed crow. How the devil had that fellow managed to get smashed into that shape. It was improbable. There was also—suspended, too, a tall melodramatic object, the head cast back to the sky. One arm raised in the attitude of, say, a Walter Scott Highland officer waving his men on. Waving a sword that wasn't there. . . . That was what wire did for you. Supported you in grotesque attitudes, even in death.[15]

Here, as throughout *Parade's End,* the impressionist vocation persists: the initial misapprehension, the deferral of understanding, the focus on immediate experience rather than the "rounded, annotated record of a set of circumstances" that he described elsewhere. Yet the attempts in *Parade's End* to meet the claims of a war exceed the subjectivity of Ford's earlier impressionism. In effect, the supersession of the individualized narrator opens the technique to a public world: the public world of war. Impressionism is no longer the working of a rarefied mind isolated by its bewilderments. Now literary experiment coincides with a scene of violence. The central device—the break with chronological sequence, the focus on disorderly perception, the replacement of "events" with "effects" (*progression d'effet*)—achieves free range in the midst of violence so that the war appears eerily as a fulfillment of impressionist technique. The scenes of physical chaos, of delayed recognition, of the uncanny dislocations of space and time, are realized on the battlefield.

The war thus remained a goad to experiment. Disenchantment, revulsion, and trauma were shocks to the world-picture of modernity—individual and social—but were also incitements to create new forms. Eliot's "Gerontion" is the first of his poems to articulate deep disillusionment. It names no battles; its references are elusive. But the sensibility of the poem is that of a stunned post-catastrophic mind. "After such knowledge, what forgiveness?" asks its voice before describing the betrayals of history.

> Think
> Neither fear nor courage saves us. Unnatural vices
> Are fathered by our heroism. Virtues
> Are forced upon us by our impudent crimes.
> These tears are shaken from the wrath-bearing tree.[16]

We are far from the personal afflictions of J. Alfred Prufrock or the speaker in "Portrait of a Lady"; we are well beyond the agony of the drawing-room. Not only does "Gerontion" give oracular statements of postwar bafflement, but the poetic world itself has changed shape. The break in Eliot's poetry after the war discloses this new constitution of space.[17] The interior realms have broken up; those rooms that contained (but also suffocated) the early protagonists are now exposed to dangerous exteriors, as in "Gerontion," with its "windy spaces" and rocky fields, and "The Hollow Men," with its "valley of dying stars" (21, 58).

The Waste Land is after all a poem in a waste-land, which owes everything to the effects of wartime geometry. The rooms are nightmare sites of failed intimacy: the dressing-room in "A Game of Chess" (part II), where the human body disappears among its sensations—the glitter of the jewels, the "strange synthetic perfumes"—or the bedsitting room in "The Fire Sermon" (part III), where the typist and the clerk perform their acts of depleted sexuality in cramped quarters. So much of the poem shows a struggle between decaying interiors (sweet smells, bad sex) and the dry, abandoned terrain outside: "Rock and no water and the sandy road." A central rhythm of the poem beats in the movement between these zones—inside and outside both unavailing—until the poem reaches a pitch of total disorientation, where bats crawl "head downward down a blackened wall / And upside down in air were towers." Nothing is fixed in space any longer, and the bewildered voice can only ask, "What is that sound high in the air," "Who are those hooded hordes," "What is the city over the mountains" (40, 47, 48).

Virginia Woolf's *Jacob's Room* marked a threshold in her career; in it she broke with the more traditional modes of her first two novels and predicted her experiments of the later 1920s. But *Jacob's Room* is also an example of a formal risk-taking inseparable from postwar mourning. As long as Jacob is alive, the room is what it often is in Modernism: a picture of singleness, of radical containment, a womb, cave, and sanctum, a box for a brain. It gives the solace of envelopment, of a refuge from the world, but also the anxiety of enclosure, of the buried self. So much of Woolf's novel is a meditation on the elusiveness of character, the way we escape one another within the rooms of selfhood. But the war is what sharpens the problem in *Jacob's Room* because it reveals the privacy and distance of selfhood as bound to the separation of death. And apart from agonizing individual mortality lies the ungraspable fact of mass slaughter, the sacrifice of a generation. The question of the room—the mysterious interior space—transforms into the question of the vast, perplexing world beyond. At the end of the novel, a noise sounds from across the English Channel. Jacob's mother, fearing for him, wakes in the night, startled by the sound.

> "The guns?" said Betty Flanders, half asleep, getting out of bed and going to the window, which was decorated with a fringe of dark leaves.
>
> "Not at this distance," she thought. "It is the sea."
>
> Again, far away, she heard the dull sound, as if nocturnal women were beating great carpets.[18]

The image discloses the paradoxical, inassimilable space opened by the war. How far can the sound of guns carry? It seems impossible to determine the distance of violence, to know how far or close it stands. Here Woolf's novel joins the imaginative project of Lewis, Eliot, Ford, and others: It undoes a map of the world; it records the loss of an intelligible diagram. The picture of modernity no longer has clear outlines: space loses sense.[19]

An analogous but inverted expression occurs in E. E. Cummings's *The Enormous Room,* a work that presents the distortions of war not as a release into violent wilderness but as confinement within claustrophobic space. Arrested by French authorities while working in the ambulance service, the protagonist (who shares a name with the author) finds himself in a detention center. Its leading feature is the room of the novel's title, a cavern containing men swept together by the chances of war. Plucked from his work in Normandy by the French authorities, "Cummings" endures the indignity and discomfort of mass incarceration. Here is his first encounter with the improbable volume where he is thrown late at night: "The hitherto empty and minute room became suddenly enormous: weird cries, oaths, laughter, pulling it sideways and backward, extending it to inconceivable depth and width, telescoping it to frightful nearness. From all directions, by at least thirty voices in eleven languages (I counted as I lay Dutch, Belgian, Spanish, Turkish, Arabian, Polish, Russian, Swedish, German, French—and English) at distances varying from seventy feet to a few inches, for twenty minutes I was ferociously bombarded."[20] Michel Foucault has written of "heterotopias," those physical sites that are marked as places socially apart, as "counter-sites" to the normative organization of space. Cemeteries, barracks, and brothels invert the social world outside them.[21] We can extend this thought to many scenes of Modernism, recognizing the heterotope both in physical manifestations—galleries, theaters, concert halls—and within the space of individual works—for instance, in the provoking spaces of a cubist painting or in the strange typography of an avant-garde manifesto. The war introduced a new set of heterotopic sites into modernity: the trench, the hut, the battlefield, the detention camp.

This network of postwar tropes also includes those of Ernest Hemingway, whose collection of stories and vignettes *In Our Time* took shape in the early 1920s. The short pieces move toward the war, in and out of scenes of violence, until apparently distant zones of experience (the American Midwest and street fighting in Europe, childhood and postwar young adulthood, crowd and solitude) resonate under pressure from each other. The emerging Hemingway style—simple sentences, repetition, concrete nouns, description without interpretation—is openly indebted to the example and advice of Pound and Stein. But it is equally a product of war. A story at the center of *In Our Time* follows the difficult readjustment of the late-returning veteran Harold Krebs. "By the time Krebs returned to his home town in Oklahoma, the greeting of heroes was over. He came back much too late. The men from the town who had been drafted had all been welcomed elaborately on their return. There had been a great deal of hysteria. Now the reaction had set in. People seemed to think it was rather ridiculous for Krebs to be getting back so late, years after the war was over."[22]

Coming home too late is Krebs's misfortune, but in a significant sense, *In Our Time* suggests that all coming home will be too late. War and home are incommensurable realms; they intersect and overlap, they dream of one another, but they never merge or integrate. Dissonance is intractable. The failure to *coincide* gives a central theme to the stories; it also gives a style. When Hemingway writes that "there had been a great deal of hysteria," the sentence itself offers a critique of what it describes. Austere, nonhysterical speech is a counter to the self-deceiving rhetoric that brought the calamity. Unlike Pound and Stein, Hemingway came to artistic self-consciousness during the war, which gave a different valence to techniques that had inspired him in their work. In a sequence such as this (the opening of the vignette "Chapter VI")—"Nick sat against the wall of the church where they had dragged him to be clear of machine-gun fire in the street. Both legs stuck out awkwardly. He had been hit in the spine. His face was sweaty and dirty. The sun shone on his face. The day was very hot"[23]—the style gets its force from the brutality it meagerly records, from the gap between undescribable disaster and short sentences, between abstract justifications of war and austere speech. What Hemingway adds to the technical reforms of Pound and Stein is the consciousness of massive, violent failure that gives verbal discipline a social dimension.

Here one other aspect of Hemingway's work, and one other author, deserve mention. Sherwood Anderson's *Winesburg, Ohio*, published in 1919, brought the short-story *collection* toward a new structural coherence, exemplary not only for Hemingway but for the developing history of the form. The volume offers reappearing characters (most prominently, George Willard, a figure for Anderson) and recurrent locations, but the continuity is perpetually broken. New situations begin again in each story; central conflicts remain inconclusive; in place of resolution stands a next problem for a next story. The town, Anderson's fictional Winesburg, gives a unity of scene, insistently exposed as a false unity. Individuals collide without meeting; they perform their lives within the terms of private will and personal obsession; they constitute an assemblage but never a community. The effect amounts to an inversion of the stream of consciousness that developed so visibly in modernist narrative. Despite the privilege given to George Willard, *Winesburg, Ohio* does not begin with the perspective of a subjectivity that aspires to reach an Other. Anderson's collection begins with the outside world, the community of Others, who look back on flailing, incomplete, and unrealized individuals.

The short story is an exemplary mode of Modernism. Often following the precedent of Maupassant—and looking further back to Poe—writers elaborated a form depending on both precision (exact views of a visible world) and evocation (of significant realms out of view). The *inconclusiveness* that Anderson developed from his precursors and that Hemingway developed and refined again—the unresolved endings, the broken dialogue that intimates (without stating) unseen troubles, the physical and emotional gestures whose meaning remains obscure—became emblems of the genre. Here we see another, perhaps surprising legacy of Symbolism. Even within a form that often aggressively embraced realist norms, ambitiously so in Anderson and Hemingway, the style of evocation—of a universe of significance beyond the terse speech of the story—recapitulates a later, modernist Symbolism. The short story addresses no higher realm of spirit, no sanctifying domain of meanings beyond the sensory world. Its symbolic work is rather to suggest a density in *this world,* a complex zone of conflicts and implications concealed beneath the rituals of everyday life. Acts of omission become as important as acts of mention. Here we recall Mallarmé's symbolist credo, that to name a thing was to destroy three-quarters of the pleasure one takes in it. Hemingway put the point in his own way, claiming that "if a writer of prose knows enough about what he is writing about he may omit things that he knows and the reader, if the writer is writing truly enough, will have a feeling of those things as strongly as though the writer had stated them."[24]

The wider issue concerns the preservation of a sphere of possibility, even in the demoralizing period of war and postwar bewilderment. The epigraph to this chapter, from Beatrice Webb's *Diaries,* records the double loss of religious faith and progressive social hope, of religion and then the religion of humanity.[25] In the face of such losses, Modernism attempted to sustain an elsewhere, a space beyond both violence and empty routine. The inconclusiveness of the short story and its more specific tactic of omission belong to this "negative dialectic," the effort to conjure alternative spaces after the breaking of hope in the catastrophe of war.

GENDER AFTER WAR

One of the alternative modernist spaces was occupied by women, who claimed and achieved a new cultural presence after the war. We know that a central current of experimental culture had been closely associated with a militant masculinism, a tendency that was pronounced but that needs to be situated alongside rival stirrings. The New Women who announced their presence at the end of the nineteenth century represented a significant provocation. The succession of feminist novels and plays and, just as notably, the contentions in a newly sex-conscious press compelled new acts of recognition, and when the cultural agitation around the New Woman converged with a militant suffragette movement, questions of gender, sexuality, and political representation became pressing.

The movement toward rights for women was primarily a legal and political campaign. Throughout the long course of the nineteenth century, the strengthening appeal was to the consistency of the law and the rights of personhood. Demands for equal status—for instance, for the right of a married woman to control and own property, the right to divorce, or the right to the custody of children—gained steadily but only partially, and by the 1890s, when Modernism was becoming a cultural force of unavoidable prominence, so too was the march toward rights for women.

The campaign for suffrage acquired power from its appeal to the logic of universalism and the claims of reason. Once legal personhood had been granted to slaves and suffrage had been granted to workers, it appeared to be only a question of time, the time of reason, before a universalizing rationality would extend full citizenship to women. Such were the claims, reiterated during the long century between Mary Wollstonecraft's *Vindication of the Rights of Women* and the granting of full suffrage. In the interval, the scenarios of resistance were perpetually restaged. Traditionalists argued that the extension of rights would bring social chaos—and those arguments proved stubborn. Women were weaker physically and subordinate biblically —and society was a delicate mechanism. To extend rights was to leap into the unknown. Indeed it was. But within the realm of bourgeois legal rationality, the force of Enlightenment reason began to seem inexorable. Under a banner of universality, the argument was that women were legally the same as men—the same in respect to personhood, to dignity, to legal rights, to the right to work, and to civic participation. The demand for Woman as the Same endured long contention with the icon of Woman as the Other: the Other as an Angel in the House, and the Other as spiritualized, as domesticated, as moralized, as chaste.

The men of Modernism engaged frequently with the liberationist campaign of women, and yet the most striking fact about the male response is that it was not symmetrical with the demands of suffrage. Most often the male modernist response was to react, not to the political-legal demands, but to the spectacle of female desire. The women who swarm through the poems, plays, and novels of modernist men are frequently apparitional and phantasmagoric, as if the campaign to extend the rights of women stimulated visions, not of political reciprocity, but of a universe of new desires. The image of the "superb" woman—Conrad's phrase—appears recurrently: the woman superb in the power of gesture and desire. She also appears as the shape-shifting, sexualized woman of Beardsley, the contorted object of fascination in Klimt. Within this context, it is not surprising that women among the modernists were often more guarded in the presentation of female desire. Stein's "Melanctha" offered itself as a portrait of a young black woman, but as readers have come to notice, lesbian desire is its carefully presented subtext. Virginia Woolf, too, keeps the desires of women in secret places, private rooms, and carefully tended corners of the mind.

What was partly at stake was a critique, a male modernist critique, of the rational demand for political equality from the standpoint of sexuality.

Sexuality was seen as the deep truth, the true asymmetry that underlies the symmetry of reason. Rationality, indifferent to gender, spoke to equal personhood. Sex spoke to desire that confounds and mocks the claims of rational selfhood, legal integrity, and universal principles of identity. In effect, male modernist sexuality stood against suffragette gender. But with few exceptions, it did not stand on the basis of a traditionalism that looked to return women to the domestic circle or to the confines of tradition and chastity. On the contrary, the far more common modernist impulse was to see the free woman as the desirous woman, a phantasm dreaded and longed for, even as so much Modernism resisted—or disengaged from—the demands of suffragettes.

But beyond this moment, the moment of phantasmagoria set against rational personhood, we can notice a certain unfolding historical logic, and also a logic of desire in the changing relations between the two sexes. We have seen in Oskar Kokoschka's play *Murderer, Hope of Women* an assertion of male will, much in the spirit of Alfred Adler's notion of "masculine protest." And yet a lasting aspect of Kokoschka's ceremony of death and desire is that in order to elevate a supreme male leader, he must imagine female strength worthy of the challenge. The conjuring of the strong woman becomes an effect of modernist masculine will. She is everywhere in works of the period, showing herself as Kurtz's "native bride" in *Heart of Darkness,* as Gudrun and Ursula in *Women in Love,* as any of the prostitutes in *Les Demoiselles d'Avignon,* as Molly Bloom in *Ulysses,* and as Maud Gonne in the poetry of Yeats. Within the logic of modernist desire, the Nietzschean male summons his female counterpart, who possesses powers and desires (almost) equal to his own. Women, demanding the political rights of the Same, receive, not the dignity of rational autonomy or reasoned citizenship, but the recognition of a comparable desire. In articulating the desires of men, stirred by the milieu of liberation, these male authors are driven to articulate the desires of women. The desires are not depicted as the same as men's, not as part of a universal appetite common to both sexes, but as *coordinate, or counterpart.* Such a relationship of men to women represents, not the achievement of legal-political identity, nor the return to woman as the site of tradition, faith, and domesticity. Within the sexual phantasmagoria of these male artists, woman is neither the Same nor securely Other but, far more unsteadily, Same and Other: parallel, comparable, tantamount.

By the 1920s women had assumed a conspicuous place within modernist movements, and some of the most important scholarship of recent years has made clear the extent of their contributions. By now the literary achievements of Stein, Richardson, H.D., Loy, Djuna Barnes, and Woolf, among others, are established within prevailing narratives of Modernism. And yet the assimilation of once-neglected works must not obscure the strains in the sexual politics of experimental art. Women were producing some of the most challenging work of the period, work acknowledged by a small group at the time and by many larger groups since. But if we hold fast to the notion of Modernism not merely as a succession of isolated works but as a social practice, then we can better recognize the fraught conditions of women's place within the communities of artists. Gertrude Stein was at the center of a major Parisian salon, but her early contributions were over-shadowed by those of the men around her, among them Picasso and Matisse. H.D. was recruited to the imagist banner by Pound, but she remained on the margins of the "men of 1914" who consolidated around Vorticism and the journal *Blast*. Virginia Woolf undertook risky experiments in the 1920s, increasingly conscious that she was writing as a woman within a literary culture informed by masculine norms.

Woolf's case remains among the most instructive, in part because she insisted so directly on the depth of the problem. "No age can ever have been so stridently sex-conscious as our own," she wrote in *A Room of One's Own*, and her work in the 1920s made that consciousness explicit and unavoidable. In *Mrs. Dalloway* (1925) she submits the rituals of male professionalism (in parliament, in medicine, etc.) to a corrosive skepticism. The argument of the novel is that only an escape from the self-infatuations of public life will allow an encounter with the thing "that mattered"—solitude, love, death—"a thing wreathed about with chatter, defaced, obscured in her own life, let drop every day in corruption, lies, chatter."[26] To recover this foundational perception is to escape from the routines of a public world that is self-deluding, complacent, and essentially male. The young philosopher Tansley's jibe in *To the Lighthouse* (1927)—"Women can't write, women can't paint"[27]—looms as a repudiation that the novel works to undo. Partly it does so through a comic reduction: if women cannot write, then how is it that Tansley appears as a character in this fiction? More substantially, the novel undoes misogyny by changing the subject. Woolf brings the demands of the New Woman of the 1890s and the agitations of the prewar suffragettes into the arena of modernist formalism. Her formal gamble in *To the Lighthouse*—the willingness to disrupt narrative continuity in "Time Passes"—is as pressing as the defense of Lily Briscoe's life as an artist outside marriage. Aesthetics and sexual politics are not the same problem in *To the Lighthouse*, but they intersect and overlap. During the transformative moments at the end of part I of the novel, Lily Briscoe resists the soft, coercive pressure to marry by recalling the demands of her painting: "She need not marry, thank Heaven: she need not undergo that degradation. She was saved from that dilution. She would move the tree rather more to the middle" (102).

The novel also moves sexuality to the middle. The novel's shift toward androgyny has been long noticed: it sets Lily Briscoe as the inheritor of both sides of the Victorian gender dyad such that her work of painting conjoins, and re-configures, the legacies of "male abstraction" and "female sympathy." This turn in *To the Lighthouse* brings it close in sympathy to a memorable dictum in *A Room of One's Own*—"It is fatal to be a man or woman pure and simple; one must be woman-manly or man-womanly"[28] —and accords more generally with yet another turn in the wheel of modernist desire. If we recall Eliot's note to *The Waste Land* where we read that "the two sexes meet in Tiresias" and the moment in *Ulysses* when Bloom appears as a "new womanly man," and if we also recall Woolf's gender-crossing protagonist in *Orlando* and numerous other examples in the novels of Proust and Djuna Barnes, in expressionist film, and in the epicene styles of the flappers, then we have good reason to speak of an androgynous moment in postwar Modernism.[29] The mingling of sexual features is too pervasive to ignore. All those uneasy negotiations over several decades— the New Woman's attack on the double standard, the suffragettes' demand for the vote, the misogynist's recoil, the erotic phantasmagoria, the masculine protest and the "worthy" female antagonist, the growing presence of women artists—brought androgyny to a brief, surprising efflorescence. It was neither stable nor abiding. But it did mark a suspension of the modernist sex war and created openings for other strange flowerings.

FROM IMAGE TO ENCYCLOPEDIA

A signal feature of transforming Modernism was the appearance of works on a new scale, works of such massive reach as to change the terms of challenge. A few years earlier, the power of art was repeatedly located in concentration and limitation—in the radiant fragment, the luminous detail, the visionary moment. The Image, the Impression, the Symbol, and the Vortex were all names for an aesthetic that resisted grand statement in favor of the resources of the miniature. Joyce's theory of Epiphany belongs to this aesthetics of compression.

Joyce wrote of his *Ulysses* that "it is the epic of two races (Israel-Ireland) and at the same time the cycle of the human body as well as a little story of a day (life). . . . It is also a kind of encyclopaedia. My intention is not only to render the myth *sub specie temporis nostri* but also to allow each adventure (that is, every hour, every organ, every art being interconnected and interrelated in the somatic scheme of the whole) to condition and even to create its own technique."[30] The remark indicates how far Joyce traveled within a brief period. From the epiphany to the epic, from the self-contained fragment to the encyclopedia—this is the arc of a career at once singular and exemplary. When Joyce explained his use of the *Odyssey* as the mythic framework for his novel—as the counterpart/parallel to Leopold Bloom's daylong journey through Dublin—he noted that Homer's Odysseus contained the fullest range of human experience. As his friend Frank Budgen reported, Joyce spoke of his protagonist as modeled upon a "complete" man, a "good" man, and it is plain that these attributes lie deep within the novel's conception.[31] Leopold Bloom is good to the extent that he is complete, where completeness includes some of the most intractable human experiences, including humiliation, sexual degradation, envy, and dread. Moreover, if the book is to offer a "cycle of the human body," then for Joyce it must unashamedly include all the organs and their functions, including defecation and masturbation, even if this caused—as it quickly did—a public outrage leading to censorship.

The epic project of *Ulysses* is at the same time, in Karen Lawrence's words, an "odyssey of style."[32] Here is the opening of the section known as "Lotus Eaters."

> By lorries along sir John Rogerson's quay Mr Bloom walked soberly past Windmill lane, Leask's the linseed crusher, the postal telegraph office. Could have given that address too. And past the sailor's home. He turned from the morning noises of the quayside and walked through Lime street. By Brady's cottages a boy for the skins lolled, his bucket of offal linked, smoking a chewed fagbutt. A smaller girl with scars of eczema on her forehead eyed him, listlessly holding her battered caskhoop. Tell him if he smokes he won't grow. O let him! His life isn't such a bed of roses. Waiting outside pubs to bring da home. Come home to ma, da. (58)

As revolutionary as it then seemed, the style is the outcome of an accumulated history. The stream of consciousness and interior monologue—in the varied techniques of Joyce, Woolf, Faulkner, Richardson, and Proust—have been taken as a culminating moment in the history of realism: Modernism discovering the very language of the mind as it talks to itself. ("If little Rudy had lived. See him grow up. Hear his voice in the house. Walking beside Molly in an Eton suit. My son. Me in his eyes"; 73.) The grammar of an ever-shifting attention—from outer world to inner reverie, from concentration to distraction, from memory to desire—offers itself as a window on immediate experience. The task of fiction was to discover the prose (and poetry) of inwardness, and in this vocation, the early episodes of *Ulysses* could seem a threshold event comparable to the discovery of the laws of perspective.

But *Ulysses* itself already suggests the obsolescence of the discovery. By the time we reach the episode "Sirens," the style flaunts its artifice. Here is Blazes Boylan as he sets off for his adulterous tryst with Molly Bloom: "By Bachelor's walk, jogjaunty jingled Blazes Boylan, bachelor, in sun in heat, mare's glossy rump atrot, with flick of whip, on bounding tyres: sprawled, warmseated, Boylan impatience, ardentbold. Horn. Have you the? Horn. Have you the? Haw haw horn" (222). *Ulysses* reprises the struggle between realism and formalism that remained one of the stimulating tensions within Modernism; indeed, Joyce's novel not only reprises the struggle but heightens and exaggerates it. If the representation of interiority must be seen as an epitome of literary realism, *Ulysses* undoes the epitome, by suggesting that realism is only one form among others. In the second half of the novel, as it sets aside the privileges of the monologue and moves through a succession of styles, it trounces the fantasy that it had once encouraged: the fantasy of an authentic speech of the self, finally achieved after generations of experiment. In its place it offers the inescapable multiplicity of styles, with each new form showing what could not be said in the others. Leopold Bloom's long quest for home and marriage, the mourning of Stephen Dedalus for his mother and for his unachieved art, Molly Bloom's turn from anticipation to the recollection of desire—there is no unmediated access to these trajectories of plot. Yet this is not to say that the novel abandons representation. It evokes the world of June 16, 1904, in richly abundant detail, confirmed in Joyce's proud boast that if Dublin were ever destroyed, it could be reconstructed from his descriptions. The commitment to the real is unwavering, but it never escapes the artifice of form.

The relativity of style belongs to Joyce's encyclopedic will, the pursuit of diversity and plenitude as a value more profound than the discovery of the one true language of mind. Early in the novel, Stephen Dedalus stands awkwardly in a schoolroom teaching history to unresponsive students. As the class puzzles over his questions, he ponders what might have happened if Pyrrhus had not died as he did, or if Caesar had not been knifed to death.

"They are not to be thought away. Time has branded them and fettered they are lodged in the room of the infinite possibilities they have ousted. But can those have been possible seeing that they never were? Or was that only possible which came to pass?" (21). *Ulysses* is a work that looks to retrieve possibility from the constraints of the actual. The novel sets itself to recover what Stephen Dedalus calls the "possibilities of the possible as possible" (159). This goal appears in the proliferation of "possible" tones and modes. It appears, too, on the plane of character in the desire to render the "complete" man, complete in every impulse, with nothing too base to represent. As Bloom comes to exemplify the cycle of human possibilities, *Ulysses* asks us to take seriously the thought in its title: that from within the constraints of social modernity, we might summon epic force. It is not that Bloom and Odysseus are identical; rather, the book suggests that their identity is a transformative possibility that might change the way modernity unfolds: a contemporary life could take on epic magnitude. The literary work is in this sense the possibility that could become actual "in the world." Two celebrated moments in the novel suggest the reach of this thought, the first when Stephen Dedalus responds to his complacent, empire-defending employer, Mr. Deasy, and the second when Bloom resists the nationalism (and anti-Semitism) of the Citizen-Cyclops.

> History, Stephen said, is a nightmare from which I am trying to awake. (28)

> Force, hatred, history, all that. That's not life for men and women, insult and hatred. And everybody knows that it's the very opposite of that that is really life.
> —What? says Alf.
> —Love, says Bloom. I mean the opposite of hatred. (273)

History appears as the merely actual, the given world of insult and hatred, the living nightmare. The characters are trying to climb out of history—not toward some unreal or ideal realm but toward the possibility of another human vocation, a "love" that is always ironized and still preserved.

MONTAGE MODERNISM

Similarly and concurrently, a poetic Modernism that placed so much emphasis on short forms, especially in the lapidary miniatures of Imagism, turned to the problem of the long poem. Pound began work on his *Cantos* during the war; Valéry published "La Jeune Parque" in 1917; Eliot brought out *The Waste Land* in 1922. The difficulty in a long work lay in avoiding what was an abomination to many modernists: laxity of rhetoric and loss of discipline. Eliot made this issue a central concern. In his essay on Blake, written shortly before he began *The Waste Land,* he wrote that "you cannot create a very large poem without introducing a more impersonal point of view, or splitting it up into various personalities."[33] In struggling to develop *The Waste Land,* Eliot in effect used both techniques. On one side, he adopts the often-biblical tones of a third-person voice that looks upon the world from an elevated perspective ("Under the brown fog of a winter dawn, / A crowd flowed over London bridge, so many"), but on the other side, and more radically, he articulates a cacophony of voices, "various personalities," which flicker and fade. The telling event is the movement from the discipline of the one-image, one-voiced poem toward a complex network of many images and voices.

"Montage Modernism" is a fit name for this synthetic moment in cultural history. The two techniques preserved the principle of the luminous details and the radiant epiphany, but these were no longer offered as self-contained achievements but were now integrated into a pattern of details, a matrix of epiphanies. This created the formidable doubleness characteristic of modernist works in the 1920s. The local fragment—whether an "episode" in *Ulysses* and *The Cantos* or a "voice" in *The Waste Land*—sustained the value of evocative, finite circumscription, while in a second movement the fragments were woven into encompassing patterns. Northrop Frye noted the meeting of these distinct values, which could create a "contrast between the course of a whole civilization and the tiny flashes of significant moments which reveal its meaning."[34] But of course the pressing question was how to bring these aims together. How could the radiant fragment participate in a larger whole without losing its force? Or to reverse the question, how could the long modernist work give value to fragments without sacrificing the coherence of the whole?

Cinema became the most prominent example and ultimately the strongest influence on the montage aesthetic.[35] The first film of the Lumière brothers, *La Sortie des usines Lumière* (Workers Leaving the Lumière Factory, 1895), holds a steady point of view as the camera records the workers streaming through the gate at the end of the day. Here was a first revolutionary contribution of cinema: the creation of a static, spatial volume as a container for movement, gesture, animation. The breakthrough toward montage occurred when the point of view became as mobile as the scenes it recorded. Although there were many stages along the way, some of the most important experiments coincided with the literary events of the 1920s, most notably the work of the Soviet filmmakers, especially Sergei Eisenstein and Dziga Vertov. Their films and their theories represent the most self-conscious stage of montage Modernism. Montage, writes Eisenstein, is a response to the "two-fold process (the fragment and its relationships)"; therefore it "becomes the mightiest means for a really important creative remolding of nature."[36]

The *construction, not the replication, of reality:* this was the emphasis in Soviet theory and practice. The individual shot, the photographic image, represented the given reality—the "granite" truth of the world—but the arrangement of shots achieved the montage effect, the reconstruction and interpretation of the world. In the first years after the Russian Revolution, artistic experiment flourished alongside social transformation. For both Eisenstein and Vertov, innovations in form were at the same time signs of political conviction. So, for instance, in *Battleship Potemkin,* the story of a shipboard mutiny during the failed 1905 revolution, a first effect of cross-cutting is to contrast repressive authority and the afflictions of the sailors: an image of privilege yields to a scene of deprivation. The blatant irony in such juxtaposition is one resource of the new aesthetic. The most celebrated sequence in the film occurs when the mutiny spreads to shore. The headlong rush down the Odessa steps builds to a controlled frenzy of inter-cutting when the citizens of the city—including a desperate mother and a runaway baby carriage careening downward—confront the soldiers who have arrived to suppress the revolt. For Eisenstein, the principle of contrast exemplified the Marxist theory of the new Soviet state. He saw montage as an art of dialectics, with the cinema, like history itself, working by means of negation and synthesis. As each frame contends with the previous, it enacts the political struggle and also points beyond it. The clash between two forces—working class and bourgeoisie, revolutionaries and the state—yields a third possibility: the act of meaning that unites them and that reveals an escape from the historical impasse.

As Eisenstein emphasized in the later 1920s, cinematic montage can become the basis for a complex political aesthetic. He distinguished between metric montage (the rhythm or beat of the cutting), rhythmic montage (the relation between movement within each frame and movement to a next frame), tonal montage (emotional colors and textures), overtonal montage (which encompasses all the relations, including those between dominant and minor tones), and intellectual montage (where the "conflict-juxtaposition" of frames brings insight into "the very heart of things").[37] All the arts, according to Eisenstein, confront the problem of montage—how to combine the units into wholes—but the special force of film is that it "is able, more than any other art, to disclose the process that goes on microscopically in all other arts."[38] Film can lay claim to be the consummate modernist medium, both because it encompasses other media and because it is supremely suited to encounter what Eisenstein recognized as the defining event of modernity: the revolution in Russia.

From our historical distance, it is clear that the achievements of Soviet filmmaking, momentous though they were, belonged to the broader movement of montage Modernism. The effort to construct complex artifacts by reassembling the smaller units—impressions, frames, images, sounds—cut across many media in the 1920s. Montage joins *The Waste Land, The Cantos,* and the "Wandering Rocks" episode of *Ulysses* just as surely as it links *Battleship Potemkin* and Vertov's *The Man with the Movie Camera* with the works of Gertrude Stein and Picasso. Image and frame no longer appear as self-contained units of meaning; now they are seen as unfinished fragments that depend upon a matrix of fragments. The difficulty of these works lies in the abruptness of transition; the gap between two moments is unfilled, it remains for the reader, the viewer, or the listener to construct the synthetic view.

DEPTH OF FIELD

A lasting legacy of Modernism, the montage aesthetic still informs our new millennial culture. But it would be a mistake to see it as the defining style of a mature Modernism. Here we can make a distinction by way of a controversy within film studies. In the influential essays written just after the Second World War and collected under the heading *Qu'est-ce que le cinéma?* (What Is Cinema?), André Bazin develops a subtle theory of the history of film. For Bazin the art first ripened among the Soviets, especially Eisenstein, and among the German expressionists. But he sees a decisive change in a later generation, led most notably by Jean Renoir and Orson Welles. Their achievement was to break with the obtrusive editing of Soviet montage and also with the spatial distortions of Expressionism in order to achieve (at last) a convincing cinematic verisimilitude. Central to the change were the new *depth of visual field,* which opened a spatial volume containing more information, and the *long take,* which let the eye linger over the image. The latter, in particular, repudiated the rapid shifts of attention in

Soviet montage and offered the absorption of gazing as a rival source of meaning.

Because Bazin cast the issue in terms of progress toward realism, he clearly thought of expressionist film as a phase to be surpassed. But viewing it another way, we can see continuities between cinematic Expressionism —in such examples as Wiene's *The Cabinet of Dr. Caligari* and Lang's *Metropolis*—and the later style of the 1930s and 1940s. It is true that Expressionism relied on extravagant gestures and illusory spaces, but it is equally true that these distortions were justified in terms of a deeper realism, an expressive truth unavailable within prevailing norms. The rapidly shifting basis of realism has been a mark of Modernism. Apart from Bazin's concern over which style reflects the Real, the issue here is the shared concern with depth. The expressionist filmmakers, like Welles and Renoir, pursued significance in wide volumes, which were valued not because they can be quickly juxtaposed with one another but because each contains a plenitude that can be patiently disclosed.

Deep Modernism can be contrasted with montage Modernism in a way that goes beyond the question of film and film theory. Montage looks to the resources of speed, discontinuity, and juxtaposition that appear in many works of the period; it exploits the challenge of the gap and emphasizes construction and assemblage. Deep Modernism, on the other hand, sustains its attentions. What Bazin emphasizes as the "shot in depth" in film reflects a much broader aesthetic attitude.[39] Psychoanalysis, which emerged around the same time, offered itself as a depth psychology, initially specifying an interest in subterranean and invisible regions of the mind: the unconscious as a cavern of impulses, desires, fantasies. But just as important to its development was the advent of psychoanalytic interpretation, both in therapy and in the genre of the case study. Sudden or simple cures (through "abreaction") gave way to the long therapeutic encounter with a patient's mental history; and the psychoanalytic case study, as we have seen, involved an exacting account of interpretation and reinterpretation. The assumption is that the volume of meaning is vast, even limitless, and that the heroism of psychoanalysis will lie in traversing its reach.

Proust's novel stands as a supreme work of the aesthetic of depth in the sense developed here. Its aim is not primarily to penetrate the cavern of the unconscious; it offers instead a depth of field spreading through time. The long rhythms of the sentences correspond to the endless patience of the narrative. Life here is not a sequence of juxtaposed moments; it is rather a long circuit moving backward as it moves forward, a cycle of repetitions and returns, a continuous process of amplification and revision. To make memory a supreme vocation is to construe life in terms of deep time. That Proust's work grew ever longer is a material sign of this vocation. The value of compression that predominates in montage is replaced by the values of elaboration and distension, duration and accumulation.

There is no need to force the distinction between montage Modernism and deep Modernism upon complex works, which often move between the two techniques. William Faulkner's novels make an illuminating case. The remarkable works that come in a rush at the end of the 1920s and in the early 1930s—*The Sound and the Fury, As I Lay Dying,* and *Absalom, Absalom!*— owe a great deal to the experiments of the prewar generation, especially those of Conrad, Ford, and Joyce. The representation of interior states, the resources of spoken testimony, the concern with reliable and unreliable narration—Faulkner found these devices in his predecessors' work and exploited them in new contexts. While he radicalized the formal challenges, creating even more formidable demands on the reader's grasp of event, speaker, and sequence, he also embedded the experimentation within the particularities of American regionalism. In the Sutpen of *Absalom, Absalom!* the legacy of Conrad's Kurtz now belongs to the history of the South, the Civil War, and racism. We recall how Yeats assimilated Symbolism to Irish folklore and Irish political struggles, and we recognize again how modernist internationalism can be absorbed within local urgencies. The new techniques were like other resources and commodities in a globalizing marketplace. Younger artists studied the virtuosity of their predecessors, and although Modernism prepared for grand universalizing projects—with Joyce's *Finnegans Wake* marking one limit of a universal Modernism—it also opened the way to local immediacy. Picasso's response to the Fascist bombing of Guernica is an illustrious case.

Montage Modernism shows itself in Faulkner in the radical multiplicity of perspectives. The shifting views in the novels—fully marked in *The Sound and the Fury* and *As I Lay Dying* and complexly implied in *Absalom, Absalom!*—follow Eliot's impulse to construct ambitious works out of separate voices. The competition among perspectives discloses the logic (and illogic) of American history, the circuit of power and love within the family, and the ambiguity of ethics. The plurality of montage is indispensable in all these respects. Nevertheless, Faulkner brings its resources to meet the aims of temporal depth. For all the looping and tangle of Faulknerian plot, all the difficulty in reassembling chronology, the accumulating effect is precisely to uncover deep time. The long duration of family trauma is one aspect. But the archaic reach of history and the ancient wound in private psyches—these, too, are embedded in the rigorous, deep temporality.

THE DADA CARNIVAL

The montage of surfaces and deep time gives one contrast in the postwar moment, but it should not obscure another contrast that we can approach by way of Dadaism and Surrealism, the avant-garde and Modernism. Surviving accounts of the first eruptions of Dada—in Zurich in 1916—make clear that these early events were often spontaneous, always exuberant, and openly indifferent to the decorum of art. In *Theory of the Avant-Garde,* Peter Bürger offers an account of Dadaism as the culmination of the history of art within postreligious modernity. As the middle classes came to dominance at the end of the nineteenth century, art completed the mission of autonomy that had first been broached within the Renaissance. "Aestheticism"—by which Bürger above all means late-century Symbolism —established an autonomous space in which the form and the content of art at last coincided. Set free from realism, the subject of art was now nothing other than the workings of its form. And yet, suggests Bürger, the autonomy of aestheticism, even as it liberated artists to make their own processes into a subject matter, was essentially a social event: an act of the bourgeois middle classes to preserve an ideal space separate from material struggle. Dadaism, in this view, was a reaction to the triumph of autonomy. It was a moment of massive refusal and renunciation, but it only became possible when the history of autonomy was complete and self-conscious. In place of the separation of art and life perfected by aestheticism, Dada moved toward the long-deferred reunion. Art returned to life, entered the realm of ordinary practice, abandoned its separate identity.[40]

Bürger's theory is elegant, stimulating, and influential. But conducted as it is on a plane of high abstraction, it ignores a history that we need to preserve. Between aestheticism and Dada, much happened within the milieu of Modernism. The performance of *Ubu roi,* the example of Rimbaud, the provocations of Fauvism and Cubism, the international spectacle of Futurism—all represent breaks with the varied practices that Bürger reduces to aestheticism. Moreover, the social challenges of realism—in the drama of Ibsen and Strindberg, in the fiction of Zola and Dreiser—were simultaneous with the growth of aestheticism, not surpassed by it. As for the later phase of the movement, Richard Murphy has convincingly argued that Expressionism satisfied most of the criteria that define Bürger's Dadaism.[41] This is not to say that Dadaism offered nothing new, only that it belonged to a wide field of oppositional art, in which the contrast between art and life was continually tested. What most distinguished Dadaism was its extravagance—in both its gestures and its manifestos—and its indifference to norms of comprehension. Bürger has persuasively said that Dada lacked a "style": that it aimed at no recognizable mode, manner, or technique, that it perpetually changed media and altered tones. The anti-style and the genius for public disturbance carried over long distances and put Dadaists in conversation with artists often reserved for the polite category of "Modernism."

As T. S. Eliot was beginning the most important stage of writing *The Waste Land,* he composed a brief response to Dada in *The Tyro,* Wyndham Lewis's new journal. "With regard to certain intellectual activities across the Channel," wrote Eliot, "which at the moment appear to take the place of poetry in the life of Paris, some effort ought to be made to arrive at an intelligent point of view on this side." Cautious about any practice that might replace poetry, Eliot still perceives a seriousness within the antic mood of Dada, whose value, such as it is, "depends upon the extent to which it is a moral criticism of French literature and French life," and this is because "all first-rate poetry is occupied with morality." In writing these words, Eliot was no doubt considering his own next risky turn in *The Waste Land,* a poem that would incite outrage comparable to that aroused by Dada but that also made clear its "moral criticism."[42] Some months earlier, Joyce, too, had mentioned the romping life of Dada in a teasing letter to his brother that asked him to squelch several rumors in the Irish newspapers, including the rumor "that I founded in Zurich the dadaist movement which is now exciting Paris."[43] Joyce was then in the midst of his own struggles with "Circe," an episode that shows just how much he had seen in the spectacle of Dada and how much in Dada he wanted for purposes of his own. The sheer liberatory release of "Circe"—the talking soap, the camel that plucks a mango, the End of the World as an octopus in a kilt—must be seen as part of the Dada carnival in Paris that Joyce watched with curiosity and fascination. Like Eliot, he kept a distance from the "exciting" events, but both writers recognized the lure of Dadaist liberation and its nearness to their own experiments.

One more distinguishing feature of the Dada movement should be stressed. Especially in its beginnings, Dadaism erupted as a succession of gestures that ignored the demands of permanence. The performances at the Cabaret Voltaire were often improvisatory and chaotic, the effect of chance actions by artists and audience, a sign of high-spirited disdain for the usual expectations. But still more striking was the willingness to let art vanish into the air. Here we need to ponder a different kind of contrast between styles of Modernism: a contrast between what we can call *textual* and *gestural* Modernism. I understand textual Modernism in a large sense, as referring to any act of inscription—in a text, on a canvas, or on a sculptor's stone—that allows a work of art to stand as a resonant and memorable artifact. We know that the modernist masterworks—from Mallarmé to Joyce, Proust to Woolf, Picasso to Eisenstein—offered themselves as objects of fascination and boundless intricacy, demanding and capable of sustaining the labor of interpretation. Modernist difficulty is one effect of this strenuous textualism: the commitment to a complexly designed artifact, one that can never be exhausted because it is always open to a further glance, a new synthesis. The period after the First World War can be seen as the great age of modernist textualism. The decade of the 1920s, with *Ulysses, The Waste Land,* Pound's *Cantos,* and the novels of Woolf and Mann, might be taken as a summit of textuality, when artifacts became dense with formal intricacy and thematic ambition.

The gestural life of Modernism, on the other hand, includes all those events that live beyond the artifacts but that nevertheless play an indispensable role in the developing movement. To some extent, this is a question of the physical disposition of artists and their audiences—a question of personal style, of dress and costume, men in capes, women on bicycles, workers in the square, suffragettes on the street, audiences in the theater. The increased visibility, not only of modernist art works but of modernist bodies, was central to the cultural milieu. Still more significantly, gestural Modernism appears in those ephemeral happenings staged by writers and artists— the spectacles engineered by Marinetti and the futurists and the riotous evenings at the Cabaret Voltaire among the Dadaists. We need to acknowledge the special character of gestural Modernism, a major lineage within the period constituted by unrepeatable spectacles. The performances were not offered as texts, nor were they made permanent in paint. If they survive at all, and this was not their aim, it is only in half-reliable newspaper reports or memoirs. But the unrepeatable event and the evanescent gesture that "take the place of poetry" were crucial to the adversary culture.

An entrenched position in twentieth-century studies continues to accept a radical contrast between the avant-garde and high Modernism and to leave these movements to separate scholars writing separate books. Within this picture, the Continental movements—especially Futurism and Dadaism—are seen as aesthetically extreme and socially transformative, whereas the monuments of high Modernism—often epitomized by *Ulysses* and *The Waste Land*—are still accused of aesthetic autonomy and social disengagement. I regard that position as a slack historical complacency and offer the distinction between gestural and textual manifestations—the punctual event and the durable text—as important but not final. High Modernism frequently took on the guise of a Dadaist gesture, not only in its willingness to shatter norms of intelligibility but also in its address to the wider culture, its appearance as a defiant act that might last only long enough to erupt in a public circle. Moreover, many of the "gestures" of Dadaism began to take on the longer life of text. Leah Dickerman has pointed out that despite the vehemence of the Dadaist critique of art, the number of its artifacts, as well as its self-consciousness of artistic tradition, suggests not mere iconoclasm but a "commitment to the production of works of art."[44] After the war, the Dadaists in Berlin turned a negative critique into a positive political program. George Grosz and John Heartfield joined the Communist Party, devising works of political art—visual satire and photomontage—that were not just fleeting manifestations but works meant to circulate within chaotic postwar Berlin. More generally, we can say that even some of the most ephemeral events in gestural Dada took on the life of texts. Reported in the press, captured in photographs, or described in memoirs, Dada manifestations have had a long and influential afterlife. To see this interplay between text and gesture is to see the high modernist masterwork and the avant-garde eruption as reciprocal events that both repel and require one another.

SURREALISM BETWEEN ART AND POLITICS

The fissiparous quality of the avant-garde group was a special risk for Dada. The bid for spontaneity, improvisation, and disorder invited opposition among allies, sometimes friendly, but increasingly not. During the early 1920s the Parisian Dadaists became more fractious among themselves, even while their influence spread, and after a new series of disputes, some young French members made a break. Their leading figure, André Breton, offered curt reasons for the rupture: "I never aspire to amuse myself. It seems to me that the sanction of a series of utterly futile 'Dada' acts is in danger of gravely compromising an attempt at liberation to which I remain strongly attached." Breton undermined Tristan Tzara's claim to leadership and continued to stress Dada's failure, arguing that it signified "a state of mind essentially anarchic . . . a deliberate refusal to judge . . . and, perhaps, in the last analysis, a certain spirit of negation which . . . had brought about a dissolution of the group . . . whose germinating force has nevertheless been decisive."[45] For Breton, Dada's historical justification lay in preparing for the movement that he himself founded.

"Surrealism" was the name he chose, borrowing the term from Apollinaire, who had never defined it. Breton, on the other hand, was nothing if not definitive. He largely abandoned the experimental form of earlier avant-garde manifestos with their screaming typography, their indifference to argument, their similarity to the more daring texts of the period. His ambitions for Surrealism were high, but he preferred the strategy of exposition and explanation. The founding surrealist manifesto of 1924 offers both dictionary and encyclopedia versions of the term.

> SURREALISM, n. Psychic automatism in its pure state, by which one proposes to express—verbally, by means of the written word, or in any other manner—the actual functioning of thought. Dictated by thought, in the absence of any control exercised by reason, exempt from aesthetic or moral concern.

> ENCYCL. *Philosophy.* Surrealism is based on the belief in the superior reality of certain forms of previously neglected associations, in the omnipotence of dream, in the disinterested play of thought. It tends to ruin once and for all all other psychic mechanisms and to substitute itself for them in solving all the principal problems of life.[46]

Working with patients during the war, Breton had employed some of the techniques of Freud, whose influence on Surrealism was profound. The psychoanalytic emphasis on dream life and the unconscious and on the liberatory power of free association was turned to the purpose of cultural revolution. Unlike the futurists, surrealists were eager to acknowledge precursors; Breton enjoyed making lists of those who had prepared for a revolution that could now transform the world. If Freud was the early intellectual inspiration, Rimbaud, Jarry, and, most crucially, the Comte de Lautréamont were the key literary predecessors. Isidore Lucien Ducasse, writing under the pseudonym Lautréamont, was the author of *Les Chants de Maldoror,* and if Freud offered a theoretical model, Lautréamont was seen to exemplify the practice of Surrealism before it knew its name. The nightmare extravagance of *Les Chants,* the release from all canons of rationality, the exploration of extreme states of mind and threshold experiences—these made the book a touchstone for surrealist experiment.

Surrealism offered itself as an affirmative movement in contrast to what Breton saw as the merely negative tendency of Dadaism. To abandon the "realistic attitude," including the realism of novels and the domi-nance of rational thought, was to prepare for the age of freedom.[47] In what Breton spoke of as the heroic first phase of Surrealism, his young adher-ents became absorbed in their dreams, spoke in hypnotic states, and at-tempted to record their unconscious desires through automatic writing. Here, too, art as the production of individual artifacts became less im-portant than the broader movement, which for the surrealists meant a transformation in psychic life, a change available to every human being, at least in principle. If logic could be overthrown and the unconscious liberated, then a broken humanity might be healed. This was the unembar-rassed visionary claim. "I demand," wrote Breton, "that he who still refuses, for instance, to see a horse galloping on a tomato should be looked on as a cretin. A tomato is also a child's balloon—surrealism, I repeat, having sup-pressed the word 'like.'"[48] To change the structure of thought was to change the world.

A fierce discipline undergirded the movement. As Roger Shattuck has written, Surrealism was "one of the most highly disciplined and tightly or-ganized artistic schools that ever existed."[49] With determination and inge-nuity Breton, the "Pope of Surrealism," strove for rigorous consensus, and when members differed with their chief, he was willing to banish them from the group. In this respect, Surrealism epitomizes the social complexity of the avant-garde. On the one hand, Breton pursued strong individual lead-ership; on the other hand, he insisted on collective liberation. Within this productively unstable community, striking individual works emerged, in-cluding the collages of Max Ernst, the paintings of Salvador Dalí and Yves Tanguy, the films of Luis Buñuel and Dalí, the poetry of Louis Aragon, and Breton's own experimental narrative *Nadja* (figs. 12–13).

The ecstatic overcoming of limits remained the beckoning goal. Breton writes of the "future resolution of these two states, dream and reality, which are so seemingly contradictory, into a kind of absolute reality, of surreal-ity." And further: "Everything suggests that there exists a certain point of the mind at which life and death, the real and the imaginary, the past and the future, the communicable and the incommunicable, the heights and the depths cease to be perceived contradictorily."[50] Soon after the first ripening in the middle 1920s, however—the initial manifesto, the automatic writ-ing, the simulation of madness, the absorption in dream—the surrealists faced new historical conditions that unsettled their projects. The attempt to revolutionize human experience inevitably brought them into contact with political revolutionaries, in particular with those on the left intent on completing the work of the Bolsheviks in Russia. What did surrealist exploration have to do with political struggle? This question remained urgent and unresolved. Here, in the later stages of Modernism, the problem of art as a social practice returns with vehemence. It appears in many guises throughout the late 1920s and 1930s—in the early poetry of W. H. Auden, Pound's *Cantos,* the German *neue Sachlichkeit* (new objectivity), the political plays of Clifford Odets, the novels of John Dos Passos. But Surrealism is perhaps the central case of a mature avant-garde obliged to confront the demands of politics.

From the perspective of Marxist theory and Leninist practice, Surrealism could seem merely another form of bourgeois whimsy. Dreams, madness, liberated imagination—what could these offer to the social emergency of the interwar period? For their part the surrealists accepted the goals of revolutionary politics; they called for the end of capitalism and the beginning of socialism; they named themselves allies of the Communists. But Breton and his closest collaborators refused to surrender the autonomy of their project to a widely inclusive campaign. Because he was committed to both aims—to the independent contribution of Surrealism and to a social-political-economic revolution—he worked arduously, and subtly, to maintain an equilibrium between culture and politics.

In the important statement "What Is Surrealism?" Breton conceded an initial point to the Marxists. It was true, he said, that in the first stage of his movement he had affirmed the "all-powerfulness of thought" and had considered the mind "capable of freeing itself by means of its own resources." The movement had nourished a "total nonconformism." Now Breton recognized this claim as "extremely mistaken," a naive belief that "thought is supreme over matter," when in fact matter holds supremacy over thought. If the transformation of the world remained the inspiriting goal, Breton now conceded that economic struggle must lead the way: "Today more than ever the surrealists rely entirely, for the bringing about of human liberation on the proletarian revolution."[51]

While some surrealists stepped across the divide and joined the Communists (Louis Aragon being the most celebrated case), Breton held fast to his distinct radicalism and his continuing faith in liberatory desire. He distinguished interior and exterior realities, subjective and objective liberation. The inner realm generated all those problems that Surrealism had dedicated itself to resolve, whereas the latter was the zone of social struggle that could be resolved only through political revolution. Even if Surrealism could achieve its ecstatic synthesis only after communism produced a just society, Breton held that its contribution was indispensable, and that the difference between material and mental liberation must never be confused.

AMERICANS LATE AND LOCAL

No account of Modernism can ever be comparative enough. Surrealism represents one culmination of the European avant-garde as its history unfolded after the emergence of Symbolism in the 1880s. But here it will be useful to consider the arc of postwar American Modernism, which offers the illumination of similarity-in-difference. The formation of artistic subcultures energized by the young, the shock effect of their experimental art, the division of the audience into the sympathetic and the outraged, the production of manifestos and journals—these events played out in familiar style. But Modernism in the United States differed in revealing ways.

A sense of belatedness pervaded the coming of the American avant-garde. The dominant early examples came from Europe and suggested that the work being created in the United States lagged well behind the advances across the Atlantic. On the other hand, America was an unsurpassed site of technological modernity. In 1915 an admiring Marcel Duchamp remarked, "If only America would realize that the art of Europe is finished—dead—and that America is the art of the future. . . . Look at the skyscrapers! Has Europe anything to show more beautiful than these?"[52] At the same time, a new national pride created resistance toward a culture imported from abroad. The grand example of Whitman loomed large in the early years of the twentieth century, and as Mark Morrisson has shown, even an "advanced" magazine such as *Little Review* betrayed a tension between Whitman, the American as national poet, and Pound, the American as international modernist.[53]

Alfred Stieglitz played a leading role in the remaking of American culture. Having achieved success as a photographer in the early 1890s, Stieglitz founded the Camera Club of New York, traveled to Europe, and reaffirmed his commitment to photography as an advanced form of art. In 1902 he initiated the Photo-Secession, inspired by the Secession groups in Vienna and Munich that had excited controversy just before the turn of the century. Part of the European example was the convergence of the arts, and Stieglitz began to look well beyond photography, as well as beyond New York, to promote a campaign of the New. His gallery 291 displayed Auguste Rodin and Henri Matisse, Cézanne and Picasso, just as their reputations were beginning to form, and his journal, *Camera Work*, published the theoretical writings of Bergson and Kandinsky.[54] Stieglitz and others, including Walter Arensberg and Alfred Kreymborg, fostered a loose circle of young American artists eager to widen the course of experiment. Various currents met in 1913, the year of the historic International Exhibition of Modern Art, known as the Armory Show because of its site. Major figures of the European scene were represented, with an early work by Duchamp, *Nude Descending a Staircase,* producing the kind of sensation seen in many other capitals between 1890 and the First World War.

The careers of Wallace Stevens and William Carlos Williams emerged within this context of rapidly coalescing American experiment. The Armory Show, the shock of the new paintings, the ambitious journals led by *Poetry* and the *Little Magazine,* the scene of urban modernity—these created a milieu of risk and aesthetic self-consciousness. The two poets, who were beginning their careers after a period of artistic radicalism and a traumatic war, willingly brought root assumptions into question: assumptions about language, word, idea, thing, and conditions of beauty. During the period Williams often makes the struggle toward poetry into a subject of his verse, as in "The Wind Increases."

The harried
earth is swept
    The trees
the tulip's bright
  tips
    sidle and
toss—

    Loose your love
to flow

Blow!

Good Christ what is
a poet—if any
    exists?

a man
whose words will
    bite

        their way
home—being actual

havgin the form
        of motions

At each twigtip

new

upon the tortured
body of thought
      gripping
the ground

a way
      to the last leaf tip[55]

The revision of the poetic line is the first effect. To compose short lines with only one or two accents, but also to let the structure of sentences carry the rhythms across the lines, creating effects of acceleration followed by sudden pauses, and then to use the resource of white space to set off brief phrases or even single words—these became favored techniques. As Albert Gelpi puts it, the "line units work against, rather than with, the sentence and the resulting line fragments remake the sentence—and the scene."[56] The gestures reflect an effort, which we have seen elsewhere, to achieve a poetic radicalism that can stand alongside the conspicuous extremities in the visual arts.

From both Imagism and the new painting Williams drew the power of the tableau: the arrangement of objects—often homely, familiar, or natural objects—until they become, in Pound's words, "an intellectual and emotional complex in an instant of time." James E. Breslin has emphasized the role of "edges" in Williams ("It is at the edge of the / petal that love waits"— "The Rose") as signs of the singularity of things, their radiant integrity.[57] And yet as "The Wind Increases" suggests, Williams also resisted the self-containment of the image, as well as its restriction to an "instant of time." Much as the canny use of enjambment flows between the broken lines, so Williams's singular objects open outward, linked to other scenes and networks. The wind of the title, a familiar, much-remarked figure in Williams's work, serves as an elemental binding force that breaks past boundaries. The universe shows itself as a field of coursing energies; the energy that shakes the trees and flowers also blows through love and through the poet who tries to speak of such matters.

When "The Wind Increases" answers the question at its center ("what is / a poet—if any / exists?"), it does so in terms that Williams will refine but never abandon. On one side is the call for words that "bite . . . home" into the pith of things, "gripping / the ground" of the world we share. This is a figure for Williams's "realism," his demand that poetry stay close, or even penetrate, material life. But words in Williams can grip the world only by "being actual." J. Hillis Miller, reflecting on Williams's view of the poem as a "field of action," has emphasized how the poetry is not a window onto the world but a world in its own right, how for Williams the poem "creates a new object, a play, a dance which is not a mirror up to nature."[58] The words are not names but things. One result is that parts of the poems often struggle against other parts. "The Black Winds," for instance, turns back against its own rhetoric with these rueful final lines.

> How easy to slip
> into the old mode, how hard to
> cling firmly to the advance—[59]

Still, to speak of the poem as its own field of action is not to say that it breaks ties with the world.[60] Poetry *engages reality by itself being a reality;* words, which are things, evoke the things around them; they enact, as much as they describe, the procession of life.

Stevens, too, has a keen sense of place and thing; he, too, stages spatial tableaux as incitements to lyric quickening. But to bring these poets together is to see how Stevens always displaces place, bringing landscape toward artifice, where it can meet the artifice of our concepts. Of Stevens's two early ambitious works, "Sunday Morning" and "Peter Quince at the Clavier," the latter poem is more important to us here because it devises the mode that will grow dominant within his work. Even as it evokes a complex visual/dramatic atmosphere—Susanna bathing, walking, sighing "in her still garden," with the "red-eyed elders" watching, waiting, lusting—the poem depends on the play of concepts in a game of thought.

> Music is feeling, then, not sound;
> And thus it is that what I feel,
> Here in this room, desiring you,
>
> Thinking of your blue-shadowed silk,
> Is music.

Concepts are as sensuous as things of the world. Like people and objects in the poem—Susanna and the elders, the green water and the winds—ideas are mobile, unfixed, and open to change. The lyric discursiveness of the poem—

> Beauty is momentary in the mind—
> The fitful tracing of a portal;
> But in the flesh it is immortal.
> The body dies; the body's beauty lives.[61]

—opens lines of inquiry that resemble philosophic thought, but from within the frame of artifice. In Stevens the activity of thought is itself a sensory event. Like music, an idea declines to settle in either body or mind, and the work of thought is to show continuity between the two.

It is often said of Stevens's first volume, *Harmonium,* that it shifts between two contrary positions: the form of the world as a projection of consciousness ("man is the intelligence of his soil,/The sovereign ghost") and consciousness as an emanation of the world ("his soil is man's intelligence") —from the poem "The Comedian as the Letter C."[62] But in fact what often gives impetus to the poems in *Harmonium* is that neither philosophic position can sustain itself. The conscious will and the imagination come to know themselves as makers and as made, as objects as much as subjects. The world is profuse in its "perpetual undulation" ("The Place of the Solitaires," 60), but we see, scent, and taste it only through the medium of a mind living through the senses. As we project a world, we discover ourselves in its midst.

> I was the world in which I walked, and what I saw
> Or heard or felt came not but from myself;
> And there I found myself more truly and more strange.
>   *("Tea at the Palaz of Hoon," 121)*

We find the self we are; we discover consciousness like another object in the field; we sometimes face the world as two mirrors might face each other—

> One must have a mind of winter
> To regard the frost and the boughs
> Of the pine-trees crusted with snow;
>
> And have been cold a long time
> To behold the junipers shagged with ice.
>   *("The Snow Man," 9)*

—and sometimes we inhabit the earth as unearthly beings who can no longer coincide with our world.

> The time of year has grown indifferent.
> Mildew of summer and the deepening snow
> Are both alike in the routine I know.
> I am too dumbly in my being pent.
>
> *("The Man Whose Pharynx Was Bad," 96)*

Stevens composes a poetry of thought that enjoys and exploits the power of the discursive proposition, that can depend on metaphysical ideas such as death, reality, imagination, nothingness. But the continuous force of the poetry is to return those words to less rarefied contexts where they rub shoulders with homely words like "ice cream," "ten o'clock," "yokels," and also eruptive, arch or nonsense words like "rou-cou-cou," "Homunculus," "Ti-lill-o," "Fat! Fat! Fat! Fat!" and "Gubbinal." Placed within a verbal environment where no words, including philosophic words, can secure their foundation, *thinking becomes a fictive exercise.* This gesture belongs to a far broader turn in Modernism, which we might think of as a "theoretical" turn, one that appropriates ideas as favored instruments but makes no attempt to achieve clinching arguments. In this sense, the theories that circulated through the 1920s differed substantially from the ideological investments that were so prominent at the end of the nineteenth century.

When Stephen Dedalus completes his long disquisition on Shakespeare (in the "Scylla and Charybdis" episode of *Ulysses*), he is asked whether he believes his own theory. "No, Stephen said promptly." Here, too, theory is made fictive. Concept and debate have no special authority; they are literary performances among others. The many intellectuals moving through literature of the 1920s—among them, Lawrence's Birkin, Robert Musil's Ulrich, Mann's Hans Castorp (between Settembrini and Naphta), Woolf's Mr. Ramsay (and also Lily Briscoe), Joyce's Dedalus, Wyndham Lewis's Tarr, Proust's Marcel—offer no final judgments within the play of tones, images, and events; their ideas are vivid without authority.

Frank Kermode describes the history of the "romantic image" as a repudiation of intellect, a commitment to "image-making powers of the mind at the expense of its rational powers."[63] Such a view captures a lineage that Kermode traces from Blake and the French symbolists toward one epitome in the career of Yeats. We have seen its importance to the formation of Modernism. And yet as the parade of intellectuals suggests, a pronounced countermovement arose, a shift from the intuitive, ineffable image toward the explicitness of theory—fictive theory. Even if these characters (and authors) can never expect to utter an authoritative word, there can be no doubt that the image is now challenged by garrulous concepts. These figures of the 1920s are often detached and self-conscious, and their voices—sometimes mild, sometimes belligerent—sound the notes of critique and self-critique. They contrast not only with traditional protagonists conceived in terms of quest and deed but also with characters of an earlier modernist generation who assumed passive and receptive attitudes and who often sought extremes of sensation that resist cognition.

Part of Williams's importance was his self-conscious resistance to this tendency, his staunch refusal of cosmopolitan intellectualism. Like Stevens, Williams gave high value to *activity,* to a quickness, even a volatility, in the movement of verse corresponding to the velocity of the postwar world. But without overstressing the point, we can say that for Stevens poetic action belongs first to the velocity of the mind as it makes nervous transactions with non-mind, while for Williams poetic action participates in the movement of an existence that perpetually excites but exceeds thought. Poetry must find moving words to disclose (and imitate) the kinetic flow of the world. The car plays a distinctive role in this regard; Williams gladly accepts its fast-moving modernity. In "The Right of Way" he goes out "spinning on the / four wheels of my car" (259), which releases vision to motion. The sense of churning flux links Williams to the futurists, as does the embrace of automobile culture. But crucially, Williams refuses to make a cult of speed, machinery, or even modernity as such. His perception of flows and circuits, energies and motion, includes the natural world; indeed, he places the mobility of wind, trees, and flowers at its center. The title poem of *Spring and All* concludes with the prospect of grass, leaf, bush, and tree prepared for the turn of season.

> the profound change
> has come upon them: rooted, they
> grip down and begin to awaken

(242)

The rootedness of the ever-changing world, the way that kinesis always belongs to some physical place, is what makes the American scene inexhaustible for Williams. The poet finds himself in the midst of twentieth-century national life, with its unsettled mix of leafy landscape and steel modernity, and his commitment to the "actual" means that he must confront the world as it is given to him. Writing from his conviction in his techniques and from his place in everyday America, Williams repudiated Eliot and *The Waste Land,* giving this account in his *Autobiography:*

> Then out of the blue *The Dial* brought out *The Waste Land* and all our hilarity ended. It wiped out our world as if an atom bomb had been dropped upon it and our brave sallies into the unknown were turned to dust.
>
> To me especially it struck like a sardonic bullet. I felt at once that it had set me back twenty years, and I'm sure it did. Critically Eliot returned us to the classroom just at the moment when I felt that we were on the point of escape to matters much closer to the essence of a new art form itself—rooted in the locality which should give it fruit. I knew at once that in certain ways I was most defeated.
>
> Eliot had turned his back on the possibility of reviving my world.[64]

THE HARLEM RENAISSANCE

During the first decades of the twentieth century, a set of intersecting events set the stage for the episodes we know as the Harlem Renaissance and the New Negro movement. The events included a determined African American response to racism and racist violence, the writings of Booker T. Washington, Paul Dunbar, and especially W. E. B. Du Bois, and the Great Migration of black Americans northward and toward the metropolis. Mark A. Sanders has usefully characterized the term "New Negro" as connoting a "sense of political self-awareness, aggressiveness, and dedication to the cause of black citizenship and empowerment."[65] Within the context of these meanings, Du Bois laid out a program of social action that set the "color line" as the foundational problem of American injustice and that called for vigorous resistance to both social oppression and the psychological burden of "double consciousness." Through his writings and his editorship of the journal *The Crisis,* Du Bois articulated a plan for struggle, writing in an editorial of 1920 that "a renaissance of American Negro literature is due; the material about us in the strange, heart-rending race tangle is rich beyond dream and only we can tell the tale and sing the song from the heart."[66] It is clear, however, that the cultural events of the 1920s resisted, as much as they depended on, the writings of Du Bois.

Harlem, and Greater New York City, became the center for an African American culture far wider than the area now identified with the Harlem Renaissance. The success of the musical *Shuffle Along* in 1921 and, more spectacularly, the international success of jazz created a milieu of creative achievement beyond the focused politics of *The Crisis.* In a much-quoted remark the Austrian director Max Reinhardt observed that the "chief contribution of America to the drama of tomorrow would be its development of Negro folk-drama," while Antonín Dvořák was said to have claimed that "if America ever had a national music, it must be based upon the songs found among the southern Negroes."[67] These comments circulated as part of the work of affirmation within a re-forming cultural community. But the power of a self-constituting and self-legitimating population was clearly more important than the validation provided by European eminence. The young black writers who encountered one another in the early 1920s— among them Claude McKay, Langston Hughes, Countee Cullen, Jean Toomer, and Zora Neale Hurston—certainly recognized modernizing precursors such as Whitman, Shaw, Eugene O'Neill, and Sherwood Anderson, but it was their mutual recognition that was crucial. As they met, collaborated, and published together, they established a movement in culture, an art-practice, that did not simply coincide with a political program.

"All Art is propaganda," wrote Du Bois, "and ever must be, despite the wailing of the purists. I stand in utter shamelessness and say that whatever art I have for writing has been used always for propaganda for gaining the right of black folk to love and enjoy. I do not care a damn for any art that is not used for propaganda."[68] As George Hutchinson has emphasized, a significant theoretical turn came with the emergence of the journal *Opportunity,* edited by Charles S. Johnson, which offered an alternative to Du Bois's doctrine of art as propaganda. Within *Opportunity,* as Hutchinson shows, art appeared as a legitimate social engagement in its own right: it could express, but also form, an African American consciousness.[69] The other decisive figure in this discussion was Alain Locke, who also recognized cultural expression as an independent good and resisted what he called the "hampering habit of setting artistic values with primary regard for moral effect."[70]

Here the question of art and social practice is visible and sharply debated. Would it harm the struggle against racism—as Du Bois intermittently worried—if a naturalist-inspired aesthetic portrayed sordid aspects of black experience? "In *The Crisis,* at least, you do not have to confine your writings to portrayal of beggars, scoundrels and prostitutes; you can write about ordinary decent colored people if you want," Du Bois said, before immediately adding, "On the other hand do not fear the Truth." The problem of realism is unsettled for Du Bois. But he remains clear in his resistance to independent aesthetic values: "We do not believe in any art simply for art's sake. . . . We want Negro writers to produce beautiful things but we stress the things rather than the beauty."[71] Alain Locke, by contrast, argued that New Negro expression began with a realist claim in order "to counter-act the false drawing and values of popular writers," but it grew toward "the few finer talents" who were "motivated by more truly artistic motives of self-expression."[72]

The struggle between art as propaganda and "truly artistic" work be-longs to an ongoing modernist debate, including debates among the sur-realists that were almost exactly contemporary but whose development made a striking contrast with the development in Harlem. Whereas Sur-realism arose under the banner of its first manifesto and through the strong leadership of Breton, the Renaissance in Harlem brought forth a range of works, a series of statements (none of which could be called a manifesto), and a diversity of leaders. The visible divisions, especially between Du Bois and Locke, gave openings to artists who were constrained by no single doctrine or theory. The closest thing to a defining event came when Locke was asked to edit a collection of writings from and about those in the new movement. The first version was a special issue of *Survey Graphic* called "Harlem, Mecca of the New Negro"; the volume was then recast as a book, *The New Negro.* Although scholarly controversy has arisen over changes from journal to book—especially over whether Locke muted the tone to achieve a broader acceptance—the two publications, however viewed, con-solidated a sense of collective movement. Yet the most striking feature of both volumes is the diversity of their contents. The sheer presence of so many black writers, so many of them young, appearing under a single cover, constituted a significant event.

But what prepared for and sustained the movement was the writing itself, which recast the terms of Modernism, in particular the question of modernist form. The leading poets of the movement differed sharply. Lang-ston Hughes built flexible structures of varying rhythms, inspired by music and also the open forms of Whitman. His early poem "The Negro Speaks of Rivers" appeared in *The Crisis* in 1921.

> I've known rivers:
> I've known rivers ancient as the world and older than the
>   flow of human blood in human veins.
>
> My soul has grown deep like the rivers.

I bathed in the Euphrates when dawns were young.
I built my hut near the Congo and it lulled me to sleep.
I looked upon the Nile and raised the pyramids above it.
I heard the singing of the Mississippi when Abe Lincoln
    went down to New Orleans, and I've seen its muddy
    bosom turn all golden in the sunset.

I've known rivers:
Ancient, dusky rivers.

My soul has grown deep like the rivers.[73]

The poem gives color to the Whitmanian "I." Through the light, unforced gesture of its title, it asserts the power of incorporation—knowing and speaking of rivers, living through ancient times, becoming deep like the rivers—and turns that power toward the question of race. This is the Whitmanian speech of the New Negro. Then, even as the rhythms extend in long lines and contract in short ones, the poem keeps announcing the unbroken presence of selfhood: "I," "I," "I," "I," "my soul," the indelible subjectivity of the black speaker. This is an ancient, undying consciousness, a "soul" as old as legendary rivers and therefore as "deep." But the poem also plays a clever game with verbs. The title "speaks" of rivers, but "I" of the first line has "known rivers," where *knowing* shows itself as more than an abstract mental process, one that involves bathing, building, looking, and hearing. Like much of Hughes's early work, the poem absorbs changing musical rhythms within a transpersonal consciousness that knows itself by knowing the history of its acts (its verbs). The subjectivity is modern just to the extent that it is aware of all the lived past—"I am a Negro . . . I've been a slave . . . I've been a worker . . . I've been a singer . . . I've been a victim . . . I am a Negro"—that has brought it to this moment.

With two other poets of the Renaissance, Claude McKay and Countee Cullen, the puzzle of form takes on a different aspect. Both worked in traditional lyric modes; both favored metrical regularity and depended on the resources of rhyme. The question has been how to understand the challenge of the verse, given its reliance on an English lyric tradition, and of the two, Cullen is the more difficult case. He made an early commitment to Keatsian aesthetics; his first volume, *Color*, not only invokes Keats repeatedly but also often takes on the aim of lyric transcendence.[74] The power of the dream vision, the struggle with earthly constraint, the yearning for transfiguration, and the richness of imagery—these are dominant elements of the volume, which near its end asks,

> And you and I, shall we lie still,
> John Keats, while Beauty summons us?

(103)

The summons of the "Vision Splendid" is the vocation that Cullen accepts. Indeed, part of his importance within the movement is precisely that his poetry resisted classification as "Negro writing." Cullen was much praised for his mastery of lyric technique, and in one respect, the content of his first volume was exactly its escape from the expectations of a white audience prepared to sort it according to their norms of content and category. But the further challenge of Cullen is that in the midst of high Keatsian mode he (intermittently) asserts his blackness. The opening poem in *Color* ends with a well-known couplet in which the "I" reflects on the inscrutable mysteries of God in a tone that mixes pride, pleasure, and irony.

> Yet do I marvel at this curious thing:
> To make a poet black, and bid him sing!

(3)

Blackness and brownness move especially through the first section of the book, even as the language of dream, imagination, and transcendence refines its ambitions. The teasing question—how should a black man sing?—reappears when Cullen invokes his spiritual concerns and thinks provokingly about blackness and redemption. Addressing Christ in "Heritage," the poet is playing his "double part":

> Ever at Thy glowing altar
> Must my heart grow sick and falter,
> Wishing He I served were black,
> Thinking then it would not lack
> Precedent of pain to guide it,
> Let who would or might deride it;
> Surely then this flesh would know
> Yours had borne a kindred woe.

(40)

The move between embodiment and transcendence (Keatsian or Christian) is the stimulating tension of the early poems. But just here it is worth stressing that the "traditionalism" of Cullen's forms is no surrender to convention; rather, it constitutes part of the wider challenge of the Harlem Renaissance to the history of Modernism, as well as to regressive distinctions between form and content. Any view that identifies form as only a collection of stylistic features—sonnet, iambic pentameter, rhyme—ignores the fact that content is inevitably also a form. No content is unformed: it is always a structure of idea and emotion, as "formed" as the structure of rhyme and rhythm. The meeting of Cullen's Christ with a Keatsian dream of blackness is not just a new content but a significant formal act, the weaving of histories of transcendence.

Alongside the growing body of poetry, a new prose fiction at once broadened and complicated the collective identity of the Harlem Renaissance. Nella Larsen's two novels, *Quicksand* and *Passing,* employ a broadly realist form that owes much to the work of Jessie Fauset, literary editor at *The Crisis,* who published her first novel, *There Is Confusion,* in 1924.[75] But Larsen turns middle-class portraiture to complexly subversive purposes by developing the mulatta as a protagonist and a rhetorical instrument. *Quicksand*'s Helga Crane is a fierce critic of systemic racism, who resists a return to America:

> To America, where they hated Negroes! To America, where Negroes were not people. To America, where Negroes were allowed to be beggars only, of life, of happiness, of security. To America, where everything had been taken from those dark ones, liberty, respect, even the labor of their hands. To America, where, if one had Negro blood, one mustn't expect money, education, or, sometimes, even work whereby one might earn bread.[76]

Despite the vehement clarity of this view, Helga, daughter of a black father and Danish mother, knows herself to be a "disturbing factor" to those African Americans—teachers, lecturers, activists—who struggle for racial uplift. Repeatedly she accuses the black community of wanting to imitate the lives of their oppressors. They "didn't want to be like themselves. What they wanted, asked for, begged for, was to be like their white overlords" (104). As a mulatta, Helga moves between black collectivity and exotic individuality. She takes on the burden and privilege of the double view: outside, inside. Her ambiguity carries her across communities, nations, races, leaving her perpetually unsettled but also exposing the hollowness of the lives she encounters: the respectable black middle class, the bohemian Danes, the religious South. As Anna Brickhouse has shown, Larsen's fiction depends on its own various acts of "passing": it assimilates and appropriates a tradition of white literary accomplishment, and its language displays mastery of standard white literary speech even as it challenges the clarity of racial distinction.[77] The critique of racism in *Quicksand* is direct and bitter, but the outside-inside perspective of the mulatta includes resistance to African American life, which is seen to be "as complicated and as rigid in its ramifications as the highest strata of white society" (43). The effect, important throughout the writings of the Harlem Renaissance but especially pointed in Larsen, is of a double oppositionalism: distance from both the perpetrators and the victims of racism.

Most of the pieces of Jean Toomer's *Cane*—poems and short stories—appeared separately in a variety of journals, including *The Liberator, Modern Review, Broom, Little Review,* and *The Crisis.* Their reappearance together in *Cane* implicitly asserted the claims of the composite text, in which the bounded form of a sonnet or a story can find its place within a wider flexible structure. Sherwood Anderson's *Winesburg, Ohio* was a key precedent for Toomer; the two writers were in close touch during the composition of *Cane.*[78] But Toomer looked beyond the novel-of-stories toward other forms of mosaic. In a letter to Waldo Frank, he wrote, "From three angles, [*Cane*'s] design is a circle. Aesthetically, from simple forms to complex ones, and back to simple forms. Regionally, from the South up into the North, and back into the South again. Or, From the North down into the South, and then a return North."[79]

Cane carried one kind of banner for the Harlem Renaissance as the work that most clearly belonged among the formal experiments of high Modernism, especially the works of montage Modernism. But it also created agitation, especially for Du Bois, who praised its successful moments for their "strange flashes of power, their numerous messages and numberless reasons for being," while expressing doubt at "much that is difficult or even impossible to understand." Du Bois described himself as "unduly irritated" by Toomer's decision "to make his art a puzzle to the interpreter."[80] Still, the challenges in *Cane* are only partly due to the difficulty of its composite form; the "puzzle" of the work that vexed Du Bois lies equally in its portrait of race and nation.

As the comment on the book's "circle" makes plain, Toomer never saw the structure of the book in abstract formalist terms: the design is that of American regionalism (North and South), specifically the regional provocation of African American history and its conflict with white modernity. As with the poets of the Renaissance, Toomer shows an attentiveness to form that is inextricable from historical self-consciousness, as is evident in another of Toomer's remarks about the book: "I realized with deep regret, that the spirituals, meeting ridicule, would be certain to die out. With Negroes also the trend was toward the small town and then toward the city—and industry and commerce and machines. The folk-spirit was walking in to die on the modern desert. The spirit was so beautiful. Its death was so tragic. Just this seemed the sum of life to me. And this was the feeling I put into *Cane. Cane* was a swan-song. It was a song of an end."[81]

Yet for all of Toomer's longing to recover a "folk-spirit" before it died, *Cane* is much more than a work of archaeology. Just as the book summons the soil-consciousness that animates old and rooted life, it avoids what it calls "impotent nostalgia" (86). Twice it refers to slavery as not long ago, as still recent enough to chill the early twentieth century, and throughout the volume lynching is a real and present threat. When *Cane* turns northward in its middle third—to Chicago and Washington—it records the failures of modernity. As the montage narrative plays out, any hope for civic revival is seen to require a memory of the South, at once rooted and traumatized. "Kabnis," the intricate story that concludes the volume, brings its title character down to Georgia, completing Toomer's circular design and staging a last confrontation with the "pain and beauty of the South." Kabnis is the would-be artist trapped within the conflict of pain and beauty. Meaning to shape beautiful words, he remains thwarted by the "mold that's branded on my soul" and that turns his speech into "misshapen, split-gut, tortured, twisted words" (111). Kabnis cannot reach the detachment of the critical intellect (Lewis), nor can he coincide with the mute black preacher (Father John) who finally speaks out to name "th sin th white folks 'midded when they made the Bible lie" (117). The story, like the volume, ends inconclusively, with recognition just out of reach. The fragmented form repeats within the broken subjectivities of characters and narrator, but also in the fractured community they inhabit. These dislocated figures reenact a life of missed connections and are left within the intensities of private consciousness, caught up in longings obscure to themselves and agitating to one another. The sense of a possible transformation haunts *Cane,* but like the continuity between the stories and poems, it remains an intimation.

6

the ends of modernism

Modernism was always ending—ending, one might say, as soon as it began. The eruption of novelty immediately faced the question of how novelty could live in time. Was Modernism a permanent revolution? This is how it has often been understood, as a vocation of experiment, an endless pursuit of the new. Harry Levin spoke of the "ultraism" of the movement: a compulsion to keep reaching beyond the last achievement.[1] Certainly this image captures an abiding aspect of the modernist decades. The career of Picasso, passing so swiftly from "analytic" to "synthetic" Cubism; the passage of Woolf from the comic realism of *Night and Day* to the lyric abstraction of *The Waves;* Marinetti's turn from Symbolism to Futurism; the movement of Joyce from the radicalism of *Ulysses* to the even-greater extremities of *Finnegans Wake*—these are a few among countless examples.

Such changes also registered a consciousness of the death of experiment. When Joyce writes that Stephen Dedalus no longer interests him because he has a shape that cannot be changed, or when Eliot speaks of *The Waste Land* as a "thing of the past," they acknowledge the risk of petrification that haunts modernist novelty.[2] Their polemical refusal of previous styles opened the modernists to a repudiation of their own experiments. Part of what is startling in any synoptic view of the modernist decades is the distance between the first brazen assertions and the more brazen utterances of ten or twenty years later. In one aspect, especially in the visual arts, the labor of novelty continued. And yet in another aspect, Modernism presented itself not as ongoing experiment but as discovery. The restless testing of new forms can be seen as the search for an ideal form, the technical solution to the problem of modernity.

Modernism, after all, was not simply a succession of styles; it was also an epoch of now-canonized masterworks. The supremely ambitious artifacts that aim toward finality are as distinctive as anything else produced in the late nineteenth and early twentieth centuries. The works were often composed over many years, in an invented language of their own, and demanded a prodigious devotion from their audiences. Pound's *Cantos,* Proust's *À la recherche du temps perdu,* Joyce's *Finnegans Wake,* Stein's *The Making of Americans,* and Musil's *Der Mann ohne Eigenschaften* (The Man Without Qualities) are some of their names. The sense of arrival, of the discovery of a style that can be sustained and elaborated for years, appears also in works like Eliot's *Four Quartets* and the cutouts of Henri Matisse. At a certain point in many modernist careers, there emerged a decision to settle upon a form and to pursue it to the very end so that an arduously achieved style could become the vocation for the long, last phase of a life.

We know that the distinctive forms of Modernism were not the effect of merely individual ingenuity. Joyce found stylistic clues in Édouard Dujardin, much as African statuary gave Picasso the technical recognitions that he went on to exploit; as Laforgue suggested modulations of irony that opened a path for Eliot; as Robert Browning gave voices that Pound could test. But these sources are no more self-contained than their effects. The articulation of characteristic modernist forms—montage and fragmentation, expressionist gesture, interior monologue, mythic contextualization, deep time—depended, too, on social and material conditions. Could montage have developed without the context of the new metropolis, with its physical disruptions and its rapid shifts of scene? Can we imagine sustained experiments with poetic form in the absence of the micro economy of little magazines? And without the growth of the mass press and its reviewing apparatus, would Modernism have taken on the aspect of a prominent and influential movement, paradoxically nurtured through the opposition of its enemies?

At the same historical moment, the absorptive powers of the media and advertising industries created new pressures on experimental artists. The successes of modernist movements were assured within a widening cultural sphere, and as Michael North has shown, the postwar years quickly brought the transfer of modernist techniques into mainstream and official styles of presentation.[3] Even Gertrude Stein, the writer so often accused of hermetic insensitivity, pondered the connection between aesthetic challenge and the historical situation of her audience. In "Composition as Explanation," written in the mid-1920s, she suggests that difficult works will not remain obscure or exclusive, that difficulty is only a stage in the process of acceptance. "Those who are creating the modern composition authentically are naturally only of importance when they are dead because by that time the modern composition having become past is classified and the description of it is classical. That is the reason why the creator of the new composition in the arts is an outlaw until he is a classic, there is hardly a moment in between. . . . For a very long time everybody refuses and then almost without a pause everybody accepts."[4]

From within the logic of its own development, then, Modernism offers two ways of thinking about its ends, two ways that correspond to differences in its realization. Seen from one point of view, the succession of new forms—the self-succeeding, self-canceling pursuit of novelty—led ultimately to exhaustion. The repertory of modernist possibilities was large but not infinite; radical though the experiments often were, they were bound to become repetitive and no longer productive. But seen from another point of view, those long (and in principle endless) works, such as those by Musil, Stein, Proust, Joyce, and Pound, suggest that a technical resolution was found and that an era of experiment had arrived at a point of destination. But both perspectives, that of exhausted novelty and that of achieved technique, suggested that an epoch of experiment was approaching its end.

Then, too, as we have repeatedly seen, the heightened political circumstances of the 1930s placed heavy pressure on the vocation of formal difficulty, intellectual demand, and challenge to the senses. A burden of the avant-garde was that it lived past a period of relative cultural stability that accommodated the extremism of young artists and provoked them. In the years before the First World War, the threat to culture seemed to be lethargy and fatigue. Under the inspiration of such leading writers as Marinetti, Apollinaire, and Lewis the challenge was insistent, noisy, and radical. But when the social world moved toward cataclysm, first in the war and then again in the economic and international crises of the 1930s, the militant avant-garde was engulfed by events and also by the rhetoric that attended them. Avant-garde theatricality lost much of its visibility and some of its point. Wyndham Lewis describes how the violence of the war overwhelmed the provocation of his journal *Blast*: "The War had washed out the bright puce of the cover of the organ of the Great London Vortex. Too much blood had been shed for red, even of the most shocking aniline intensity, to startle anybody."[5] In the 1930s, economic emergency, the rise of Fascism, civil war in Spain, and the imminence of a second world war overwhelmed the independent practice of radical art. One way or another, almost every modernist confronted the question of aesthetics and politics.

I move toward conclusion with an account of two political aesthetics, that of Ezra Pound, as he moved sharply rightward, and that of Bertolt Brecht, as he developed a rigorous theory of art and leftwing politics. An Anglo-centric view of the modernist moment tends to overemphasize the convergence of art and reactionary politics. Certainly the examples are notorious. Eliot's dalliance with the theory of totalitarianism, Yeats's drift toward fantasies of social hierarchy, and Lawrence's cult of leadership shared a contempt for liberal democracy that came perilously close to Fascism. Yet it is vital to remember the revolutionary leftism of many European experimentalists, including the Dadaists George Grosz and John Heartfield, many surrealists, the Russians Vladimir Mayakovsky and Kazimir Malevich, Eisenstein and Dziga-Vertov, John Dos Passos in America, Hugh MacDiarmid in Scotland, and, in certain phases, Picasso. The cases of Pound and Brecht may help to bring into focus the abiding puzzle of modernism and politics.

Pound came to England with an intense consciousness of the literary past, which was above all an array of memorable particular achievements. His first axiom was that "the study of literature is hero-worship," and he never abandoned the view that imaginative life can carry us, lifted by the genius of writers, to a plane of grandeur and transport.[6] But after the war the worship of the hero extended and altered. The first attempts toward *The Cantos*—both in "Three Cantos," written during the war, and then in the revised opening—still take their impetus from literary history, from the vigor of heroic literary agency (whether in writer or in character). Moreover, the impetus depends on a scene of struggle. Pound contends with his predecessors ("Hang it all, Robert Browning,/ there can be but one Sordello") as his Odysseus contends with the sea, in the rough accents of Anglo-Saxon verse.

> And then went down to the ship,
> Set keel to breakers, forth on the godly sea, and
> We set up mast and sail on that swart ship,
> Bore sheep aboard her, and our bodies also
> Heavy with weeping.[7]

The surpassing of Imagism during the war years was a movement beyond lyric as precision and toward epic as agon—agonistic in its local texture as well as its central climaxes. The compression that shapes *The Cantos*—itself a legacy of Imagism—means that the past is summoned not as the sweep of history but as the scene of immediate ferocity. Background, stage setting, and context are seen as excess. What remains is contest.

This last point needs to be qualified on two counts. First, even though the staging of a struggle is the animating force of *The Cantos,* the agon does expend itself. Phases of conflict come to an end, most often through death, but also through rare moments of release into a new state.

> Cloud over mountain; hill-gap, in mist, like a sea-coast.

> Leaf over leaf, dawn-branch in the sky
> And the sea dark, under wind,
> The boat's sails hung loose at the mooring,
>   Cloud like a sea inverted

> *(108)*

Sometimes these scenes of release come to the gods, sometimes to human beings. In either case, they appear as exemptions within the life of struggle. During the decades of work on the poem, Pound repeatedly invoked the promise of Paradise that would enfold the poem and bring it to wholeness. But his failure to arrive at paradisal closure—a perpetually deferred outcome that stands as another monument of modernist incompletion—is congruent with the rhythm of this epic. *The Cantos* enacts a pulsation between scenes of strenuous tension (to win a love, to build a temple, to construct a railway) and much less frequent scenes of release. These, whether for gods or for people, characteristically feature natural processes (stirring winds, moving waters, the clarity of light) that exist outside the walls of the city and beyond the changes of history.

Here we come to the second point of qualification, because when the poem returns to its zones of struggle, it does so by reaching beyond literary heroism. The poetically productive decision in the early 1920s was to look back to the Italian Renaissance and to invoke the life and career of Sigismondo Malatesta, as a lover, as a leader of mercenaries (condottiere), and as a great cultural patron. Malatesta stands as the fully embattled citizen, the illegitimate son of Pandolfo Malatesta who fought to become a self-legitimating man of will. Entangled within the conflicts of the Italian city-states, his military services bestowed on all sides, his career was a succession of violent struggles with blood relatives, rival lords, and the Pope. The first of the Malatesta cantos (canto VIII) ends in this way.

> And that year they fought in the streets,
> And that year he got out to Cesena

And brought back the levies,
And that year he crossed by night over Foglia, and . . .

From this point forward, the cantos turn to political (and economic) history as readily as to literary topoi. Pound, in his early years, looked to the literary heroism of the troubadours; now in addition to Malatesta, he summons Jefferson, Adams, Mussolini, Confucius. Moreover, this turn to historical hero-worship brings a new attitude toward language. The much-recognized formal breakthrough of the Malatesta cantos is the appropriation of documents, often directly quoted and typically without any conventional "literary" value. Long blocks of prose text (translated letters) both disrupt the metrical patterning and become startling typographical events that change the norm of the poetic page.

The turn to history—its documents, its personages, its flourishing, and its decadence—became central to Pound's understanding of the epic (his epic being defined as a "poem containing history"), and above all, it registered a turn from individual destinies to the public world.[8] The great act of cultural will that looms over The Cantos is Malatesta's rebuilding of the church of San Francesco in Rimini to the revolutionary design of Leon Battista Alberti. Even the love poetry is characteristically the strenuous public love that Pound found celebrated by the troubadours of Provence. As several readers have remarked, The Cantos declines to look inward for its stresses and its resolutions. The excavation of interiority—this abiding modernist occupation—has no deep purchase in Pound's work. As the epic takes its shape through the 1920s, it effectively empties out subjectivity, as if what was inward was never really private anyway.[9] In Pound's case the epic movement outward is inseparable from his absorption of new political and economic views.

As Pound developed his active engagement in politics after the war, he threw many backward glances at the fast-receding period that he once knew as the London Vortex, the brief time of tumult that he had done so much to stir up. In recalling this time, he sometimes placed it between 1900 and 1915, sometimes between 1908 and 1919, but whatever its boundaries, he always identified it as a definitive period of cultural change. What becomes marked in his retrospection, however, is the way the early phase now appears as self-contained. Pound wrote of looking back over the Little Review of twenty years earlier and finding almost no significant achievement "between that date and the present": no development, no novelty.[10] He saw Surrealism as a dead end, Joyce as staggering after Ulysses, Eliot as reduced to the mumble of his "mortuary ethics."[11] The work of Wyndham Lewis lived on, but even with Lewis, Pound regarded the early work as the notable accomplishment: "Enemy of the Stars," *Tarr, Blast.* Still, none of this troubled Pound, because the first quarter of the century had completed its task—it had dissolved the "oatmeal porridge" of the arts; it had performed the "necessary dissociative process of cutting" each medium clean from the others; it had cured muddle; it had allowed music to be understood as music, painting as painting. "Let that stand as the phase for the first quarter of the century."[12]

In the story of Modernism that Pound constructed, which was at the same time a story of his own career, the Fascist march on Rome in 1922 began the second and concluding phase. Now the focus fell on "men in action," not on "secluded artists." The Fascist will of Mussolini, the volition that asserts the power of "mind" over "mud," not only made possible a political revolution but carried the revolution in the arts past its long impasse. The first task, the dissociation of the arts into their separate essences, could now give way to a new settlement, their reunion within the Fascist embrace. Or, as Pound puts it, "Back in the war years we began to talk about design in terms of design and about music in terms of vibration," but now, "we are concerned with the reintegration of the arts in totalitarian synthesis."[13]

Within the new dispensation, the avant-garde changed its oppositional character. It ceased to be an alternative to politics. Now its goal was to find a secure and officially guaranteed place within the state apparatus; among the many guilds of the national economy, experimental writing will form one. Thus, in his farewell to Harriet Monroe, Pound interpreted her editorship of *Poetry* as the creation of "a trade journal in the best sense of the word. You might say it preceded the guild sense."[14] And then he gave a riper version of this image, writing, "The nearest thing to a guild in the arts in our time has been (past tense) the group"[15]—that is, the group of experimental writers whose names he lists as Joyce, Eliot, Lewis, and Pound. In the fully achieved corporate state, experimental writers would organize in a guild; they would be represented in a final council and be financially supported by the state.

Pound emphasized the discontinuity between his two phases—the phase of the separation of the arts and the phase of a synthetic Fascism that would reunite the arts within the state. And yet his earliest literary writings had prepared for the political challenge, which in many ways extended and fulfilled the ambitions in art. The perpetual aim of Pound's circle in the years before the war was to transform literary incitement into a disturbance of the wider public sphere. Pound spoke of "order[ing] the 'public' . . . to take note of certain poems."[16] The triumph of will that he celebrated in Fascism, the volitionist push against the tide of circumstance, was *his* will as the impresario of the avant-garde and as a propagandist, the only one in London, he insisted, "with guts enough to turn a proselyte into a disciple."[17] The links were deep and sustained between the revolutionary political party and the original avant-garde sect with its utopian hopes, its unyielding manifestos, its rhetorical violence, and its manipulation of the press.

For Pound the issue ran still deeper. What, after all, is a poem? And what a polis? Each is a spatially extended field, alive with contending pressures, vulnerable to decay and disintegration, tense with the relationship between the local part and the encompassing whole; and for Pound, more than for others, the critique of failed aesthetics met the critique of decaying politics, while the vision of the successful poem began to resemble that of a flourishing polis. The demand for aesthetic discipline transformed into the leader cult. Terms of abuse that had once been reserved for that low part of speech, the adjective—superfluous, intrusive, wasteful, parasitic—now attached to the adjective's social equivalent: the bank. Standing above all else was Mussolini, who, like art itself, became a "lord over fact." Pound's imagist manifesto had enjoined poets "to use absolutely no word that does not contribute to the presentation,"[18] a remark uncannily echoed nearly four decades later when he wrote: "The Fascist creed is that a man ought to make a positive contribution to the general well being. If he doesn't he is unfit to belong to the executive. He is unfit to join."[19] What is startling is the ease with which a polemic in the arts transposed itself into a political campaign and the way that pleasure in figural violence became pleasure at the thought of the real thing. A language militant from the start kept assimilating the brutal images that the world offered to it. In 1914 Pound had enjoined the modernist artist to "live by craft and violence."[20] Twenty years later the metaphor became an image of Confucian thought as an axe for clearing away the jungle of Christian theology. Then, on the eve of the war, Pound wrote chillingly that "usury is the cancer of the world, which only the surgeon's knife of Fascism can cut out of the life of nations."[21]

An enduring double focus unsettles Pound's poetics: a defense of a poetic form that controls the anarchy of details but also the celebration of particularity against convention and cliché. Within his criticism, the powerful general conceptions—"The WHOLE of 18th century literature was a cliché";[22] "Christian theology is a jungle"[23]—contended with "unsquashable" facts: "True criticism will insist on the accumulation of these concrete examples, facts, possibly small, but gristly and resilient, that can't be squashed, that insist on being taken into consideration."[24] The conflicts were at once literary and political.

The politics of Modernism was not imposed on Pound's aesthetic mission. The problem of modernist poetics had already assumed a political valence in which the form of the poem was a question of power and order, representation and governance, freedom and discipline. The gristly fact appeared sometimes as the oppressed citizenry, sometimes as the untamed rabble. Both politics and poetics involve transactions between distant poles, between the Lord and the Fact, between the long sentence and the short one, between the complete idea and the single phrase, between the state and the subject. The difficulty is how to achieve a synthesis, or, as Pound put it: "A man working on a large project may often seem a bit mad. He speaks in large terms at one moment and in the next is discussing minute details which, on the surface, have little to do with the main problem. A man whose mind moves faster than a snail finds it tedious to have to explain the connecting links of his thought."[25]

But of course the difficulty had another source besides a disdain for a snail's pace, the boredom of connecting links. It sprang from a refusal of the claims of the linking thought. So we find Pound regretting that the early Wyndham Lewis had not carried through the logic of contraction: he "had escaped from the polite paragraph but the old inertia of momentum still led him to finish his sentences, often when the complete revelation of idea had been made in a single phrase."[26] The contempt for the paragraph and the suspicion of the sentence were restaged in the Fascist contempt for the mediating institutions of liberal democracy. Nothing needs to stand between the single phrase and the complete idea, nothing between the boss and the small citizen subject. The Fascist state offered a solution to the problem of parts and wholes: "A thousand candles blaze with intense brightness. No one candle's light damages another's. So is the liberty of the individual in the ideal and fascist state."[27]

Set against this arc of political reaction, the career of Brecht stands as a contrast, but also as a surprising mirror image. Notably, he began within the milieu of Expressionism just after the war; his early play *Baal* is frequently and persuasively associated with that movement. Yet in Brecht's postwar rendering, the expressionist New Man no longer appears as the unique visionary, whose gifts prefigure universal human liberation. Baal is coolly destructive and self-annihilating, caught in the irritations of sexual cruelty, capable of inspirational song but equally capable of murder—a kind of Ubu living after the slaughter of war, an Ubu who feels the lure of power but who has lost both hope and high spirits. Baal moves through extravagant nighttime tableaux with the nihilism of his poetic gift, his sexuality, his indifference. His is an expressive individualism fallen into a corrupt world, which it can only carry to destructive extremity. No individual could be strong enough to heal a world like the one that surrounds Baal.

The plays that immediately followed, *Drums in the Night* and *In the Jungle of Cities,* render life after war as competitive anarchy, fed by the will to power and the itch of desire, with both urges covered over by social manipulation and self-deception. *Drums in the Night* records the late homecoming of the soldier Kragler, who has been held prisoner after the end of hostilities and who comes home only to find his fiancée Anna pregnant with another man's child. Those at home quicken to the postwar thrills of easy profit and trashy desires even as the Spartacist League launches its revolutionary uprising. The sound of the workers demonstrating at the newspaper offices intrudes on the drunken, complacent bourgeoisie while the play builds to the reunion of Kragler and Anna, who walk without hope (and "without touching one another") amid the pandemonium of the unreal city. As Kragler puts it in the final lines, "The bagpipes play, the poor people die in the newspaper district, the houses fall on them, the day dawns. They lie in the street like drowned cats, I'm a stinker, and the stinker goes home. . . . The shouting will all be over tomorrow morning, but I'll lie in bed tomorrow morning and multiply, so as not to perish from the earth."[28]

In the Jungle of Cities transposes the crisis of modernization to hypercapitalist Chicago, where the pace of tawdry profiteering accelerates. The play teases its audience with a false contrast between the innocent and the fallen: the modest domestic George Garga, a clerk in a lending library, and the blood-seeking sharks called Shlink, Skinny, Worm, and Baboon. In fact, no one is free from the money/desire machine. Garga becomes a capitalist boss, and his sister Mary is caught in the pain that in this world passes for love.

The disenchantment with affirmative aesthetics, with Expressionism above all, and an encounter with the social crisis were inescapable in Germany. The disorder of the postwar city was an impetus to theatrical experiment. Brecht's early works brought him a mix of celebrity and notoriety; they also brought him into contact with leading figures in the arts, most notably Max Reinhardt. Reinhardt's experimentalism, which had led to landmark productions of Strindberg, Ibsen, Shakespeare, and Hauptmann, among others, gave a widening field for Brecht's dramatic experiments. The texture of the writing—rough speech, popular song, sexual frankness, the perpetual clink of money, strong drink, aggressive gestures—gave his early plays their startling tone. But at least as provocative was the irreverence toward values that prevailed across the political spectrum: art, love, heroism, hope. Characters who pursue decency and defend innocence were favorite targets, and in these early works, although Brecht unmasks the deceptions of power and privilege, he offers no persuasive alternative.

A turning point came in the middle and later 1920s, with *Mann ist Mann* (A Man's a Man) as the crucial instance. As the title suggests, the play forces "humanity" and "identity" into question, following from Strindberg's defiant claim "that we continually adapt ourselves to people and to circumstances" and "that reality, so varied and shifting, makes us changeable" and also from the expressionist hope for the transformation of human character. In Brecht's case, however, the transformation is not an event of the inner life but an episode in shared history. As he put it a few years later, the individual "becomes increasingly drawn into enormous events that are going to change the world. No longer can he simply 'express' himself."[29]

Galy Gay is an Irish porter who sets off to buy some fish for his wife. But when a machine-gun battery loses one of its four members, Galy is appropriated by the others. They press and persuade and reconstruct him until he takes the name of the straying comrade, Jeraiah Jip. With the name comes the role and the function. And what more makes a man a man? Just before the play was produced, Brecht gave an interview in which he described the new work.

A. A comedy called *Mann ist Mann*. It's about a man being taken to pieces and rebuilt as someone else for a particular purpose.

Q. And who does the re-building?

A. Three engineers of the feelings.[30]

Gone is the expressionist liberation of inward selfhood. For Brecht, the crucial turn is toward character as engineering, as an effect of social construction. Galy Gay is called Jip, so he comes to call himself Jip; he is placed in a uniform, so he becomes a soldier; he is given a gun, so he slaughters the innocent. The comedy of *A Man's a Man* lies in the exuberance of instability: it has been persuasively suggested that Charlie Chaplin was a model for Galy Gay. If a man can be remade—with new beliefs, new appetites, new hopes—then no social form is immune to change, and no orthodoxy can resist challenge. Brecht's play came at a moment when he was reforming his aesthetics alongside a new theory of history and politics. In a radio broadcast, he declared, "What matters most is that a *new human type* should now be evolving, at this very moment," and any artistic work ignoring this fact "has nothing to do with anything." Galy Gay, he suggests, is a "new sort of type" or "possibly an ancestor" of the new type—and this is exactly because he is susceptible to re-engineering. He has no opinions of his own; he lies; he can fit in anywhere: "I imagine also that you are used to treating a man as a weakling if he can't say no, but this Galy Gay is by no means a weakling; on the contrary he is the strongest of all. That is to say he becomes the strongest once he has ceased to be a private person; he only becomes strong in the mass."[31]

Brecht became immersed in Marx at this moment in his career. Although *A Man's a Man* is still a transitional work, it points both to his emerging radical politics and to his comparably radical technical ambition. The detached perspective of the play—which prevents sympathy or "identification" with Galy Gay—the satiric tone, the interruption of the plot with song and spectacle, the analytic reflection of characters back upon their own predicament, all shift the base of drama and political art. Notably, Brecht was thinking back to Shaw. "Three Cheers for Shaw," published in 1926, praises the Shavian outspokenness, which "broke with the unthinking custom of speaking in a whisper, instead of loudly and cheerfully, in anything resembling a place of worship"; it embraces the sense of "fun" in Shaw's work. Still more significantly, the essay endorses Shaw's "delight in dislocating our stock associations" and his unhesitating appeal to reason.[32]

Marx, Shaw, and Chaplin, in descending measure, incited the change. But at least as important to Brecht's career were the political context and the immediate artistic milieu. As Germany moved toward the catastrophe of Nazism and as Communist opposition became organized and militant, Brecht identified himself as an engaged revolutionary, intent on working with others, notoriously willing to take credit for their efforts, but also willing to change in response to suggestion or critique. In the later 1920s he and Kurt Weill collaborated on a series of operas—*The Threepenny Opera, Happy End* (written with Elisabeth Hauptmann), and *The Rise and Fall of the City of Mahagonny*—which crystallized Brecht's thinking on the relation between revolutionary forms and revolutionary politics. Although *The Threepenny Opera* was an enormous popular success, Brecht was determined to resist an audience that saw art as just an "evening entertainment." When *Mahagonny* premiered in 1930, he composed one of his most important essays. Under the heading "The Modern Theatre Is the Epic The-atre," he attacks the "purely hedonistic approach" to art, which he called "culinary." He explains that even though his opera gives pleasure, "one of its functions is to change society; it brings the culinary principle under discussion, it attacks the society that needs operas of such a sort." His opera also attacks the integrated operatic form that derives from Wagner.[33]

Wagner's importance to the formation of Modernism has been de-scribed, but for later artists he was more significant as a point of resistance. To Brecht, the Wagnerian ideal of the synthetic work with all its formal ele-ments (music, drama, gesture, scene) fused into unity (*Gesamtkunstwerk*) was precisely what a new drama must resist. Brecht aimed toward a "*radical separation of the elements,*" a "struggle for supremacy" among the parts instead of a synthesis. Fusion was not a goal, since it only bewitches the spectator. On the contrary, "*words, music and setting must become more in-dependent of one another.*"[34] The essay contains Brecht's schematic opposi-tion between a Dramatic Theatre, dominant since the time of Aristotle, and an Epic Theatre, which he identifies as the theater of the present historical moment. The terms of the famous contrast are worth invoking here.

DRAMATIC THEATRE
plot
implicates the spectator in a stage situation
wears down his capacity for action
provides him with sensations
experience
the spectator is involved in something
suggestion
instinctive feelings are preserved
the spectator is in the thick of it, shares the experience
the human being is taken for granted
he is unalterable
eyes on the finish
each scene makes another
growth
linear development
evolutionary determinism
man as a fixed point
thought determines being
feeling

EPIC THEATRE
narrative
turns the spectator into an observer
arouses his capacity for action
forces him to take decisions
picture of the world
he is made to face something
argument
brought to the point of recognition
the spectator stands outside, studies
the human being is the object of the inquiry
he is alterable and able to alter
eyes on the course
each scene for itself
montage
in curves
jumps
man as a process
social being determines thought
reason[35]

It has often been said that Brecht's own work could not sustain this austere contrast and that especially his later plays—*Galileo* and *Mother Courage and Her Children*, for example—give the satisfactions offered by Dramatic Theatre. But the schema captures both the extent of the ambition and the nature of the formal and political challenge. Brecht saw the existing avant-garde as all too ready to make its challenge from within existing forms, from the inherited apparatus of art. While this judgment seems unfair to many of the radical artists of the period—from Apollinaire to Cendrars, from Picasso to Stein—it sharpens the terms of critique and reveals its urgency.

In a celebrated and illuminating dispute with Lukács, Brecht resisted the claim that a socially engaged art must follow the methods developed by the realist novel of the nineteenth century—the methods of Balzac and Tolstoy that Lukács saw as exemplary. "As we have in mind," wrote Brecht, "a fighting people that is changing the real world we must not cling to 'well-tried' rules for telling a story, worthy models set up by literary history, eternal aesthetic laws. We must not abstract the one and only realism from certain given works, but shall make a lively use of all means, old and new, tried and untried, deriving from art and deriving from other sources, in order to put living reality in the hands of living people in such a way that it can be mastered." He went on just as briskly: "Copying the methods of these realists, we should cease to be realists ourselves.... Methods wear out, stimuli fail. New problems loom up and demand new techniques. Reality alters; to represent it the means of representation must alter too."[36]

Brecht has plausibly been seen to have the better of the argument here. Even so, the question notoriously persists. What relation holds between artistic forms and political effects? How can any aesthetic technique reliably yield a social outcome? Certainly one advantage in placing Brecht alongside Pound is the opportunity to consider how these artistic radicals are similar in many respects—in mixing modes (language, quotation, music, visual media), in juxtaposing high and low tones, in exploiting discontinuity and abrupt shifts of scene, in alienating the reader/spectator from familiar forms of perception and feeling—and how they came to such opposed political convictions. Pound the Fascist and Brecht the Communist were cousins in their technical ambitions. Then, too, they shared with many other modernists a belief that art could be of great social consequence and, more controversially, that it could, and should, make common cause with politics. The two modernists displayed supreme confidence in the power of the artist to sway audiences and to direct the course of events. Moreover, what both Pound and Brecht suggested is that experimental forms are not only compatible with urgent political action but are a privileged arena of political radicalism.

Let me conclude by noting the extent of the historical change over just a few decades. Within the generation that matured before the First World War can be found some of the most defiant assertions of the independent radicalism of the arts: not art as a self-enclosed and socially indifferent autonomy, although such views certainly appeared, but art as the insistence on a *culturalism,* a conviction that art must follow its own course to social flourishing. Modernism emerged by resisting the claims of rival social practices and by insisting on the specificity of its contribution to a shared history. But in the cataclysm of war and its aftermath, many modernists reengaged with the practice of politics that the movement had once strenuously refused. In one aspect, this is a sign of the power that Modernism claimed for itself, the power to lead history through a time of emergency. But in another aspect, it is a concession to those forces that live beyond the aesthetic and that determine its goals and hopes.

NOTES

INTRODUCTION

1 Susan Stanford Friedman, "Definitional Excursions: The Meanings of Modern/ Modernity/Modernism," *Modernism/Modernity* 8, no. 3 (2001), 504.

2 Friedrich Nietzsche, "Richard Wagner in Bayreuth," in *Untimely Meditations*, ed. Daniel Breazeale (Cambridge: Cambridge University Press, 1967), 198.

3 Miriam Alice Franc, *Ibsen in England* (Boston: Four Seas, 1919), 24.

4 George Bernard Shaw, *The Quintessence of Ibsenism* (London: Constable, 1947), 197, 134 (quotation).

5 Shaw, *Quintessence of Ibsenism*, 99.

6 Thomas Carlyle, *On Heroes, Hero-Worship, and the Heroic in History* (London: Chapman and Hall, 1894), 144.

7 Friedrich Nietzsche, *Thus Spoke Zarathustra: A Book for All and None*, trans. Walter Kaufmann (New York: Viking Penguin, 1966), 287.

8 Reinhart Koselleck, *Futures Past: On the Semantics of Historical Time*, trans. Keith Tribe (Cambridge, Mass.: MIT Press, 1985), 251–252, 257.

9 Joseph Conrad, *The Collected Letters of Joseph Conrad*, vol. 2, ed. Frederick R. Karl and Laurence Davies (Cambridge: Cambridge University Press, 1986), 418.

CHAPTER 1. THE AVANT-GARDE IN MODERNISM

1 Henrik Ibsen to Georg Brandes, *The Correspondence of Ibsen*, trans. and ed. Mary Morison (London: Hodder and Staughton, 1905), 350.

2 George Bernard Shaw, *The Perfect Wagnerite* (New York: Brentano's, 1909), 81–82.

3 Mark S. Morrisson provides an indispensable discussion of the circulation of modernist work through a transforming journalistic milieu: *The Public Face of Modernism: Little Magazines, Audiences, and Reception, 1905–1920* (Madison: University of Wisconsin Press, 2001).

4 In this context consider Lawrence Rainey's meticulous discussion of the "complex social realities informing the interaction among avant-garde, elite bourgeois, and popular cultures in the formative moments of Modernism and the avant-garde." *Institutions of Modernism* (New Haven: Yale University Press, 1998), 11.

5 Gustave Flaubert, *The Letters of Gustave Flaubert, 1857–1880*, ed. and trans. Francis Steegmuller (Cambridge, Mass.: Harvard University Press, 1982), 122.

6 Quoted in Miriam Franc, *Ibsen in England* (Boston: Four Seas, 1919), 34–35.

7 Quoted in Kirsten Shepherd-Barr, *Ibsen and Early Modernist Theatre, 1890–1900* (Westport, Conn.: Greenwood Press, 1997), 21.

8 Stéphane Mallarmé, *Selected Prose, Poems, Essays and Letters,* ed. Bradford Cook (Baltimore, Md.: Johns Hopkins University Press, 1956), 12.

9 Raymond Williams, *The Politics of Modernism: Against the New Conformists* (New York: Verso, 1989), 34.

10 Arthur Rimbaud, *I Promise to Be Good: The Letters of Arthur Rimbaud,* trans. and ed. Wyatt Mason (New York: Modern Library, 2003), 33, 35. Marjorie Perloff, *The Poetics of Indeterminacy: Rimbaud to Cage* (Princeton, N.J.: Princeton University Press, 1981). In her later work, Perloff elegantly and persuasively developed a synthetic account that looked beyond the antitheses of Baudelaire and Rimbaud, Symbolism and indeterminacy: *The Futurist Moment: Avant-Garde, Avant Guerre, and the Language of Rupture* (Chicago: University of Chicago Press, 1986).

11 George Bernard Shaw, *The Quintessence of Ibsenism* (New York: Brentano's, 1915), 36–37.

12 Richard Rorty, *Contingency, Irony, and Solidarity* (Cambridge: Cambridge University Press, 1989), 73.

13 See John Milner, *Art, War and Revolution in France, 1870–1871: Myth, Reportage and Reality* (New Haven: Yale University Press, 2000).

14 Henrik Ibsen, *Letters and Speeches,* ed. and trans. Evert Sprichorn (New York: Hill and Wang, 1964), 106.

15 See Toril Moi's critique of the "fundamentally flawed" opposition between realism and Modernism. Realism "is neither modernism's predecessor nor its negative opposite." *Ibsen and the Birth of Modernism* (Oxford: Oxford University Press, 2006), 67.

16 Algernon Charles Swinburne, "Note on a Question of the Hour," *Athenaeum* (June 16, 1877): 767–768.

17 Sigmund Freud, *Dora: An Analysis of a Case of Hysteria,* trans. James Strachey et al. (New York: Collier Books, 1963), 3.

18 Arthur Rimbaud, "Enfance" ("Childhood"), in *Illuminations,* in *Rimbaud: Complete Works, Selected Letters,* trans. Wallace Fowlie; updated and revised by Seth Whidden (Chicago: University of Chicago Press, 2005), 310. Here and elsewhere all translations not otherwise acknowledged are by Michael Levenson.

19 Maurice Maeterlinck, *Princess Maleine,* in *The Plays of Maurice Maeterlinck,* trans. Richard Hovey (New York: Herbert S. Stone, 1902), 79.

20 Havelock Ellis, "Introduction," in Émile Zola, *Germinal,* trans. Havelock Ellis (London: J. M. Dent and Sons, 1933), vii.

21 Karl Marx, *The Eighteenth Brumaire of Louis Bonaparte* (New York: International Publishers, 1994), 66.

22 Kenneth Cornell, *The Symbolist Movement* (Hamden, Conn.: Archon Books, 1970), 42.

23 Quoted in René Wellek, "What Is Symbolism?," in *The Symbolist Movement in the Literature of European Languages,* ed. Anna Balakian (Budapest: Akadémiai Kiadó, 1982), 23.

24 Stéphane Mallarmé, *Oeuvres complètes* (Paris: Édition de la Pléiade, 1961), 869.

25 Quoted in Haskell Block, *Mallarmé and the Symbolist Drama* (Detroit: Wayne State University Press, 1963), 11–12.

26 Wellek, "What Is Symbolism?," 26.

27 Arthur Symons, *The Symbolist Movement in Literature* (New York: E. P. Dutton, 1919), 194, 184.

28 Joris-Karl Huysmans, *Against Nature (À Rebours),* trans. Robert Baldick (London: Penguin, 2003), 21–22.

29 Stéphane Mallarmé, *Selected Poems,* trans. C. F. MacIntyre (Berkeley: University of California Press, 1957), 54–55.

30 Cornell, *Symbolist Movement,* 67.

31 Huysmans, *Against Nature,* 199.

32 Mary Gluck has charted a richly suggestive arc from Baudelaire's flâneur to Huysmans's decadent, by way of the example of Théophile Gautier. *Popular Bohemia: Modernism and Urban Culture in Nineteenth-Century Paris* (Cambridge, Mass.: Harvard University Press, 2005), 108.

33 Symons, *Symbolist Movement in Literature,* 201.

34 Arthur Symons, *Dramatis Personae* (Indianapolis: Bobbs-Merrill, 1923), 98.

35 Émile Verhaeren, "Un Peintre symboliste," *L'Art Moderne* (April 24, 1887): 129.

36 Ezra Pound, *The Letters of Ezra Pound, 1907–1941,* ed. D. D. Paige (New York: Harcourt Brace, 1950), 180.

37 Arthur Symons, "A Symbolist Farce," in *Studies in Seven Arts* (New York: E. P. Dutton, 1913), 373.

38 Alfred Jarry, *The Ubu Plays,* ed. S. W. Taylor, trans. C. Connolly and S. W. Taylor (New York: Grove Press, 1969), 39.

39 Peter Brook, television interview, quoted in Keith Beaumont, *Jarry: Ubu Roi* (London: Grant and Cutler, 1987), 10.

40 W. B. Yeats, *The Trembling of the Veil,* in *The Collected Works of W. B. Yeats,* vol. 3, *Autobiographies,* ed. William H. O'Donnell and Douglas N. Archibald (New York: Scribner, 1999), 265.

41 W. B. Yeats, "The Celtic Element in Literature," in *Essays and Introductions* (New York: Macmillan, 1961), 187.

42 Friedrich Nietzsche, *The Anti-Christ,* trans. R. J. Hollingdale (Harmondsworth, U.K.: Penguin, 1978), 125, 118.

43 Friedrich Nietzsche, *Thus Spoke Zarathustra,* trans. Walter Kaufmann (New York: Viking Penguin, 1966), 190.

44 Nietzsche, *Anti-Christ,* 127.

45 Nietzsche, *Anti-Christ,* 115.

46 Peter Nicholls, *Modernisms: A Literary Guide* (Berkeley: University of California Press, 1995), 72.

47 Symons, "Symbolist Farce," 371.

48 Stéphane Mallarmé, *Selected Letters of Stéphane Mallarmé,* ed. Rosemary Lloyd (Chicago: University of Chicago Press, 1988), 68.

49 Williams, *Politics of Modernism,* 50.

50 Yeats, *The Trembling of the Veil,* 115.

51 Roger Shattuck, "Foreword," in *Apollinaire on Art: Essays and Reviews, 1902–1918,* ed. LeRoy C. Breunig, trans. Susan Suleiman (Boston: MFA, 2001), xiv.

52 Quoted in Michael Meyer, *Strindberg* (London: Secker Warburg, 1985), 483.

53 Apollinaire, "Exoticism and Ethnography" (September 1912), in *Apollinaire on Art,* 244.

54 William Rubin, "Modernist Primitivism: An Introduction," in *Primitivism in 20th Century Art: Affinity of the Tribal and the Modern,* ed. William Rubin (New York: Museum of Modern Art, 1984), 11.

55 Rubin, "Modernist Primitivism," 5–6.

56 Simon Gikandi, "Picasso, Africa, and the Schemata of Difference," *Modernism/Modernity* 10, no. 3 (2003): 458.

57 Joseph Conrad, *Heart of Darkness,* ed. Robert Kimbrough (New York: W. W. Norton, 1988), 37.

58 D. H. Lawrence, *Women in Love* (Harmondsworth, U.K.: Penguin, 1976), 72.

59 Willa Cather, "A Wagner Matinée," in *Early Novels and Stories* (New York: Library Classics of America, 1986), 106–107.

60 Willa Cather, *My Ántonia,* in *Early Novels and Stories,* 838, 840.

61 Rubin, "Modernist Primitivism," 53.

62 F. T. Marinetti, "The Founding and Manifesto of Futurism," in *Let's Murder the Moonshine,* trans. R. W. Flint and Arthur Coppotelli (Los Angeles: Sun and Moon Press, 1991), 49.

63 Futurism, as Rainey puts it, "mounted a sustained interrogation of the concept of aesthetic autonomy." *Institutions of Modernism,* 12.

64 Wyndham Lewis, "The Melodrama of Modernity," *Blast* 1 (1914): 143.

65 Ezra Pound, "Vorticism," *Fortnightly Review,* 96 (1914): 461.

66 Quoted in Anna M. Lawton, *Russian Futurist Manifestoes, 1912–1928,* trans. and ed. Anna M. Lawton and Herbert Eagle (Washington, D.C.: New Academia, 2005), 51–52.

67 Vladimir Markov, *Russian Futurism: A History* (London: MacGibbon and Kee, 1969).

68 Quoted in Markov, *Russian Futurism,* 151.

69 Some excellent discussions of the manifesto have appeared in recent years. See especially Janet Lyon, *Manifestoes: Provocations of the Modern* (Ithaca, N.Y.: Cornell University Press, 1999); Martin Puchner, *Poetry of the Revolution: Marx, Manifestos and the Avant-Garde* (Princeton, N.J.: Princeton University Press, 2006); Luca Somigli, *Legitimizing the Artist: Manifesto Writing and European Modernism, 1885–1915* (Toronto: Toronto University Press, 2003).

70 Peter Bürger, *Theory of the Avant-Garde,* trans. Michael Shaw (Minneapolis: University of Minnesota Press, 1984).

71 Bürger, *Theory of the Avant-Garde,* 18.

72 Tristan Tzara, "Dada Manifesto" (1918), in *Dadas on Art,* ed. Lucy Lippard (Englewood Cliffs, N.J.: Prentice-Hall, 1971), 14.

CHAPTER 2. NARRATING MODERNITY

1 Henry James, *The Art of Fiction and Other Essays,* ed. Morris Roberts (New York: Oxford University Press, 1948), 3.

2 Ford Madox Ford, "Professor Saintsbury and the English 'Nuvvle,'" *Outlook* 32 (November 1, 1913): 605.

3 Gustave Flaubert, *The Letters of Gustave Flaubert, 1857–1880,* ed. and trans. Francis Steegmuller (Cambridge, Mass.: Harvard University Press, 1982), 119.

4 Gustave Flaubert, *The Sentimental Education,* trans. Perdita Burlingame (New York: New American Library, 1972), 89.

5 Marcel Proust, "About Flaubert's Style," in *Pleasures and Days,* trans. Louise Varese, Gerard Hopkins, and Barbara Dupee (New York: H. Fertig, 1978), 228, 227, 228, 234.

6 F. W. Dupee, "Afterword," in Flaubert, *Sentimental Education,* 427.

7 Georg Lukács, "Narrate or Describe," in *Writer and Critic,* trans. and ed. Arthur Kahn (New York: Grosset and Dunlap, 1971), 110.

8 Henry James, "Émile Zola," in *The Art of Criticism: Henry James on the Theory and Practice of Fiction,* ed. William Veeder and Susan M. Griffin (Chicago: University of Chicago Press, 1986), 430.

9 Walter Benjamin, "On Some Motifs in Baudelaire," in *Illluminations,* ed. Hannah Arendt, trans. Harry Zohn (New York: Schocken, 1968), 193.

10 Émile Zola, *Nana,* trans. Douglas Parmée (Oxford: Oxford University Press, 1992), 420.

11 Gustave Le Bon, *The Crowd: A Study of the Popular Mind,* trans. D. S. Snedden (New York: Macmillan, 1896).

12 Matthew Arnold, *Culture and Anarchy: An Essay in Political and Social Criticism* (London: Smith, Elder, 1869), 58.

13 Karl Marx and Friedrich Engels, *The Communist Manifesto,* ed. Samuel H. Beer (New York: Appleton-Century-Crofts, 1955), 18, 21.

14 Gustave Flaubert, *Dictionary of Received Ideas,* in *Bouvard et Pécuchet,* trans. A. J. Krailsheimer (Harmondsworth, U.K.: Penguin, 1976), 310, 320.

15 Émile Zola, *The Experimental Novel and Other Essays,* trans. Belle M. Sherman (New York: Cassell, 1893), 28.

16 Zola, *Experimental Novel,* 20, 3.

17 Philip D. Walker, *Zola* (London: Routledge and Kegan Paul, 1985), 142–143.

18 Thomas Nagel, "What Is It Like to Be a Bat?" *Philosophical Review* 83 (1974): 435–450.

19 Thomas Hardy, "Candour in English Fiction," in *Personal Writings: Prefaces, Literary Opinions, Reminiscences,* ed. Harold Orel (Lawrence: University of Kansas Press, 1966), 128.

20 Thomas Hardy, "Explanatory Note to the First Edition," in *Tess of the d'Urbervilles,* ed. Sarah E. Maier (Peterborough, Canada: Broadview Press, 1996), 27.

21 Thomas Hardy, "The Science of Fiction," in *Personal Writings,* 134.

22 Hardy, "Candour in English Fiction," 127.

23 Thomas Hardy, "The Profitable Reading of Fiction," in *Personal Writings,* 114.

24 Joris-Karl Huysmans, *Against Nature (À Rebours),* trans. Robert Baldick (London: Penguin, 2003), 109–110.

25 Hardy, *Tess of the d'Urbervilles,* 83.

26 Marjorie Garson, *Hardy's Fables of Integrity: Women, Body, Text* (Oxford: Clarendon Press; New York: Oxford University Press, 1991).

27 Tony Tanner, "Colour and Movement in Hardy's *Tess of the d'Urbervilles,"* in *The Victorian Novel: Modern Essays in Criticism,* ed. Ian Watt (New York: Oxford University Press, 1971), 420.

28 Kaja Silverman, "History, Figuration and Female Subjectivity in *Tess of the d'Urbervilles,"* *Novel* 18, no. 1 (Autumn 1984): 8.

29 August Strindberg, *Selected Essays,* ed. and trans. Michael Robinson (Cambridge: Cambridge University Press, 1996), 112.

30 Richard von Krafft-Ebing, *Psychopathia Sexualis* (New York: Rebman, 1922), 161.

31 Harry Oosterhuis, *Stepchildren of Nature: Krafft-Ebing, Psychiatry and the Making of Sexual Identity* (Chicago: University of Chicago Press, 2000).

32 Michel Foucault, *Discipline and Punish: The Birth of the Prison,* trans. Alan Sheridan (New York: Vintage Books, 1995); Havelock Ellis, *Studies in the Psychology of Sex,* vol. 1 (Watford, U.K.: The University Press, 1900), 29.

33 Sigmund Freud and Josef Breuer, *Studies on Hysteria,* ed. and trans. James Strachey with the collaboration of Anna Freud (New York: Basic Books, 2000), 160.

34 Sigmund Freud, *From the History of an Infantile Neurosis,* in *Three Case Histories,* trans. James Strachey et al. (New York: Simon and Schuster, 1996), 169.

35 Sigmund Freud, *Dora: An Analysis of a Case of Hysteria,* trans. James Strachey et al. (New York: Collier Books, 1963), 26.

36 Sigmund Freud, "Further Recommendations in the Technique of Psychoanalysis," in *Therapy and Technique,* trans. Joan Riviere (New York: Collier Books, 1963), 147.

37 Peter Brooks, *Reading for the Plot: Design and Intention in Narrative* (Cambridge, Mass.: Harvard University Press, 1992), 268.

38 Sigmund Freud, *Three Essays on the Theory of Sexuality,* trans. and ed. James Strachey (New York: Basic Books, 2000), 26.

39 Sigmund Freud, *Introductory Lectures on Psychoanalysis,* trans. James Strachey (New York: W. W. Norton, 1966), 353.

40 Thomas Mann, *Death in Venice and Seven Other Stories,* trans. H. T. Lowe-Porter (New York: Random House, 1963), 66.

41 Franz Kafka, *The Diaries of Franz Kafka, 1910–1913,* ed. Max Brod (New York: Schocken, 1948), 275–276.

42 Franz Kafka, "The Judgment," in *The Penal Colony* (New York: Schocken, 1976), 54, 59, 62–63.

43 Lukács, "Narrate or Describe," 77, 92.

44 James Joyce, *A Portrait of the Artist as a Young Man* (New York: B. W. Huebsch, 1916), 193–194.

45 Martin Heidegger, "'. . . Poetically Man Dwells . . . ,'" in *Philosophical and Political Writings,* ed. Martin Stassen (New York: Continuum, 2003), 267.

46 James Joyce, *Letters,* vol. 2, ed. Stuart Gilbert (London: Faber and Faber, 1966), 134.

47 Ezra Pound, "A Retrospect," in *Literary Essays of Ezra Pound,* ed. T. S. Eliot (New York: New Directions, 1968), 5.

48 James Joyce, *Stephen Hero* (Norfolk, Conn.: New Directions, 1963), 86.

49 See Pericles Lewis, "Modernism and Religion," in *The Cambridge Companion to Modernism*, 2nd ed., ed. Michael Levenson (Cambridge: Cambridge University Press, 2011).

50 Henry James, "The New Novel," in *Notes on Novelists* (New York: Charles Scribner's Sons, 1914), 348.

51 Ford Madox Ford, "Joseph Conrad," in *The Critical Writings of Ford Madox Ford,* ed. Frank MacShane (Lincoln: University of Nebraska Press, 1964), 72–73.

52 Ford Madox Ford, "On Impressionism," in *Critical Writings of Ford Madox Ford,* 41.

53 Recorded by Jean Renoir, in *Renoir, My Father,* trans. Randolph Weaver and Dorothy Weaver (Boston: Little, Brown, 1958), 174.

54 Joseph Conrad, *The Collected Letters of Joseph Conrad,* vol. 1, ed. Frederick R. Karl and Lawrence Davies (Cambridge: Cambridge University Press, 1983), 425.

55 Joseph Conrad, *Under Western Eyes* (1911; rpt., Garden City, N.Y.: Anchor-Doubleday, 1963), 1.

56 North lucidly describes the pictorial outcome as representing "the tension, the slippage, between mask and face, between impersonality and individuality, conventional representation and likeness." Michael North, *The Dialect of Modernism: Race, Language, and Twentieth-Century Literature* (New York: Oxford University Press, 1994), 71.

57 Quoted in Gertrude Stein, *Three Lives,* ed. Linda Wagner-Martin (Boston: Bedford / St. Martin's, 2000), 25.

58 Gertrude Stein, "Melanctha," in *Three Lives* (Norfolk, Conn.: New Directions, 1933), 226–227.

59 North, *Dialect of Modernism,* 64. See all of this work for its treatment of the depth of race-thinking in Modernism.

60 See Michael Bell's trenchant discussion of Frazer and Modernism in his *Literature, Modernism and Myth: Belief and Responsibility in the Twentieth Century* (Cambridge: Cambridge University Press, 1997), 43–44.

61 J. G. Frazer, *The Golden Bough: A Study in Magic and Religion* (New York: St. Martin's Press, 1990), xxv.

62 John Vickery, *The Literary Impact of the Golden Bough* (Princeton, N.J.: Princeton University Press, 1973), 26.

63 Paul Peppis, "Thinking Race in the *Avant Guerre:* Typological Negotiations in Ford and Stein," *Yale Journal of Criticism* 10, no. 2 (1997): 382.

64 Chinua Achebe, "An Image of Africa: Racism in Conrad's 'Heart of Darkness,'" *Massachusetts Review* 18, no. 4 (Winter 1977): 782–794.

65 G. W. F. Hegel, *Phenomenology of Spirit*, trans. A. V. Miller (Oxford: Oxford University Press, 1977), 110–111.

66 Corinne E. Blackmer, "African Masks and the Arts of Passing in Gertrude Stein's 'Melanctha' and Nella Larsen's *Passing*," *Journal of the History of Sexuality* 4 (October 1993): 246.

67 Quoted in David Bordwell, Janet Staiger, and Kristin Thompson, *Classical Hollywood Cinema* (London: Routledge, 1988), 191.

68 Consider here David Trotter's brisk and compelling account of the dialectic of presence and absence in early cinema: *Cinema and Modernism* (Malden, Mass.: Blackwell, 2007).

69 Wyndham Lewis, "The Crowd Master," *Blast* 2 (1915): 94.

70 Georg Simmel, *The Sociology of Georg Simmel*, trans. and ed. Kurt H. Wolff (New York: Free Press; London: Macmillan, 1950), 3.

CHAPTER 3. THE MODERNIST LYRIC "I"

1 Stéphane Mallarmé, *Oeuvres complètes* (Paris: Édition de la Pléiade, 1961), 869.

2 Charles Baudelaire, "The Painter of Modern Life," in *My Heart Laid Bare and Other Prose Writings*, ed. Peter Quennell, trans. Norman Cameron (New York: Haskell House, 1975), 37.

3 Marshall Berman, *All That Is Solid Melts into Air: The Experience of Modernity* (London: Verso, 1983), 133.

4 Charles Baudelaire, *Les Fleurs du mal*, in *Oeuvres complètes* (Paris: Louis Conard, 1923), 207.

5 See Richard D. Burton, *The Context of Baudelaire's "Le Cygne"* (Durham, U.K.: University of Durham, 1980).

6 Arthur Symons, *The Symbolist Movement in Literature* (New York: E. P. Dutton, 1919), 5.

7 Stéphane Mallarmé, *Selected Letters of Stéphane Mallarmé*, ed. Rosemary Lloyd (Chicago: University of Chicago Press, 1988), 74.

8 Stéphane Mallarmé, *Collected Poems*, trans. Henry Weinfield (Berkeley: University of California Press, 1994), 29.

9 Haskell M. Block, *Mallarmé and the Symbolist Drama* (Detroit: Wayne State University Press, 1963), 15.

10 Quoted in Frantisek Deak, *Symbolist Theater: The Formation of an Avant-Garde* (Baltimore, Md.: Johns Hopkins University Press, 1993), 59.

11 Mallarmé, *Selected Letters*, 58.

12 Mallarmé, *Collected Poems*, 38.

13 Stéphane Mallarmé, *Igitur, Divagations, Un Coup de dés* (Paris: Gallimard, 1976), 248.

14 Mallarmé, *Selected Letters,* 72.

15 Quoted in Deak, *Symbolist Theater,* 86.

16 Mallarmé, *Selected Letters,* 143.

17 Mallarmé, *Selected Letters,* 144.

18 Arthur Symons, "The Decadent Movement in Literature," in *Dramatis Personae* (Indianapolis: Bobbs-Merrill, 1923), 96.

19 Symons, *Symbolist Movement in Literature,* 4.

20 W. B. Yeats, *The Trembling of the Veil,* in *The Collected Works of W. B. Yeats,* vol. 3, *Autobiographies,* ed. William H. O'Donnell and Douglas N. Archibald (New York: Scribner, 1999), 246.

21 Denis Donoghue, "Yeats: The Question of Symbolism," in *We Irish: Essays on Irish Literature and Society* (Berkeley: University of California Press, 1986).

22 W. B. Yeats, *The Collected Letters of W. B. Yeats,* vol. 1, *1865–1895,* ed. John Kelly (Oxford: Clarendon Press, 1986), 303.

23 W. B. Yeats, "The Poetry of Samuel Ferguson I," in *Early Articles and Reviews,* ed. John P. Frayne and Madeleine Marchaterre (New York: Scribner, 2004), 8, 11–12, 27. Gregory Castle locates the anthropological basis of Yeats's turn to folklore, noting his "interest in the purity and preeminence of a folk culture." *Modernism and the Celtic Revival* (Cambridge: Cambridge University Press, 2001), 41.

24 Quoted in Douglas N. Archibald, *Yeats* (Syracuse, N.Y.: Syracuse University Press, 1983), 93.

25 W. B. Yeats, *Reveries over Childhood and Youth* (New York: Macmillan, 1916), 86.

26 Quoted in R. F. Foster, *W. B. Yeats: A Life,* vol. 1 (Oxford: Oxford University Press, 1997), 87.

27 W. B. Yeats, *The Land of Heart's Desire,* ed. Jared Curtis (Ithaca, N.Y.: Cornell University Press, 2002), xxv.

28 W. B. Yeats, *Ideas of Good and Evil* (London: A. H. Bullen, 1907), 294.

29 Anna Balakian observes that when Symbolism spread through other nations, "it did not become a foreign literary mode but was amalgamated with native trends and local propensities." *The Symbolist Movement in the Literature of European Languages* (Budapest: Akadémiai Kiadó, 1982), 9.

30 Yeats, *Land of Heart's Desire,* xxv.

31 W. B. Yeats, *The Collected Poems of W. B. Yeats* (Canada: Macmillan, 1956), 49.

32 W. B. Yeats, "The Symbolism of Poetry," in *Ideas of Good and Evil,* 255.

33 Quoted in Richard Ellmann, *Yeats: The Man and the Masks* (New York: Norton, 1978), 156.

34 For the best discussion of the suffragette context surrounding Yeats's poem, see Elizabeth Butler Cullingford, *Gender and History in Yeats's Love Poetry* (Cambridge: Cambridge University Press, 1993), 73–82.

35 W. B. Yeats, *Responsibilities and Other Poems* (London: Macmillan, 1916), 91.

36 W. B. Yeats, *Discoveries: A Volume of Essays* (Dundrum: Dun Emer Press, 1907), 14.

37 Ezra Pound, *The Spirit of Romance: An Attempt to Define Somewhat the Charm of the Pre-Renaissance Literature of Latin Europe* (London: J. M. Dent and Sons, 1910).

38 Ezra Pound, *New Selected Poems and Translations,* ed. Richard Sieburth (New York: New Directions, 2010), 11.

39 Ezra Pound, "Ford Madox (Hueffer) Ford; Obit," *Nineteenth Century and After* 126 (August 1939): 179.

40 Ezra Pound, "Vorticism," *Fortnightly Review* 96 (1914): 462.

41 Ezra Pound, "The Serious Artist," in *Literary Essays of Ezra Pound,* ed. T. S. Eliot (New York: New Directions, 1935), 43.

42 James Longenbach, *Stone Cottage: Pound, Yeats and Modernism* (New York: Oxford University Press, 1988).

43 Ezra Pound, "The Later Yeats," in *Literary Essays of Ezra Pound,* 378–379.

44 Lady Gregory, *Our Irish Theatre: A Chapter of Autobiography* (New York: G. P. Putnam's Sons, 1913), 112.

45 W. B. Yeats, *The Collected Letters of W. B. Yeats,* vol. 4, *1905–1907,* ed. John Kelly and Ronald Schuchard (Oxford: Clarendon Press, 2005), 866.

46 Yeats, "Symbolism of Poetry," 253.

47 W. B. Yeats, "Synge and the Ireland of His Time," in *The Cutting of an Agate* (New York: Macmillan, 1912), 162.

48 Gregory Castle persuasively suggests that "the controversy over Synge's *Playboy of the Western World* may have been the point at which Yeats realized that he had failed to capture the 'essence' of Irish folk culture, and it may be that his new emphasis on personality was an attempt to bypass the political dimensions of his project of cultural redemption." *Modernism and the Celtic Revival,* 84.

49 Foster, *Yeats,* 482.

50 Yeats, *Collected Poems:* "To a Shade," 108; "All Things Can Tempt Me," 95; "These Are the Clouds," 94; "At Galway Races," 95; "September 1913," 106.

51 Foster, *Yeats,* 160.

52 W. B. Yeats, "What Is Popular Poetry?" in *The Collected Works of W. B. Yeats,* vol. 4, *Early Essays,* ed. Richard J. Finneran and George Bornstein (New York: Scribner, 2007), 8, 10.

53 Ezra Pound, *Ripostes of Ezra Pound, whereto are appended the "Complete Poetical Works of T. E. Hulme"* (London: E. Mathews, 1913), 59; Pound, *The Letters of Ezra Pound, 1907–1941,* ed. D. D. Paige (New York: Harcourt Brace, 1950), 10.

54 Ezra Pound, "*Status rerum,*" *Poetry* 1, no. 4 (January 1913): 126.

55 Ezra Pound, "A Retrospect," in *Literary Essays of Ezra Pound,* 4–5.

56 H.D., "Hermes of the Ways," in *Collected Poems, 1912–1944,* ed. Louis L. Martz (Manchester, U.K.: Carcanet Press, 1984), 36.

57 Quoted in Diana Collecott, *H.D. and Sapphic Modernism: 1910–1950* (Cambridge: Cambridge University Press, 1999), 113.

58 See Edward Comentale, *Modernism, Cultural Production and the British Avant-Garde* (Cambridge: Cambridge University Press, 2004), 43–44.

59 Collecott, *H.D. and Sapphic Modernism*, 259, 131.

60 H.D., "Oread," in *Collected Poems*, 55.

61 Pound, "Vortex. Pound," *Blast* 1 (1914): 154.

62 Rachel Blau DuPlessis, *H.D.: The Career of That Struggle* (Brighton, U.K.: Harvester, 1986), 12; Collecott, *H.D. and Sapphic Modernism*, 149.

63 Ezra Pound, "In a Station of the Metro," in *New Selected Poems*, 39.

64 Pound, "A Retrospect," 4–5.

65 Harold Monro, "The Imagists Discussed," *The Egoist* 2 (May 1, 1915): 79.

66 Pound, "A Retrospect," 11–12.

67 James Joyce, *Ulysses*, ed. Hans Walter Gabler (New York: Random House, 1986), 720.

68 Guillaume Apollinaire, *Alcools*, trans. Anne Hyde Greet (Berkeley: University of California Press, 1965), 3.

69 Roger Shattuck, *Apollinaire, Selected Writings*, trans. Roger Shattuck (London: Harvill Press, 1950), 26.

70 Guillaume Apollinaire, "Reality, Pure Painting," *Der Sturm* (December 1912), reprinted in *Apollinaire on Art: Essays and Reviews, 1902–1918*, ed. LeRoy C. Breunig, trans. Susan Suleiman (Boston: MFA, 1972), 265.

71 Blaise Cendrars, *Complete Poems*, trans. Ron Padgett (Berkeley: University of California Press, 1992), 230, 4. The two page numbers refer to the French source and the English translation, which are placed in different parts of the volume.

72 Guillaume Apollinaire, "Through the Salon des Independants" (March 1913), in *Apollinaire on Art*, 291.

73 Marjorie Perloff, *The Futurist Moment: Avant-Garde, Avant Guerre, and the Language of Rupture* (Chicago: University of Chicago Press, 1986), 26–29.

74 Quoted in Arthur A. Cohen, *Sonia Delaunay* (New York: Harry N. Abrams, 1975), 35.

75 Perloff, *Futurist Moment*, 29.

76 Guillaume Apollinaire, "On the Subject in Modern Painting," in *Apollinaire on Art*, 197.

77 Quoted in Richard Cork, *Vorticism and Abstract Art in the First Machine Age*, vol. 1 (London: G. Fraser, 1976), 202.

78 Ford Madox Ford, "Preface to Collected Poems of 1911," in *Collected Poems* (New York: Oxford University Press, 1936), 327.

79 Ezra Pound, "The Serious Artist," in *Literary Essays of Ezra Pound*, 42, 44, 46.

80 Ezra Pound, "The New Sculpture," *The Egoist* 1 (February 16, 1914): 68.

81 Ezra Pound, *Gaudier-Brzeska: A Memoir* (New York: New Directions, 1974) 98.

82 Wassily Kandinsky, *Concerning the Spiritual in Art* (1912; rpt., New York: George Wittenborn, 1972), 67.

83 Pound, "Serious Artist," 44. David Trotter places will-to-abstraction within the complex conditions of psychopathology and professionalism: "What the advocacy of abstraction did for Hulme, and subsequently for Lewis, and indeed for Modernism in general, was to reunite charisma with expertise." "Modernism, Anti-mimesis and the Professionalization of English Society," in *Rethinking Modernism*, ed. Marianne Thormählen (Houndmills, U.K.: Palgrave Macmillan, 2003), 35.

84 Ezra Pound, "Vorticism," *Fortnightly Review* 96 (1914): 465.

85 See Roger Shattuck's virtuoso reading of "Lettre-Océan" in "Apollinaire's Great Wheel," in Shattuck, *The Innocent Eye: On Modern Literature and the Arts* (New York: Farrar Straus Giroux, 1984).

86 Gertrude Stein, *Tender Buttons*, in *Writings, 1903–1932* (New York: Library of America, 1998), 321.

87 Sherwood Anderson, "Introduction," in Gertrude Stein, *Geography and Plays* (New York: Something Else Press, 1968).

88 Susan Hawkins, "Sneak Previews: Gertrude Stein's Syntax in 'Tender Buttons,'" in *Gertrude Stein and the Making of Literature*, ed. Shirley Neuman and Ira B. Nadel (Boston: Northeastern University Press, 1988).

89 Gertrude Stein, *The Making of Americans*, quoted in Allegra Stewart, *Gertrude Stein and the Present* (Cambridge, Mass.: Harvard University Press, 1967), 81.

90 Quoted in Zbigniew Folejewski, *Futurism and Its Place in the Development of Modern Poetry: A Comparative Study and Anthology* (Ottawa: University of Ottawa Press, 1980), 36.

91 F. T. Marinetti, *Let's Murder the Moonshine*, trans. R. W. Flint and Arthur Coppotelli (Los Angeles: Sun and Moon Press, 1991), 92.

92 Quoted in Folejewski, *Futurism*, 185.

93 F. T. Marinetti, "Technical Manifesto of Futurist Literature," in *Let's Murder the Moonshine*, 85, 95, 96.

94 Quoted in Carolyn Burke, *Becoming Modern: The Life of Mina Loy* (Berkeley: University of California Press, 1996), 178.

95 Mina Loy, *The Lost Lunar Baedeker*, ed. Roger L. Conover (New York: Farrar Straus Giroux, 1996), 149–151.

96 August Stramm, *Twenty-Two Poems*, trans. Patrick Bridgwater (Wymondham, U.K.: Brewhouse Press, 1969), n.p.

97 Quoted in Anna Lawton, ed., *Russian Futurism through Its Manifestoes, 1912–1928* (Ithaca, N.Y.: Cornell University Press, 1988), 55.

98 Quoted in Lawton, *Russian Futurism*, 65.

99 Hugo Ball, "The First Dada Manifesto," in *Flight Out of Time*, ed. John Elderfield (Berkeley: University of California Press, 1996).

100 Ezra Pound, "Harold Monro," *Criterion* (July 1932): 590.

101 Pound, *Letters,* 40.

102 Symons, *Symbolist Movement in Literature,* 7–8.

103 T. S. Eliot, *Inventions of the March Hare,* ed. Christopher Ricks (New York: Harcourt Brace, 1996), 27.

104 T. S. Eliot, *The Complete Poems and Plays, 1909–1950* (New York: Harcourt Brace, 1952), 5. The poems quoted in the chapter come from this volume unless otherwise attributed.

105 T. S. Eliot, "Introduction," in *Selected Poems: Ezra Pound,* quoted in Hugh Kenner, *The Invisible Poet: T. S. Eliot* (New York: Harcourt, Brace and World, 1959), 13.

106 Kenner, *Invisible Poet:* 9, 21.

107 Eliot, *Inventions of the March Hare,* 48.

108 Eliot, *Inventions of the March Hare,* 49.

CHAPTER 4. DRAMA AS POLITICS, DRAMA AS RITUAL

1 "To Suffragettes," *Blast* 1 (1914): 151–152.

2 W. B. Yeats, *The Trembling of the Veil,* in *The Collected Works of W. B. Yeats,* vol. 3, *Autobiographies,* ed. William H. O'Donnell and Douglas N. Archibald (New York: Scribner, 1999), 161.

3 Alex Owen, *The Darkened Room: Women, Power and Spiritualism in Late Nineteenth-Century England* (London: Virago, 1989).

4 Henrik Ibsen, *Four Major Plays,* vol. 1, trans. Rolf Fjelde (New York: New American Library, 1992), 109.

5 George Bernard Shaw, "The Quintessence of Ibsenism," in *Major Critical Essays* (London: Constable, 1947), 40.

6 Friedrich Nietzsche, *Thus Spoke Zarathustra: A Book for All and None,* trans. Walter Kaufmann (New York: Viking Penguin, 1971), 20.

7 Kirsten Shepherd-Barr, *Ibsen and Early Modernist Theatre, 1890–1900* (Westport, Conn.: Greenwood Press, 1997), 117–137.

8 Otto Reinert, *Strindberg: A Collection of Critical Essays* (Englewood Cliffs, N.J.: Prentice-Hall, 1971), 5.

9 August Strindberg, *The Father,* trans. Michael Meyer (London: Methuen, 1986), 29.

10 August Strindberg, *Six Plays of Strindberg,* trans. Elizabeth Sprigge (Garden City, N.Y.: Doubleday, 1955), 65. The plays quoted in the chapter are in this volume.

11 Quoted in Dieter Borchmeyer, *Richard Wagner: Theory and Practice* (Oxford: Clarendon Press, 1991), 71.

12 Quoted in Martin Puchner, *Stage Fright: Modernism, Anti-Theatricality, and Drama* (Baltimore, Md.: Johns Hopkins University Press, 2002), 66.

13 Quoted in Frantisek Deak, *Symbolist Theater: The Formation of an Avant-Garde* (Baltimore, Md.: Johns Hopkins University Press, 1993), 63.

14 Haskell M. Block, *Mallarmé and the Symbolist Drama* (Detroit: Wayne State University Press, 1963), 105.

15 Puchner, *Stage Fright,* 80; Block, *Mallarmé,* 89.

16 Maurice Maeterlinck, *The Plays of Maurice Maeterlinck,* trans. Richard Hovey (Chicago: Herbert S. Stone, 1902), 274.

17 Maurice Maeterlinck, *The Treasure of the Humble,* trans. Alfred Sutro (New York: Dodd, Mead, 1913).

18 Philippe Auguste Villiers de l'Isle Adam, *Axel,* trans. June Guicharnaud (Englewood Cliffs: Prentice-Hall, 1970), 46, 69.

19 Yeats, *The Trembling of the Veil,* 246.

20 Quoted in R. F. Foster, *W. B. Yeats: A Life,* vol. 1 (Oxford: Oxford University Press, 1997), 135.

21 W. B. Yeats, *The Land of Heart's Desire,* ed. Jared Curtis (Ithaca, N.Y.: Cornell University Press, 2002), 247.

22 W. B. Yeats, "The Theatre," in *Ideas of Good and Evil* (London: A. H. Bullen, 1908), 266.

23 Christopher Innes, "Modernism in Drama," in *The Cambridge Companion to Modernism,* ed. Michael Levenson (Cambridge: Cambridge University Press, 1999), 136.

24 Edward Gordon Craig, *On the Art of the Theatre* (Chicago: Brown's Bookstore, 1912), 75.

25 W. B. Yeats, "At Stratford-on-Avon," in *The Collected Works of W. B. Yeats,* vol. 4, *Early Essays,* ed. Richard J. Finneran and George Bornstein (New York: Scribner, 2007), 76.

26 Quoted in Foster, *Yeats,* 352.

27 W. B. Yeats, *Discoveries: A Volume of Essays* (Dundrum: Dun Emer Press, 1907), 8.

28 W. B. Yeats, "Preface to the First Edition of *The Well of the Saints,*" in *The Cutting of an Agate* (New York: Macmillan, 1912), 37.

29 John Millington Synge, *The Well of the Saints* (Boston: John W. Luce, 1911), 13.

30 John Millington Synge, "Preface," in *The Playboy of the Western World* (Boston: John W. Luce, 1907), vi.

31 Yeats, *Cutting of an Agate,* 39.

32 Synge, *Playboy,* 30.

33 Leonard Woolf, "Miscellany: Tchehov," *New Statesman* 9, no. 227 (August 11, 1917): 446.

34 Quoted in Ernest J. Simmons, *Chekhov: A Biography* (Boston: Little, Brown, 1962), 604.

35 Anton Chekhov, *The Cherry Orchard: A Comedy in Four Acts,* in *The Major Plays,* trans. Ann Dunnigan (New York: New American Library, 1964), 370.

36 Raymond Williams, *The Politics of Modernism: Against the New Conformists* (New York: Verso, 1989), 34.

37 Francis Fergusson, *The Idea of a Theater* (Garden City, N.Y.: Doubleday, 1953), 189.

38 Friedrich Nietzsche, *The Birth of Tragedy,* trans. Walter Kaufmann (New York: Random House, 1967), 73.

39 Nietzsche, *Thus Spoke Zarathustra*, 107.

40 Quoted in Michael Meyer, *Strindberg* (London: Secker and Warburg, 1985), 355.

41 Quoted in Meyer, *Strindberg,* 521.

42 August Strindberg, *To Damascus,* in *August Strindberg: The Plays,* vol. 2, trans. Michael Meyer (London: Secker and Warburg, 1975), 120, 121.

43 Strindberg, "Author's Note," in *A Dream Play,* in *Six Plays,* 193.

44 Quoted in Meyer, *Strindberg,* 229.

45 See Michael Patterson, *The Revolution in German Theatre: 1900–1930* (Boston: Routledge, 1981).

46 Reinhard Sorge, *The Beggar,* in *An Anthology of German Expressionist Drama,* ed. Walter H. Sokel (Garden City, N.Y.: Doubleday, 1963), 41.

47 Walter Hasenclever, *The Son,* trans. Henry Marx, in *German Expressionist Plays,* ed. Ernest Schürer (New York: Continuum, 1997), 97, 104, 122.

48 Ernst Schürer, "Provocation and Proclamation, Vision and Imagery: Expressionist Drama between German Idealism and Modernity," in *A Companion to the Literature of German Expressionism,* ed. Neil H. Donahue (Rochester, N.Y.: Camden House, 1997), 232.

49 Georg Kaiser, *Five Plays,* trans. B. J. Kenworthy, Rex Last, and J. M. Ritchie (London: Calder and Boyars, 1971), 115.

50 Georg Kaiser, *The Coral,* in *Five Plays,* 191.

51 Quoted in Schürer, "Provocation and Proclamation," 239.

52 Mel Gordon, "German Expressionist Acting," *Drama Review* 19, no. 3 (1975), 35.

53 See David F. Kuhns, *German Expressionist Theatre: The Actor and the Stage* (Cambridge: Cambridge University Press, 1997).

54 Paul Kornfeld, "Epilogue to the Actor," in Sokel, *Anthology of German Expressionist Drama,* 6–7.

55 Kasimir Edschmid, "On Poetic Expressionism," quoted in Gordon, "German Expressionist Acting," 34.

56 Kaiser, *The Coral,* 156.

57 Georg Kaiser, *Gas I,* in, *Five Plays,* 210, 231.

58 Eugene O'Neill, *The Emperor Jones,* in *Complete Plays, 1913–1920* (New York: Library of America, 1988), 1041.

59 Quoted in Egil Tornqvist, "Strindberg and O'Neill," in *Structures of Influence: A Comparative Approach to August Strindberg,* ed. Marilyn Johns Blackwell (Chapel Hill: University of North Carolina Press, 1981), 277–291.

60 Deanna Toten Beard observes that *"The Emperor Jones* is frequently characterized as the first American expressionist play; perhaps it is also the last American experimentalist play." "Experimentalism, Expressionism, and Early O'Neill," in *A*

Companion to Twentieth-Century American Drama, ed. David Krasner (Malden, Mass.: Blackwell, 2005), 61.

61 Georg Kaiser, "Man in the Tunnel," trans. Walter H. Sokel, in Sokel, *Anthology of German Expressionist Drama.*

62 Katherine E. Kelly, "Imprinting the Stage: Shaw and the Publishing Trade, 1883–1903," in *The Cambridge Companion to George Bernard Shaw,* ed. Christopher Innes (Cambridge: Cambridge University Press, 1998), 50.

63 George Bernard Shaw, *Man and Superman: A Comedy and a Philosophy* (New York: Brentano's, 1922), 14.

64 George Bernard Shaw to William Archer, August 27, 1903, in *Bernard Shaw: Collected Letters, 1898–1919,* ed. Dan H. Laurence (London: Max Reinhardt, 1972), 352.

65 Shaw, *Collected Letters,* 474–475.

CHAPTER 5. MODERNISM IN AND OUT OF WAR

1 For a magisterial treatment of Modernism and the war, see Vincent Sherry, *The Great War and the Language of Modernism* (New York: Oxford University Press, 2003).

2 "Editorial," *Blast* 2 (1915): 5.

3 Quoted in Richard Ellmann, *James Joyce* (New York: Oxford University Press, 1983), 472.

4 T. S. Eliot, "Reflections on Vers Libre," *New Statesman* 8 (March 3, 1917): 519.

5 Wyndham Lewis, *Blasting and Bombardiering* (London: Eyre and Spottiswoode, 1937), 40.

6 James Joyce, *Ulysses,* ed. Hans Walter Gabler (New York: Random House, 1986), 310.

7 Ezra Pound, *The Selected Poems of Ezra Pound* (New York: New Directions, 1957), 61–62, 64.

8 As Vincent Sherry observes, "Lyric immediacy clearly overrides a language of Latinate abstraction, which is incompatible with the mendacities of that authorized war." *Great War and the Language of Modernism,* 142.

9 Pound, *Selected Poems,* 64.

10 John Maynard Keynes, *The Economic Consequences of the Peace* (New York: Harcourt, Brace and Howe, 1920), 3, 10.

11 Henri Gaudier-Brzeska, "Vortex Gaudier-Brzeska," *Blast* 2 (1915): 33.

12 Virginia Woolf, "Modern Fiction," in *The Common Reader,* ed. Andrew McNeillie (London: Hogarth Press, 1984), 149–150.

13 Keynes, *Economic Consequences,* 5–6.

14 Ford Madox Ford, "Techniques," in *Critical Writings of Ford Madox Ford,* ed. Frank MacShane (Lincoln: University of Nebraska Press, 1964), 68.

15 Ford Madox Ford, *A Man Could Stand Up, Parade's End* (New York: Random House, 1979), 552.

16 T. S. Eliot, *The Complete Poems and Plays, 1909–1950* (New York: Harcourt Brace, 1952), 22. The poems quoted below come from this edition.

17 Allyson Booth cannily interprets the spatial legacies of war, in *Postcards from the Trenches: Negotiating the Space between Modernism and the First World War* (New York: Oxford University Press, 1996).

18 Virginia Woolf, *Jacob's Room* (New York: Harcourt, Brace and World, 1950), 175.

19 See Allyson Booth's discussion of *Jacob's Room* in her *Postcards from the Trenches,* 45–59.

20 E. E. Cummings, *The Enormous Room* (Mineola, N.Y.: Dover, 2002), 36.

21 Michel Foucault, "Of Other Spaces," trans. Jay Miskowiec, in *Diacritics* 16, no. 1 (Spring 1986): 22–27.

22 Ernest Hemingway, *In Our Time* (New York: Scribner, 1958), 69.

23 Hemingway, *In Our Time,* 63.

24 Ernest Hemingway, *Death in the Afternoon* (New York: Charles Scribner's Sons, 1932), 192.

25 Beatrice Webb, *The Diaries of Beatrice Webb,* vol. 4, ed. Norman MacKenzie and Jeanne MacKenzie (London: Virago, 1985), 152–153.

26 Virginia Woolf, *Mrs. Dalloway* (Orlando: Harcourt, 1981), 184.

27 Virginia Woolf, *To the Lighthouse* (Orlando: Harcourt, 1981), 48.

28 Virginia Woolf, *A Room of One's Own* (New York: Harcourt, Brace and World, 1957), 108.

29 Eliot, *Complete Poems and Plays,* 52; Joyce, *Ulysses,* 403.

30 James Joyce, *Selected Letters of James Joyce* (New York: Viking Press, 1975), 271.

31 Frank Budgen, *James Joyce and the Making of Ulysses* (Bloomington: University of Indiana Press, 1967), 17.

32 Karen Lawrence, *The Odyssey of Style in Ulysses* (Princeton, N.J.: Princeton University Press, 1981).

33 T. S. Eliot, "William Blake," in *Selected Essays* (New York: Harcourt Brace, 1964), 278.

34 Northrop Frye, *Anatomy of Criticism: Four Essays* (Princeton, N.J.: Princeton University Press, 1957), 61.

35 See P. Adams Sitney on the practice of montage in postwar Russian film: *Modernist Montage: The Obscurity of Vision in Cinema and Literature* (New York: Columbia University Press, 1990), 39–42.

36 Sergei Eisenstein, "Through Theater to Cinema," in *Film Form* (Orlando, Fla.: Harcourt, 1949), 4–5.

37 Sergei Eisenstein, "Methods of Montage," in *Film Form,* 82.

38 Eisenstein, "Through Theater to Cinema," 5.

39 André Bazin, *What Is Cinema?* ed. and trans. Hugh Gray (Berkeley: University of California Press, 1971), 33.

40 Peter Bürger, *Theory of the Avant-Garde,* trans. Michael Shaw (Minneapolis: University of Minnesota Press, 1984).

41 Richard Murphy, *Theorizing the Avant-Garde: Modernism, Expressionism, and the Problem of Postmodernity* (Cambridge: Cambridge University Press, 1999).

42 Quoted in T. S. Eliot, *The Annotated Waste Land*, ed. Lawrence Rainey (New Haven: Yale University Press, 2006), 144–145.

43 James Joyce, *Letters of James Joyce*, vol. 3, ed. Richard Ellmann (London: Faber and Faber, 1966), 22.

44 Leah Dickerman with Matthew S. Witkovsky, eds., *The Dada Seminars* (Washington D.C.: National Gallery of Art, 2005), 3.

45 André Breton, "After Dada," in *What Is Surrealism?* ed. Franklin Rosemont (New York: Monad, 1978), 10, 119.

46 André Breton, "Manifesto of Surrealism (1924)," in *Manifestoes of Surrealism*, trans. Richard Weaver and Helen R. Lane (Ann Arbor: University of Michigan Press, 1972), 26.

47 Breton, "Manifesto of Surrealism," 6.

48 André Bréton, "Exhibition X . . . Y . . . ," in *What Is Surrealism?*, ed. Rosemont, 43.

49 Roger Shattuck, "Introduction," in Maurice Nadeau, *The History of Surrealism*, trans. Richard Howard (New York: Macmillan, 1965), 14–15.

50 Breton, "Manifesto of Surrealism," 14; André Breton, "Second Manifesto of Surrealism," in *Manifestoes of Surrealism*, 123.

51 André Breton, *What Is Surrealism?*, trans. David Gascoyne (London: Faber and Faber, 1936), 50, 48.

52 Quoted in Marjorie Perloff, "The Avant-Garde Phase of American Modernism," in *The Cambridge Companion to American Modernism*, ed. Walter Kalaidjian (Cambridge: Cambridge University Press, 2005), 195.

53 Mark Morrisson, "Nationalism and the Modern American Canon," in Kalaidjian, *Cambridge Companion to American Modernism*, 12–35.

54 See Bram Dijkstra, *Cubism, Stieglitz, and the Early Poetry of William Carlos Williams: The Hieroglyphics of a New Speech* (Princeton, N.J.: Princeton University Press, 1978).

55 William Carlos Williams, *The Collected Earlier Poems* (Norfolk, Conn.: New Directions, 1951), 68–69.

56 Albert Gelpi, *A Coherent Splendor: The American Poetic Renaissance, 1910–1950* (Cambridge: Cambridge University Press, 1987), 339.

57 James E. Breslin, "Spring and All: A New Lyric Form," in *Critical Essays on William Carlos Williams*, ed. Steven Gould Axelrod and Helen Deese (New York: G. K. Hall, 1995), 108.

58 J. Hillis Miller, *Poets of Reality* (Cambridge, Mass.: Harvard University Press, 1965) 309.

59 Williams, *Collected Earlier Poems*, 246.

60 In *Mosaic Modernism*, David Kadlec describes the "dynamic tension in Williams's work between representational and nonrepresentational aesthetics" and "between the aesthetics of cleanness and that of contamination." *Mosaic Modernism: Anar-*

chism, Pragmatism, Culture (Baltimore, Md.: Johns Hopkins University Press, 2000), 136.

61 Wallace Stevens, "Peter Quince at the Clavier," *Others: A Magazine of the New Verse* 1, no. 1 (1915): 31, 33.

62 Wallace Stevens, *The Collected Poems of Wallace Stevens* (New York: Knopf, 1954), 27, 36. Page numbers for quotations of Stevens's poems in the chapter are all from this volume.

63 Frank Kermode, *Romantic Image* (New York: Vintage, 1964), 43.

64 William Carlos Williams, *The Autobiography of William Carlos Williams* (New York: New Directions, 1967), 174.

65 Mark A. Sanders, "American Modernism and the New Negro Renaissance," in Kalaidjian, *Cambridge Companion to American Modernism*, 137.

66 W. E. B. Du Bois, "Negro Writers," *The Crisis* 19 (April 1920): 298–299.

67 Quoted in George Hutchinson, *The Harlem Renaissance in Black and White* (Cambridge, Mass.: Harvard University Press, 1995), 190, 180.

68 W. E. B. Du Bois, "Criteria of Negro Art," *The Crisis* 31 (January 1926): 151.

69 George Hutchinson, "Toward a New Negro Aesthetic," in *The Harlem Renaissance in Black and White*, 191.

70 Alain Locke, "Youth Speaks," *Survey Graphic* (March 1925): 131.

71 Du Bois, "Criteria of Negro Art," 151.

72 Quoted in Werner Sollors, *Interracialism* (Oxford: Oxford University Press, 2000), 274.

73 Langston Hughes, *The Collected Works of Langston Hughes,* vol. 1, ed. Arnold Rampersad (Columbia: University of Missouri Press, 2001), 36.

74 Countee Cullen, *Color* (New York: Harper and Brothers, 1925).

75 Thadious Davis has suggested that Fauset represented an ideal for Larsen, one that loomed over her early career and that she sharply resisted. *Nella Larsen, Novelist of the Harlem Renaissance: A Woman's Life Unveiled* (Baton Rouge: Louisiana State University Press, 1994).

76 Nella Larsen, *Quicksand,* in *The Complete Fiction of Nella Larsen,* ed. Charles R. Larson (New York: Anchor Books, 2001), 111.

77 Anna Brickhouse, "Nella Larsen and the Intertextual Geography of *Quicksand,*" *African American Review* 35, no. 4 (Winter 2001): 533–560.

78 See George Hutchinson, "Identity in Motion: Placing *Cane,*" in *Jean Toomer and the Harlem Renaissance,* ed. Geneviève Fabre and Michel Feith (New Brunswick, N.J.: Rutgers University Press, 2002).

79 Quoted in Jean Toomer, *Cane,* ed. Darwin T. Turner (New York: Norton, 1988), 152.

80 W. E. B. Du Bois, "The Younger Literary Movement," *The Crisis* 27 (February 1924): 161–163.

81 Quoted in Werner Sollors, "Jean Toomer's *Cane*: Modernism and Race in Interwar America," in Fabre and Feith, *Jean Toomer and the Harlem Renaissance,* 19.

CHAPTER 6. THE ENDS OF MODERNISM

1 Harry Levin, "What Was Modernism?," *Massachusetts Review* 1, no. 4 (Summer 1960): 610.

2 Recorded in Frank Budgen, *James Joyce and the Making of Ulysses* (Bloomington: University of Indiana Press, 1967), 105; T. S. Eliot, *Letters,* vol. 1, *1898–1922,* ed. Valerie Eliot (London: Harcourt Brace Jovanovich, 1988), 596.

3 Michael North, *Reading 1922: A Return to the Scene of the Modern* (New York: Oxford University Press, 1999).

4 Gertrude Stein, "Composition as Explanation," in *Writings,* vol. 1, *1903–1932* (New York: Library of America, 1998), 521.

5 Wyndham Lewis, *Blasting and Bombardiering* (London: Eyre and Spottiswoode, 1937), 90, 95.

6 Ezra Pound, *The Spirit of Romance* (New York: New Directions, 2005), 5.

7 Ezra Pound, *The Cantos of Ezra Pound* (New York: New Directions, 1970), 6, 3.

8 Ezra Pound, interview with Donald Hall, *Paris Review* 28 (Summer–Fall 1962): 27.

9 See James Longenbach, *Modernist Poetics of History: Pound, Eliot and the Sense of the Past* (Princeton, N.J.: Princeton University Press, 1987), 142–143.

10 Ezra Pound, "D'Artagnan Twenty Years After," in *Selected Prose* (New York: New Directions, 1973), 452.

11 Ezra Pound, "The State Should Move Like a Dance," *British Union Quarterly* 2, no. 4 (October–December 1938).

12 Ezra Pound, "Totalitarian Scholarship and the New Paideuma," ed. Douglas Fox, *Germany and You* (Berlin) 7, nos. 4–5 (April 5, 1937): 95–96, 123–124.

13 Pound, "Totalitarian Scholarship," 123–124.

14 Ezra Pound, "Vale," *Poetry* 49, no. 3 (December 1936): 137–138.

15 Pound, "The State Should Move Like a Dance."

16 Ezra Pound, *The Selected Letters of Ezra Pound, 1907–1941,* ed. D. D. Paige (London: Faber and Faber, 1971), 38.

17 Pound, *Selected Letters,* 26.

18 Ezra Pound, "A Retrospect," in *Literary Essays of Ezra Pound,* ed. T. S. Eliot (New York: New Directions, 1968), 3.

19 Ezra Pound, "Was the Ideal Liberty?," *Action* 160 (March 12, 1939): 12.

20 Ezra Pound, "The New Sculpture," *The Egoist* 1 (February 16, 1914): 68.

21 Ezra Pound, "What Is Money For?" in *Selected Prose,* 300.

22 Ezra Pound, *Guide to Kulchur* (New York: New Directions, 1970), 180.

23 Ezra Pound, "Immediate Need of Confucius," in *Selected Prose,* 78.

24 Ezra Pound, "A Visiting Card," in *Selected Prose,* 333–334.

25 Pound, "Totalitarian Scholarship," 118.

26 Pound, "D'Artagnan," 456.

27 Pound, "Visiting Card," 306.

28 Bertolt Brecht, *Drums in the Night,* in *Collected Plays,* vol. 1, ed. Ralph Mannheim and John Willett (New York: Random House, 1970), 106.

29 Bertolt Brecht, "The Modern Theatre Is the Epic Theatre," in *Brecht on Theatre,*
    ed. and trans. John Willett (New York: Hill and Wang, 1964), 35.

30 Brecht, interview, in *Brecht on Theatre,* 16.

31 Brecht, "A Radio Speech," in *Brecht on Theatre,* 18–19.

32 Brecht, "Three Cheers for Shaw," in *Brecht on Theatre,* 10–12.

33 Brecht, "Modern Theatre," 41, 39, 36, 41.

34 Brecht, "Modern Theatre," 37, 38.

35 Brecht, "Modern Theatre," 37.

36 Brecht, "The Popular and the Realistic," in *Brecht on Theatre,* 109–110.

ILLUSTRATION CREDITS

1 Photo credit: Erich Lessing / Art Resource, NY.

2-5, 8, 12 Digital Image © The Museum of Modern Art / Licensed by SCALA / Art Resource, NY.

7 Photo: Allan Macintyre © President and Fellows of Harvard College.

9 Image copyright © The Metropolitan Museum of Art / Art Resource, NY.

11 Image © Tate, London, 2010.

13 Photographer: Hickey-Robertson, Houston.

INDEX

Abbey Theatre, 129, 134, 188, 190, 194

Achebe, Chinua, 115, 306

Adams, John Quincy, 272

aestheticism, 17, 26, 29, 33, 34, 46, 49, 50–52, 57, 73, 89, 104, 114, 119, 153, 155, 160, 181, 186, 194, 221, 224, 226, 236, 240, 243, 245, 247, 253, 268, 278, 281; adversary, 133; affirmative, 276; anti-representational, 265; autonomy, 248, 286n63; choices, 218; collective, 7; dream-state, 27; erotic, 113; eternal laws, 280; evocation, 182; experiment, 32, 99; failed, 274; formalism, 90; independent, 261; Keats, 262; labor, 14; limitation, 141; montage, 242; naturalist-inspired, 260; and politics, 13, 14, 58, 138, 241, 270; radicalism, 158; post-symbolist, 47; Pound, 275; realism, 20; representational and non-representational, 300n60; seclusion, 31; and sexual politics, 235; of ultimacy, 25; Vorticism, 221; weakness, 51; will, 195

Aldington, Richard, 138–139

allegory, 75; contradictions of, 68; political, 70; transparent, 68; Wagnerian, 3

Alving, Oswald, 11

Anderson, Sherwood, 157, 260; *Winesburg, Ohio,* 231, 265

anthropology, 40, 56, 100, 291n23

Apollinaire, Guillaume, 49, 98, 149–152, 156, 157, 168, 269, 280;

Alcools, 143, 145, 146; "Cortège," 144, 146; "Et Moi Aussi Je Suis Peintre" (And I Too Am a Painter), 155; "Exoticism and Ethnography," 40; "I," 146, 147, 149, 160; "Lettre-Océan" ("Ocean-Letter"), 155; "On the Subject in Modern Painting," 153; in Paris, 147, 152, 155; shallow eye, 142–146; Surrealism, 249; "Zone," 143–145

Arnold, Matthew, 91; *Culture and Anarchy,* 66

Arnoux, Frédéric, 60

Arnoux, Madame, 60, 61, 62, 63

artist as solitary, 86

audiences, 3, 5, 6, 8, 18, 31, 36, 48–50, 52, 78, 94, 102, 120, 134, 174, 176, 179, 182, 183, 188, 189, 191, 193, 208, 246, 247, 252, 268, 276, 278, 281; art, 220; large, 181; pleasure-seeking, 215; response to tragedy, 199; suspicious, 38; sympathetic, 221; white, 263

autonomy, 105, 120, 121, 251, 281; aesthetic, 248, 286n63; of art, 50; loss of, 66; mission of, 245; rational, 234

avant-garde, 2, 12–53, 126, 154, 211, 245, 273–274, 283n4; and Brecht, 280; burden of, 269; characteristics, 7; concept, image, word, 17–23; contrast between high Modernism and, 247, 248; European, 252; experiment and antipathy, 12–17; Futurism, 45–48; general, 170;